How to Do *Everything* with

Macromedia Flash MX

35

```
on(release) {
    trace(_root.shape._y);
    trace(_root.shape._x);
}
```

About the Author

Bonnie Blake is an award-winning designer who specializes in web and multimedia design. She also teaches web, multimedia, and graphic design at Ramapo College in Mahwah, New Jersey. She is the author of *The Premiere Virtual Classroom*, *How To Do Everything with Macromedia Flash 5*, and co-author of *Flash DeCONSTRUCT*, and of the bestselling online course "*Flash 5 ActionScript*" on E-Handson.com.

Bonnie authors online courses for *Education to Go* and is currently authoring "*Animation and Interactivity*," which will be published in summer 2002. She is also the current host of the Adobe Premiere forum for the World Wide Users Group (wwug.com).

About the Technical Editor

Gordon Banks is a web developer from Boulder, Colorado. His design goals are to build dynamic front-end and back-end web content integrating Flash with XML, PHP, and SQL technologies. He is the webmaster for www.kayakingcolorado.com, a paddling resource for boaters in Colorado. His dream gig is a tech editing assignment from a cabin in the Wasatch Range, skiing 3000 feet vertical of powder every morning before remote wireless tech editing, and some high-test java.

How to Do *Everything* with

Macromedia Flash™ MX

Bonnie Blake

```
on(release) {
    trace(_root.shape._y);
    trace(_root.shape._x);
}
```

McGraw-Hill/Osborne

New York Chicago San Francisco
Lisbon London Madrid Mexico City
Milan New Delhi San Juan
Seoul Singapore Sydney Toronto

McGraw-Hill/Osborne
2600 Tenth Street
Berkeley, California 94710
U.S.A.

To arrange bulk purchase discounts for sales promotions, premiums, or fund-raisers, please contact **McGraw-Hill**/Osborne at the above address. For information on translations or book distributors outside the U.S.A., please see the International Contact Information page immediately following the index of this book.

How to Do Everything with Macromedia Flash™ MX

34567890 FGR FGR 019876543

ISBN 0-07-222250-6

Publisher	Brandon A. Nordin
Vice President & Associate Publisher	Scott Rogers
Acquisitions Editor	Megg Morin
Project Editor	Jennifer Malnick
Acquisitions Coordinator	Tana Allen
Technical Editor	Gordon Banks
Copy Editor	Bill McManus
Proofreader	Linda Medoff
Indexer	Jack Lewis
Computer Designers	Lucie Ericksen, Lauren McCarthy
Illustrators	Michael Mueller, Lyssa Wald
Series Design	Dodie Shoemaker

This book was composed with Corel VENTURA™ Publisher.

Dedication

This book is dedicated to my mother, Mary Jane,
whose humor and spirit will always live on.

Contents at a Glance

Contents

Acknowledgments

I would like to thank the team at Osborne for doing such an outstanding job in coordinating all facets of this book—this includes Megg Morin, Tana Allen, and Jennifer Malnick. Thanks also to Gordon Banks, whose technical editing was precise and complete with great suggestions. And thank you to Roger Stewart for giving me the opportunity to write another edition of this book.

Thanks to Doug Sahlin for being supportive, funny, and incredibly helpful while life as we know it was put on hold to write this book. I wish you much success with your Flash and Fireworks books. I know firsthand how great your books will be and how hard you worked on them.

Thank you, Mary Cicitta, for your research and input. I also want to thank Erlene Healy for contributing her professional photographs for the book. Special thanks to Dale, Matthew, Kelly, and my friends (Laura, Linda, Gail) who patiently waited for me to finish this project. Also, thank you Margot Maley Hutchenson for making this all possible.

Introduction

There is so much to say about Flash and so much to do in the program. Yet as designers, developers, other professionals, students, and just plain human beings, we are severely limited by time. Does anyone really have the luxury of setting aside weeks to learn an application like Flash MX nowadays? If you do, you're a very lucky person. For most of us, though, I can safely say that you probably need to get up and running as fast as possible (like last week) with Flash. By this I mean learning the basics—understanding the general concept behind the Flash architecture, and collecting an arsenal of impressive techniques that you can quickly use in a Flash movie to impress your boss or clients. From this plateau, you can master the Flash building blocks. If the time ever comes when you feel you want to absorb more (and it may never), you can confidently climb on to the next plateau.

One of the things that makes Flash unique is that so many people in diverse professions use it. For example, graphic designers and web designers use Flash as a creative tool. Then there are developers whose sole purpose is to script a Flash movie after the interface has been built. There are many other people making Flash movies, too, from educators to doctors. So what's the point? Well, since Flash attracts such a diverse population, the skill level and direction of various Flash users varies from person to person. The person who's a designer by trade is going to make beautiful-looking Flash movies. The audio engineer is going to hone in on the many different things you can do with sound in Flash. The videograper will discover cool things he can do with the new FLV format. The programmer is going to make incredible games and all sorts of other interactive movies that will baffle the designer. Depending upon your skill set, you will contribute different virtues to your Flash movies.

Because Flash is such a diverse and potentially complex program, it is a rare individual who will master each and every facet of the application. People study Flash and its native programming language, ActionScript, for years and still don't fully grasp the vastness of it. So don't allow yourself to stress over learning each and every facet of the program. Flash users are always in the process of learning something new about Flash.

On the bright side, with just a basic understanding of Flash, and a creative spark, you can create graphics that will dazzle even a more-seasoned Flash user. This book focuses on getting you up and running as quickly and efficiently as possible.

I have designed the book with just this in mind. I explain the basics of Flash in simple language and show you how to put these ideas to work. In other words, I tell you how to make things and, if they're interactive, I tell you how to get them to work. All of the exercises in the book can be altered to fit your own projects. You change the images, the colors, and voilà, you have an original design. This is kind of like learning some new recipe in a cookbook. Once you've got the basic ingredients mastered, you start feeling a little cocky. You start adding a little of this spice, and a little of that. Before you know it, you've changed the recipe so much that now it's your own unique creation. In no time, you will be creating original movies in Flash too.

One thing is for sure: You will never tire of this program—nor will you ever stop wanting to learn more, even if you don't have the time.

The Flash Community

Would you believe it? There is this vast community of Flash users all around the world. Want to talk about Flash in the middle of the night when everyone you know is sleeping? Take heart. There is always someone, somewhere on a Flash message board who will respond. There must be a lot of fellow Flash insomniacs out there. The amount of information on Flash, availability of this information, and the number of users is staggering. What's even more surprising is the camaraderie among users. If you too become addicted to Flash (and believe me, this is a good addiction), there are a number of resources you should investigate. I have listed many of these in Appendix A. I encourage you to get on that computer, start asking questions, and chatting with fellow Flash users. Take advantage of the fellowship you can find with this program. This is one of the many fringe benefits of being a Flash user.

Web Site

There are examples throughout the book of various techniques that can be created in Flash movies. All the major figures in the book are posted on the web site (**www.osborne.com**) for you to refer to and, in some cases, modify and customize for your own purposes. I believe you will find this particularly helpful, especially when more advanced techniques are covered toward the second half of the book. I'm sure you'll find that having access to the source code of a Flash movie, in conjunction with this book, will truly augment your learning experience.

The Structure of this Book

There are five parts to this book. The chapter subjects are arranged in order of complexity, starting with the more basic aspects of Flash and building up to the final chapters, which examine the program's more advanced features, including ActionScript and publishing Flash files. The parts of this book are organized into the following categories:

Part I: Learn the Building Blocks of Flash MX

Part I is designed to give you an overview of what Flash is all about, its fabulous capabilities, and the process one would use to actually build a movie in Flash. It sets the stage for the rest of the book and familiarizes you with language of Flash and concepts associated with the application while covering the basic drawing tools, the Flash interface, and how to use it.

Part II: Add Graphics to Your Flash Movies

Part II introduces the very important concept of creating objects in Flash and manipulating the properties of these elements—like scale, color, position, and so on. Also discussed is the transformation of objects and the many special techniques you can use to create exciting visual effects. Importing and exporting vector art, bitmaps, and audio and video from today's most popular programs are also examined in detail, as is creating static, input, and dynamic text. The virtues of making objects into graphic symbols is introduced in this section, as well as the concept of instances. It provides you with a solid overview of all facets of beginner to intermediate Flash, as well as providing an excellent reference for more experienced Flash users.

Part III: Animate in Flash

Part III covers all facets of animation including frame by frame, shape, and motion tweening. The concept behind animation and how it works is also discussed in depth. Symbols are expanded upon in this section, including buttons, movie clips, and understanding how to add objects to the Timelines of these symbols. Step-by-step examples of projects are provided to accelerate your learning curve, and key figures are posted on the web site for you to deconstruct and examine how they were created.

Part IV: Lay the Groundwork for Flash Interactivity

In Part IV, ActionScript, the scripting language behind Flash interactivity, is introduced in a simple, easy-to-understand manner. This information is particularly useful for the non-programmer because scripting concepts are discussed in laymen's terms. This makes it fairly easy for you to jump right in and immediately start adding simple interactivity to your movies. Again, the source code for figures are posted on the site for you to examine further and incorporate into your own work.

Part V: Move Full Throttle into ActionScript

For those of you who are ready to take ActionScript to the next level, Part V provides you with an analysis and examples of ActionScript on a more advanced level, providing step-by-step instructions on how to create common interactive effects, with some complex tasks reviewed as well. Movie clips and their relation to interactivity are also examined in depth. Many new features in Flash MX ActionScript are covered, such as the drawing object, the button movie clip, and components. You will also have an opportunity to fine-tune your ActionScript skills in the Expert mode.

Finally, Part V ends with a complete synopsis on how to prepare your movie for publishing to the web or other media. Key figures are also posted on the web site for you to deconstruct and examine how they were created. Once again, the Flash source files referred to in the figures and illustrations are posted on the web site for you to examine.

Appendix A: Multimedia Resources

This Appendix provides a list of various resources you can call upon when you're ready to take you Flash studies to the next level. This includes a comprehensive list of Flash-based award-winning web sites, sites that range from the simple to complex, and ActionScript-driven movies that will keep you up nights wondering how these authors made them.

For those of you who have the idea but just can't figure out how to execute it, this Appendix is equipped with a complete list of sites you can visit to download source code and see how others might have created that effect you're looking for.

Also included are learning resources, technical references, tutorials, and sites that offer audio, sound loops, and video downloads for use in your Flash movies.

Appendix B: Frequently Used Shortcut Keyboard Commands

Finally, this Appendix provides you with a list of all the commands you need to know to navigate in Flash—on the menu, and with keyboard shortcuts, both in Windows and on the Mac.

Conventions Used In this Book

Since Flash is for PC and Mac users alike, there are certain things to keep in mind when reading this book. Because the interface is nearly identical on both platforms, the screen captures were done on the Mac platform.

When shortcut keys are listed next to menu commands, the Windows version is listed first and the Mac version second with a slash separating the two. The shortcut keys themselves are abbreviated.

Notes are set apart from the body copy and include important issues you should be aware of regarding Flash. Tips are set apart as well and include helpful hints to streamline the creation of your Flash movies. New to this book are Did You Know sidebars. Here you can find insights and interesting information on Flash-related subjects. Lastly, the How To sidebars provide step-by-step instructions on complex Flash and ActionScript techniques

Conclusion

My goal was to produce a book that provides more than just a reference for Flash. I wanted this book to explain why things work the way they do in Flash, for what purpose would you use various techniques, and, most important, how to make things happen in Flash. This was not intended to be a book you would read once, put away, and never use again. Instead, my expectation was to write a desktop companion you would be able to keep at your fingertips and refer to time and time again, whenever you had a question or issue with Flash. I also invite you to correspond with me if you have any questions or comments on the book at **bblake@ optonline.net**. I believe I achieved my desired goals in writing this book, and I hope you enjoy reading it as much as I did writing it.

Part I

Learn the Building Blocks of Flash

Chapter 1

Examine the Dynamic Features of Flash MX

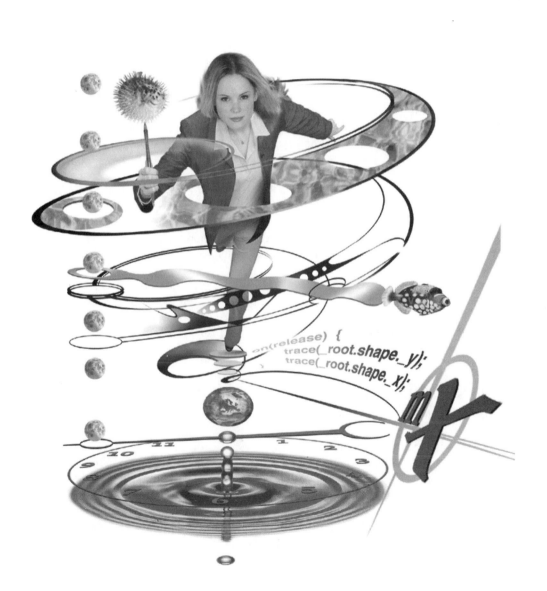

How To...

- Understand the language of Flash
- Get Flash files on the Web
- Use vector graphics in Flash
- Use bitmaps in Flash
- Use the Flash Player
- Examine movie clips
- Understand Flash and relevant technologies

If you're new to Flash, you may be surprised to know that it has actually been around for a few years. In 1997, Macromedia purchased the rights to a program called FutureSplash Animator, owned at the time by a company called FutureWave Software, Inc. Macromedia re-engineered the product, added some tantalizing bells and whistles, and renamed it Flash.

The Flash that was introduced back in 1997 is a far cry from the Flash we know today. Back then, not too many people could enjoy Flash animation because most browsers were not equipped with the plug-in software that enabled them to see Flash movies. Also, compared to the capabilities of Flash today, the old Flash really didn't do much.

Move forward to 2002 and Macromedia Flash is one of the most exciting multimedia applications to hit planet earth, ever. At least millions of designers and developers think so. Flash not only is an exciting application, but its animation has changed the face of the Web forever. Because of Flash, complex animation and interactivity on the Web is technology we all take for granted nowadays—you know, when you go on the Web and you see a really cool web site that has sound and animation. Maybe things move on the site when you hover your mouse over an object on the screen, and it changes in some way. Or perhaps you have seen mind-addicting games on the Web that keep you challenged and entertained (see Figure 1-1). Chances are, one of those sites, or at least part of one, is Flash driven.

Understand the Language of Flash

So how do I begin introducing the wonders of such an awesome program? Let's start with the very basics and try to pinpoint what Flash is and exactly how it works.

Flash is a global multimedia authoring tool used by millions of web designers, developers, programmers, educators, students, and many others—too numerous to mention. In Flash, you can create text and graphics, change the properties of these objects, and then animate them. You can import bitmapped images, video, and sound, and create user-controlled designs. When you're done with your Flash creation, it can be output in a variety of ways. Your Flash Player file (or SWF file) can be exported as a QuickTime file, sequential file format, or as a self-playing movie, and there are other output options available. These features are just the tip of the iceberg with Flash, but at least you have some idea of the capabilities of the program.

FIGURE 1-1   Rocketsnail.com, creator of online Flash games, serves as an outstanding example of Flash creativity in action (www.rocketsnail.com).

NOTE *Whenever I see the file extension .swf, I always think of "single white female." You can probably guess that's not what "SWF" stands for. Some people think it means "Shockwave Flash File." Wrong again. It actually means "Small Web Format," a nomenclature perfect for a Flash movie, since they tend to be smaller than animations generated from other applications.*

Get a Flash File Up on the Web

Well, you've got Flash loaded on your computer. You've probably opened it up, clicked around, and made a circle or two with the drawing tools. But how do you get a page up on the Web? Let me walk through the basic process of doing this.

Let's say you've created a Flash file. These are generally known as Flash movies because, often, you're creating something that moves in time, or is animated. Not all Flash movies are animated, however. You can make something that stands still and it can still be considered a Flash movie.

Your Flash movie is saved as a Flash file. The extension for this is .fla, and this is the root document that you return to if you need to make revisions. This is not the file version that goes up on the Web.

Once you're ready to go live and put your movie on the Web, your Flash movie is published as a Flash Player file. The original FLA file is still intact, and the Flash Player file now becomes a noneditable copy of the original. The extension for this Flash Player file is .swf.

So now you have two copies of your movie: a FLA version, which can be edited, and an SWF version, which can't be edited.

To see your SWF file on the Web, you have to embed it in an HTML document. The easiest way to do this is to generate an HTML page automatically with an SWF file using the Publish Settings dialog box (see Figure 1-2). The Publish Settings dialog box is discussed in Chapter 16.

You could also insert the file in an HTML page manually. Since a Flash Player file (SWF) requires a plug-in to be viewed in a browser, the <EMBED> tag is used for the SWF file. Once the SWF file is in the HTML document, the document just needs to be uploaded, along with the HTML file it is embedded in, to a server.

As long as your viewers' browsers are equipped with the Flash plug-in, you will be able to see your Flash Player file on the Web. That's all there is to it, aside from learning the actual application.

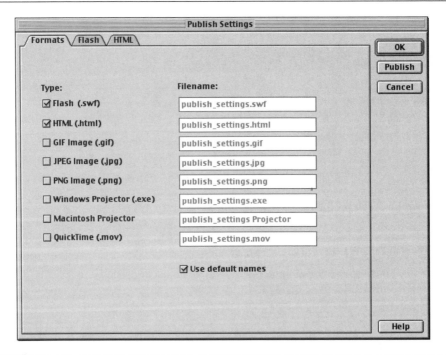

FIGURE 1-2   In the Publish Settings dialog box, you can generate an HTML document and an SWF file.

It's important to note that Flash Player files can be saved for different versions of the Flash Player. As of this writing, the latest Player version is version 6. This version can open all older Flash Player (SWF) files. When you are publishing your movie, keep in mind that since Flash Player version 6 is still relatively new, a portion of your audience won't yet have downloaded this player. They probably have an older version—like version 5 or, heaven forbid, version 4, or even 3 (from a very long time ago). With this in mind, you generally want to offer a link to the latest free download plug-in on the Macromedia site (www.macromedia.com/downloads).

Of course, a portion of your audience may not have the time to download a plug-in, and as a result they will browse elsewhere on the Web. To combat lost hits on your site, you can always save your SWF file down to be compatible with earlier versions. Flash 5 is probably safe because it's been around for about two years. However, keep in mind that when you save an SWF file down to an earlier plug-in version, it will not recognize features from newer application versions. So, if I use a new technique to create my Flash MX movie (like the new masking feature discussed in Chapter 15), and I publish or export the movie in a Flash Player 5 format, I will not get the results I expect.

Macromedia posts the latest Flash Player statistics on its web site so that you can get an idea of how many people out in cyberspace might have access to your Flash files (www.macromedia.com). As of this writing, Macromedia polls claim that over 98 percent of all web users have the Flash Player. Although these users may not all have the latest Player, this constitutes a pretty substantial slice of the web audience.

Part of your learning journey in Flash will be balancing a myriad of output issues. Outputting Flash files is discussed in Chapter 16.

NOTE *All versions of Netscape 4.06 and over contain the Flash Player. Beware, though, because older browsers contain older versions of the Flash Player. As of this writing, the Flash Player is up to version 6. Flash movies can also be viewed with ActiveX controls in Internet Explorer (Windows 95, 98, and NT) and Flash Java Edition (present on Java-enabled browsers).*

The Advantages of Flash on the Web

All you need to do is browse the Web to realize that sites that are serious about design are Flash driven. Sure, there will always be sites that deal primarily with data and reference. But even on those sites, you have little Flash-driven banners popping up all over the place. When it comes down to it, as much as we hate to admit it, everyone is selling something on the Web. Unfortunately, the Web doesn't pay for itself. Even if you've created a small banner to attract an audience, your product or service is competing with billions of other products. Solid multimedia can keep people on your site a little longer, increasing the chances that they will indulge.

We know you can make beautiful movies with Flash, which is one reason to use it for web design, but there are other benefits of using Flash on the Web. Let's take a look at some of them.

Flash is *streaming* technology, which means that while your movie is playing on the Web, the rest of the movie is loading in the background. Your viewer doesn't have to read a book while waiting for the movie to appear. Of course, you have to create the movie to work correctly, but streaming is a definite benefit to Flash technology. People don't like to wait.

Flash generates low-bandwidth files. People with slower connections don't have to wait forever to see your movie, provided you monitored the file size while you were making it.

Flash movies are high quality. Compare a gradient object on the Web created in Flash to a gradient picture in an HTML file. The Flash gradient looks perfect and smooth. The other one looks terrible. Text in an SWF file looks terrific, too. We talk about this in the next section.

Flash has far more capabilities than HTML. Sure, DHTML and JavaScript help enhance your web pages, but the capabilities of Flash pack more power in a single application than HTML in conjunction with a scripting language.

Flash Player files offer more cross-browser consistency than HTML. For the most part, you can be assured that the movie you create locally on your computer in Flash (assuming you've handled fonts the right way—text is discussed in Chapter 4) will look consistent on that compatible browser. As I write this, I'm cringing, because I know there is no such thing as a perfect world when your web audience consists of millions of computer users with a variety of browsers (each spanning several versions). Although Flash is generally a safer bet than HTML for cross-browser consistency, the files must be prepared correctly to ensure accuracy and must be tested anywhere and everywhere—forever.

Flash is capable of creating a total multimedia experience. Yes, you can get out the popcorn and forgo the movies for some Flash Player files. In Flash, you can see streaming video, hear sound, play games, listen to stories, and chat with people online, as well as numerous other things. If you can imagine it, you can probably create it in Flash.

There are additional design issues you should know about before you begin using Flash. It's a good idea to understand the nature of Flash graphics. Let's take a look at the different kinds of images you can create in Flash.

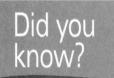

Font Management

Flash MX has a wonderful new feature for font management mishaps. If a Flash Player file with type loads on a system that is missing the font used, a dialog box is displayed allowing the user to substitute the missing font with a new one. If a font was missing in previous versions of Flash, the area where the text was located would often come up blank. This could cause a lot of embarrassment for the Flash author, especially if you were trying to impress a client.

Choose Flash as Your Design Tool

In the earliest release of Flash, the reference manual was so sparse, and the examples were so uninspiring, I remember thinking to myself, "Who would ever want to use this silly program?" The fact that it was such a robust application with so many capabilities wasn't communicated well. The authors were developers, not artists. Designers and developers had yet to merge their talents together. That would take a little time.

The first Flash reference manual suggested that, if you wanted, you could just use Flash as a drawing application for print media and disregard the program's animation capabilities. I didn't understand why Macromedia marketed it that way back then, when there were other solid drawing programs that were more equipped to get the job done. But, in retrospect, I understand that very few people at that time had the capability of seeing your Flash Player file. Not many people were going to configure their browser just so they could see your Flash site online. So, to make it seem like you were getting more bang for the buck, Macromedia offered alternative suggestions on how you might use the application. There's another aspect suggested here that made, and still makes, Flash technology so valuable. Because it's based on the model of a drawing program, or vector-based program, the graphics and text in Flash look crisp and clean, and Flash Player files (SWF files) load quickly when viewed in a browser. So, let's look at the difference between vector images and bitmaps to further understand how both kinds of images are utilized in Flash.

Examine the Difference Between Vector Graphics and Bitmaps

There are two types of graphics you can create on a computer: vector and bitmaps. Let's examine the difference between the two and see how Flash processes both of these kinds of graphics.

Vector Graphics

Vector art is commonly associated with drawing programs such as Adobe Illustrator and Macromedia Freehand. In fact, when you create text and shapes in Flash, you are creating vector art. Designers most often use vector graphics for logos, art with flat color, and illustrations. Anything that requires straight lines, precision, and sharpness best lends itself to vector images. In a vector-based program, drawing curves is done with mathematical precision (see Figure 1-3) and points are connected with paths.

For certain projects, vector-based graphics would have a distinct advantage over bitmaps. For one, vector art is crisper than bitmapped images—so for logos or text, the output is cleaner. Vector art, under most circumstances, is also more compact in size than bitmaps. It takes a lot less information to mathematically describe a vector curve than it does a bitmap. Because of this, vector images, like Flash generates, are smaller in file size. The third consideration with vector art versus bitmaps is that vector art is scalable. If you display a logo at various sizes, from very small to big, the quality will generally be maintained from one extreme to another (see Figure 1-4).

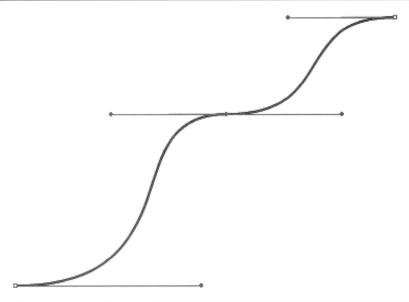

FIGURE 1-3   Flash offers a Bézier curve tool that enables you to connect points with curved lines.

FIGURE 1-4   A vector image created in Flash (or any other vector-based program) will maintain its integrity when enlarged or reduced in size.

Display Vector Art on the Web

Although vector art is crisp and clear, it is inherently associated with print media as opposed to the Web. Line art, or vector art, is commonly printed out at high-resolution quality. Screen resolution (or what you see when you browse the Web), on the other hand, is very low quality compared to print: 72 dpi to be exact. If I created text in Adobe Illustrator, a vector program, and wanted to insert it in an HTML document, I would export it as a GIF file because HTML doesn't recognize file formats like EPS that are commonly associated with vector art. A GIF file is a bitmap format that I can insert into my HTML page. The text that originated as vector art is now bitmap. So, in this scenario, I wouldn't have a strong reason for having created my text in a vector program instead of a bitmap program. It wouldn't have made a difference either way because the output on the Web is still a screen resolution bitmap, regardless of how it originated. HTML is limited and can only hold bitmap images.

So what's the point of even discussing vector art and the Web? Well, had I imported a vector-based image into Flash, saved it as a Flash file, and embedded my Flash Player file (SWF) into the same HTML page, the text would be crisp and scalable and would contain all the attributes of a vector graphic. Another wonder of Flash is its ability to antialias images. Antialiasing mathematically blends surrounding pixels together to create the illusion of smoother edges in an image. So Flash pages are antialiased, explaining why they look so much crisper than the bitmap graphics on a regular web page. This also explains why Flash Player files (from now on, I will refer to them as SWF files) are generally compact in size if made the right way.

Vector art sounds great, doesn't it? Yes, but sometimes you need to use images of a more photographic nature, and vector art just isn't appropriate for that project. This would be a good time to consider using a bitmap image in Flash.

Bitmap Images

Although vector graphics generally are crisper, smaller, and more scalable than bitmaps, it doesn't mean you should rule out using bitmaps altogether. Sometimes your project will be better stated using bitmap images in Flash.

Bitmap graphics, sometimes referred to as *raster art*, are commonly edited, manipulated, and created in programs like Adobe Photoshop or Macromedia Fireworks. The difference between vector art and bitmaps can best be understood by examining the two, side by side (see Figure 1-5).

Bitmaps are created with a series of bits, the measurement system on a computer. You can call them rectangles, dots, bits, whatever you like. But the illusion of an image is created when these dots are juxtaposed next to one another. Some dots are turned off, some are turned on, and the color and color intensity changes from dot to dot to complete the illusion of a picture. You can't see all this detail going on unless the image is enlarged or you're examining it under a magnifying glass. If your Flash movie screams out for a photographic or continuous tone image, it probably lends itself to a bitmap image. Although you cannot edit individual pixels in a bitmap image in Flash, you can import bitmaps into your Flash movie (see Figure 1-6).

Once these images are imported, you can manipulate bitmaps a little. You can scale them, change their opacity level, use them as part of an animation, and make them interactive. If you

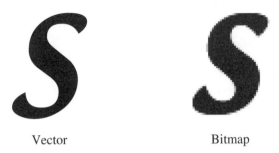

Vector   Bitmap

FIGURE 1-5   An enlarged bitmap letter next to the identical enlarged letter that was saved as vector art

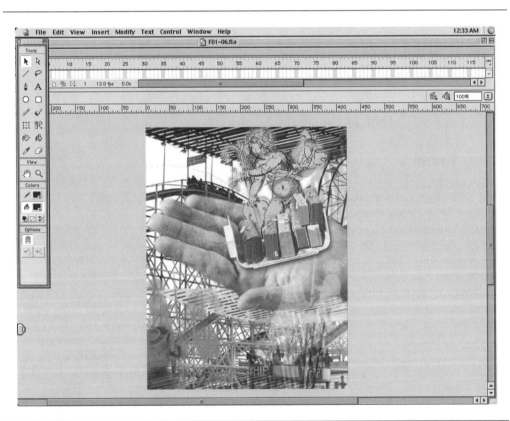

FIGURE 1-6   A bitmap image imported into Flash

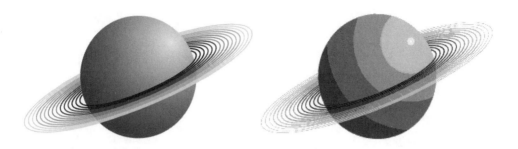

FIGURE 1-7   Compare the quality of the image on the left (Flash SWF) and the right (GIF).

do use bitmaps in Flash, careful consideration must be given to optimizing bitmaps before importing them into Flash and within Flash, if necessary. Otherwise, the file size can get out of hand. We'll discuss techniques for optimizing graphics in Chapter 7.

The beauty of Flash is that you can work with both vector and bitmap images, even in the same file. This way, you can combine the crispness of vector text and curves with the changing colors and shades of a photographic image and be assured the quality of the output is going to look great and the file size will remain manageable for slow-poke computers viewing your Flash movie on the Web (see Figure 1-7).

Antialias Features in the Flash Player

Another reason you would prefer a Flash-driven web site is that your audience can have some control over how a Flash file appears on the Web. The image in Figure 1-8 is an SWF file embedded in an HTML page. In Windows, if a user right-clicks the Flash image, a pop-up menu appears that gives the user some control over the display of the file. On the Mac, the user simply needs to CTRL-click to access the same pop-up menu.

In this pop-up menu, the user can zoom in or out on an SWF file. Because of the antialiasing capabilities of Flash, objects you've created in Flash, from text to drawings, will maintain their quality even when they're enlarged. Try the pop-up menu on a page in any of the Flash-driven web sites listed in Appendix A and try to zoom in and out of the image. Notice, as you zoom up, that the quality readjusts itself so the integrity of the image remains as close as possible to the original. You'll see how convenient a feature this is, especially if you're like me and need a little help reading very small text.

TIP   *This pop-up menu in the Flash Player is more commonly called a* context *menu. Context menus are always accessed by right-clicking (Windows)/CTRL-click (Mac). Their purpose is to streamline production by offering you a list of options available to the element you're clicking on. We will be using context menus a lot throughout this book, so they will become a familiar sight.*

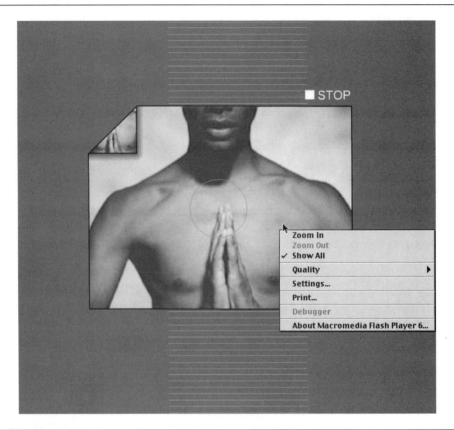

FIGURE 1-8 A pop-up menu with viewing selections becomes available when you right-click (Windows)/CTRL-click (Mac) on an SWF file.

A user not only can zoom in and out on an SWF file with this handy little tool, but also can change the resolution of the image from high to medium or low. Why would someone want to do this? If someone in your audience is using an old, slow computer, they can change the quality of the display by adjusting the Quality setting. When the Quality setting is lowered, a slow CPU has less processing to do, and the movie will render quicker.

Flash Image Quality

The Flash Player default setting assumes the user wants to see the image that's displaying in high quality. Let's face it, high quality is one of the major benefits behind Flash technology. However, if the file is set to a low quality using this handy little pop-up menu, the low-bandwidth user (the unfortunate user with the old, slow configuration) can speed things up a little so the file plays more efficiently. So the balance shifts from the quality of the movie being most important to the speed of the display.

Printing in the Flash Player

Another wonder of the Flash Player is that your audience can print a Flash page from the browser. If you've ever tried to print an HTML file from a web browser, you know it usually looks bad. Images that look terrific on the screen appear jagged and illegible on the printout. If text is a bitmap and it's on a certain color background, it may not print out at all.

Flash Player files printed from a browser look crisp and clear, which is another benefit of using Flash. In the Flash Player context menu, a user can easily select Print to display their system's Print dialog box.

You can provide the visitor to your site with a button they can click to print a frame in your online Flash movie. This technique involves a little scripting, but it will give your visitor some direction in deciding which screens may be important to print. Also, in ActionScript, you can control the quality of the print. Printing specifics are covered in Chapter 15.

Examine the Movie Clip Object in Flash

When you've finished reading this book, you will understand why the movie clip is one of the most important aspects of Flash. In fact, movie clips provide the springboard for most of the cool interactivity you'll be creating in Flash.

Understanding movie clips is actually quite simple. A movie clip is an object that is a self-contained movie. This movie is just like any movie. It can have animation, sound, graphics, even video. It can be one frame or multiple frames. A movie clip even can have more movies contained within it, a concept known as *nesting*.

If you assign a name to these movie clips (known as an "instance" name), you can talk to them and order them around. Movie clips can even talk to other movie clips, and talk to movie clips within movie clips. Amazingly enough, movie clips can also have split personalities; they can simultaneously act as buttons in addition to being movie clips. The benefit of this is that it gives the object tremendous flexibility in terms of interacting with other objects. Movie clips are one of the elements that make Flash ActionScript so powerful and complex. So, all those eye-popping interactive effects you see on Flash-driven web pages are bound to be chock full of movie clips ordering other movie clips around (see Figure 1-9). As the director of the movie, you write the actors' scripts (the movie clip objects) and they do exactly what you tell them to do. Movie clips and how they work are discussed in Chapters 9 through 14.

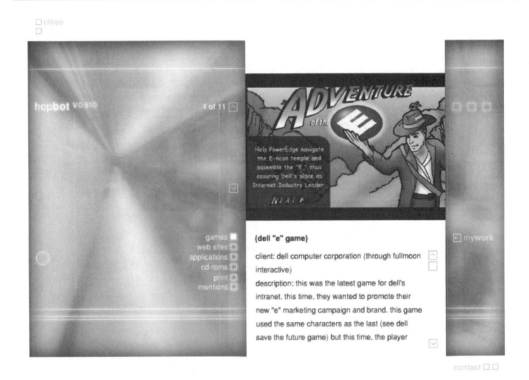

FIGURE 1-9 Movie clip objects are always working behind the scenes in complex and beautiful Flash-driven movies (www.hopbot.com).

Understand the Relationship Between Flash and Other Web Technologies

Flash enables you to create some pretty amazing movies for web delivery, but it arguably doesn't meet all the needs of every developer for every project. A Flash project might require something simple like hyperlinks to an HTML document. Many clients, on the other hand, require complex data-driven Flash sites. Sometimes, gaming applications on the Web require server-side scripting because of their enormous complexity. For these types of projects, Flash works side by side with other programming and scripting languages. This section discusses the technologies that might commonly be used in conjunction with Flash movies for certain projects.

HTML

HTML is the core language of the Web. As a markup language, HTML is quite limited, as it only displays static text and graphics. HTML tags are read in browsers, like Internet Explorer and Netscape Navigator. It's important for Flash users to know a little about HTML because, if your Flash movie is web-bound, you will be inserting it in an HTML page in order for your web audience to see it.

You see multimedia on the Web, like the dynamic movies you'll soon be creating in Flash, only because your web browser contains a plug-in that allows you to see it. Plug-ins are modules in your browser that enable you to view multimedia files. Flash offers publishing settings for HTML so that you can automatically generate an HTML page, complete with your Flash Player movie intact. In addition, Flash offers you the ability to create HTML links in text fields (see Chapter 4).

With the help of some scripting, in Flash, you can also launch a URL based on the occurrence of an event, such as the user clicking an object. So, HTML and Flash can work well together to help give you more flexibility in your web site design.

JavaScript

JavaScript is a scripting language created by Netscape. You've probably seen many simple web sites that contain interactive buttons. Often, these buttons just contain a simple JavaScript script, instructing objects to swap places with one another when a mouse event occurs.

ActionScript, the native programming language that drives Flash interactivity, is closely related and very similar in syntax to JavaScript. Since JavaScript is a popular scripting language, it's no surprise that there are methods available in Flash that enable the two languages to work together. For example, with the FS command in Flash, you can pass data along to JavaScript to perform functions like sizing a movie a certain way in a browser or opening up an external program from the SWF file.

XML

XML, Extensible Markup Language, is becoming more commonplace on the Web because of the flexibility it provides programmers in creating custom tags. XML, like HTML, is a derivative of the language SGML, but is a more robust and varied language than HTML.

Flash ActionScript contains XML objects that enable you to send, load, and manipulate XML data on a remote server via an SWF file. XML and Flash are commonly used together for web sites that contain elements like sophisticated shopping carts, for financial institution web sites, and for sites that publish information that is continuously updated—like weather, news, and so on.

In the near future, you will see an abundance of XML applications on the web. If you are serious about Flash and web development, you should make it a point to learn more about XML in order to stay abreast of current technologies.

There are other programming and scripting languages that are used in conjunction with Flash, such as ASP, JSP, CFML, ActiveX, PHP, Java, C++, and many others. On large sites, Flash is often enhanced on the back end with the assistance of one or more of these languages. Keep in mind, however, that there are still many sophisticated things you can do in Flash MX just using the application alone.

Some advanced Flash capabilities and techniques will be covered in this book. But keep in mind that people study Flash for years and still learn new things every day. There are people who use Flash only for design, and others who use it strictly for programming and development. It's hard to become a master of every element of Flash, if not impossible, because it's such an extensive and complex program. You won't often meet someone who is a fabulous designer, yet knows all the ins and outs of ActionScript. So, in this book, we will try to aim for somewhere in the middle to get you started on the right track to learning Flash.

In the next chapter, we will jump right into the basics of Flash, take a look at the tools, and learn how to drive the sports car of all multimedia-authoring tools.

Chapter 2

Get to Know the Flash Workspace

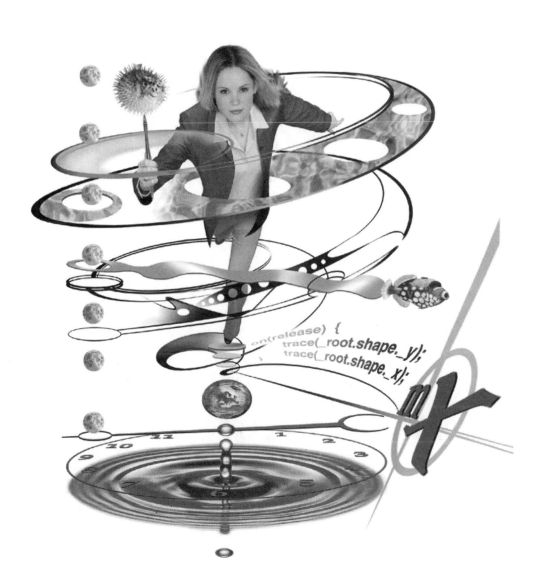

How To...

- Grasp the stage concept
- Control the way your movie looks
- Work in the Timeline
- Understand the Toolbox
- Dissect the Properties Inspector
- Explore the Library
- Create a new document

My guess is that you have launched Flash and probably poked around a little, too. Hopefully you have, because it means you have gained at least a cursory familiarity with your new surroundings. Of course, some readers will have more experience than others with the principles we are about to review in this chapter. If you've worked in other Macromedia applications or drawing programs, the Flash interface will be much easier to master. You'll find that some of the Flash features work in a similar manner to how corresponding features work in other graphics applications.

In this chapter, we explore the Flash workspace. What you learn here will serve as your springboard to more intermediate and advanced Flash concepts. In other words, we should review the basics first in order to achieve our ultimate goal of making beautiful movies in Flash.

Grasp the Stage Concept

One of the most important elements of the Flash workspace is the *stage*. Your movie comes alive on the Flash stage, and this is the first thing you'll see when you begin a new file in Flash. The stage is used to create, assemble, and edit graphics that eventually become your Flash movie. You can see the stage within the Flash workspace in Figure 2-1.

The stage defines the size of each frame in your finished Flash movie. In this sense, a frame on the stage would be the equivalent of a page if you were working in a typical graphics program. Just like in a drawing program, if you create or drag objects off the page, or stage—as is the case in Flash, the objects won't appear in the Flash Player file.

Since Flash is a multimedia application, and your movie consists of frames, the language of Flash is a little different than in an application whose final output is bound for print. The stage represents the area where your cast of characters will be performing, just like in a real movie. In Flash, your cast will include text, graphics, maybe buttons, and movie clips. Just like in a real production, your actors (or objects in this case) will be chatting and interacting with one other. Events will take place and the actors will respond to those events. You are the director of the movie, and, as such, you are in control of all the action on the stage.

The other important element regarding the stage is that it also displays the current frame, or the frame that's playing at that moment. The current frame can have the same contents as the frame before it, or the contents of a frame can change to display different objects. You, the individual

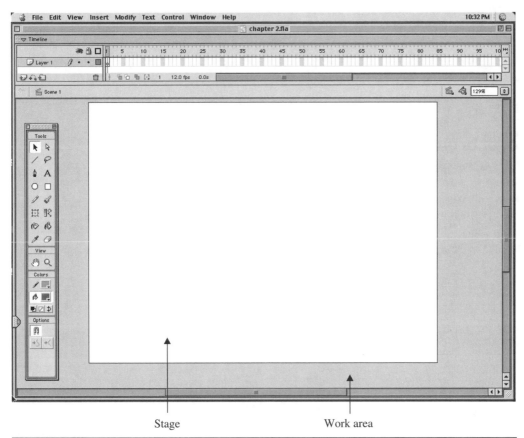

Stage   Work area

FIGURE 2-1   The stage in Flash MX and the workspace

who controls the contents of your movie, make all the decisions on how the movie plays out. Frames are made and controlled in the Timeline, which we discuss in the next section.

Use the Work Area

You probably noticed in Figure 2-1 that the default stage is depicted as a white rectangle and the surrounding area is gray. The gray area is the Flash work area. Any element you place within this area can't be seen on the stage. Why, you may ask, would you need an area like this? Well, suppose you have an animation where an object enters the stage to the left and departs on the right of the stage. In this scenario, you would need to place the object off the stage in the beginning and the end just as if it were an actor that walked on and off the stage. So, the work area becomes the back stage area, and your audience can't see the stage in the Flash Player file. Flash users can store all sorts of components of a movie in this area and bring them onto the stage when needed.

View the Movie on the Stage

While working on a Flash document, you will often need to enlarge a portion of the stage or an object on the stage. Enlarging an area makes it easier to draw or edit an element very precisely. Concurrently, you need to be able to reduce the view of the stage from time to time so that you can get a feel for the stage as a whole.

Flash offers many convenient features to change the view of the stage, as well as to navigate quickly on a single page once you've enlarged an area. Let's take a look at these tools.

Zoom In and Out

Although Flash possesses a graphical user interface complete with easily identifiable icons, most selections are also listed in the menu. So, if you prefer selecting from a menu, you can work with the program by using menus. In addition, the shortcut key associated with each particular function is always listed to the right of the menu item.

Zooming gives you the ability to enlarge or reduce the view of the Flash work area to make it easier to work in. The Zoom functions can be found in the View menu.

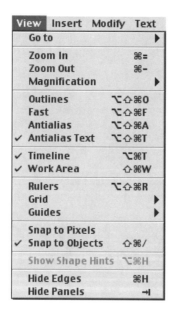

Selecting View | Zoom In magnifies the image, and selecting View | Zoom Out reduces the image. The Zoom function enlarges and reduces in increments of 100 percent.

Selecting View | Magnification presents a flyout menu with various magnification settings ranging from 25 percent to 800 percent, as shown next.

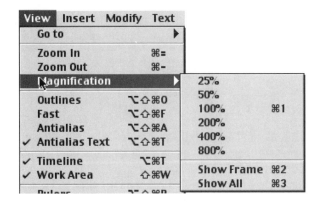

2

View | Magnification | Show Frame and View | Magnification | Show All provide you with two quick ways to preview the entire frame, as opposed to an individual element on the stage.

Set the Zoom Control Window

You can also zoom in and out of the stage using the Zoom Control located in the upper-right corner of the stage, just under the Timeline:

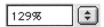

Here, you can zoom in and out in either of two ways. You can select a preset zoom from a flyout menu by clicking one of the arrows, or you can highlight the zoom number and type in a custom view. With this tool, the stage can be enlarged all the way up to 2000 percent and reduced all the way down to 8 percent. These zoom ranges are a little extreme, but, if you wanted to, you could hone in on a minute detail using this tool.

Zoom Tool

Although we're going to cover each element in the Toolbox in detail later on, it's important to mention the Zoom tool in the context of viewing a document in Flash. The Zoom tool is under the View options in the Toolbox, to the right of the Hand tool.

This icon is a familiar sight to users of graphics programs and it essentially works by the same rules as most programs.

To use the Zoom tool to enlarge an object, click the tool. When you do this, the cursor becomes the Zoom icon, and options for the Zoom tool appear at the bottom of the Toolbox.

On the left is the Enlarge Zoom icon with the plus sign (+), and on the right is the Reduce Zoom icon with a minus sign (−). These tools allow you to hone in on a specific object or area, as opposed to selecting Zoom from the menu.

To zoom in or out on an object or a portion of the stage, either click in the area you want to zoom in or out of, or draw an invisible marquee around the area with the Zoom tool (see Figure 2-2).

You can use this marquee method with the Zoom tool if you want to quickly isolate a particular element on the stage. That way, you don't have to scroll the page to target a particular area each time you try to enlarge the page.

TIP   *If you hold down the ALT key in Windows or the OPT key on the Mac while using the Enlarge Zoom tool, it turns into the opposite tool, + or −.*

FIGURE 2-2   You can draw a marquee around an area on the stage to zoom in on an area.

Scroll on the Stage

When any of the View tools are used to enlarge an area of the stage, you will often need to scroll to a different area of the stage to target a specific object or area. Of course, you can always use the scrolling arrows and scroll bars on the bottom and right side of the Flash window to redefine the area of the stage that is visible.

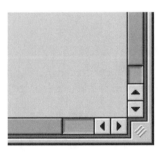

Another quick way to navigate around a stage is to use the Hand tool. The Hand tool is located in the View Tools section of the Toolbox, right next to the Zoom icon:

When you click this tool in the Toolbox, your cursor becomes a hand icon. To use this hand to scroll around on the stage, click an area and drag. The Hand tool allows you to scroll very precisely and is perfect for honing in on a particular object.

Another quick way of scrolling when you're using another tool in the Toolbox is to hold down the SPACEBAR. When you do this, the hand scroll will replace the cursor while the SPACEBAR is down. When you release the SPACEBAR, the cursor returns to its previous state.

Additional Control View Options

When you create a complex Flash movie, the various components of the movie are stored in your processor's memory. As your Flash projects increase in complexity, the demands on your processor increase—sometimes to the point where Flash slows down the redrawing of an object—or slows down an animation as you test the movie in the authoring mode. When this happens, you can speed things up again by changing the way Flash draws objects on the stage. You have four commands from the View menu that will speed up a movie's display in the authoring mode:

- ■ **View | Outlines**   Flash displays all objects as outlines (see Figure 2-3).
- ■ **View | Fast**   Flash displays the shapes and colors of objects without antialiasing.

- ■ **View | Antialias**   Flash applies antialiasing to all shapes and bitmaps in your movie. This display option gives you the best idea of what your finished Flash production will look like, but might slow down the display speed when previewing animation. Use this mode if you have a fast processor and a video card capable of displaying 24-bit color.

- ■ **View | Antialias Text**   Flash applies antialiasing to all text objects in your movie. As a rule, you want to choose this option (which is enabled by default) to accurately display text used in your movies.

Use Grids

Although it is not visible when you create a new document, Flash always provides you with a grid, which you can use to align objects to each other and the grid. You can choose to display the

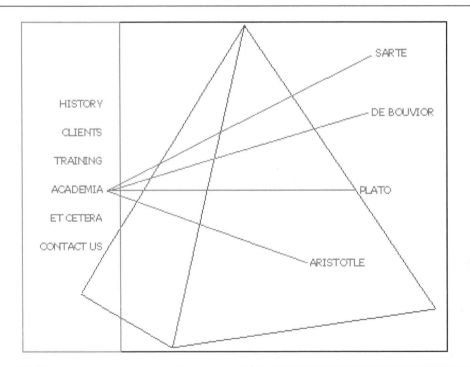

FIGURE 2-3   Viewing a Flash document as outlines

grid, change the grid's spacing and color, and choose whether objects snap to grid points. If you choose View | Grid | Show Grid, Flash will display the grid shown in Figure 2-4.

Use Grid Snapping

You can use the Flash grid in two ways: as a visual reference when you manually align objects to grid intersections, and as a virtual reference where Flash snaps objects to intersecting grid points. If you choose View | Grid | Snap To Grid, Flash will snap an object to grid points as you move it across the stage.

When you employ Flash to align objects to grid points, the point where an object aligns to the grid is dependent on where you select the object. Every object you create has a bounding box with a handle in its center, and a handle for each extremity of the bounding box. As you drag an object, the handle (an unfilled dot) you are dragging the object by becomes larger and darker when it nears a grid intersection point.

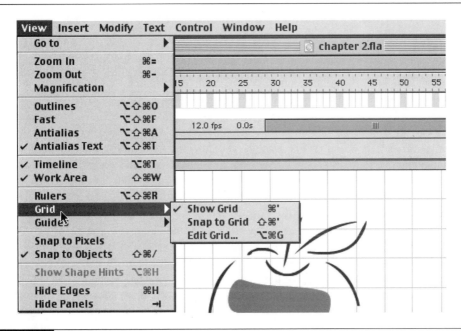

FIGURE 2-4   A grid on the stage in Flash

Edit the Grid

The default grid will display a light-gray line every 18 pixels along the document's width and length. You can modify the grid spacing and color to suit the document you are editing. Choose View I Grid I Edit Grid, and Flash displays the Grid dialog box shown here.

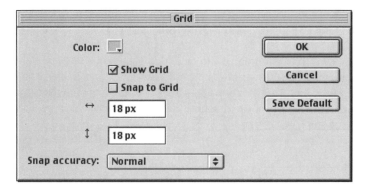

Change Grid Color

To modify the color of the grid lines, open the Grid dialog box (View I Grid I Edit Grid), click the Color swatch, and select a color from the palette. Select a color that contrasts well with the background color of your document. Click OK and Flash changes the grid to the color you specified.

Change Grid Spacing

To change the grid spacing, open the Grid dialog box (View I Grid I Edit Grid), and enter the desired values in the width (the horizontal double-headed arrow) and height (the vertical double-headed arrow) fields. Click OK and Flash redraws the grid lines using the spacing you specified.

Change Grid Snapping Accuracy

You can change how close an object must be to a grid intersection before Flash snaps the object to the grid. To change grid snapping accuracy, open the Grid dialog box (View I Grid I Edit Grid). Click the vertical, double-headed arrow to the right of the Snap Accuracy field and choose an option from the pop-up list. The effect of the different options will vary depending on the size of your document and the spacing of the grid. Normal works best in most instances. Choose Must Be Close or Always Snap if you have specified wide grid spacing.

Use Rulers

Flash has another hidden tool that you can use to align objects in your movies: rulers. When you choose View I Rulers, Flash displays a vertical and horizontal ruler, as shown in Figure 2-5. The rulers use the unit of measure you specified in the Document Properties dialog box. If you did not modify the Ruler Units option when you set up the movie, the rulers use pixels, the Flash default, as their unit of measure.

When you select an object on the stage and move it, Flash displays two small lines on each ruler that correspond to the object's width and height. As you move an object across the stage,

2

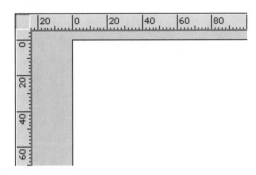

FIGURE 2-5   Use the rulers in Flash to measure elements on the stage.

these reference points follow, giving you a preview of the object's current position. You can use these reference points to accurately position an object on the stage. You also use rulers to create guides for your document.

Use Guides

Another option you can use to align and position objects in your movies is guides. Guides are visual references that you create and position where needed. You can create horizontal and vertical guides. You can create as many guides as you need. Guides will not be visible when the movie is published. An example of using guides would be aligning a series of navigation buttons to a vertical guide. To create guides for your document, you must first make the rulers visible by choosing View | Rulers.

To create a vertical guide, click the vertical ruler and drag to the right. As you drag, a small vertical line appears on the horizontal ruler, giving you a preview of the vertical guide's position. When the guide is in the desired position, release the mouse button, and Flash creates a lime-green horizontal guide.

To create a horizontal guide, click the horizontal ruler and drag down. As you drag, a small horizontal line appears on the vertical ruler, indicating the current position of the guide. When the guide is in the desired position, release the mouse button. The following illustration shows vertical and horizontal guides added to a document.

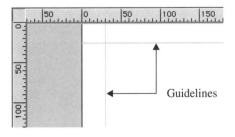

To toggle the visibility of guides, choose View | Guides | Show Guides. When you choose this command, Flash hides all visible guides from view. Select the command again, and Flash reveals the hidden guides.

```
✓ Show Guides        ⌘;
  Lock Guides       ⌥⌘;
✓ Snap to Guides    ⇧⌘;
  Edit Guides...   ⌥⇧⌘G
```

Use the Snap To Guides Feature

After you create a series of guides, you can have Flash snap objects to the guides by choosing View | Guides | Snap To Guides. After you choose this option, Flash will snap objects to guides as you drag the objects across the stage. The snapping takes place at the handle you chose when you selected the object. For example, if you select the object by its center, snapping will occur when the center of the object approaches a guide. If you select the object by one of its corners, snapping will occur when the corner approaches a guide. The object's handle (an unfilled dot) becomes darker and slightly larger when it approaches a guide that it can snap to.

When you use the Snap To Guides feature, it's a good idea to disable snapping to the grid. If you have both options enabled at the same time, Flash has so many targets to snap to, it will be difficult to ascertain when Flash is snapping an object to the grid or to a guide.

Move Guides

After you create a guide, you can easily move it. As you near a vertical guide, a small arrow appears to the right of the cursor. Click the guide to select it, and then drag it to the desired position. As you near a horizontal guide, a small downward-pointing arrow appears to the right of the cursor. Click the guide to select it and drag it to the desired position.

Lock Guides

When you have a series of guides positioned just the way you want them, you can lock them to prevent inadvertently selecting and moving a guide when you meant to select an object. To have Flash lock all guides used in your document, choose View | Guides | Lock Guides.

Edit Guides

You can edit guides after you create them. You can change the color of guides and modify the snapping accuracy Flash employs when you align objects to the guides. Choose View | Guides | Edit Guides, and Flash opens the Guides dialog box.

Change Guide Color

To change the color of guides in your document, open the Guides dialog box (View | Guides | Edit Guides), click the Color swatch, and select a color from the palette. Select a color that contrasts well with the background color of your document. Click OK and Flash applies the selected color to all guides in your document.

Change Guide Snapping Accuracy

You can specify the amount of accuracy Flash uses when snapping an object to a guide. Snapping accuracy determines how close an object must be to a guide before Flash snaps the object to the guide. To modify guide-snapping accuracy, open the Guides dialog box (View | Guides | Edit Guides). Click the arrow to the right of the Snap Accuracy field and choose an option from the pop-up list. Click OK and Flash applies the new setting.

The default snapping accuracy of Normal works well in most instances. If you choose Must Be Close, the object must be close to a guide before Flash will snap the object to it. If you choose Can Be Distant, the object can be farther away from a guide before Flash will snap the object to the guide.

NOTE   *There is also a new Snap To Pixels feature in Flash. You can activate this feature by selecting View | Snap To Pixels. This feature allows you to snap objects to their nearest pixel. Use this feature if you need pinpoint accuracy in aligning objects.*

Control the Way Your Movie Looks

The stage, of course, doesn't work alone. There are many props you'll be using that work in conjunction with elements on the stage so you can dress up your Flash movie. We'll be going over each and every one of these elements so you can get the true feel of the Flash interface. The Timeline is one of these important elements, and it works very closely with the stage in creating your movie.

ToolTips

There are many features in Flash that help speed up productivity. One of the favorite features of new users is ToolTips. ToolTips are little labels that appear under most icons and text elements in the work area when you position your cursor over them, identifying the function of the icon or text element. So if you forget what something does, try using this method to find out the name of the icon.

Work with the Timeline

As the name suggests, the Timeline is where elements on your stage can change in time. Objects in Flash can move, change size, rotate, and perform many other functions while time elapses. As with every other element in Flash, you are fully in charge of how objects behave over time. This may seem like an abstract concept, but if you look at the way the Timeline is built, it logically makes sense (see Figure 2-6).

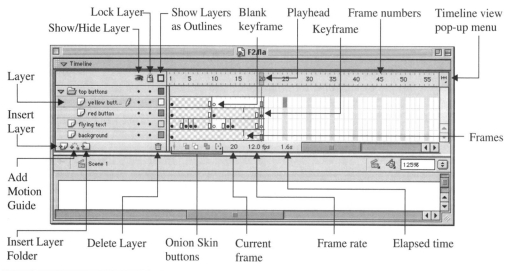

FIGURE 2-6   The Timeline is a major component of the Flash interface.

The Timeline consists of layers and frames. If you're familiar with other graphics applications, you've probably worked with layers and understand the concept. Just in case you're not familiar with them, I'll explain them here.

Work with Layers

Layers are like transparent sheets of acetate, sitting on top of one another. The top layer can obscure objects on a lower layer. When you're working on a complex Flash document, layers can make it easier to separate and sort out all the elements you're using. You can also lock a layer, which freezes the objects on that layer in place, and you can turn off a layer's visibility. By turning off the visibility, you can make it easier to selectively see layers sitting behind one another. It should be noted here that locking layers and making layers invisible does not affect your exported Flash Player file. These features are just bells and whistles that help streamline your production in Flash.

Layers in Flash can be stored in their own folders in the Timeline. This allows you to conserve space by neatly organizing groups of related layers in their own folder. Create a layer folder by clicking on the Insert Layer folder on the bottom left of the Timeline. Create a layer by clicking on the Insert Layer icon on the bottom left of the Timeline. Layers are defined, examined, and used extensively throughout Flash. As we travel through this book, you'll get to know them intimately.

Dissect the Timeline

Now that you've had an overview of layers, you are ready to look at how the other half of the Timeline works. To the right of each layer is a series of frame rectangles that appears in gridlike fashion. Each frame is numbered chronologically.

In these frame cells, you create the frames for your movie. Have you ever seen a filmstrip outside a camera? The film exists as a series of frames. However, when the movie is projected, the audience only sees one frame at a time. So it is with Flash, but instead of a celluloid filmstrip, frames exist in the Timeline. You, as the director, can control the length of time layered objects are on the stage, pause time, or stop time altogether.

The actual frames you create can exist as keyframes, frames, or blank keyframes. Keyframes are represented with a black circle and are used for changing the contents of a frame. For example, if you wanted an object to appear blue on one frame and then yellow on the next, a keyframe would be required on both frame cells because the object changes from one color to another. If an object on a keyframe remained the same and you wanted to extend the length of time this object appeared, you would create regular frames. Frames that have not been filled yet are depicted as white rectangles, and every fifth frame is depicted in light gray to make it a little easier for you to keep track of frames.

Blank keyframes are depicted as white circles. Blank keyframes are exactly that—blank. We will be examining keyframes in more depth in Chapter 8.

Understand the Toolbox

We have already looked at the View options in the Toolbox, and many of the other Flash icons
likely look familiar to you (see Figure 2-7).

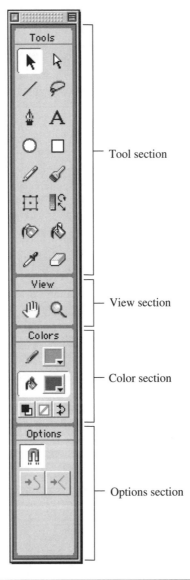

FIGURE 2-7   The Toolbox houses drawing, editing, transforming, and viewing tools,
among others.

The Toolbox is divided into four sections:

- **Tools**   This is where tools related to drawing and editing objects are stored.
- **View**   These tools give you options for viewing the stage.
- **Colors**   In this segment of the Toolbox, you can select and edit colors of elements on the stage.
- **Options**   Additional options become available depending upon which tool is selected.

When you select a tool and position your mouse over the stage, the cursor changes its appearance, depending upon the tool you selected. For example, if you click the Zoom tool and position the cursor on the stage, the cursor becomes a magnifying glass. If you click the Circle or Rectangle tool and position the cursor on the stage, the cursor becomes crosshairs. When you gain more proficiency with Flash, you will become increasingly more familiar with Flash visual terminology.

When you position your pointer over a tool on the Toolbar, you see a letter in parenthesis to the right of the ToolTip. This letter represents the shortcut key for that tool. In addition to accessing tools by clicking them, you can access them by selecting their keyboard equivalent. Do an experiment in the Toolbox and try it out for yourself. If you press the V key, the Selection tool becomes highlighted in the Toolbox. The following are a few other shortcut keys. Press them and see what happens in the Toolbox.

- **T**   Text
- **B**   Brush
- **P**   Pen
- **E**   Eraser

By selecting tools with the keyboard equivalent, you can quickly move through the Toolbox. It is very productive to memorize the shortcut keys for your most frequently used tools. It may save some strain on your wrist if you're hopping a lot from one tool to another.

We will be going over all the tools in the Toolbox throughout this book as they become relevant to the subject at hand.

Dissect the Properties Inspector

The Properties Inspector is a new feature in Flash MX. If you don't see the Properties Inspector (or the PI, as it is sometimes called) when you launch the application, you can open it by selecting Window | Properties from the menu. Let's talk about what this window is, what it does, and how it works (see Figure 2-8).

Packing a big wallop in a small amount of space, the Properties Inspector displays current information about a selected element of your Flash document. If an object is selected, the Properties Inspector displays information about the object in context and also allows you to edit certain properties of the element. There are additional sets of windows, called panels, that you can use for editing elements in the movie. Panels are covered in the next section.

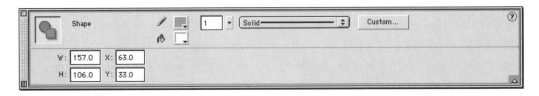

FIGURE 2-8 The Properties Inspector in Flash allows you to display and edit information about elements in your movie.

Get Information and Edit Your Movie in the Properties Inspector

If you're curious about how the Properties Inspector works, open a Flash file from the Samples | FLA folder in your Flash MX folder. In Figure 2-9, you see a sample movie named 360_degrees.fla, from the Samples folder.

If you click the little circle to the right of center stage in this document, the Properties Inspector displays data on this object. It tells you the object type, which happens to be a movie clip. It also tells you where it's located and the width and height of the object.

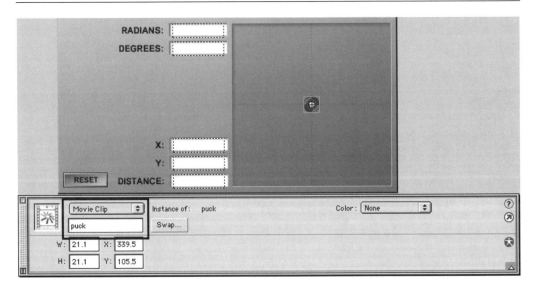

FIGURE 2-9 Sample files can be found in the Samples folder in the Flash MX folder on your hard drive.

If you continue to click other elements in the movie, the Properties Inspector changes in context to whatever you have selected. If you click the gray work area, the Properties Inspector displays information about the actual movie, including its size, background color, and so forth.

The little arrow in the bottom-right corner of the Properties Inspector expands or collapses the window when clicked. The purpose of this is to provide you with a set of secondary options related to your selection.

The data in the Properties Inspector is editable, so you can modify any elements in the Properties Inspector that have an editable field. You can also get information and edit properties of elements using panels. Panels are much more involved than the Properties Inspector, as you will see in the next section. The Properties Inspector, however, can sometimes help save screen real estate if you're working on a smaller monitor. Since the Properties Inspector is contextual, it only displays information one selection at a time.

Ultimately, when you work on a project, you will be customizing your workspace for that particular project. Having data so readily available to you in the Properties Inspector and in panels is a convenient feature in Flash.

Use Panels

In addition to the Timeline and Properties Inspector, myriad other little windows are available in Flash that assist you in creating and editing elements in your movie, including the movie itself. These small windows are known as *panels* (see Figure 2-10).

You can customize your workspace with panels, displaying only the panels that are relevant to your current work session. You can arrange them any way that helps you be more productive. Twenty panels are available, inclusive of the Timeline, Toolbox, Library, and Properties Inspector. You could really clutter up your screen with all of these panels if you wanted to. Flash fortunately provides some assistance in helping you maintain a neat and well-organized work environment.

If you don't see a panel you need to use because it's been closed or isn't listed in the default panel layout, you can access it by going to the Window menu. Here, all panels are listed and can be selected.

Dock Panels

Panels can dock to other panels. "Docking" refers to anchoring one or more panels together to form one big window or panel. When a panel is not docked, it can float freely around the workspace and you can place it in an easily accessible area of the workspace.

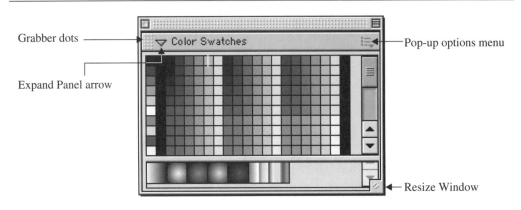

Grabber dots

Expand Panel arrow

Pop-up options menu

Resize Window

FIGURE 2-10 The free-floating Color Swatches panel is typical of most panels.

When Flash is first launched, you'll see the default workspace that includes several docked panels, as shown in Figure 2-11. To tear off a docked panel, grab the little dots in the upper-left corner of the panel and drag the panel outside the docked set.

You will know you have selected the grabber dots because a hand will appear over the dots when the cursor is positioned in the right part of the panel.

Once a panel is floating freely, you can close it by clicking the little rectangle (Mac) or X (Windows) in the upper-left corner of the window. To open a panel, select Window | (panel name).

Sometimes you may not like the order of your docked panels. You can rearrange the order of the panels to suit your needs. To rearrange docked panels, tear off the panel that you want to move, grab it with the grabber dots, and place it over the panel you want it to be docked with. The panel will assume a position underneath the other panel. When you do this, the new panel snaps to the docked panels. Once you get used to the technique, you'll discover it's quite easy to customize docked panels.

Manipulate Panels Around the Workspace

The top strip on a panel has a slightly different appearance in Windows versus the Mac platform. The grabber dots in the upper-left corner form sort of an arrow shape in Windows.

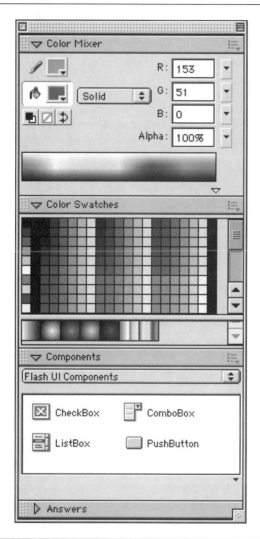

FIGURE 2-11   The default Flash workspace on the Mac platform includes a few docked
panels that appear on the right side of the workspace window.

On the Mac platform, the top strip in a panel used for grabbing the panel forms a
rectangle shape.

When panels are torn off, in Windows, the top panel strip appears in blue. On the Mac, the panel strip remains the same gray color. There are subtle differences between the Flash Windows and Mac graphical interfaces—since this book addresses both platforms, it's important to point that out. To move a panel around the workspace, click either on the top strip or the outer boundaries of the panel and drag.

Since the Properties Inspector, the Toolbox, and the Timeline are also panels, they, too, can be docked within the workspace. The Toolbox can be docked to the work area in Windows; and the Properties Inspector can be docked to the bottom of the workspace in Windows, too. The Timeline can be docked to the top of the workspace window in both Windows and Mac (see Figure 2-12).

Once you get the feel for panels, your workflow will become more productive. You also need to become familiar with the many options available in panels. We will be using panels and their contents throughout this book to create and edit our Flash files.

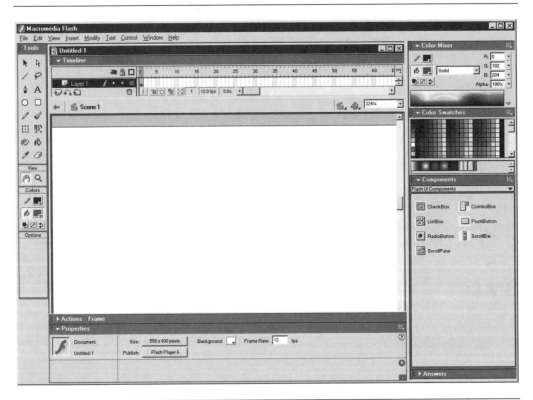

FIGURE 2-12   The default Flash workspace in Windows docks the Toolbox, Properties Inspector, and default panels to the Flash workspace window.

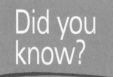

2

Flash News and Info

The Answers panel is also part of the default panel layout. Here you can connect to Macromedia to get the latest Flash news and update information.

Use a Preset Panel Layout

New to Flash MX is the ability to make your own custom panel layouts. Custom panel layouts allow you to quickly select a set of panels customized to your particular needs. To view the panel layout selections, choose Window | Panel Sets to preview the flyout menu selections.

Default Layout
Designer [1024x768]
Designer [1280x1024]
Designer [1600x1200]
Developer [1024x768]
Developer [1280x1024]
Developer [1600x1200]
my layout

Flash authors are comprised of many different people, inclusive of designers and developers. For example, if you choose to display the Designers set (1024×768), the panels that are displayed in this set will most likely be related to the functions a designer might use Flash for. The numbers in parentheses to the right of the set name are the screen resolution settings. Flash is optimized for screen-resolutions of 1024×768 and above.

If none of these presets works for your projects, then you can create your own custom panel layout. So, if there is a set of panels you find yourself always using, this may be the best alternative for you.

To create a customized panel layout, open and arrange the panels you want to use. Then select Window | Save Panel Layout. In the dialog box that appears, type in a name for your new panel set.

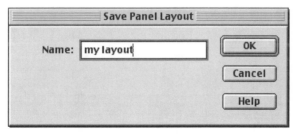

The next time you open this document or another document, or begin a new document, you will see your new custom panel set listed with the other panel sets.

Customized layouts can be quite useful. Depending upon what you use Flash for, there may be some panels you may never use and others you use all the time.

Explore the Library

Another panel you'll be using a lot in Flash is the Library panel. The Library panel is a dockable panel where you store various elements you'll be using in your movie. These elements can be graphics, buttons, movie clips, and imported elements. You can import vector graphics, bitmaps, sounds, and video in a variety of different formats. Then, when you want to call upon one of these elements to perform on your stage, you drag it onto the stage from the Library (see Figure 2-13).

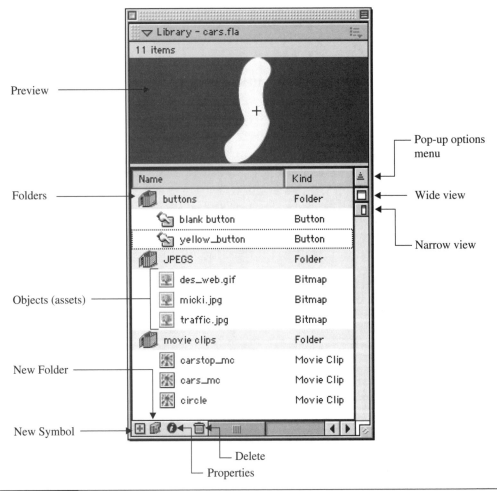

FIGURE 2-13 The Library panel in Flash

To display the Library panel, select Window | Library or press CTRL-L in Windows/CMD-L on the Mac.

When you become a more experienced Flash user, you'll discover that the most efficient way to work is to organize as many elements as possible into symbols. Symbols are elements you create that are stored in the Library of a movie. A symbol can just be a simple graphic. However, a symbol can also be a movie, which is referred to as a *movie clip*.

Symbols are edited on their own stage with their own timelines and layers—so, in effect, you're creating contained images or movies within your main movie. What's more, symbols can be reused throughout your movie, as well as in other movies. The important thing here is to understand that their home is the Library. Since symbols are probably the single most important mechanism in Flash, you'll be using the Library a lot. We will be examining the Library in detail in Chapter 6.

Use Keyboard Shortcuts

There are many keyboard shortcuts in Flash. For those of you who may not know, keyboard shortcuts are combinations of keystrokes that are assigned to specific functions in Flash. Once you become more experienced in the application and determine which aspects of the program you are going to use frequently, it will be well worth learning some of the keyboard shortcuts.

Shortcuts can also be customized in Flash if you don't like the default shortcut given in the application. Since many of the functions in Flash—like drawing objects, grouping objects, and so on—mirror functions in some of your favorite programs, it can get kind of confusing if both programs have different shortcut keys. You can change these shortcuts to suit your needs by selecting Edit | Keyboard Shortcuts to open the Keyboard Shortcuts dialog box.

The default menu shortcut keys are listed to the right of the menu selection, if one exists. Not all menu items have shortcut keys.

Create a New Document

When you launch Flash, the program creates a blank document set to the default parameters. There will be times when you need to create a new movie while editing another one, or create a new movie after saving a Flash document for another project. To create a new movie, choose File | New. Flash creates a new document that is 550×400 pixels with a frame rate of 12 fps (frames per second) on a white background. You can change these settings to suit the final destination of your movie.

Choose Your Movie's Size

The default size of a Flash movie is 550×400 pixels. The size of a Flash movie determines the size of the published SWF file. You can, however, modify the HTML publish settings so that the movie occupies a certain percentage of the Web browser, no matter what the size of the original document is. However, this might distort the graphics, especially if you use bitmap images in your movie. It is best to decide upon the size of the movie prior to the beginning of the project. To modify the size of your movie, enter the desired Width and Height values in the Document Properties dialog box, as shown in Figure 2-14.

You can access the Document Properties dialog box in one of four ways:

- Select Modify | Document from the menu or press CTRL-M in Windows/CMD-M on the Mac.
- In the Properties Inspector, click the box indicating the movie size.
- Right-click in Windows/CTRL-click on the Mac either a blank part of the stage or the work area. From the pop-up menu, select Document Properties.
- Double-click the FPS setting at the bottom of the Timeline.

In the Document Properties dialog box, you can type in a new movie size, background color, frame rate for animation, and ruler unit (pixels, points, inches, and so on).

To apply the new size to the movie, click OK and Flash will resize the document.

Decide on a Frame Rate

The frame rate you choose for your movie determines how many frames Flash uses to display one second of action in your published Flash movie. The default frame rate for a movie is 12 fps, which is well suited for most interactive movies you create. If, however, you are packing a lot of action

```
                   Document Properties

   Dimensions:  [550 px      ]  (width      x    [400 px     ]  (height)

        Match:   [ Printer ]    [ Contents ]    [ Default ]

   Background Color:  [ ▾]

   Frame Rate:  [12        ]  fps

   Ruler Units:  [ Pixels        ▾]

   [ Help ]  [ Make Default ]              [ Cancel ]  [ OK ]
```

FIGURE 2-14   The Document Properties dialog box

into a movie, you might need to increase the frame rate. Select a higher frame rate, between 15–24 fps, to create smoother action in your movies. The only penalty you pay for an increased frame rate is a larger file when the movie is published. To change your movie's frame rate, enter a new value in the Document Properties dialog box's FPS field (refer to Figure 2-14), and click OK to apply the new frame rate. You can also change the frame rate by clicking the Frame Rate button on the bottom of the Timeline and typing in a new number.

Keep in mind that if members of your audience are working on a low-bandwidth configuration, the movie may not play back at the same rate on their computer as it does on your local configuration. If increasing the frame rate is important to the delivery of your movie, you might need to design it so the integrity of your movie won't suffer at a slower playback speed.

After initially setting up the movie, you might find it necessary to change the frame rate. If the motion in your action sequences appears jerky, increase the frame rate. If you increase the frame rate, you will need to add frames between the start and finish of any sequence to maintain the timing of the movie. For more information on working with frames, see Chapter 8.

Choose Background Colors

The background color you choose for your Flash movie is displayed behind the artwork you create and animate on the stage. The default background color of a Flash movie is white. To change the default background color, click the Background Color swatch in the Document Properties dialog box, as shown here:

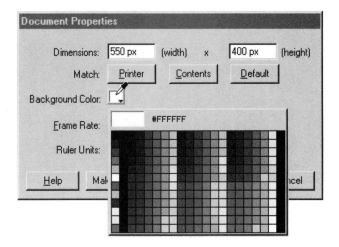

Flash opens the color palette and your cursor becomes an eyedropper. Click a color from the palette to select it. Flash displays the new color in the Background Color swatch. Click OK to apply the new background color to the document.

Choose Ruler Units

The default ruler unit for a Flash document is pixels, which means that Flash uses pixels as the unit of measure to record the position and size of objects in your movie. Most of your Flash work will end up being displayed on the Internet. Web pages and desktop sizes are all measured in pixels— a good reason for sticking with pixels as the ruler unit for the document. If, however, your movie will incorporate imported assets that use a different unit of measure, open the Document Properties dialog box, click the arrow to the right of the Ruler Units field, and choose a unit of measure from the drop-down menu. Your choices are Inches, Points, Centimeters, Millimeters, and Pixels (the default). Click OK to apply the change.

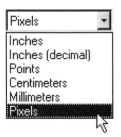

Save a Flash Document

During the course of a typical Flash project, you create objects, import graphic images, animate objects along the Timeline, and add interactivity to your movie. Given the complexity of a typical Flash movie, you might find yourself creating the finished project over the course of several work sessions. When you save a Flash document in its native FLA format, you can open the file at a later date to edit it, or share the file with another Flash author working on the project. You can also share the document across platforms.

To save a Flash document, choose File | Save, and Flash will open the Save As dialog box. Navigate to the folder where you want to save the file, name it, and then click OK. Flash will save the file and all the assets used to create it to your hard drive for future use.

As with other graphics programs, frequently saving your file is a wise idea. If your project is growing in size, you want to use Save As frequently as opposed to a plain old Save. This will help keep the file size smaller.

Open Existing Flash Movies

After you save a Flash file, you can edit it at any time by opening the file. To edit an existing Flash project, you open the document as saved in Flash's native FLA format. Upon opening an FLA file, you can edit any element used to create the file, or add additional elements to the file. To open an existing Flash file, choose File | Open, and Flash displays the Open dialog box. Navigate to the folder where the file is stored, select it, and then click OK to open the file.

You also can preview a published Flash movie in the authoring environment by opening it. When you open a movie published in Flash's native SWF format, the Flash Player plays it in a preview window within the authoring environment. To open a published Flash movie, choose File | Open, and Flash displays the Open dialog box. Navigate to the folder where the published movie is stored, select it, and then click OK to open and play the file.

Break a Movie into Scenes

When you create a complex movie with lots of action, you end up with a Timeline of equal complexity. To prevent having to scroll past an endless procession of frames and framesets to find a particular action sequence, you can break your movie into scenes. A movie with scenes is like a three-act play; after the finale of one scene, another starts.

When you create a new Flash document, it has one scene by default. If you know your production is going to involve a lot of frames and interaction, you can break it down into scenes right after you create the document. You also can create a new scene when your production reaches a point where it becomes obvious that editing the movie as a single scene would be a logistical nightmare. If your movie has a discernable beginning, middle, and end, you can break it down into three scenes, which will make editing your movie easier.

Use the Scene Panel

You use the Scene panel to create, delete, and arrange the order of scenes in your movie. To open the Scene panel, shown here, choose Window | Scene. The Scene panel is essentially a window with a list of the scenes in your movie. The buttons at the bottom of the panel are used to duplicate, add, and delete scenes from your movie.

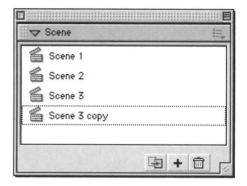

Create a Scene

You can create all your scenes after you create the document, or create a scene on-the-fly when it becomes obvious that the magnitude of your movie requires an additional scene. After you create a scene, you can cut and paste frames and layers from another scene into the new scene. To create a new scene, open the Scene panel. Click the Add Scene button (the + icon at the bottom of the panel), and Flash will add a new scene to your movie.

Name the New Scene

You can name the scenes in your Flash movies. Naming scenes is a good habit to get into. The proper naming of scenes will make it easier for you to identify the scene's contents by its name. In addition, Flash will add the scene name to drop-down menus that are associated with certain actions you use when writing your own ActionScripts. When you name a scene, choose a name that has meaning, one that will make the scene's contents identifiable by the name alone.

When you create a new scene, Flash gives it the default name, of Scene followed by the next available scene number. To name a scene, click its current name, and Flash will highlight it. Type a new name for the scene and then press ENTER or RETURN. Flash will now identify the scene by its new name.

> **TIP** *If you have created more than one scene, you can select a scene to edit from the Edit Scene button on the upper-right corner of the Timeline.*

Delete a Scene

You can delete a scene when it is no longer needed. To delete a scene, open the Scene panel and click the Delete Scene button, which looks like a trash can. Flash removes the scene from your movie.

NOTE *Deleting a scene cannot be undone.*

Duplicate a Scene

You can duplicate an existing scene and use the entire scene or parts of it to create a new scene. When you duplicate a scene, Flash creates an exact copy, preserving the original scene's layer names, frame names, and action. To duplicate a scene, open the Scene panel (Window | Scene) and click the Duplicate Scene button, which looks like an arrow pointing from one document to another. Flash creates a new scene duplicating all the elements in the original scene. Flash names the new scene by appending the original scene's name with "copy." Rename the duplicated scene and delete any unwanted frames or layers.

Change the Order in Which Scenes Play

The scenes you create in Flash play in the order in which they were created. When you open the Scene panel and view the list of scenes in your movie, the last scene created appears at the bottom of the list. To rearrange the order in which scenes play, click the scene's name and drag it to a new position in the Scene panel.

Set the Preferences

Like most graphics applications, Flash has preferences that can be set. Preferences offer you yet another way to customize your workspace so it works more efficiently for you. You can change the way you select elements or the way the drawing tools work, among other things.

To display the Preferences dialog box, select Edit | Preferences. The Preferences dialog box consists of five tabs: General, Editing, Clipboard, Warnings, and ActionScript Editor, as shown in Figure 2-15. When a tab is selected, check box preferences related to that particular subject become available.

On the General tab, you can change the number of undo levels in Flash. The default number is 100. The Undo Levels setting indicates the number of times you can undo the last move to get back to a particular point in time. Preferences can be reset at any point in your Flash production to affect any task you perform after resetting it.

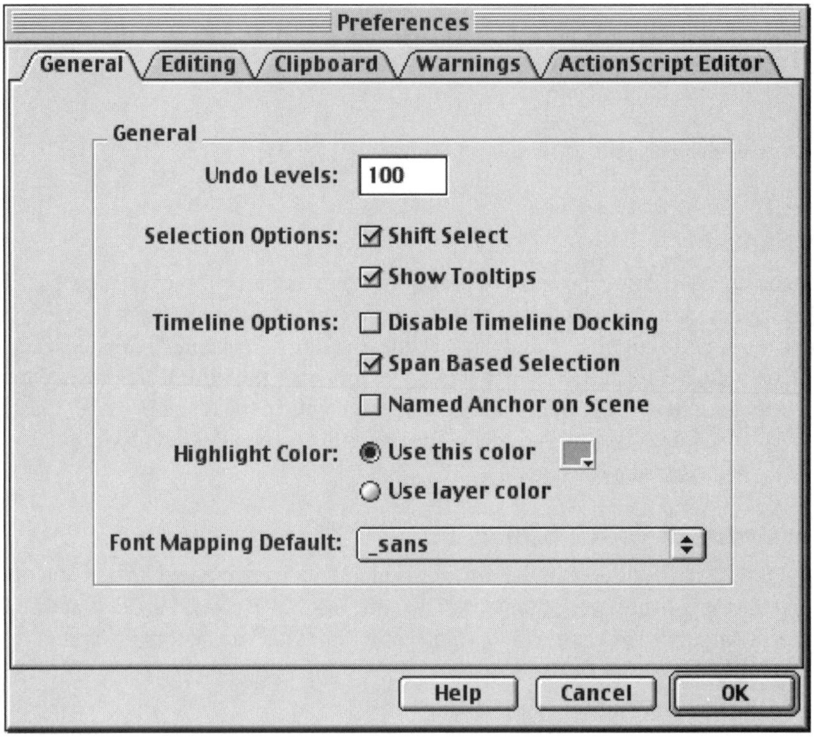

FIGURE 2-15   The Preferences dialog box is used for customizing preferences in Flash.

Although the beginner may not have cause to change the Preferences dialog box in a document now, it would be well worth your time to browse through this window and at least become familiar with the settings. You never know when you might need to select one in the future.

Flash is a rich and complex program, and there are many other features that are essential in your Flash journey. This chapter has provided you with a foundation on which to base your future studies. In the next chapter, we will begin to use some of the tools we've been talking about.

Part II

Add Graphic Elements to Your Flash Movies

```
on(release) {
    trace(_root.shape._y);
    trace(_root.shape._x);
}
```

Chapter 3

Incorporate Graphic Objects into Your Flash Movie

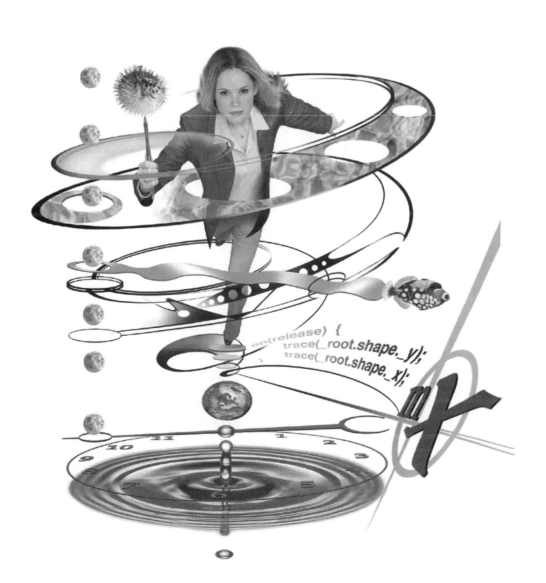

How to...

- ■ Use the Toolbox
- ■ Make objects
- ■ Apply fill and stroke colors
- ■ Draw lines and curves
- ■ Create basic shapes
- ■ Combine shapes to create new objects
- ■ Sample and apply colors to objects

In this chapter, we are going to study the basics of drawing in Flash. For some designers, drawing will become a major component they will rely on heavily to create Flash movies. Others will prefer to do their drawing in external vector-based applications like Adobe Illustrator or Macromedia Freehand—and that's okay, too. All they need to do is draw in their favorite program, import art into Flash, and build the rest of the movie from there. We'll be covering all the ins and outs of importing graphics in Chapter 7.

For those of you who are accustomed to working in programs like Adobe Illustrator or Macromedia FreeHand and you are new to Flash, the drawing interface may seem a little strange. This is because some of the tools you'll meet are not commonly associated with drawing programs, like the Lasso tool, or even the Eraser. You'll find that once you get used to the feeling of drawing in Flash, it's not as strange as it looks. With that said, let's learn how to use the tools in the Toolbox.

Locate the Right Tool in the Toolbox

Drawing in Flash begins with selecting a tool in the Toolbox (see Figure 3-1). This window is home to all of the tools you use to create and modify objects that will eventually become your movie. I briefly introduced you to the Toolbox in Chapter 2. In this chapter, we will take all the tools out for a test drive.

The Toolbox is comprised of four sections:

- ■ **Tools** Houses the tools you use to create, select, and modify objects.
- ■ **View** Includes two tools that you use to zoom in or out on objects, and pan your view of the stage.
- ■ **Colors** Includes two color wells, one that modifies the object's stroke (outline) color and one that changes the object's fill color.

3

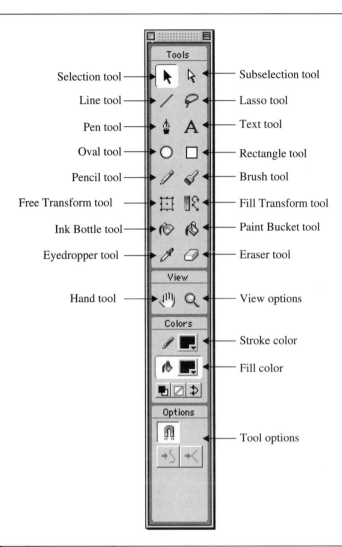

Selection tool ——————▶ ◀—————— Subselection tool
Line tool ——————▶ ◀—————— Lasso tool
Pen tool ——————▶ ◀—————— Text tool
Oval tool ——————▶ ◀—————— Rectangle tool
Pencil tool ——————▶ ◀—————— Brush tool
Free Transform tool ——————▶ ◀—————— Fill Transform tool
Ink Bottle tool ——————▶ ◀—————— Paint Bucket tool
Eyedropper tool ——————▶ ◀—————— Eraser tool
Hand tool ——————▶ ◀—————— View options
◀—————— Stroke color
◀—————— Fill color
◀—————— Tool options

FIGURE 3-1   The tools in the Toolbox

■ **Options** Contains the modifiers for a selected tool. Many of the tools have multiple modifiers; some have none. For example, if you select the Oval tool, the Options section comes up blank. In contrast, if you select the Brush tool, you then can choose various options for the size and shape of the brush.

 *When you select certain tools like the Paintbrush tool, the Properties Inspector also offers certain properties that can be set or modified as they relate to that specific tool.*

To select a tool from the Toolbox, simply click it. After you select a tool, Flash updates the Options section to display the tool's modifiers, if any.

 *The Toolbox can dock to the work area in Windows. On the Mac, you don't have this docking option for the Toolbox. Instead, it can float freely within the work area.*

Create Objects for Your Movies

It's quite easy to create a simple object in Flash. Once you travel beyond the simple rectangle or brushstroke, things appear to become a little more complicated. For now, let's begin with understanding simple drawing and then progressively build on our knowledge as we go along.

Basically, creating a simple object involves selecting a tool from the Toolbox, sometimes setting properties related to a particular object, and specifying the fill and/or stroke color for the object you are creating. You adjust the tool's modifiers to control the performance of the tool and modify the type of shape it creates. To draw the object, you simply position your cursor on the stage and draw. Let's take a look at this process in more detail.

Select Fill and Stroke Color

After you select a drawing tool, you use the Colors section of the Toolbox to specify the object's stroke (outline) and fill colors before you draw the object. When I am drawing, I often forget to select a color before I create an object. The color of the new object then assumes the last color I selected. This is no problem because you can also select an object after you create it and change the color later.

Apply a Fill Color to an Object

To select a fill color for an object, click the Fill Color swatch in the Options section of the Toolbox. After clicking the swatch, Flash opens a color palette and your cursor becomes an Eyedropper. This is the identical color palette that you use to create a stroke color.

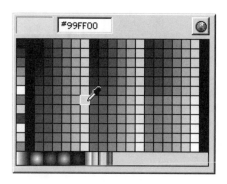

TIP *You can also change the fill and stroke of an object in the Properties Inspector.*

The only difference between the Fill and Stroke palettes is that the Fill Color palette includes gradient fills, too. The default gradient colors are depicted on the bottom row of swatches. A *gradient fill* is a blend of two or more colors. Click a color or gradient to select it. Flash then applies the selected fill to the shape you create.

You can create your own custom colors and gradient fills, too. We will be learning more about how to create and apply color to objects in Chapter 5.

TIP *To copy a solid color from an existing object, click the Stroke Color or Fill Color swatch, and then drag the Eyedropper on the stage. Move the Eyedropper over the object whose color you want to sample and release the mouse button. Flash displays the sampled color in the swatch's window and will apply it to the shape you create with the tool.*

Apply a Stroke Color to an Object

The Stroke Color well is used to select the color for a line or a stroke of an object. To set an object's stroke color, click the color swatch to the right of the pencil icon in the Color Options portion of the Toolbox. After you click the swatch, the cursor becomes an Eyedropper and Flash opens a color palette. Then, click a color in the palette to select it. This is the identical process you use to select a fill color.

If you do not want a stroke color for the object you are creating, click the No Color button. When you create the shape, Flash applies the selected fill color, but no stroke color.

 *The stroke of an object can't be made with a gradient fill color. It can only be a solid color.*

At the bottom of the Color Options section are three buttons that you use to modify the stroke and fill colors. Click the first button to restore the swatches to Flash's default black stroke color and white fill color.

Click the No Color button after clicking the Fill Color button, and Flash will create a transparent fill for the object you create with the selected tool. For example, if you wanted to create two rectangles with an outline and no fill, they could appear to intersect when placed on top of one another because their fill is nonexistent.

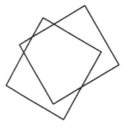

Click the Swap Colors button, and Flash will swap the fill color with the stroke color, and vice versa.

Select the Line Style

When you use a drawing tool to create a line or an object with an outline, the default style is a solid one-pixel-thick line (or "stroke," as it is referred to in Flash). You use the Properties Inspector, shown next, to change a line's style, height, and color.

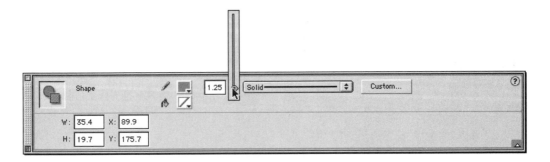

To change a stroke height of a line in the Properties Inspector, click the arrow to the right of the stroke height. This displays a vertical slider. Drag up or down to select an appropriate height. With the slider, you can make a line as thin as .25 pixel and as thick as 10 pixels. You can also type the exact size into the Stroke height box if you don't want to use the slider. You can type in a stroke height between .10 and 10 pixels.

To change the stroke style of a line in the Properties Inspector, click the Stroke Style pop-up menu.

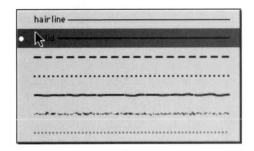

Here, you can choose from a variety of line styles. In the Properties Inspector, the styles are visual, so you can make your selection based upon what the style looks like, as opposed to selecting only a name.

When you modify the line style of a selected line, Flash updates the image in real time on the stage. Line styles don't just stop here. You can use the Custom Stroke Style dialog box to do more with lines. There, you can customize the standard stroke styles.

Create a Custom Line Style

Let's say you want to do something a little different than just your everyday solid or dotted line. In the Properties Inspector, you can click the Custom button to display the Custom Stroke Style dialog box to get a larger variety of choices.

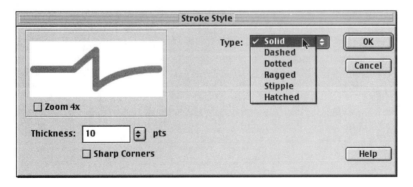

To begin creating a custom line style, click the pop-up menu to the right of Type. Here, you can select from six line styles that have self-explanatory names. For example, the Dotted style creates a dotted line, and so on.

You also can set the thickness of your custom line in the Custom Stroke Style dialog box, as well as see a preview of that line. You can see it in the thumbnail preview located at the right of the dialog box.

To specify the line's thickness, click the triangle to the right of the Thickness field and select a number. Alternatively, you can also type in a value between .10 and 10. In other words, the same rules that apply to selecting a stroke height for a line in the Properties Inspector apply to selecting the thickness of a custom line. The thickness of the custom line you create is the same as the stroke height of a line.

For the custom strokes, there are additional properties that can be set. For a dotted line, you can select the number of points you want between dots. For dashed lines, you can customize the size of the dash and the space between the dash.

For Ragged, Stipple, and Hatched lines, additional custom menu selections appear that enable you to customize every element of the line, as shown in Figure 3-2.

Enable the Sharp Corners option by checking it and Flash will render abrupt transitions in the lines you create as sharp corners. To finish creating the custom line style, click OK. Flash will display the line style in the Stroke Style window and apply it to all the shapes you create until you once again modify the line style.

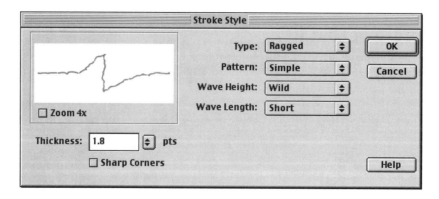

FIGURE 3-2   With a ragged line, you can adjust the pattern, wave length, and height.

Draw Lines and Curves

The Flash Toolbox provides you with one tool for drawing lines and three tools for drawing lines and curves. The Line tool enables you to create the simplest geometric shape, the straight line. You use the Pencil tool to create lines or geometric shapes. The tool has extensive modifiers that give you the freedom to create anything from a freeform line to a recognizable geometric shape, such as a circle, rectangle, or triangle. You use the Brush tool to add calligraphic splashes of color to your movies. To create a line, path, or shape with point-to-point control, the Pen tool can be used.

With the Line Tool

The Line tool is used to create straight lines that go from point A to point B. To create a straight line, select the Line tool, adjust the line style, and select a stroke color, as outlined previously.

Click and drag on the stage to create the line. Hold down the SHIFT key while dragging to constrain the line to 45-degree increments. Keep in mind that a line only has a stroke color, and no fill. You can also change the stroke and style of a line in the Properties Inspector. We will discuss using the Properties Inspector further in Chapter 5.

NOTE   *You can also use the Ink Bottle tool from the Toolbox to modify the color of a line. We will discuss using this tool later in this chapter.*

Freeform Draw with the Pencil Tool

The Pencil tool has a more freehand feel to it, as opposed to the Line tool. If the outline you create with the Pencil tool is closed (the beginning and ending points meet), you can fill it with the Paint Bucket tool. In other words, if you make an object from the Pencil tool, you can fill it with color.

You can actually set the Pencil tool's modifiers to achieve a little more precision with your pencil. If you're used to working with Bézier curves in a drawing application and prefer the precision associated with it, the Pencil tool will feel like a very strange alternative. You won't quite be able to achieve the accuracy you can with a Bézier curve, but this tool can be used to create some very cool freeform graphics.

There are three different pencil modes that give you varying degrees of assistance while creating the line. To create a line with the Pencil tool, select the tool from the Toolbox, and then select a line style, thickness, and stroke color, as outlined earlier. In the Options section, click the Pencil Mode button and choose Straighten, Smooth, or Ink. Pencil modes are discussed in the next section. To create the line, click the stage and drag. To constrain the line to 45-degree increments, hold down the SHIFT key while dragging.

What Are Pencil Modes?   When you select the Pencil tool, the Pencil Mode button appears in the Options section of the Toolbox.

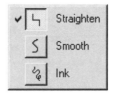

You have three different modes that modify the performance of the Pencil tool. Figure 3-3 shows lines created with the Pencil tool in each mode.

FIGURE 3-3   With the Pencil tool, you can create straight lines, smooth lines, and totally freeform lines.

To select a mode, click the Pencil Mode button, and Flash expands the button to a pop-up menu. To select the desired mode, click the appropriate button. You have three Pencil modes to choose from:

- **Straighten**   Choose this mode to create a line comprised of straight-line segments and interconnecting curves.
- **Smooth**   Choose this mode when you want to draw smooth-flowing curved lines.
- **Ink**   Choose this mode when you want to create a freeform line with no assistance from Flash. You might prefer this mode if you are an accomplished artist working with a digital tablet or if your movie calls for an irregular line.

TIP   *To quickly create a geometric shape with the Pencil tool, select the tool and then select the Straighten mode. Draw a shape resembling an oval, a rectangle, or a triangle, and Flash will transform your creation into its proper geometric shape.*

With the Brush Tool

You use the Brush tool when you want to add splashes of color that appear as if they came from a paintbrush. This is actually one of my favorite drawing tools in Flash because you can achieve a painterly kind of effect.

The Brush tool has modifiers that let you vary the shape of the brush tip, as well as the width of the brush. There's even a modifier you can use to vary the width of the brush stroke when drawing with most pressure-sensitive tablets. However, you will only see this icon if you have a pressure-sensitive tablet installed on your system. The modifiers for the Brush tool are shown here.

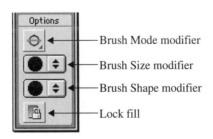

Unlike the Line tool, the color of objects created with the Brush tool is the fill color.

To create a brush stroke, select the Brush tool and select a fill color as just outlined. Click the Brush Mode button and choose an option. Brush modes will be discussed in the next section.

To create a brush stroke that varies in width with your computer's pressure-sensitive tablet, click the Pressure Sensitive button. Click the triangle to the right of the Brush Size window and choose a brush size from the drop-down menu. To select a brush-tip style, click the triangle to the right of the Brush Shape window and choose an option from the drop-down menu. To create the brush stroke, click anywhere on the stage and drag the tool.

What Are Brush Modes?   The Brush tool has four different modes that you use to control where color is applied with the tool. To select a Brush mode, select the Brush tool, click the Brush Mode button in the Toolbox's Options panel, and choose one of the following options:

- ■ **Paint Normal**   Applies paint over existing lines and fills on the selected layer.
- ■ **Paint Fills**   Applies paint to all filled shapes and blank areas on the stage while leaving lines unaffected.
- ■ **Paint Behind**   Applies paint behind existing lines and fills, and applies color to blank areas of the stage.
- ■ **Paint Selection**   Applies paint within a selected filled shape while leaving lines and blank areas of the stage unaffected.
- ■ **Paint Inside**   Applies paint within the filled shape where you begin the brush stroke without affecting surrounding lines, surrounding fills, and blank areas of the stage. If you like painting within the lines, choose this mode. Figure 3-4 shows how you can modify where brush stokes are applied with the different Brush modes.

Paint Normal   Paint Fills   Paint Behind   Paint Inside

FIGURE 3-4   The Brush Mode button lets you choose how paint is applied with the Brush tool.

With the Pen Tool

The Pen tool works in a similar manner to other drawing- or vector-based applications. So, if you're accustomed to the quirks of a Pen tool, you'll get the feel for the Flash Pen tool in no time. If you've never worked with a Pen tool, using this will probably seem a little frustrating at first. If you fall into this category, you will probably want to turn to the Pencil tool for comfort.

You use the Pen tool to create lines, outlines, and point-to point and/or curved paths. In other words, it's kind of like the Pencil tool in that the lines yield a similar result. It's different in that it handles differently and can also be used for drawing that requires extreme precision.

Another difference between the Pen and Pencil tool is that with the Pen tool, you create your object going from point to point instead of just drawing as if the tool were a real pencil. In effect, it's like manipulating a string (the line) between two needles (the points connecting the lines). Sound confusing? I'll try to clear it up for you.

To create a straight line with the Pen tool, select the tool, and select a line style, stroke, and/or fill color, as outlined earlier. Click the spot on the stage where you want the line segment to begin, and Flash creates a single corner point. Click the spot where you want the segment to end, and Flash adds another corner point, connecting the points with a straight-line segment, as shown next. You can keep on clicking other spots on the stage like this to create an object or shape with more sides. The result will be straight lines connecting to one another via points.

TIP *To constrain a line segment to 45-degree increments, hold down the SHIFT key.*

To complete drawing an open path with the Pen tool, double-click the last point. Alternatively, you can CTRL-click in Windows/OPT-click on the Mac anywhere on the stage. To create a closed path, click the first point you created, and Flash closes the outline and applies the currently selected fill color.

Creating a curved path with the Pen tool involves the same technique as outlined previously with a slight variation. Wherever you need to add a curve point to the path, you click and drag. As you drag, Flash creates a pair of tangential handles that define the shape of the curve. Remember the knitting needle analogy I used earlier? The handles are almost like knitting needles and the curve becomes the yarn between them. The tip of the needles would be the equivalent of the points on the path. The only difference between Pen handles and the knitting needle analogy is that, in the case of Pen handles, they point the direction of the curve, as shown in Figure 3-5.

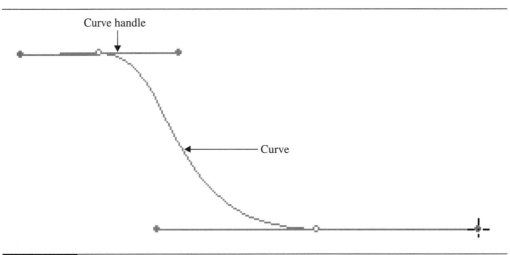

Curve handle

Curve

FIGURE 3-5   On a curved path, handles point in the direction of the curve.

The direction and the distance you drag on the end of the handle (either side) after clicking determines the length and slope of the handles. When the curve segment is the shape you desire, release the mouse button. You can now add curve points or corner points to create a path. If the shape of the path is not satisfactory, you can modify each point along the path with the Subselection tool to the right of the Arrow tool, or you can add additional points to the path or delete unneeded points with the Pen tool. When you draw with the Pen tool, you can combine curve points and corner points, as shown here.

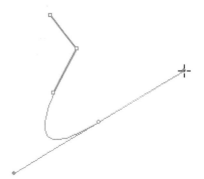

Modify Paths   Once you create a path with the Pen tool, you can easily modify it by manipulating the points that make up the path. You can add points or delete points, convert corner points to curve points and vice versa, or move points to modify a path. By default, Flash displays selected corner points as hollow squares and selected curve points as hollow circles.

The following are several ways to change the way your path looks:

- To move a point along a path, select the Subselection tool, click the point you want to move, and drag it to a new position. When you release the mouse button, Flash readjusts the shape of the path to reflect the point's new position.

- To nudge a point, select it with the Subselection tool and then use your keyboard's arrow keys to nudge the point in the desired direction. To nudge more than one point, select the first point with the Subselection tool, and add additional points to the selection by clicking them while holding down the SHIFT key. Alternatively, you can drag a marquee around the points you want to select with the Subselection tool. Use the arrow keys to nudge the selection of points to a new location.

- To add a point to a path, select the path with the Pen tool and then click on the path. As you approach the path, the cursor's icon changes to a plus (+) sign. Click to add a point to the path. Flash creates a new point along the path that you can modify with the Subselection tool.

- To delete a corner point from a path, select the path with the Pen tool and move toward the corner point you want to delete. As you approach the point, the cursor becomes a minus (–) sign. Click the point to delete it.

■ To delete a curve point from a path, select the curve with the Pen tool and move toward the curve point you want to delete. As you approach the point, the cursor becomes an angled (<) sign. Double-click the point (the first click converts the point to a corner point; the second click deletes it) to delete it. Alternatively, you can delete any point from a path by first selecting it with the Subselection tool and then pressing DELETE.

■ To convert a corner point to a curve point, select the point you want to convert with the Subselection tool and, while holding down the ALT/OPT key, drag. As you drag, Flash creates a pair of tangential handles that define the shape of the curve point. When you release the mouse button, Flash redraws the path.

■ To convert a curve point to a corner point, click the point with the Pen tool. Flash collapses the point's handles as it converts it and redraws the path.

TIP *The Pen tool is a little tricky and requires a lot of practice for a novice. For practice, you may want to try tracing over images you have created with the Pencil tool.*

Adjust Pen Tool Preferences   You can edit the Pen tool to change the appearance of the Pen tool cursor, display line segments as you draw, or change the appearance of selected points to suit your working style.

You modify the Pen tool's performance by choosing Edit | Preferences and then clicking the Edit tab. In the Pen tool section, you can adjust the following options:

■ **Show Pen Preview**   Flash creates a preview of each line segment as you move the cursor across the stage, before you create the end point of the segment.

■ **Show Solid Points**   Select this option, and Flash displays selected points as hollow points and unselected points as solid points.

■ **Show Precise Cursors**   Select this option, and Flash displays the Pen tool as a cross hairs. Use this option when you need to align path points to precise locations along the grid.

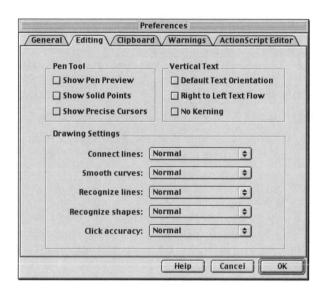

Use the Text Tool to Create a Text Object Quickly

When you want to add the written word to your Flash movie, one way to do it is to use the Text tool. Text in Flash can be animated, become a dynamic interactive element of your movie, or be used to display a static message or word. In fact, some designers only design with text. Check out Jimmy Chin's site, www.typographic.com, for an excellent example of a beautiful Flash-driven web site that uses text as the main design element.

The usage of text in Flash movies is covered in detail in Chapter 4. This section simply gives you a quick overview on how to create a block of text, since it is by most definitions in the graphic object category, too.

Creating a text object in Flash is pretty simple. Select the Text tool in the Toolbox, position the cursor (which now has become an "I" beam) on the stage where you want the text to begin, click, and start typing.

If you want to specify the attributes of the text before you start typing, you can do so in the Properties Inspector.

At the top of the Properties Inspector, you can change text properties such as font, size, style, type, and many others. In the bottom half, you can change properties such as width, height, and position, and assign a URL. In the next chapter, we will hone in on all the details of creating text in Flash.

Create Basic Shapes

Flash gives you two basic shapes to work with: a rectangle and an oval. Although these are certainly rather humble shapes, they can be combined to become a whole greater than the sum of its parts because, after you create a basic shape, you can modify it, move it, rotate it, skew it, or combine it with other shapes to create a new shape.

Basic Flash shapes are vector-based objects. If you are a veteran user of vector-based drawing applications such as Macromedia's FreeHand or Adobe's Illustrator, you will quickly realize that Flash has a decidedly unique way of handling overlapping shapes and intersecting lines. After you become familiar with the way Flash treats vector objects, you will learn to use this unique behavior to your advantage.

With the Oval Tool

You use the Oval tool to create circles and ellipses for your Flash movies. The shapes you create with this tool can be outlines, solid shapes with outlines, or simply a filled shape. You can use the Oval tool to create shapes for your buttons, or use the tool to create artwork such as a cartoon character's eyes.

If you're using a stroke and you want to further hone in on the stroke's properties, use the Properties Inspector. As with the other tools, you can set the properties of the oval before you begin to draw, or select the object later and then change the attributes using the Properties Inspector.

Modify the line style for the shape's outline as discussed previously in this chapter. To create the ellipse, click and drag the tool on the stage. As you drag the tool, Flash creates a bounding box that gives you a preview of the shape's size and position. To finish creating the oval, release the mouse button. To constrain the tool to draw a perfect circle, hold down the SHIFT key while dragging. Remember to release the SHIFT key before releasing the mouse button; otherwise, the tool will revert to its unconstrained ellipse mode.

With the Rectangle Tool

To add rectangular shapes to your movies, use the Rectangle tool. This tool, like the Oval tool, works the same way similar tools work in desktop publishing, drawing, and word processing applications. This Rectangle tool has one modifier that lets you create a rectangle with rounded edges.

To create a rectangle, select the Rectangle tool and, in the Options section of the Toolbox, select a stroke and fill color for the rectangle. If you're creating a rectangle with a border, you can modify the border's line style by using the Properties Inspector, as outlined previously.

To create the rectangle, click anywhere on the stage and drag. As you drag the tool, Flash creates a rectangular bounding box, giving you a preview of the rectangle's size and position. When the rectangle is the size you want, release the mouse button. To constrain the tool to drawing a square, hold down the SHIFT key while dragging the tool. Remember to release the SHIFT key before releasing the mouse button.

To create a rounded rectangle, select the Rectangle tool and then select a stroke and fill color. Click the rounded rectangle radius button in the Toolbox's Options section.

This will open the Rectangle Settings dialog box. In the Corner Radius field, enter a value between 0 and 999. A value of 0 will create a rectangle with 90-degree corners. A value of 999 creates a rectangle with a gently curved corner. If you constrain the Rectangle tool to a square shape and enter a Corner Radius value of 999, you create a circle. After selecting a corner radius, click the stage and drag to create the rounded rectangle. As you drag the tool, Flash creates a bounding box, giving you a preview of the rounded rectangle's shape and size. Release the mouse button to complete creating the shape.

Select and Edit Graphics with the Arrow Tool

The Arrow tool has a revered position in the upper-left corner of the Toolbox for good reason. It is one of the most versatile tools you have at your disposal. You use the Arrow tool to select objects, move objects, scale objects, rotate objects, and modify the shape of editable objects.

Select an Object Fill

When you create a stroke and a fill, you're actually creating two separate objects that can be selected and edited independently. This is where the Flash drawing interface departs from the usual vector-based application. When you draw a rectangle in another drawing application, the fill and stroke move as a single entity. This is not the case in Flash. The fill and stroke must be selected separately. In Chapter 5, we will cover this process in detail; but for now, let's just try to understand the basics.

To select an object's fill, select the Arrow tool, position your cursor over the filled section of the object, and click. Flash selects the fill, as shown next. Notice that when the fill is selected, a screen appears over the selected area. This screen appears because it's an editable object. Graphics as editable objects will be discussed in Chapter 5 also. You can now edit the fill independent of the object's outline.

Select an Outline

You also can select only an outline with the Arrow tool. After the outline is selected, you can modify it with menu commands or other tools. To select an object's outline, select the Arrow tool and move your cursor over the object's outline. Click the outline to select it, as shown here.

Select an Entire Object

You also use the Arrow tool to select an entire object. To select a filled object and its outline, select the Arrow tool and position your cursor in the middle of the object's fill. Double-click to select both the object and its fill. When the entire object appears to have a screen over it, it is selected.

Once the object is selected, you can modify the properties of the object. We cover modifying objects in Chapter 5.

Select a Line

When you create a line with the Line tool, it is a single segment. However, when you create a line with the Pencil tool, it is a series of connected line segments. You can use the Arrow tool to select either a single line segment or the entire group of segments that make up the line.

To select a single line segment, select the Arrow tool, position your cursor over a line segment, and click it; Flash selects the single line segment. To select a single line segment and attached line segments, position your cursor over any line segment and double-click it; Flash will select the entire line.

Move an Object

After you select an object with the Arrow tool, your cursor becomes an angled arrow with a four-headed arrow just below it. Once this cursor appears, you can move the object anywhere on the stage.

Use the Arrow Tool's Modifiers

When you select an object with the Arrow tool, Flash reveals the tool's three modifiers in the Options section of the Toolbox, as shown next. By selecting the proper modifier, you can align one selected object to another, smooth a line segment, or straighten a line segment. After you select an object with the Arrow tool, you activate the desired modifier by clicking its button.

Snap To Objects

When you enable the Arrow tool's Snap To Objects modifier, you can precisely align one object to another. When you move one object toward another with this option enabled, Flash will snap the selected object to the other object. The actual point of alignment will depend upon where you select the object. If you select the object by its registration point (the object's center, by default), the object's center will align to other objects. If you select the object by one of its corners, snapping occurs at the selected corner. If you select the object by top center, bottom center, right center, or left center, snapping occurs at the center selected.

Flash creates an unfilled dot to designate the point at which you selected the object. When you move close to an object that the selected object can snap to, the unfilled dot becomes larger and its outline becomes thicker. Release the mouse button, and Flash will snap the objects together.

TIP *You can also turn on and off Snap To Objects on the menu by selecting View | Snap To Objects.*

Smooth a Line

You can use the Arrow tool to take the kinks out of a line drawn with the Pencil tool. To smooth a line with the Arrow tool, select the line you want to smooth. If you're smoothing a line that is a series of connected segments, remember to double-click the line to select all attached segments. After selecting the line, click the Smooth modifier, and Flash smoothes the line. When you smooth a line, in addition to creating a smoother line, you optimize it, reducing the number of points that are used to make up the line. Click the modifier as many times as you need to produce the desired smoothing.

This tool, as well as the Straighten tool described next, is a little tricky and doesn't always deliver the desired results. I suggest you save the document before you play with this tool. This way, if you mess it up, you can just select File | Revert to return to the last saved copy.

Straighten a Line

You also can use the Arrow tool to straighten a line. This Arrow tool modifier optimizes a line by converting curved segments to straight line segments. To straighten a line with the Arrow tool, select the line and its associated segments and click the Straighten modifier; Flash will straighten the line. Click the modifier as many times as needed to produce the desired level of straightening.

So, for those of you who can't learn to love the Pen tool, the Smooth and Straighten tools may be the next best thing to use to change the shape of an object.

Reshape Objects with the Arrow Tool

You can use the Arrow tool to reshape any editable object you create with the drawing tools. When you select the Arrow tool and move it toward an editable object without clicking, the cursor changes, alerting you to the type of change you can apply. When you approach a curved line segment, or a curved segment that is part of a filled shape, a small curve appears below the cursor. An angled line appears when you approach a corner point.

You can modify an editable object with the Arrow tool by altering the shape of curved segments, or adding corner points and then moving them. To alter a curved segment, select the Arrow tool and move your cursor toward the object you want to modify. When a curved-line icon appears below the cursor, click and then drag the segment to modify it. If the curved segment is part of a filled shape, the entire object is modified, as shown here.

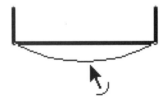

You can use the Arrow tool to add corner points to a curved segment, too. Add a corner point when you need to create an abrupt transition in the middle of a curved segment. To add a corner point to a curved or straight segment, select the Arrow tool, hold down the CTRL (Windows)/OPT (Mac) key, and then click and drag the point on the curved segment where you want to add the corner point, as shown next.

Create a Selection of Objects

You create a selection of objects when you need to edit several objects in one action, move a selection of objects, or create an object group. When you need to create a selection of objects, you can use the multifunctional Arrow tool or the Lasso tool.

With the Arrow Tool

When you use the Arrow tool to create a selection of objects, there are two ways you can go about it. The default method of selecting several objects with the Arrow tool is to click one object, and then, while holding down the SHIFT key, click other objects you want to add to the selection.

The other way you use the Arrow tool to select objects is by creating a marquee selection. To create a marquee selection, select the Arrow tool, and then click and drag the tool down and across the stage, creating a rectangle around the objects you want to select. As you drag the tool, Flash creates a rectangular bounding box that gives you a preview of the marquee selection's area. Release the mouse button, and Flash creates the selection. Selected objects will be highlighted for visual reference.

With the Lasso Tool

The Lasso tool looks like a cowboy's lariat. You use the Lasso tool in its default mode to create a free-form selection of objects, or in Polygon mode to create a point-to-point selection of objects.

In Free-Form Mode   To create a free-form selection, select the Lasso tool, click anywhere on the stage, and drag around the objects you want to select. As you drag the tool, Flash creates a line that gives you a preview of the selection area, as shown next. When you have surrounded (lassoed) the objects you want to select, release the mouse button.

In Polygon Mode   When you use the Lasso tool in Polygon mode, you create the selection area by creating a point-to-point bounding box to define the boundary of the selection area. To create a point-to-point selection, select the Lasso tool. In the Options section of the Toolbox, click the Polygon Mode modifier, as shown next.

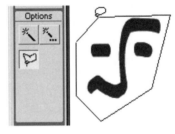

Click anywhere on the stage to define the first point of the selection; click to create the second point, and Flash creates a straight line between the two points. Continue adding points until you have defined a selection area that encompasses all the items you want to select. Double-click to complete the selection, and Flash highlights the items you have selected.

Work with Intersecting Lines

Every line you create with the Line tool is a single line segment. However, when you create one line and then place another line over the top of it, the top line neatly cuts the bottom line into two sections, which you can select and treat as individual line segments. If you select the top line first, it is the one that loses its identity and is severed into two segments. Figure 3-6 shows two identical sets of intersecting lines. The set at the right has been separated with the Arrow tool.

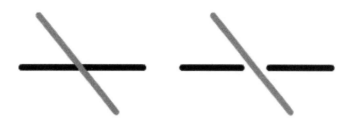

FIGURE 3-6   When you intersect lines in Flash, they lose their identity.

Combine Shapes to Create New Objects

In most vector-based drawing programs, when you create one shape and then create another shape on top of the first shape, both shapes retain their identities. This, however, is not the case in Flash. When two shapes overlap, they either combine to create a new shape or one shape will cut away from the other. At first, veteran users of vector-based drawing programs might be frustrated by the way Flash handles overlapping shapes, but you will soon learn to use this characteristic to create interesting shapes that would otherwise be extremely difficult to create. If you convert a shape to a symbol, it will retain its identity. See Chapter 6 for more information on creating symbols.

TIP   *You can group a single shape and it also will retain its identity. To group a single object, select it, and then choose Modify | Group or CTRL-G (Windows)/CMD-G (Mac). For more information on creating object groups, see Chapter 5.*

Expand a Shape

When you overlap two objects of the same color, Flash combines them and they become a single entity that you can select and modify. This kind of behavior between objects is more like a raster, or paint, program than a drawing program. In due time, we will cover how *not* to make this happen if you don't intend for two objects to join together. But for now, the process will be explained.

You can use any of the Flash drawing tools to create the overlapping shapes you are going to combine. When creating shapes for the specific purpose of combining them, remember to create a shape with no stroke. If you overlap shapes with a stroke outline, the outline will thwart your intended purpose and cut out the shape you select first. To expand a shape, create a second shape overlapping the first. Use the Arrow tool to move the second shape and overlap the first shape if the object you want to overlap is located somewhere else on the stage. Click anywhere on the stage to deselect the shapes and then use the Arrow tool to select the new shape. You'll notice they are now conjoined.

Subtract from a Shape

When you overlap two shapes of differing colors, one shape will cut a piece out of the other. For example, if you place a small green oval inside a large red oval, deselect the green oval, and then reselect and move the green oval beyond the red oval's boundary, there will be a hole inside the red oval, the same size as the green oval you removed. You also can overlap shapes of differing colors. When you select one of the shapes and remove it, the shape you remove will take a cut out of the remaining shape. The area of the cut is equal to the area where the two shapes overlapped each other. You can use this Flash characteristic to create eyes for cartoon characters in your movies or to create windows for buildings. In Figure 3-7, you see the two circles from the previous illustration separated. The circle on the left is now a crescent because the circle to the right cut a hole in it from overlapping it.

Sample and Apply Colors to Your Objects

Color is a major component of any Flash movie, even if the designer opts to use a palette of all gray. Color of course helps set the tone of your movie. The combination of color and animation can be a very potent duo.

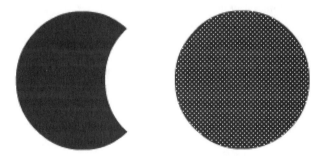

FIGURE 3-7　Overlap a shape on top of another and Flash will cut the top one out.

Did you know?

Stacking Order

When you select and create objects the way we've been doing throughout this chapter, they do not have a stacking order if placed on top of one another like in a drawing program. Instead, they become one entity on a flat plane. In the next chapter, we'll learn how to group objects in order to create a stacking order that will allow you to place objects in front of and behind each other. You can also create a type of stacking order by placing objects on separate layers. This is discussed also in Chapters 7 and 8.

There are a couple of other tools in the Toolbox that can help you set or modify a spot fill or stroke on an object. These tools are the Ink Bottle tool; the Dropper tool; and the Paint Bucket tool, used to apply colors to the objects in your movie. In many ways, they replicate functions in the menu, Properties Inspector, and Options area of the Toolbox. When you become a Flash expert, you will undoubtedly settle upon the color selection method that works best for you, and you will tend to favor it over other methods.

Use the Ink Bottle Tool

You use the Ink Bottle tool to apply colors to lines and outlines in your movie, or, as they are referred to in Flash, strokes. For example, when you use the Pencil or Line tool, the property you are modifying is the stroke—if you create a circle or rectangle with an outline, it is referred to as a "stroke." The Ink Bottle tool is a handy way to quickly apply a stroke color to lines and the outline of a shape in your movie. The Ink Bottle tool looks similar to the old-fashioned ink bottles used to fill fountain pens, although this tool gives you a bit more latitude.

To fill the Ink Bottle, select the tool; and then, in the Colors section of the Toolbox, click the color swatch to the right of the Pencil icon. You can also change the stroke color in the Properties Inspector, as well as change the stroke height and style as outlined earlier.

To apply the stroke, click an object on the stage. Click a line segment to apply the stroke to it, or click the center of a filled object to apply the stroke to the object's outline.

Use the Paint Bucket Tool (Including Gap Size)

You use the Paint Bucket tool to apply solid colors, or color blends known as *gradients,* to objects in your scene. You can use the tool to fill an existing outline you create with one of the drawing tools or change an object's fill. The tool has modifiers that enable you to fill an outline with gaps.

To apply a fill with the Paint Bucket tool, select it; then, in the Colors section of the Toolbox, select a solid fill color or gradient from the palette. You also can create a custom fill color using the Properties Inspector. We discuss this in Chapter 6. If the object you are filling was created with one of the drawing tools and has gaps, click the Gap Modifier button shown next and choose one of the following options:

- **Don't Close Gaps** The default setting. Flash will only apply the fill to objects with no gaps.
- **Close Small Gaps** Tells Flash to apply the fill to an outline with small gaps.
- **Close Medium Gaps** Tells Flash to apply the fill to an outline that has medium gaps.
- **Close Large Gaps** Informs Flash that you want the fill applied to an outline with large gaps.

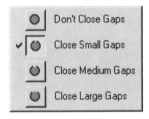

Click an object on the stage to apply the fill.

Use the Eyedropper Tool

You use the Eyedropper tool to sample fill and stroke colors and apply them to other objects in your movie. You can also use the tool to sample a bitmap fill, a technique that is covered in Chapter 7.

To sample an object's stroke or fill, select the Eyedropper tool. As you move the tool toward an object, the cursor will change to signify what you can sample with the tool.

If a Pencil icon appears under the Eyedropper tool, it is over a stroke; a Paintbrush icon signifies you can sample a fill. Click the stroke or fill to sample it. When you sample a fill, the Eyedropper tool becomes the Paint Bucket tool; sample a stroke, and the Eyedropper tool becomes the Ink Bottle tool. To apply a sampled stroke, click a line or an outline. To apply a sampled fill, click an enclosed outline or filled object.

Use the Eraser Tool

When the rare occasion pops up and you do make a mistake, use the Eraser tool to right your wrong. The Eraser tool has modifiers that you use to control exactly what is erased. Use the tool to erase only lines, fills, or a combination thereof. When you select the Eraser tool, you have three modifiers, as shown next: a modifier that lets you control which areas are erased, a modifier to soak up all an object's fill, and a modifier that lets you change the shape of the eraser.

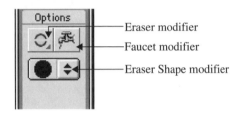

Eraser modifier
Faucet modifier
Eraser Shape modifier

Erase Shapes   To erase an object with the Eraser tool, select the tool. In the Options section of the Toolbox, click the Eraser Mode button and then select one of the following options:

- ■ **Erase Normal**   Causes strokes and fills on a layer to be erased as you drag the tool across them.
- ■ **Erase Fills**   Causes only filled shapes to be erased; strokes and outlines are not affected.
- ■ **Erase Lines**   Causes only strokes to be erased; filled objects are not affected.
- ■ **Erase Selected Fills**   Causes a fill from a selected shape to be erased without altering its stroke.
- ■ **Erase Inside**   Causes an object's fill to be erased from the point where you begin the eraser stroke without altering surrounding fills or strokes.

Click the Eraser Shape modifier and choose a shape from the menu shown here.

Drag the tool on the stage to erase objects.

TIP *To erase everything on the stage quickly, double-click the Eraser tool.*

Erase Fills The Eraser tool's Faucet modifier makes it easy for you to soak up all of an object's fill or stroke. To completely erase a stroke or fill, select the Eraser tool; then click the Faucet modifier, as shown previously. Click an object's outline to erase a stroke; click its center to remove a fill.

We've covered a lot of ground in this chapter. As you can see, Flash is no kids' program. With the many features of Flash MX, we have just about scratched the surface of what you'll need to know in order to build movies. In the next chapter, we will concentrate on learning all about creating text in Flash. This will help add to your library of Flash knowledge.

Chapter 4

Design with Text

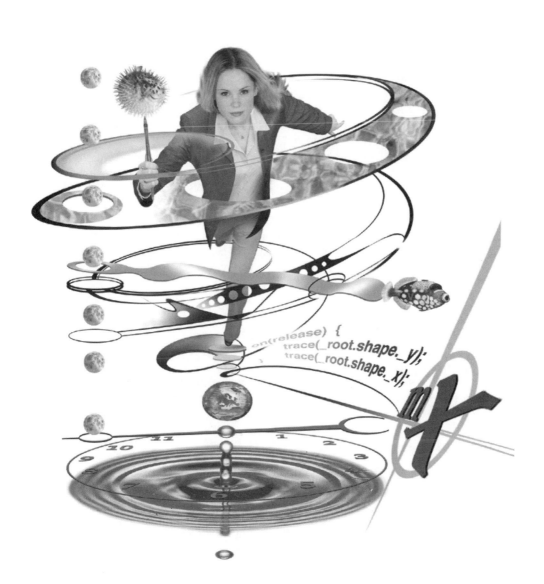

```
on(release) {
    trace(_root.shape._y);
    trace(_root.shape._x);
```

How to…

- Create and edit text
- Change the look of your text
- Create input text fields
- Create dynamic text fields
- Break apart text

Basic text—or Static text, as it is called in Flash—is easy to create; and the interface is so simple, it's almost self-explanatory. In addition to making Static text, you can also create Input text and dynamic text in Flash. Input text allows your audience to enter text in a text field right in the Flash movie, making the movie "form-like" in behavior. Dynamic text fields, among other things, can receive text that is generated from an external source.

Once you create text in Flash, it doesn't just have to sit still on your stage. There are many exciting techniques you can achieve with text. For example, you can make breathtaking motion graphics, with text zooming across the screen and fading out. You can create scrolling text boxes, too. The many uses of the text object is only limited by your imagination. The other important point about Flash text is that it is vector based. Fonts, therefore, not only are scalable, but also look crisp and clean in a Flash movie. If you compare HTML fonts on the Web to Flash fonts, there is no comparison in quality.

As easy as making text may sound, there are many things you need to know about text creation in Flash. In this chapter, we will discuss how to display fonts correctly, embed fonts in Flash movies, work with device fonts, and transform your text into an object, among other things. So let's get to it and start designing with text.

Create and Edit Text Objects

As mentioned before, creating basic text in Flash is fairly easy. After you create it, there are many ways to design your text. Just like any object, you can modify the size, color, scale, rotation, and skew, as well as change paragraph formatting. This chapter shows you how to modify the basic look and feel of your text. In subsequent chapters, you will return to the text object and continue to build on your base knowledge.

Understand Text in Flash

Flash text works with Postscript Type 1, TrueType, or bitmap fonts (Mac only) installed on your system. When you create basic text in a movie, Flash embeds font information in the Flash Player file so that when the movie is played, the fonts display as you originally intended. Fonts, however, are far from being an exact science. There is little guarantee that your fonts will display correctly once the movie leaves your desktop. Some font types aren't capable of embedding; if that is the case, a portion of the audience will not see the text as they were supposed to. This can be pretty embarrassing for you as the designer. If you want to be sure the fonts look okay

Did you know?

Font Fixes

Wondering whether your fonts are going to display properly in your SWF file? If you're using a font that may be suspect, turn on View | Antialias Text from the menu. Although this is not an entirely foolproof method for all occasions, if the font appears bitmapped (jaggy-looking), it means that Flash cannot interpret the outline for that font.

in your movie, there are a couple of things you can do to have more control over the fonts your audience will see.

Use Device Fonts

One way to play it safe with fonts in Flash is to use device fonts. Device fonts may be appropriate for lengthy chunks of text throughout your movie. For example, if you're telling a story, and the text is more for informational purposes as opposed to part of the design, you may opt to use device fonts.

There are three device fonts that come with Flash: sans, serif, and typewriter, as shown here.

```
_sans
_serif
_typewriter
```

If you use device fonts in your movie, the sans font will default to a font similar in appearance to Helvetica, Arial, or Verdana. A serif font will default to a font that looks like Times Roman. A typewriter font will default to a font that looks like Courier. Ultimately, testing your movie on many different computers, platforms, and browsers is the best way to detect potential problems with fonts. But using the device fonts that come with Flash will give you a reasonable idea of what you can expect the viewer to see on their computer.

Unlike regular fonts, device fonts are not embedded in the Flash Player files. Embedded fonts make the size of the movie larger because there is additional font information that accompanies the movie. This is another element to take into consideration when making font decisions. If your Flash file is ultimately being put on the Web, you want the size of the file to be as small as possible because smaller files will mean faster download times for users.

The second alternative is to break your text apart so the text becomes a bitmap instead of an editable font. We discuss breaking apart text at the end of this chapter.

NOTE   *To view Postscript Type 1 font correctly, you should have Adobe Type Manager (ATM) 4.1 or later installed on your system. Windows 2000 does not require the use of ATM to display Postscript fonts.*

Create Basic Text

Let's go over the process of creating basic text in Flash:

1. Go to the Toolbox and select the Text tool.

2. Drag the tool onto the stage where you want the text positioned. Notice the cursor transforms into a text-input icon (cross hairs with the letter *A* in the bottom right).

3. Start typing, and you'll see that the Text input icon becomes an I-beam and a text box surrounds the text.

As you type, the text box expands in width to accommodate the text you're typing. To move a text box to a different location, select the Arrow tool and click, drag, and drop the box in its new position.

To modify text, select the Text tool from the Toolbox and highlight the text you want to modify. With the text area highlighted, start typing over the old text. The new text will automatically appear where the old text was located.

Manipulate the Extended Text Box

Flash allows you to easily modify the shape of your text box. The simplest way to create text is to select the Text tool in the Toolbox, set the text properties in the Properties Inspector, choose a location on the stage where you want the text to be, click, and start typing. This encloses your text in something called an *extended text box*. An extended text box displays the boundaries of the text you're inputting. If you were to modify the text (for example, by scaling or rotating), the text box would serve as a reference point for aligning the text. The text box enables you to view the text as a whole object instead of as separate characters.

Notice the round handle in the upper-right corner of the text block you just created. This indicates a text box handle (see Figure 4-1).

A *round* handle indicates a text box that will expand and contract in length indefinitely (unless you press ENTER to start a new line). The extended text box is primarily used for small lines of text. To enter more than one line of text with an extended text box, simply press ENTER and continue typing. Otherwise, the text will continue on one line indefinitely.

Manipulate a Fixed-Width Text Box

A fixed-width text box has a width that is predetermined. Fixed-width text boxes are similar to extended text boxes in that they indicate the boundaries of the text they're enclosing. A fixed-width text box is a better choice when you're typing in a substantial amount of text, such as a paragraph.

FIGURE 4-1   An extended text box is identified by the round handle in the upper-right corner.

Unlike an extended text box, a fixed-width text box will constrain to the width of the box you created. You can use the fixed-width text box for a small line of text, too. In fact, some designers who are accustomed to this method prefer to create their text with a fixed-width text box. The selection of an extended text box versus a fixed-width text box is a matter of designer preference.

To make a text box with a fixed width, click the Text tool in the Toolbox, set the text properties, drag the icon to the stage, and click and drag the text box to the desired width. When you type text in a fixed-width text box, the type constrains to the parameters of the text box. The constraining function of the fixed-width text box is similar to the left and right margins in a word processing program. It creates its own soft return that conforms to the width of the box. Both the extended text box and the fixed-width text box have no depth limit. You can make them both as long as you want. A square handle in the upper-right corner indicates that you've created a fixed-width text box.

To modify the width of a text box, select the Text tool and click the text box to be modified. Drag your mouse over the square or round icon in the upper-right corner. The icon transforms into a double-headed arrow. Click and drag the square or round icon to reduce or enlarge the width, as shown in Figure 4-2. Modifying the width of both kinds of text boxes does not distort the actual text within the box. It just rewraps the text within the box, like changing margins in a word processing program.

Convert a Text Box

To convert an extended text box into a fixed-width text box, select the Text tool and click the text box to be modified. Drag your mouse over the round icon in the upper-right corner. The icon transforms into a double-headed arrow. Click and drag the icon to reduce or enlarge the width, as Figure 4-3 shows. When you deselect the icon, it will transform into a square.

To convert a fixed-width text box into an extended text box, select the Text tool and click the text box to be modified. Double-click the square icon. The square icon transforms into a circle and snaps back to the last character in the text box, indicating that the text box can now be extended.

Control the Look of Your Text

All objects in Flash, including the text object, have properties that can be set and changed. Just like any other object, there are numerous ways you can change the look of your text in Flash. The easiest way to control the look of text is to use the Properties Inspector, which enables you to set or change the font, size, and paragraph attributes, among other things, to new or existing text (see Figure 4-4).

FIGURE 4-2   Change the size of the fixed-width text box by dragging on its square handle.

FIGURE 4-3   Change an extended text box into a fixed-width text box by extending the round handle.

NOTE   *Some of the text options in the Property Inspector will be dimmed if Static text is selected as a text type because these options are not applicable to Static text. Likewise, other selections are dimmed for both Input and Dynamic text fields.*

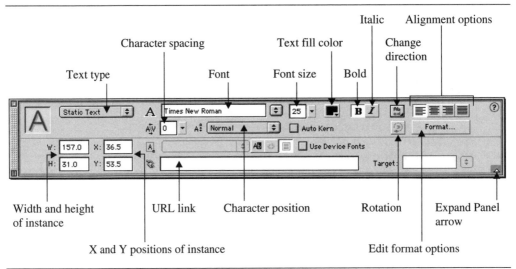

FIGURE 4-4   When text is selected, the Properties Inspector allows you to change the properties of text.

If you're a menu kind of person, font properties also can be changed in the menu. The Text menu offers font, size, style, and tracking selections. You can set these properties either before or after you input text. If you wait until after, you simply highlight and modify the text.

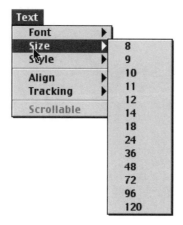

In the Text menu, you can select from the following choices: Font, Size, Style, Align, or Tracking. As shown in the previous illustration, each entry has a pop-up selection menu. Choose your options, and then click the Text tool on the Toolbox. Click the stage and start typing. The text will display according to your menu selections.

To modify already existing text with the options from the Text menu, highlight the text with the Text tool. Go to the Text menu and select your new options. The text will now reflect your new choices.

Set the Text Properties in the Properties Inspector

We have mentioned the Properties Inspector quite a few times in this chapter. Now we will discuss the specifics of how to use it. As you will see, it's quite easy to use because all the property selections are located in the same place.

■ To set the appearance of text *before* you input text, select a font, color, size, style, alignment, spacing, and so on, in the Properties Inspector. Then select the Text tool on the Toolbox, click the stage, and begin typing. The font will reflect your choices.

■ To change the appearance of already existing text using the Text panels, highlight the text with the Text tool from the Toolbox. Using the Properties Inspector, select the properties you wish to change.

Now let's hone in on the specifics in the Properties Inspector. Some properties are obvious and don't need much explanation on how to use them. For example, to change the font, you simply click the pop-up font list and select a new font. The fonts available to you in this list will reflect the fonts available on your system.

The Text fill color is a swatch panel that is identical to the Fill color on the Toolbox, and the Bold, Italic, and Alignment features are self evident. What may look different to you is the Change Direction Of Text option.

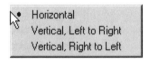

This pop-up list is located to the left of the Alignment icons. It enables you to change the direction of the characters in a text box, as shown in Figure 4-5.

You can change the character spacing (more commonly known as "tracking") by clicking the Character Spacing arrow and displaying a pop-up list. To use it, slide the arrow up for more space between characters and slide it down for less space between characters.

If Auto Kerning is checked, Flash will attempt to automatically determine the best pair-kerning ratio between characters.

You can change character spacing on any selected text. For example, if an entire word is selected, and you adjust the Character Spacing setting, it will apply to the entire word. If you

horizontal text

V
E
R
T
I
C
A
L

VERTICAL

| FIGURE 4-5 | The Change Direction Of Text optionand the Rotation text tool in the Properties Inspector. |

were to select three characters in a sentence, only those characters would be spaced as per your new setting.

You also can change the character spacing between a highlighted block of text or in between two characters by selecting the text (or in between two characters) with CTRL-ALT on the PC or OPT-CMD on a Macintosh and simultaneously clicking the left and right arrow keys. To kern or track in larger increments, hold down SHIFT-CTRL-ALT on a PC or SHIFT-OPT-CMD on the Mac.

The Character Position box is a pop-up menu from which you can specify a baseline for your text.

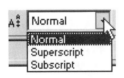

This is useful for special text effects, scientific equations, or any design when you need the text to have an irregular baseline. The baseline of the text is the bottom of the text block. The default setting is Normal. Superscript puts the text above this normal baseline and displays the text in a smaller font. Subscript displays the text underneath the normal baseline and displays the text in a smaller font.

TIP   *In addition to using the sliding arrow options to set the font, size, and tracking in the Properties Inspector, you also can manually input this information in the boxes next to Font, Size, Tracking, and so on, or wherever there is an input box in the Properties Inspector.*

Identify a URL in the Properties Inspector

You also can specify a link to a URL in this panel. If you include a link to a URL on some text, when your web viewer clicks the text you selected for linking, it will lead them to the location you indicated as your URL. URL stands for *uniform resource locater,* which, in plain English, is a Web address. The address can be an HTML file or a Flash Player file (SWF). The URL address will determine where the file is located. To link to another page (URL), select the text you want to link and type in the address of the URL.

Set Formatting in the Properties Inspector

Once you've created your text and set the appearance of this text, you may need to finish it off by setting paragraph formatting attributes. If your text is in a paragraph format, you need to make additional design decisions, such as indents, margins, and line spacing. By clicking the Format button, you can change the leading, or the space between lines.

When you click this button, the Format Options dialog box appears. Here, you can adjust various paragraph attributes, such as indents, line spacing, and margins. To change any of the formatting in this box, select the text you want to change, and click the slider to the right of the input box. The new value will appear in the input box. As with the other input boxes in the Properties Inspector, you can manually type a number in, too. To see the adjustments you're making in real time, position the Format Options dialog box next to the selected text. When you adjust the settings, you will be able to preview them, as shown in Figure 4-6. Once you've decided upon an appropriate setting, click the OK button.

Because the Format Options dialog box can be put away when not in use, it makes for a neater, more organized work area in Flash.

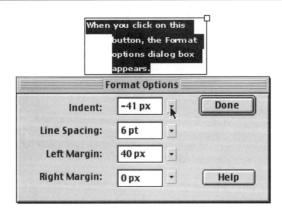

FIGURE 4-6   You can preview formatting in real time if you position the dialog box next to the selected text.

Create Input Text and Dynamic Text Using the Properties Inspector

Up until now, we have been working with Static text. As mentioned in the beginning of this chapter, you can also create Input text and Dynamic text.

You could use text input fields in a Flash movie to gather information about your audience, or you may use them for Flash-driven, interactive games, among other things. Basically, the concept here is that text input fields can pass information from one source to another. Input text fields, like Dynamic text fields, work with a script action called a variable. A *variable* is a name that's assigned to the text field. Variables are called such because they can change or vary at the designer's discretion. Variables can be assigned to objects as well as text. This in itself has amazing implications. It means you can transform an object into another object by changing a variable in a script.

Variables need to be defined, so they are assigned a value. Your value can be either text or numeric. If you prompted your viewers to fill out a form where you wanted them to indicate their age, the *variable* may be a text box named "age," but the *value* of the variable is whatever number the user types in the text field. Variables are discussed further in Chapter 12.

A variable, as suggested by its name, can change, depending upon the nature of the formula that is attached to that variable. Sounds complicated, doesn't it? Actually, it will all eventually fall into place. For now, you just need to know that Input and Dynamic text fields require variable names to perform fancy tricks.

A good example of Input and Dynamic text fields is in the Samples\FLA folder in your Flash MX folder. The file named Paycheck_Calculator.fla contains both Input and Dynamic text input fields. I encourage you to open this file, click the text fields, and check out the Properties Inspector. Here, you will notice the type of field you're clicking, and you will see the variable name given to the text field, as shown in Figure 4-7.

When you're done examining the components, select Control | Test Movie to see the text fields and variables in action. This way, you'll develop a cursory understanding of how these features work. You will see that information you input is combined with other information you input and then passed on to another text field where a calculation is done. At this point in your

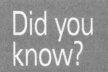

The Text Object

In Flash MX, Input and Dynamic text fields are both instances of the text object. Because text is an object, just like movie clips, they can be assigned instance names. As such, you can manipulate text instances with ActionScript. There is a long list of text methods that enable you to do some pretty fancy interactive tricks with text. We will discuss this more in Part IV.

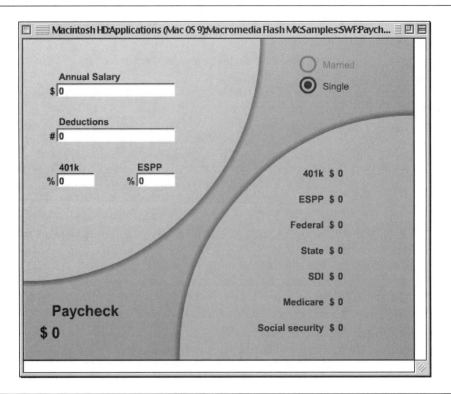

Macintosh HD:Applications (Mac OS 9):Macromedia Flash MX:Samples:SWF:Paych...

Annual Salary
$ 0

Deductions
0

401k   ESPP
% 0   % 0

Paycheck

$ 0

○ Married
◉ Single

401k $ 0

ESPP $ 0

Federal $ 0

State $ 0

SDI $ 0

Medicare $ 0

Social security $ 0

FIGURE 4-7   The sample file, Paycheck_Calculator.fla, is a good example of Input and Dynamic text fields in action.

studies, you don't want to overburden your learning experience by trying to create something this fancy. Toward the end of this section, we'll do a simple exercise so you can experience what it's like to create Input and Dynamic text fields.

Input text is created just like static text, but some of the settings in the Properties Inspector will differ. You do so by selecting Input Text from the pop-up text type list.

Setting dynamic text in the Properties Inspector works the same way. When Input or Dynamic text is selected in the Properties Inspector, you will be offered additional options. For example, you can now select the line type from a pop-up menu. The Line Type setting will determine how the text field displays.

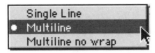

If you want user input on a Flash movie, you may want to restrict the user from typing in more than one line of text (Single Line). Or you may want a user to enter an encrypted password before continuing their navigation in your movie. You can customize the user input in this way to suit the nature of your project.

To the right of the Line Type selections are three additional settings related to input and dynamic text:

- ■ **Selectable (Dynamic Text Only)**   Clicking this setting enables the user to select, type, and edit text in a field.

- ■ **Render Text As HTML**   Click this selection if your text was created with rich text formatting and you want to retain this formatting.

- ■ **Show Border Around Text**   Select this setting if you want your text field to be displayed with a border instead of the boundaries being invisible.

- ■ **URL (Dynamic And Static Text)**   Here, you can enter a URL link for text in the text field, the same way you would create a hyperlink in HTML. You can set a link to a remote URL, a local URL, or an SWF file. When you create a link to an SWF file, the SWF file will open in a browser.

- ■ **Target**   If you create a URL link, you can also decide how you want it to display in the browser. Generally, you would want to specify a target if the SWF file was opening within a URL with framesets and you wanted to have some control over how it displays.

- ■ **Character Options**   For Input and Dynamic text, you can selectively choose to embed all or no characters in the text field, or only certain characters. To do so, click the Characters button in the bottom right of the Properties Inspector. In the Character Options dialog box, select the desired setting. This setting will be determined by factors surrounding your movie, such as desired file size versus the importance of a font in the overall design of the movie.

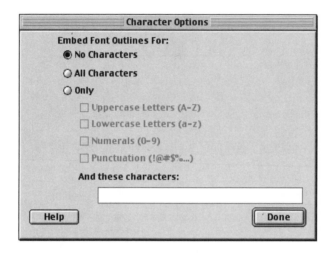

For input text and dynamic text, you can also indicate an instance name as well as a variable name in the Properties Inspector. Variables were discussed previously, and an instance name assigned to a text field allows you to add a script to that instance.

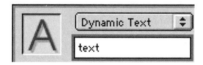

How to Create a Dynamic Text Field Using Rich Text Formatting

To help you understand Dynamic text fields a little better, we will now cover one of the many ways you can use a Dynamic text field. And, as you will see, this example has several interesting things going on in it. You're going to learn how to create a Dynamic text box, format it, and assign a variable to it. We will also be using a text file that contains rich text formatting (RTF), text that contains basic HTML formatting. The formatting will not be seen in the Flash movie (unless we select the Render Text As HTML option) but Flash will translate the formatting and apply it to the text in the Dynamic text field.

Then we are going to create our first ActionScript. ActionScript, in case you don't know yet, is the native programming language of Flash. ActionScript enables you to do some incredible things to Flash movies, inclusive of interactivity. In fact, the last part of this book is devoted to learning more about ActionScript. For now, just know that there is a simple "frame action" applied to the movie we are working with. This frame action, loadVariables, is going to load an external text file named textsample.txt (the text file with RTF) into a Dynamic text field when the movie first opens.

As you can see in Figure 4-8, the finished file we are about to create doesn't look like anything very exciting. However, this exercise will help you understand a little about how Dynamic text fields work on a larger scale. For example, Flash sites that contain frequently updated information, like sports and weather sites, although far more complex than this example, could have been constructed using a similar technique.

Figure 4-8 was created using the following steps:

1. Create a new Flash file and save it with the filename "ch4 dynamic text.fla."

2. Select the Text tool, and in the Properties Inspector select Dynamic in the Text Type pop-up menu. In addition, choose a font, size, and alignment.

3. In the Properties Inspector Line Type pop-up menu, select Multiline. This option is for Dynamic text fields that contain more than one line of information.

4. Draw a text field. Do this by positioning the pointer on the stage and drawing a text field rectangle that is big enough to contain the text represented in Figure 4-8.

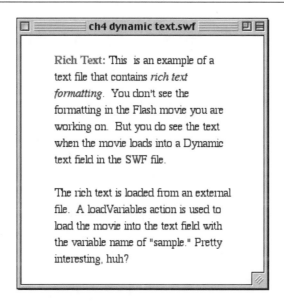

FIGURE 4-8   This RTF file was loaded into a Flash movie from an external source.

5. Select the text field and give it a variable name in the Variable box in the Properties Inspector. Use a variable name of "sample."

6. In Notepad or Simple Text, type in the following text, save it as "textsample.txt", and store it in the same folder as your Flash file, ch4 dynamic text.fla.

```
sample=<P><FONT COLOR="#cc0000"> <B>Rich Text: </B></COLOR>

<P><FONT COLOR="#000000">
```

This is an example of a text file that contains rich text formatting. You don't see the formatting in the Flash movie you are working on. But you do see the text when the text file loads into a Dynamic text field in the SWF file.

The rich text is loaded from an external text file. A loadVariables action is used to load the text into the text field with the variable name of "sample." Pretty interesting, huh?

What's different about this text is that it contains some HTML formatting tags. These tags are contained in brackets. The other element that differs from a regular text file is that the variable name we assigned to the Dynamic text field ("sample") is the very first thing you see on this page with an equal sign to the right of it. This is interesting because the loadVariable action is assigned to the first frame of the movie, and when the text loads into the movie, it knows to go to the Dynamic text field that was assigned the name of "sample."

7. Getting back to the movie, assign an action to the first frame of the movie by clicking the first frame in the very top of the Timeline. Then launch the Actions panel right from the Properties Inspector. To launch the Actions panel, click the little diagonal arrow on the right of the Properties Inspector.

8. In the Actions panel, assign a loadVariables action the selected frame. To do this, go to the top right of the Actions panel and click the options panel icon to display the pop-up Options menu.

9. In the Options pop-up menu, select Expert mode. This enables you to type in your own ActionScript with very little assistance from Flash. In Part IV of this book, you will learn how to input scripts using Normal mode. Normal mode is the default setting in the Actions panel and it helps beginner-to-intermediate ActionScript users find actions and build scripts without having to memorize a lot of the code. In Normal mode, you can pick and choose various actions from the Toolbox list on the left and apply them to the script you're building on the right of the panel.

10. In the area to the right of the panel, in the Actions tools column, type in the following:

```
loadVariablesNum("textsample.txt", 0);
```

```
loadVariablesNum("textsample.txt", 0);
```

11. Save the movie. When you test it (Control | Test Movie, or CTRL-ENTER in Windows or CMD-RETURN on Mac), the formatted text appears in the Dynamic text field that you named "sample."

Let's just review what's going on in this movie. The text file named textsample.txt was formatted using HTML tags. It also declared the variable name (given to the Dynamic text field in the Flash File) at the beginning of the text file. A loadVariables action was applied to the first frame of the movie that instructed the text file, textsample.txt, to load into the variable named "sample" (the Dynamic text box) after the first frame of the movie loaded. So, the Dynamic text field is capable of loading text from external sources. The location of the text file must be clearly defined in order for this to work correctly. In this case, both the text file and the Flash file are located in the same place (see Figure 4-9).

One final point regarding this example is that the rich text formatting from the text file does not show up in the movie. Rather, the formats are preserved in the text displayed. This little example is small in comparison to the many things you can do with Dynamic text fields. In later sections, we will return to these techniques to expand upon what we've learned here.

Did you know?

Rich Text

Not all HTML tags are supported in rich text formatting. In fact, only the very basic ones like <FONT COLOR>, <FONT FACE>, <FONT SIZE>, <B>, <I>, <P>, <U>, and <A> are supported. Still, text that has a little formatting applied to it is a little more visually interesting than plain old text.

loadVariables action on frame 1   Dynamic text box   Script in Expert mode

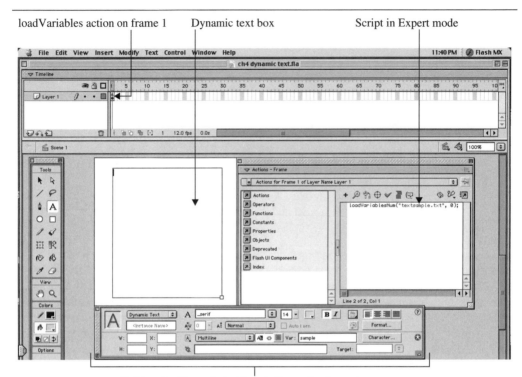

Settings for Dynamic text box in Properties Inspector

FIGURE 4-9   When the LoadVariable action is used to load text into a Dynamic text field, the text resides in an external text file.

Set Variables in a Text Field with Input Text

Just like Dynamic text fields, Input text fields can possess powerful interactive capabilities, too. Although the capabilities of an Input text field can be very complex, the basic premise behind its inner workings is simple. Creating an Input text field is almost identical to creating a Dynamic text field. However, with Dynamic text, you can enter a URL and a target, which you can't do with Input text. In addition, the user cannot input text in a Dynamic text field as he or she can Input text.

To create an Input text field, select Input Text in the Properties Inspector pop-up menu. Now create a fixed-width text box. Notice that when Input Text is selected in the Properties Inspector, the rectangular handle that's located in the upper-right corner is now located in the bottom-right corner. To review, this is how you tell the difference between an Input, Dynamic, or Static text field.

Just like with Dynamic text fields, you need to type in a variable name for the Input text to work the right way. Generally, you will use Input text because you intend to add some sort of interactivity to your movie. You can name your variable anything you like. You would also set the additional text properties like size, color, alignment, and so forth. After performing these tasks, you're ready to go. Since you may not know where "go" is at this point in your Flash career, the following section provides a simple example of what Input text does. Also, this should help you understand the bare-bones function of how Input text works with variables.

Create a Simple Input Text Field with a Variable

In this example, we will create an Input text field and duplicate the text field. The duplicate will have the same variable name as the original, so the value that the viewer types in will always match the text field with the same variable. We will also create a couple of Static text boxes to tell the user what they are supposed to do in the Input text field. The static boxes just serve as instructions on what to do next (see Figure 4-10).

4

This concept is often used on the Web where a site may prompt you for your name. Then, throughout the site, your name is remembered, so the site appears to be personalized. You can obviously expand upon this idea later with something a little more imaginative than a name. Until then, the following steps show you how to accomplish this technique:

1. Select the Text tool and go to the Properties Inspector.

2. In the Text Type pop-up list, select Static. You can then select a font, size, alignment, and so forth.

3. Click somewhere on the left of the stage, draw a text field, and type in some text. For this example, I typed in the word "Name."

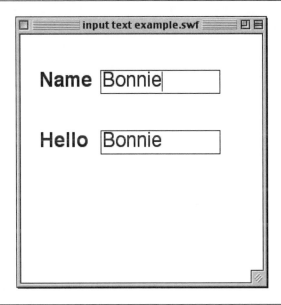

FIGURE 4-10   An example of an Input text field

4. Duplicate the word you type in (in this case, it's the word "Name") by clicking the word with the Arrow tool. Then, hold down CTRL-SHIFT in Windows/SHIFT-OPT on the Mac, and drag downward a couple of inches. This duplicates the selected text and constrains its vertical alignment. In the *new* text box, highlight the text and replace it with the word "Hello."

5. You will now create an Input Text box to the right of "Name." Select Input Text from the Properties Inspector pop-up menu. Click the Show Border Around Text icon. The text field box will now have a border around it in the movie. This helps if you need the user to see where they should input type.

6. Click and drag to make a text box to the right of the word "Name" that's large enough to accommodate a viewer's first name. Under Input Text, select Single Line. For Variable, type **Name**. To speed up the process, duplicate this text field the way you did previously, and place the new text field to the right of the word "Hello." Now, both text fields are identical, with the same variable name.

7. With the Text tool selected on the Toolbox, click the top and bottom-right blank Input text fields. Hold the SHIFT key down so you can select them together. In the Properties Inspector, choose the font, color, and style of the text the viewer will see in the Input fields when he or she types. Our sample illustration has the same properties as the Static Text block that says "Name" and "Hello."

8. Align the Input text fields left. Test the Input text field by typing a couple of characters in the blank text field box. You want the baseline of the Static text, "Name," to be aligned with the baseline of the text the viewer will input. Use the sample text you typed to align the baselines of both text boxes. In the sample illustration, a guideline was placed on the baseline of the Static text and the sample Input text was used for alignment purposes. When you're finished aligning, *delete* the sample text in the text box. Repeat this alignment process for the Text Input box next to "Hello."

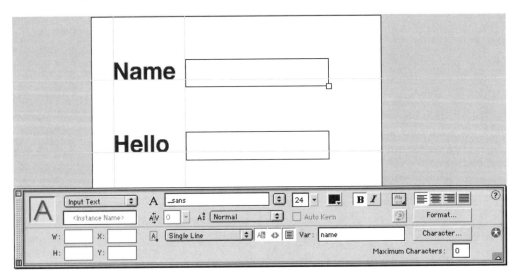

> **NOTE** *If you don't delete the sample text, it will show up in the actual movie. Because you're just using it for alignment purposes, you don't want it to appear.*

Test the movie by selecting Control | Test Movie. Next to "Name," type in your name. Your name will appear simultaneously next to the "Hello" Text Input box because both text fields have the same variable, as shown previously in Figure 4-10.

To review, variables can be assigned to text fields and movie clip instances. In our simple exercise, when the viewer inputs his or her name, that becomes the *value* of the text field, "Name," and that variable and value remain consistent throughout this movie.

Break Apart Your Text

As mentioned earlier, text is not always predictable when it displays on your viewer's system because you have no control over the way your movie will look. One way to ensure the font you've selected will display the way you want it to is to break text apart so it becomes an editable bitmap. This technique is great for a special font or a complex animation that uses text as a design element.

Breaking apart text is generally used for display text rather than lengthy paragraphs because once you break the text apart, it's no longer editable as text. The text is treated as a graphical object rather than a font. In fact, it no longer is a font once you break it apart.

To use the Break Apart feature, create some Static text. Then, assign properties to the text, such as font, color, size, and so on. Select the text with the Arrow tool. Select Modify | Break Apart. This breaks the text up into individual characters.

break this text

With the text still selected, select Modify | Break Apart again. This time, the text looks shaded, because it is now editable like a graphic instead of a font. In other words, you can no longer go back and change the font size, alignment, and so forth.

break this text

To group the letters together so they're not floating around as separate objects, select all the letters by either SHIFT-clicking on each of them or drawing an invisible marquee in the work area around the group. Then, select Modify | Group. Now you can manipulate the letters individually, too, if your design calls for it.

In the next chapter, we will focus on the numerous ways you can modify and transform text and graphics once you create them. The depth of this application is amazing, and we are just beginning to chip at the iceberg.

Chapter 5

Manipulate Graphics and Text

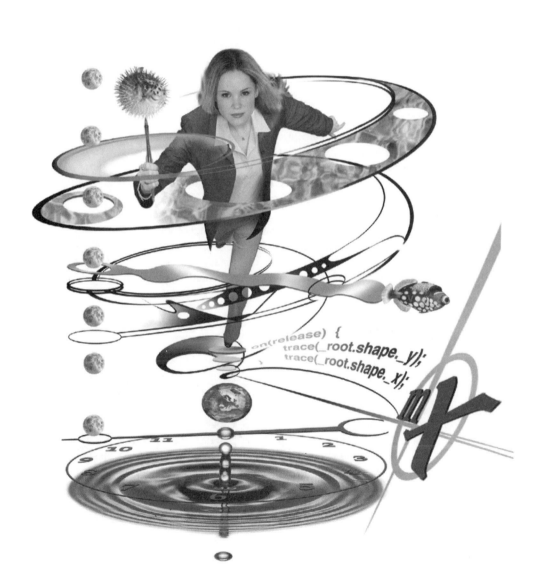

```
on(release) {
    trace(_root.shape._y);
    trace(_root.shape._x);
}
```

How to...

- ■ Group objects in Flash
- ■ Control the stacking order of objects
- ■ Apply transformations to objects
- ■ Use Snap To functions
- ■ Lock and unlock objects
- ■ Arrange objects on the stage
- ■ Get details on a movie
- ■ Apply colors to objects
- ■ Use the Fill Transform and the Lock Fill tools

Creating basic shapes and text is easy in Flash. However, for most Flash movies, you'll need to learn all the ways you can build more complex images. There are many different ways you can modify and control graphics and text in Flash for this purpose. Although you can import both raster and vector graphics into Flash, bypassing the need to draw in Flash, the drawing and modifying tools in Flash are pretty complete. Because of this, it's easy for some designers to create their entire movie in Flash. If you're willing to put the time into familiarizing yourself with all these tools, you will sail through your movie productions quickly and with minimal problems.

The tools used to modify graphics and text can be accessed a few different ways, including the Toolbox and the Properties Inspector. The way you access transformations is a matter of personal preference that ultimately hinges on which method simplifies your creation of Flash movies.

Control Graphics in Flash

If you are new to the Flash drawing environment, the tools may feel kind of strange to you. You draw an object, then you draw another, and, if they're overlapping, they connect. You may not have wanted them to connect as one, but they do anyway. Before you get the feel for the tools, it may seem as if you have no control over what's going on.

When you draw in Flash, the graphics you create are "editable." The "editable" state that is being referred to here is almost akin to working in a paint program where the graphics you create are malleable, as if you were working with digital paint and rearranging pixels on a page. In other words, your cursor can change the shape of an element by drawing another element over it or dragging an eraser over it, giving it sort of a "wet" feeling. These "wet" (or editable, as they are really called) elements can be identified by their distinct screen pattern when they're selected.

Editable elements can be annoying if you don't want to work in this paint-like mode. Fortunately, you can group graphics within themselves or with other groups to bypass this paint-like behavior. By grouping editable elements, you can easily move them around, put them on top of one another, and transform them, making Flash feel more like the vector program it's supposed to be. Fortunately, you can still retreat back to the editable state of graphic elements to change their color and shape when needed. Let's take a look at the Flash grouping features and see how they work.

Group Graphic Elements in Flash

Grouping elements in Flash makes it easy for you to move them around the stage and perform additional modifications in a single-layer environment. In Chapter 8, you'll be learning how to create multiple-layer movies, which will afford you even more creativity when making your Flash production.

It is quite easy to group a graphic in Flash. You can group an object unto itself by first selecting it. With the entire object selected, select Modify | Group or press CTRL-G in Windows/CMD-G on the Mac (see Figure 5-1). After the graphic is grouped, the boundaries of the object will display as a rectangle around the object, so you can no longer perform edits on the graphic by positioning your cursor over an edge. Now the graphic is a separate entity that can be moved on top of other objects.

In addition to clicking an editable element to select it, you can select it by drawing an invisible marquee around the graphic, as outlined in Chapter 4. If you have a graphic element like the stripes depicted in Figure 5-2, comprised of more than one piece, you need to select all parts in order to group it together. In such a case, you can either use the marquee method on all objects or SHIFT-click each object to select them all. If you use the SHIFT-click method on objects that contain both a fill and a stroke, you must also SHIFT-click the stroke of the element as well to include it in the selection.

To ungroup an object from itself, click the grouped object and go to the menu. Select Modify | Ungroup, or press CTRL-SHIFT-G/CMD-SHIFT-G. Once the graphic is ungrouped, it will return to its original editable state.

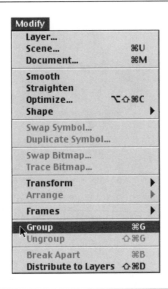

FIGURE 5-1   The Group command in the menu

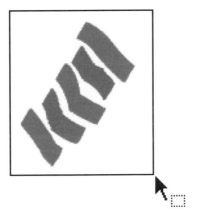

FIGURE 5-2   A marquee selection around several editable graphic elements

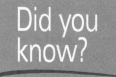

Symbols

Understanding the concept of containing objects within one another as you do when you group will help prepare you for making symbols in Flash. Symbols possess group-like qualities, too, and also can contain any combination of groups and symbols, or symbols within symbols. In other words, symbols can exist on different levels relative to the main stage. Symbols are one of the most important aspects of Flash, and also help keep things neat and well organized in your movie. Graphic symbols are covered in Chapter 6.

Group and Ungroup Graphics

Not only can you group individual objects unto themselves, you can group several objects together to form one big group. This can be done with grouped objects, ungrouped objects, or symbols. In using this technique, you're essentially creating groups within groups. Groups of objects can contain or "nest" other groups within groups. The levels of these groupings can go on and on. There is no limit to the number of objects and levels that can be grouped together.

To nest groups inside of one another, simply select the grouped elements, either using the marquee method or by SHIFT-clicking each object. Then, select Modify | Group or use the shortcut key.

Edit Grouped Graphics

If you try to click a group and change the color, it won't work. Remember, an element has to be in its editable state in order for you to change the color. Fortunately, it's easy to edit an element once it's grouped.

To do so, you need to enter the editing mode of the graphics. Enter Editing mode in one of two ways:

- Double-click the graphic.
- Select the object and choose Edit | Edit Selected from the menu.

When you do so, you enter Group Editing mode. The stage will look a little different in this mode. The band above the Timeline indicates the mode you are in with a graphic icon and the name "Group" to the right of the Scene icon as shown in the next illustration.

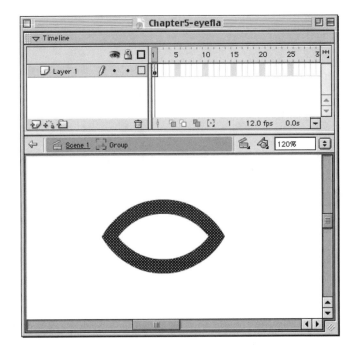

Additional modifications can be applied while in Editing mode, such as changing the shape, color, size, and so forth. When you're done, you can exit this mode in one of two ways: click the Scene name in the upper-left corner of the stage or select Edit | Edit All. This returns the object to its grouped state.

You can also edit groups nested within one another using this method. When you double-click nested groups to enter Editing mode, to get to the nested level where you want to edit a graphic, you must continue to click. The hierarchy of your nesting is indicated in the upper-left corner, to the right of the Scene icon. Each time a level within the group is accessed, another Group icon appears next to the previous one, as shown in Figure 5-3.

This convenient little feature enables you to navigate to whatever group you want to edit by clicking the appropriate group in the hierarchy list. To return to the group, click the Scene icon to the left of the group hierarchy or select Edit | Edit All.

The grouping hierarchy addresses the last group as the first one in the edit chain. In other words, the last group created becomes the highest-level group. You can ungroup this hierarchy by applying the Ungroup command to each group in the hierarchy.

Break Graphics and Text Apart

Breaking apart text was examined in Chapter 4 when we talked about text. In addition to text, the Break Apart command works with graphics, symbols, and even imported bitmaps.

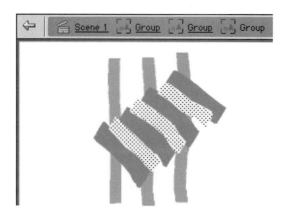

| FIGURE 5-3 | Groups nested within groups assume a nesting hierarchy, as indicated in the upper-left corner of the stage. |

Break apart objects by clicking the object and selecting Modify | Break Apart or pressing CTRL-B in Windows/CMD-B on the Mac.

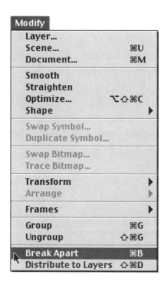

You break objects apart to separate the elements into editable objects. For example, if you wanted to modify the color of a grouped graphic, you could break it apart to do so. So, in this sense, the Break Apart command would be used in the same way you would use the Ungroup command, which would also break the object down into an editable graphic. Because you can ungroup graphics easily to make them editable, Break Apart is generally used for text and bitmaps.

NOTE *When you import clip art into Flash or graphics you created in other vector programs like Illustrator or Freehand, they come in as grouped objects. If you need to modify the graphics as editable objects, you need to ungroup them or break them apart. If the graphics were grouped in the program they were created in, you may have to apply the Break Apart command more than once.*

The main difference between the Ungroup command and the Break Apart command is that the Break Apart command is not reversible in some cases. For example, you can break apart a Symbol instance, but the Break Apart command discards what may be important information about that instance, such as frames and layers, and breaks the link between the instance and the master symbol. When the master symbol is updated, it no longer carries through to the instance that has been broken apart. For more information about symbols, see Chapters 6 and 11.

As mentioned previously, imported bitmap pictures can be broken apart, too. Flash provides some fun tools to manipulate a broken-apart bitmap. This is covered in Chapter 7, where importing bitmaps is discussed in detail.

Change the Stacking Order of Objects

As discussed previously, when you draw editable objects on top of one another, they conjoin and become one object. Grouped elements, on the other hand, allow you to select each element separately, place them on top of one another, deselect them, and select them again, and they are still perceived as separate pieces.

So, grouped elements on a single layer possess the ability to be stacked on top of one another. If graphic elements are capable of having a stacking order, the next logical question is, which graphic element takes precedence over the other? In other words, which one gets the top position? The answer is actually quite logical. The stacking order is determined by the last element that was created on the Flash stage. The first element created takes the position behind subsequent elements. If you were to create a grouped rectangle as an element on the stage, create another grouped graphic element on the stage, and position the second element on top of the first, the first element would be hidden by the second element. This is the natural stacking order of grouped elements in Flash (see Figure 5-4).

Layer Order

In the Timeline, the order of layers creates a type of stacking order, too. Each layer created is behind subsequent layers, and this is evident in the list structure of the layers; so the first layer in the layer list is always on top of the layers underneath. Layer order can be reshuffled simply by clicking a layer and dragging it up or down in the layer list to reposition it. We'll be using multiple layers frequently in subsequent chapters.

FIGURE 5-4   A single-layer drawing with grouped elements stacked on top of one another

You can change the stacking order of grouped elements in a single-layer Flash document. To change the stacking order of one grouped graphic in relation to another, select one of the objects. In the menu, select Modify | Arrange | Send To Back or press CTRL-SHIFT-DOWN ARROW/ CMD-SHIFT-DOWN ARROW. This puts a graphic element all the way to the back in the stacking order.

NOTE *When you draw an editable element without grouping it and it overlaps a grouped element, the editable graphic will always assume the last place on the stacking level until it is grouped.*

Selecting Modify | Arrange | Bring To Front or pressing CTRL-SHIFT-UP ARROW/OPT-SHIFT-UP ARROW places the selected graphic element at the top of the stacking order.

To move the stacking position of your grouped element *up* one level or *down* one level instead of all the way to the back or all the way to the front, select Modify | Arrange | Bring Forward (CTRL-UP ARROW/CMD-UP ARROW) or select Modify | Arrange | Send Backward (CTRL-DOWN ARROW/CMD-DOWN ARROW). This works well if your single-layer design requires multiple stacking, as is most often the case when working on a design of medium-to-difficult complexity.

When an experienced Flash designer tackles a complex movie with a lot of graphic elements, most often, he or she will create all the ancillary parts of the drawing as symbols. This makes all

the pieces more modular and easy to organize. Symbols, like groups, stack easily and are simple
to edit. Chapters 6 and 11 cover symbols in more detail.

*The stacking order of text in Flash is like that of a grouped graphic element. In other
words, you can stack text elements on top of one another. The exception to this is if text
is broken apart. In this case, the object is editable and doesn't have a stacking order
unless grouped.*

Change the Look of Graphics and Text

There are many ways to modify the graphics you create in Flash. The Flash user interface is easy
to use once you understand where everything is located and how it all works. The Free Transform
tools, as the name implies, are used to change the appearance of graphic elements you create.
You can scale and rotate graphics to change the size and angle of them. You also can skew an
object if you want to distort its perspective, or flip it for a mirror effect. For the most part, text
can be transformed in the same way that graphics can. In addition, grouped graphics can be
transformed, as can editable graphics and symbols.

Let's examine the different ways you can change graphics in Flash. Probably the quickest
and easiest way is to use the Free Transform tool in the Toolbox.

There are also several different ways to modify graphics using the menu and the Properties
Inspector. Let's take a look at these different methods.

Scale an Object

You can make a selected object smaller or larger by applying the scaling features. Before modifying
the scale of an object, you must select the object first and then perform the scale. This is true of all the
Free Transform tools. The tools must know what it is they're transforming before they do their job.

Use the Transform Tool to Scale an Object

Scale an object visually by clicking the object and selecting the Free Transform tool in the Toolbox.
Eight square handles surround the boundaries of the object when you do this. When you position
your cursor right on top of any of these handles, the cursor turns into a double-headed arrow.
Depending upon which handle you're over, the double-headed arrow will change direction. The
direction indicates which way the object is going to scale. The following list describes the various
ways the double-headed arrow scales:

■ The double-headed arrow that appears when you position your cursor over any of the
four corner handles is in a diagonal direction. The arrow icon shown next indicates that
you can scale the width and height of the graphic.

■ The double-headed arrow that appears when you position your cursor over the right or left handle is depicted in a horizontal direction. This indicates that you can scale the width of the graphic.

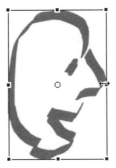

■ The double-headed arrow that appears when you position your cursor over the top or bottom handle is depicted in a vertical direction. This indicates that you can scale the height of the graphic.

To scale a graphic, position your pointer directly on top of one of the square handles until the pointer turns into one of the icons just mentioned. Then, click and drag in the direction you want the object to enlarge or reduce.

You can also rotate and skew with the Free Transform tool. When you position your pointer slightly *off* the transform handles, the icon for the Scale features or the icon for the Rotate features will display, depending upon where your pointer falls. We will cover that process in the next section. However, it needs to be mentioned here because if you are new to the Free Transform tool, you may find it hard to access the correct transform tool using this mouse-over method. To ensure your tool will only scale, as opposed to activating the Rotate icon or Skew icon, in the Options section of the Toolbox, you can select the Scale icon. This way, you will only be able to access the Scale icon.

Concurrently, if you select the Rotate icon, you will only be able to access the Rotate icon in the four corners. Also, with the Scale Rotate tool selected in the Options section of the Toolbox, you can access the Skew tool by clicking right on the transform handles, in between the four corners.

To constrain the scale of an object, hold down the SHIFT key while dragging on one of the square handles in the four corners. This scales the graphic in exact proportion to its original size.

To remove a transformation, select Modify | Transform | Remove Transform or press CTRL-SHIFT-Z/SHIFT-CMD-Z.

Scale Using Menu Options

You also can use the Scale command in the Modify | Transform menu to scale an object. Scale an object in this manner by clicking the object and selecting Modify | Transform | Scale.

This works the same way as the Scale icon in the Options section of the Toolbox. Scale by clicking and dragging one of the eight scaling handles located on the boundaries of the object.

There are other ways to scale an object, too. The Free Transform option in the Menu is identical to using the Free Transform tool in the Toolbox. The same scaling handles appear around the graphic and it is manipulated in the same way.

Another method that's used frequently (when an object requires a specific size) is to scale an object with a numeric percentage. This is done by clicking the object and selecting

Modify | Transform | Scale And Rotate from the menu or pressing CTRL-ALT-S /CMD-OPT-S.
This displays the Scale And Rotate dialog box.

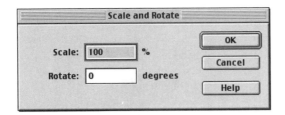

In the Scale setting, type a percentage number and click OK. This method will always
constrain objects to the proportion you're entering. For example, if you wanted to scale a
rectangle to 50 percent, the width and the height of the rectangle at 50 percent would be in
perfect proportion to the original at 100 percent.

Undo a scale by clicking the object and choosing Modify | Transform | Remove Transform
or pressing CTRL-SHIFT-Z/CMD-SHIFT-Z. This removes any of the transformations applied and
returns the object to its original state. Selecting Edit | Undo or pressing CTRL-Z/CMD-Z will return
the object to its previous state before you applied the transformation.

Change the Size from the Properties Inspector

Although you can't scale an object from the Properties Inspector, you can change the width and
height of an object. This method would be appropriate if you knew beforehand that an element
had to be in exact proportion. The Properties Inspector can assist you in targeting the exact size
of a graphic element.

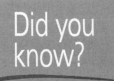

Undo Levels

By selecting Edit | Preferences | General, you can specify the number of undo levels that can be
applied, up to 200 times. The default number of undos in the Preferences | General dialog box is
100. This means you can apply Edit | Undo to an object to return back to a previous state up to
100 times. Flash keeps track of the progression of your movie so elements can be undone to a
certain point. Keep in mind that setting the Undo Levels all the way up to 200 times is not a
good idea because it requires more system memory. If you're running Flash on an older system,
increasing the Undo Levels could slow down your system's performance considerably.

To use the Properties Inspector in this way, select a graphic first. Then, in the Properties Inspector, you can type in a new width and height for the graphic. The graphic now assumes the new dimensions you typed in.

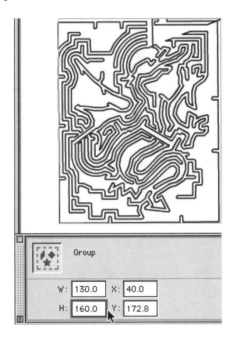

Rotate a Graphic Element

When you rotate a graphic element, the angle of its direction is changed. Many interesting visual effects can be achieved by applying simple rotations to objects. As mentioned in the "Use the Transform Tool to Scale an Object" section, you can rotate an object visually by selecting the graphic and using the Transform tool.

To rotate a graphic with the Transform tool, select the object first. Then, position your pointer slightly off and to the outside of one of the four square handles in the corners until it assumes the shape of the Rotate icon.

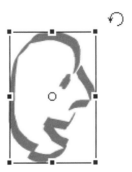

Notice that if you actually touch the handle, it turns into the Scale or Skew icon, which will not yield the correct results if your intention was to rotate.

Drag the handles in a circular motion to rotate the graphic. When you are done, click the Arrow tool or press the V key to return to the default Arrow tool.

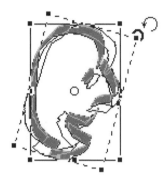

To constrain the rotation of a graphic, hold down the SHIFT key while dragging on one of the four rotation icons. This will constrain the graphic in 45-degree increments.

To make your selection of the Rotate icon easier when using the Free Transform tool, you can click the Rotate icon in the Options section of the Toolbox. As mentioned in the last section, this makes the Free Transform tool only address the Rotate and Skew properties of the tool. The Rotate tool is only available when the Free Transform tool is selected. When using the Rotate tool from the Options section of the Toolbox, you can position the pointer directly on the handle in any of the four corners to rotate, as opposed to placing the pointer near the four corners to rotate.

Rotate Using Menu Options

As an alternative, you can also use the Rotate command in the Modify | Transform menu. To do so, select the graphic and go to Modify | Transform | Rotate And Skew. This works the same way as using the Rotate tool in the Options section when using the Free Transform tool on a graphic.

Rotate an object to a predetermined numeric degree by clicking the object and selecting Modify | Transform | Scale And Rotate or pressing CTRL-ALT-S in Windows/CMD-OPT-S on the Mac, as shown before. In the Rotate setting, type a specific angle degree and click OK.

To further your choices, the Modify | Transform menu offers you two more rotation-related options: Rotate 90° CW, which rotates the object 90 degrees clockwise, and Rotate 90° CCW, which rotates the object 90 degrees counterclockwise. Use these Free Transform tools by clicking the object to be rotated and selecting the desired transformation from the menu. Click OK and the transformation will be completed.

A rotation can be undone by clicking the object and choosing Modify | Transform | Remove Transform (CTRL-SHIFT-Z/CMD-SHIFT-Z). This command completely removes the transformation. The Edit | Undo (CTRL-Z/CMD-Z) command returns the objects to their previous state, right before you applied the transformation.

Skew and Flip an Object

To skew a graphic, you distort it by applying a slant effect along an axis. This gives the object a quasi-3-D effect on a two-dimensional plane.

To apply a skew technique to an object using the Free Transform tool, first select the object. Position the pointer over the outer transform rectangle edges.

The pointer turns into the Skew icon. Click and drag left or right if you selected the top or bottom center handles. Click and drag up or down if you selected the left or right edge center handles. The further you drag the handle, the more distorted the object becomes. With all the transform tools, you can track the result of your transformation because an outline is displayed during the transformation.

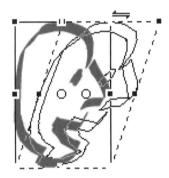

Skew Using Menu Options

You can perform a skew on a graphic by selecting Modify | Transform | Rotate And Skew from the menu. This works the same way as using the Rotate tool in the Options section when using the Free Transform tool on a graphic. When you select this option, the eight transformation handles appear around an object. To skew an object, position the pointer over one of the middle handles on the outer transform rectangle edges. The handle turns into the Skew icon. Use this icon the same way you use it with the Transform tool.

You also can flip a graphic horizontally or vertically to create a mirror effect. The flip transformation options can be found in the menu under Modify | Transform | Flip Horizontal or Flip Vertical.

Use the Snap To Functions

The Snap To functions in Flash give you some assistance with positioning graphic elements on the Flash stage. When the Snap To Objects feature is turned on, the edge (or the center) of an object "magnetically" jumps to a grid, guideline, or another object when the object is dragged close to the grid, guideline, or other object. This allows you more accuracy in the positioning of your graphics. You can also snap to pixels, as well as objects. There are a few different ways to set up and control snapping in Flash. Let's take a look at them.

Snap to Grid and Guides

To snap an object to a guide or a grid, you first need to set up and display guides or a grid. Guides can be displayed by selecting View | Guides | Show Guides. Then the ruler needs to be displayed (View | Rulers). The guides are dragged from out of the ruler. From the menu, select View | Guides | Snap To Guides. Now the edges and center of objects can be precisely aligned on a guide.

If you want graphics to snap to guides, it's best to lock the guides in place by selecting View | Guide | Lock Guides. This way, the guides won't move if you need to reposition an object. The grid and guides are only visible on the Flash stage and they don't display when the movie plays.

To prepare the stage to snap to a grid, first turn on a grid by selecting View | Grid | Snap To Grid or pressing CTRL-'/CMD-SHIFT-'.

You also want to make sure that View | Grid | Show Grid is selected in the menu so the grids won't be invisible. You can customize the grid size and color by selecting View | Edit Grid or pressing CTRL-ALT-G/CMD-OPT-G. In the Edit Grid dialog box, the color, space between the horizontal and vertical grid lines, and snap accuracy level (Normal to always snap) can be adjusted.

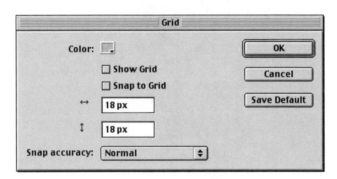

TIP   *Default guides can be edited by selecting View | Guides | Edit Guides.*

With your Snap To settings selected in the menu, to snap an object to a guideline or a grid, select it on an edge or in the center. When you click and drag the object to snap it to the guide or grid, a little ring appears on the edge or in the center where you are grabbing it.

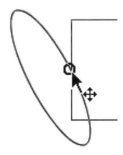

To snap the object to the guide or grid, drag it to the guide/grid you want it to snap to. When you locate the guide or grid you want to snap the object to, the little ring grows in size.

Snap To Objects

If you want to assure that objects are aligned with one another, you can use the Snap To Objects command. This feature works in a similar manner to Snap To Guides and Grid. The difference is that instead of snapping an object to a guide or a grid, you're snapping to another object.

To snap one object to another, first select View | Snap To Objects or press CTRL-SHIFT-/ or CMD-SHIFT-/. You can also select Snap To Objects from the Options settings in the Toolbox when the Arrow tool is selected. Snap To Objects appears as a magnet icon in the Toolbox.

Click the edge or the middle of the object, and you will see the little snap-to ring. Drag the ring to the area on the other object you want to snap the current one to. You will feel the magnetic pull as it snaps into place on the other object. When the ring hits the snap-to target, it grows in size.

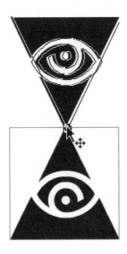

The Snap To Objects feature is also used for animation when you are aligning objects to a motion guide. Snapping objects to a motion guide object is discussed in Chapter 9.

Snap To Pixels

When you turn on Snap To Pixels, a pixel grid appears when the magnification level is set to 400 percent or above.

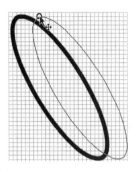

To activate Snap To Pixels, select View | Snap To Pixels. When the edge or the center of the object is selected, you see the same ring handle as previously outlined. You can use the Snap To Pixel grid for projects that require very precise placement of graphic objects.

NOTE   *In a text block, the snap-to rings are active on the center of the text. So, if you want to snap a graphic object to a text block, select the object first, and then locate the center of the text block. When the graphic hits the center of the text block, the ring handle grows in size and it snaps to this point.*

Lock and Unlock the Position of an Object

On a single-layer drawing with many components and multiple stacking orders, you may want to lock an object into place so you don't accidentally move or change it while modifying other objects around it. This can be done with any grouped elements or symbols. To lock a grouped object or a symbol, select it in the menu, and select Modify | Arrange | Lock or press CTRL-ALT-L/CMD-OPT-L. The object will be visible, but you will be unable to manipulate it. To unlock the object, select Modify | Arrange | Unlock All or press CTRL-ALT-SHIFT-L/CMD-OPT-SHIFT-L. This unlocks all the elements on the stage that were previously locked.

Arrange Objects on the Stage

When you're creating a Flash movie with many objects on the stage, arranging the objects on this stage precisely becomes an important issue. If your stage layout demands balance and it's cluttered with many objects, Flash offers a lot of options to help you make your layout appear symmetrical.

You can align and distribute objects in relation to one another using the Align panel, as shown in Figure 5-5. The Align panel is a floating panel that can be docked to other panels on the stage.

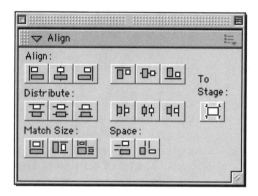

FIGURE 5-5   Use the Align panel for aligning objects to one another.

In addition to standard alignment features in the panel, the size, height, and width of two or more objects can be matched. You also can space objects evenly on a horizontal plane and/or a vertical plane. Aligned and distributed objects can be aligned and distributed to the actual stage if you click the Stage button. Within this panel, every possible scenario for alignment of two or more objects exists. The alignment options in the panel are represented as icons that are easy to interpret. The following are the elements of the Align panel:

- **Align options**   From left to right, the six options are Left Edge, Horizontal Center, Right Edge, Top Edge, Vertical Center, and Top Edge. The Align options align two or more selected objects (grouped object or symbol) according to the alignment icon you selected.

- **Distribute options**   From left to right, the six options are Top Edge, Vertical Center, Bottom Edge, Left Edge, Horizontal Center, and Right Edge. The Distribute options distribute two or more selected objects (grouped object or symbol).

- **Match Size options**   From left to right, the three options are Match Width, Match Height, and Match Width And Height. The Match size options match the dimensions of two or more selected objects (grouped graphics or symbol).

- **Space options**   From left to right, the two options are Space Evenly Vertically and Space Evenly Horizontally. The Space options space evenly either horizontally or vertically two or more selected objects (grouped graphics or symbol).

- **To Stage icon**   Enables you to use the alignment features in conjunction with the stage as a whole. When this icon is selected, objects can be aligned in relation to the stage, as well as to one another.

FIGURE 5-6   Graphic elements aligned and distributed evenly

To use the options in the Align panel, first select the objects, and then click the appropriate icon(s) in the panel.

Figure 5-6 illustrates five individually grouped objects with different alignment features applied. In the Align options, Align Vertical Center was selected. For Distribute, Distribute Horizontal Center was selected, and all selected objects have been aligned to the stage.

In Figure 5-7, the same selected objects have now had the Match Size option, Match Height and Width, applied to them. Note the heights of all selected objects are now identical.

You can use the Align panel instead of the Snap To Grid and Snap To Guides features to align several selected objects. Personal preference will dictate which method will be more effective for your project.

FIGURE 5-7   The Match Size option is set on these graphic elements.

Get Details About Objects

Flash movies can become very large and complex. This, coupled with the fact that your movie architecture will contain many levels of nested groups and symbols, means you will need many tools to help you navigate through the movie structure. Fortunately, Flash comes equipped with many tools to assist you in getting information about elements and finding them, too. We have looked at the Properties Inspector, which provides information on select elements and allows you to edit them. Another helpful tool for getting information about elements is the Info panel. The Info panel is a floating panel that displays information about objects currently selected. You can also dock the Info panel to other panels in the work area.

Another tool, which is sometimes useful for getting information about your movie, is the Movie Explorer. The Movie Explorer provides you with an ongoing synopsis of the structure of your Flash movie. It gives you a detailed history of all the movie's components, including frames, symbols, levels of symbols, and so forth. The Info panel provides information on currently selected objects, whereas the Movie Explorer window gives you the blueprints of the bigger picture.

Use the Info Panel

Use the Info panel by clicking an object, and selecting Window | Info or pressing CTRL-I in Windows/CMD-I on the Mac.

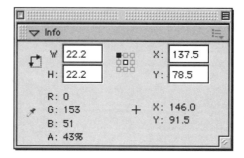

The Info panel displays the width, height, X and Y coordinates, RGB, and Alpha percentage of the selected object. You can find out the exact location (X and Y coordinate) of a selected object on stage. The reference point icon in this panel allows you to reference the XY coordinate from either the upper-left corner or the center of an object. You can also modify the properties of a selected object right in the Info panel. To do this, type in the new data in the appropriate box. For example, if you want to change the width and height of a selected object, just type in new data in the width box and the height box.

The RGB setting indicates the color of the selected, editable graphic when you position your pointer over the graphic. The Alpha percentage indicates the level of transparency that's applied to the graphic. A setting of 100 percent alpha is an opaque color, and 0 percent is the absence of color (transparent). RGB and Alpha data is only available on editable objects.

Get Movie Information from the Movie Explorer

The Movie Explorer panel gives you a complete description of the components that make up your movie, including objects, symbols, layers, frames, actions, sounds on different Timelines, and more (see Figure 5-8).

When your movies become complex, with multiple layers, frames, movie clips, scenes, and complex actions, the Movie Explorer keeps a running track of the components of the movie as you build it. Sometimes, you may know there is an object or a script hidden somewhere in the movie and you just can't find it. That's when you want to turn to the Movie Explorer.

5

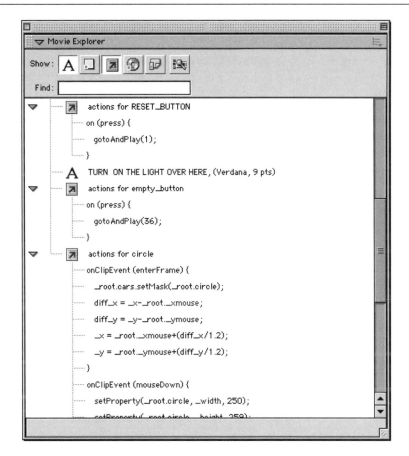

FIGURE 5-8   The Movie Explorer helps keep track of the structure of the movie.

It also can help you find and modify elements in the movie. This is particularly important when multiple users are building the same movie. On large Flash productions, teams of people often work on different chunks of the same movie at different stages. One person can track the work of another with the aid of the Movie Explorer. It's even difficult to dissect components of your own movie when it becomes very involved. The Movie Explorer can sometimes help bring the project back into focus for you.

Display the Movie Explorer by selecting Window | Movie Explorer or pressing F4. The window displays a collapsible hierarchy of all elements and events that are part of the current movie. Each time you change the movie, the Movie Explorer window is updated to include new additions. Elements are arranged in a folder-like hierarchy with scenes, layers, symbol definitions, and other titles, acting as a container to organize elements in the movie. Plus and minus signs reside next to each container, enabling you to expand and collapse its contents. A plus sign indicates the presence of contents, whereas a minus sign indicates an empty container.

On the top of the Movie Explorer, you can extract the display of specified elements in the movie. The icons display in the following order, from left to right:

- Show Text
- Show Symbols
- Show ActionScripts
- Show Video, Sounds, And Bitmaps
- Show Frames And Layers
- Customize Which Items To Show

The last selection, Customize Which Items To Show, enables you to customize your display selection to only include elements that you are interested in seeing.

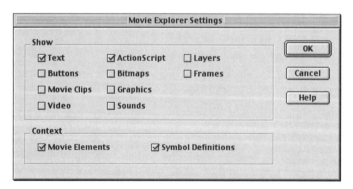

If you know the name of an element, you can find text, ActionScripts, video, sounds, bitmaps, frames, and layers by entering the name of the item in the Find field. The Movie Explorer will go to that item in the Movie Explorer list.

Elements of your movie also can be edited right from the Movie Explorer. For example, text can be edited directly in the Movie Explorer window, and the change is immediately reflected on the stage. Edit text by double-clicking the text in the Movie Explorer you want to change. You also can access Editing Mode for symbols by double-clicking the appropriate icon. This is a convenient feature when your movies contain a great deal of nested or invisible elements that are difficult to spot on the stage.

Once you get the feel for the many tools available in Flash, it's easy to transform the properties of objects in your movies. Because Flash movies are rich with multimedia elements, color is also an important property in your Flash movies that you often need to edit. Let's examine some important things you need to know about colorizing graphic elements in Flash.

Apply Colors to Graphics and Text

Earlier in this book, we applied color to objects using the Stroke and Fill swatches in the Toolbox and in the Properties Inspector on a selected graphic element. As you can see, applying color to editable objects in Flash is a pretty simple, straightforward process. There are additional ways to apply color in Flash, and that's what we are going to take a look at in this section.

You can also set the color on an editable element using the Color Mixer or Color Swatches panels. These panels have a multitude of selections and allow you to create and store custom colors and gradients.

Modify Color on a Selected Element

To apply a fill or stroke color to an object or text *before* the object is created, select a Fill and/or Stroke color from the Toolbox, Properties Inspector, Color Mixer, or Color Swatches panel. When you apply a fill color and a stroke color to an object, these colors become the current color in all of the Fill Color and Stroke Color boxes. After you select a color, create the object or text. The item will display in the currently selected Fill and Stroke color. The Color panels that display when you click a color in any of these panels look and behave the same (see Figure 5-9).

To modify the fill or stroke color of an editable object, select the object and then select the color from the Toolbox, Properties Inspector, Color Mixer, or Color Swatches panel. The object will display the chosen color. To modify the stroke of an editable object, click the stroke until the entire stroke is selected, and then modify the color in one of the previously mentioned panels.

> **NOTE**   *Stroke color cannot be applied to a text object. To apply a stroke to text, it must be broken apart and made into an editable object. To break the text apart, click the text with the Arrow tool and select Modify | Break Apart or press CTRL-B/CMD-B.*

Modify Color in a Grouped Object

To modify the color on a grouped element, double-click the element to enter the Group Editing mode (or select Edit | Edit Selected), where the object becomes editable. If the grouped object is

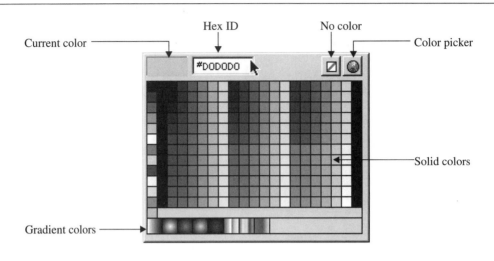

FIGURE 5-9   The color swatches for Fill and Stroke color in the Color panels and
Properties Inspector

nested within other groups, continue to click the graphic until you reach the level where the
element becomes editable. You can distinguish between the editable element and the other elements
on the stage because the editable element will not be dimmed on the stage and the other elements
will be, as shown in Figure 5-10.

Change the fill or stroke color of the graphic in Editing mode just as you would any other
graphic. Then exit Editing mode by clicking the Scene icon in the upper-left corner or selecting
Edit | Edit All from the menu.

Modify Fills with the Shape Menu

Flash comes equipped with a few creative ways to manipulate fills. These can be found in the
Modify | Shape menu.

The selections in this menu can only be applied to editable objects. You can do things like
change a line into a fill and make the fill of an object grow larger or smaller, thereby changing
the size of the object You also can soften the fill edges of an object in the Soften Edges dialog

FIGURE 5-10   Surrounding objects on the stage that are not being edited become dimmed.

box to make it appear soft and blurry. The Soften Edges option works well for creating a blurry edge effect usually associated with bitmap graphics.

Convert a line to a fill by clicking a line and selecting Modify | Shape | Convert Lines To Fills. Use this to convert what was previously a line into an object made from a fill.

Expand or contract the size of a fill by clicking an editable element and selecting Modify | Shape | Expand Fill. The Expand Fill dialog box will appear. Here, you can indicate the amount you want to enlarge or reduce the fill in the Distance box. Click Expand to make the fill larger and click Inset to reduce the size of the fill.

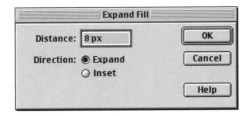

Expanding the fill changes the dimensions of the object. If you compare the size of the object in the Properties Inspector or the Info panel before and after applying the Expand fill, you will notice an increase or decrease in size, depending upon whether you chose Expand or Inset in the dialog box. Expand makes the size bigger and Inset reduces the size of an object.

Blur the edges of a fill by selecting Modify | Shape | Soften Fill Edges. In the dialog box that appears, indicate the distance amount you want the fill to expand or reduce.

The default distance is four pixels. Select the number of steps the object will soften to. A large number of steps will create a softer edge, but the file will be larger. A small number of steps will create either a harder fill or more banding, depending on the distance you entered. A smaller number of steps will result in a smaller file size. Caution should be used when entering a large number of steps. It can take forever to display in a browser. Applying soft edges with a limited number of steps is generally a safer choice. The default number of steps is four pixels.

Set the direction of the soft edge by clicking Expand to make it larger or Inset to make the blur effect go inward. You can achieve some spectacular effects by experimenting with the Soften Fill Edges settings.

Set Colors with the Flash Color Panels

In addition to picking colors from the Fill and Stroke color swatch pop-up menus, you can select or mix custom RGB colors in the Color Mixer panel. Once an RGB color is created, you can store your new custom color in the bottom of the Color Swatches panel. Custom mixed colors are saved with the current Flash movie, not with the default application palette.

Use the Color Mixer Panel to Set Color

The Color Mixer panel offers a multitude of ways to set colors. Display the Color Mixer panel by selecting Window | Color Mixer. You may not have to display this panel because the Color Mixer panel and the Color Swatches both appear as part of the default layout panel set when Flash launches.

The Color Mixer panel gives you the option of selecting a color from the Fill and Stroke color boxes, mixing an RGB color, changing the Alpha of a color, or selecting colors from the Color Picker (see Figure 5-11).

To set a solid Fill or Stroke color on an existing object using the Color Mixer, first select either the fill or the stroke of the object. Then, select Solid from the Fill style pop-up menu to the right of the Fill color. Select a color from the pop-up Fill colors, too.

If you want to select a custom color, click and drag in the color space with the cross hairs pointer until the current Fill or Stroke color is acceptable to you. You can also adjust the

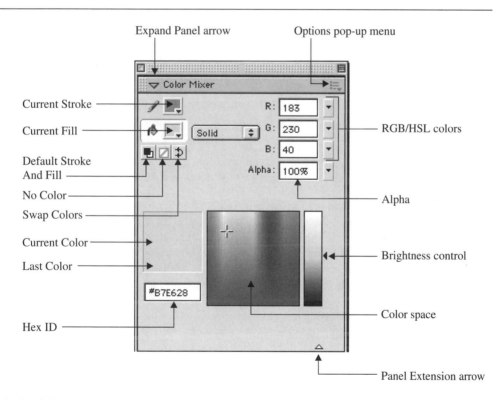

The Color Mixer panel in Flash

brightness of the custom color by dragging the Brightness control slider up and down. Using this control gives you a greater selection of colors. The selected object will reflect your color choice.

Of course, you can select a color prior to making an object, too. To do this, simply set the colors, and then create the object.

You also can set the Alpha from the Color Mixer, which is the transparency index of a color. Type a number in the Alpha value field or use the sliding arrow to select an alpha percentage of a color. When two objects are overlapping one another and the top object has an alpha percentage applied, you can see the bottom object through the alpha color.

Change the Color Mixer to reflect different color models by clicking the pop-up menu at the top right of the panel.

The following color model options are available in this menu:

- **RGB**   Select RGB mode if you want to create an RGB color.

- **HSB**   Select HSB to make a color using the hue value, saturation, and brightness.

- **Add Swatch**   Select this to add a color to the Color Swatches panel. You also can add a swatch to which an Alpha value was applied. This means you can create colors that are partially transparent. New colors display on the bottom of the Color Swatches panel.

In the Color Mixer panel, there is a Default Fill And Stroke button under the Paint Bucket. This is the same Default Stroke And Fill button as is in the Toolbox. Click this to return the Stroke to white and the Fill to black. Next to the Default Fill And Stroke button is the None button. Select the None button if you want a Fill without a Stroke, or vice versa. To use the None button, an object must first be selected. Otherwise, None will not be an available option. Next to the None button is the Swap Colors button. Swap the Fill color with the Stroke color, and vice versa, by clicking this button.

To add a custom color swatch you mixed to the Color Swatches panel, select either the Stroke or the Fill color in the Color Mixer. Then, in the pop-up menu, select Add Swatch. The custom color will then appear in the bottom of all the swatch color windows.

To save a custom color palette, add the swatches to the color palette using the method outlined previously. In the Color Swatches pop-up menu, select Save Colors. In the Export Color Swatch dialog box, save the colors.

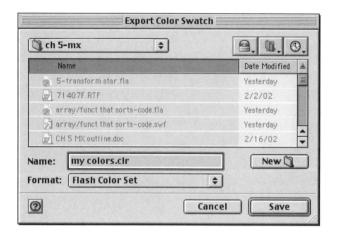

You can reload the color palette into other Flash movies by selecting Add Colors from the Color Swatches pop-up menu. We'll discuss this process in the next section on creating gradients in the Color Swatches panel.

TIP   *To eliminate a stroke from an existing object, select it (the selection must be editable) and manually delete the stroke. To delete a fill, select it (it, too, must be editable).*

Use the Color Swatches Panel to Select Color

The Color Swatches panel mimics the colors in the Fill and Stroke color pop-up menus. The difference is that this panel can remain on the stage, making it easier for you to compare colors.

The top of the Color Swatches panel lists the default Flash color swatches. The bottom strip is reserved for gradient colors and custom mixed colors. New gradients that you create also are stored in this panel.

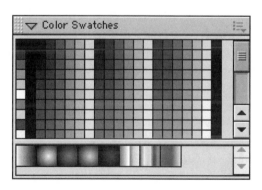

The pop-up menu in the upper right of the panel enables you to further customize the Color Swatches panel settings.

```
┌─────────────────────────────┐
│  Duplicate Swatch           │
│  Delete Swatch              │
│                             │
│  Add Colors...              │
│  Replace Colors...          │
│  Load Default Colors        │
│                             │
│  Save Colors...             │
│  Save as Default            │
│                             │
│  Clear Colors               │
│                             │
│  Web 216                    │
│                             │
│  Sort by Color              │
│                             │
│  Help                       │
│  Maximize Panel             │
│  Close Panel                │
└─────────────────────────────┘
```

The options in the pop-up menu are as follows:

- **Duplicate Swatch and Delete Swatch**   To duplicate or delete a swatch, click a swatch you want to modify, and select Duplicate Swatch or Delete Swatch in the pop-up menu. If you duplicate a swatch, it will appear in the bottom of the swatch window. Deleting a swatch removes it from the swatch color table of this file.

- **Add Colors and Replace Colors**   Add or replace colors by selecting these options in the pop-up menu. The Import Color Swatch dialog box appears. You can add or replace color sets from other Flash files, color tables created in other programs (such as Photoshop, Fireworks, and Director), and colors from GIF files.

- **Load Default Colors**   To reload the original Flash default colors, click this option, and then navigate to the Flash application folder where the default color table is located. Select it to return the panel to its original state.

- **Save Colors**   Colors can be saved in the Flash Color Set format or as a Color Table. Save colors by selecting Save Colors. A Save dialog box will appear. Target a place where you want the color palette saved. Color Table files are saved with an .act extension. Files with this extension can be imported into other programs, such as Photoshop or Fireworks. Flash Color Set files are saved with a .clr extension. These color sets can be imported and exported into Flash movies.

- ■ **Save As Default**   This makes the selected color palette the new default for that movie, which replaces the current default color set.
- ■ **Clear Colors**   This deletes all colors from the current selection, leaving only black-and-white swatches.
- ■ **Web 216**   Use this option if you want to display the web-safe palette.
- ■ **Sort By Color**   Select this option to sort current colors by hues ranging from light to dark.

> NOTE   *The difference between Add Colors and Replace Colors is that Add Colors loads the new color set and retains the old set. Replace Colors loads the new color and deletes the old color set. When you mix custom RGB colors and gradients, they are saved with the Flash movie. They are not saved in the program's preference file.*

Apply a Gradient Color

Gradient color changes from one hue, saturation, alpha, color, or tint to another. There are many different effects you can create using gradient color. You can start with a solid color and fade out to no color; or you could have several colors in a gradient that gradually transform into one another. In Flash, you have a lot of control over the way a gradient appears, as well as the way that colors blend into one another.

Generally, Flash produces pretty impressive gradients. Although colors are restricted on the Web, a Flash movie with gradients generally displays clearly with minimal banding on most monitors. Banding is an (sometimes) undesirable result of gradients created in vector programs that makes the gradual transition of color appear as a series of rectangle boxes, or bands. Gradients made in vector programs are created from a series of bands of color that give the illusion of color gradually changing.

> NOTE   *Gradients can't be applied to strokes or text unless the text is broken apart.*

If a monitor isn't capable of displaying 16- or 24-bit color, the banding in a gradient can become very noticeable. Banding becomes even more of an issue if your beginning and end colors in the gradient are similar in hue and intensity. In this case, because the colors are similar, there are less color steps for the computer to interpret. Gradients in a Flash movie are far better quality than a gradient in a GIF file. Still, there's little guarantee that your gradient will look smooth on every viewer's platform, because there's such a wide variety of different configurations in cyberspace.

In Flash, you create gradients with the Color Mixer, and you can create them before you select an element or while an element is selected. There are two types of gradients you can create:

- ■ **Linear fill**   Gradates color in a straight horizontal or vertical direction. Use linear fills for rectangular shapes or objects where you want the fill to appear in a straight line.
- ■ **Radial fill**   Gradates color in a circle. Use radial fills for ellipses or any object where you want the gradation to appear radiating.

5

You'll notice in the bottom of the color swatches that there are a few default gradients already. There's not much of a choice, so it's good to know how to mix your own. Let's now review the process of creating a new gradient on a selected object:

1. Select the fill of an editable object.

2. In the pop-up Fill style menu in the Color Mixer, select a gradient type of either Linear or Radial. In this example, we will apply a linear gradient to a selected object.

3. When you select a gradient type of color style, a gradient definition bar appears in the Color Mixer. Slide the pointers (color proxy) on the bottom of the gradient bar to set the color and position of the gradient color. The pointers mark the entrance and exit of a color, and they slide left and right on the bar. If you slide a pointer to the left or right, the color on the bar changes, altering the balance of the gradient mix.

4. To change the color on a pointer, select the pointer and click the current color fill box to access the color swatch pop-up menu. From this menu, pick a new color. Your gradient color instantly changes on that pointer in the gradient bar. Use the same method to change other pointers on the bar. You can also create custom colors from the Color space box by clicking and dragging in this space. The current custom color is reflected in the color fill box. The Brightness control slider can be used in conjunction with the Color space box to create a greater range of colors.

5. To *add* more color to the gradient bar to create a multicolor gradient, click anywhere on the bottom of the bar to create more pointers. The Arrow tool will have a + sign on the bottom right when you position it under the gradient bar. To add a color, repeat the process as previously outlined.

6. To *delete* a color from the gradient bar, click a pointer and drag it outside the Color Mixer.

To change the direction of the gradient on the selected object, select the Paint Bucket tool from the Toolbox, and click and drag the object in any direction. The direction of the gradient will change to reflect the direction you moved the Paint Bucket.

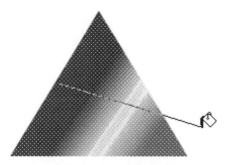

Gradients can be used on the currently selected object(s) or added to the current movie's Color Swatches palette. If you like a gradient you create, you can store it in the Gradient Swatch panel as we did earlier with solid colors. To do this, click the pop-up menu in the upper-right corner of the Color Mixer, and select Add Swatch. The swatch will now appear in all of the color swatch menus as a color option. If you create a bunch of good-looking gradients, you can save them in a Flash Color set that you can load into another Flash file, as outlined in the last section.

To save the gradient to the Color Swatches panel, go to the pop-up arrow to the right and click Add Swatch. The gradient you just created appears in the bottom of the Color Swatches panel. You can customize the way Linear and Radial gradients display, too, which we discuss in the next section.

NOTE   *Gradients cannot be applied to the stroke of an object.*

Modify Gradients with the Fill Transform and the Lock Fill Tools

To change the angle of a gradient on an object quickly, you can use the Paint Bucket method, as discussed previously. But for more control over the process, you need to use other techniques. Once you've assigned a gradient color to an object, there are other ways to adjust the angle of the gradient on an object. You can also apply a gradient across several selected objects and change the way the gradient appears. The Fill Transform and Lock Fill tools can be used to achieve some interesting gradient effects.

Use the Fill Transform Tool

The Fill Transform tool is located in the Toolbox. This is a fun tool to use because you can create some dramatic effects by manipulating the size and the angle of the gradation.

To adjust a linear fill on an object, follow these steps:

1. Click the Fill Transform tool in the Toolbox. Then click an object that has a gradient whose direction you want to change. If you chose an object with a linear fill, two vertical lines will appear on either side of the object. A ring handle appears in the center of the

object and on the top of the line to the right. On the right centerline, a square adjustment handle appears, too.

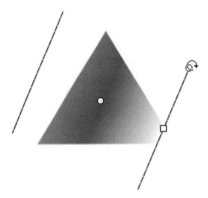

2. To reduce or enlarge the gradient in the object, click and drag the square adjustment handle. This can dramatically change the look of the gradient. By shortening or elongating its length, you can give the gradation a completely different look. Rotate the angle of the gradient by clicking the top-right ring handle and dragging clockwise or counterclockwise to change the angle of the color.

3. Change the center point of the gradient by clicking and dragging the ring handle in the center of the object. This makes the center point of the gradient start at the new point you've chosen.

Transform a Radial Fill

Transforming a fill on a radial gradient is slightly different from transforming a linear fill. Because the color radiates in a circle, it requires a different kind of adjustment.

To apply a radial gradient to an object, follow these steps:

1. Select the Transform Fill tool as previously outlined. Click an object with a radial fill. An ellipse appears around the circumference of the object. There is a ring handle in the middle of the ellipse, and two ring handles and a square handle on the right edge of the ellipse.

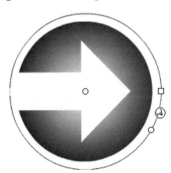

2. Adjust these handles by clicking and dragging. One ring handle rotates in the direction of the gradation, and the second ring handle reduces or enlarges the gradation. The square handle controls the radial gradient's perspective. The ring handle in the center of the object changes the center point of the object much like the center ring handle on a linear gradation.

Use the Lock Fill Tool

Use the Lock Fill tool to adjust your color in a continuous gradation across several objects. Figure 5-12 demonstrates how the Lock Fill can be used. In this figure, the text is broken apart and a gradation with a Lock Fill has been applied separately to each character in the word. Instead of the gradation treating each character as a separate object with a separate gradation for each character, the characters are treated as one object with one gradation applied. This technique displays a kind of masking effect on a group of objects. It creates the illusion of a gradient in the background being masked by the objects you've created. The Lock Fill tool becomes available in the Options section of the Toolbox when you choose the Paint Bucket and the Paintbrush tools. Fills can be locked on bitmap fills also. Bitmap fills are discussed in Chapter 7.

To create a Lock Fill, let's review the steps that were used to create Figure 5-12:

1. Create some text on the stage. If you're using text for your Lock Fill, it's a good idea to select a heavy weight font, so the locked gradation will stand out more. For Figure 5-12, 100-point Arial Black was used.

2. Click the text and break it apart using Modify | Break Apart or CTRL-B in Windows/CMD-B on the Mac.

3. Select a gradient fill color from the color fill swatches.

4. Select the Paint Bucket and click the Lock Fill icon in the Options section of the Toolbox.

5. Click each one of the characters, starting from the middle and going outward, and the gradient will be locked in position, as if the text graphics were one object.

You can also span the gradient fill over several objects by selecting the editable objects and clicking the Paint Bucket tool. Make sure the Lock Fill button is unlocked. Select a gradient fill, and click and drag the Paint Bucket tool over the span of objects. Depending upon how you drag and the direction angle, the gradient will appear differently.

FIGURE 5-12   Apply a Lock Fill to objects to create a continuous gradation on several objects.

Transform Fill

After applying a Lock Fill to a series of objects, you also can apply a Transform fill to change the size and direction of the gradient across the span of objects. To do this, select all Lock Fill objects and follow the procedure in the section "Use the Fill Transform Tool."

Use the Brush Tool with Locked Fills

The Brush tool can also be used to create locked fills. To lock a fill within a series of brush strokes, select a gradient fill color. Then, select the Paint Brush tool and click the Lock Fill button in the Options section of the Toolbox. When you use the Paint Brush to draw a series of separate brush strokes, the gradient color will span the series of brushstrokes. You can create some interesting effects using this technique.

Up to this point in the book, symbols have been mentioned periodically. In the next chapter, we will review graphic symbols and instances. The introduction to symbols will help you understand how they're used, as well as the potential power they will yield in your movies.

Chapter 6

Use Graphic Symbols, Instances, and Libraries

How to...

- Create graphic symbols
- Convert a graphic into a symbol
- Edit symbols
- Nest symbols
- Place and edit instances
- Transform an instance
- Break apart an instance
- Modify instances
- Get information on symbols and instances

Symbols are an important feature of Flash. They are powerful because they lay the groundwork for interactivity in Flash. When you learn how and when to make symbols, you'll be on your way to understanding advanced Flash concepts.

There are three kinds of symbols you can make in Flash. These symbols include graphic symbols, button symbols, and movie clip symbols. Although buttons and movie clips are symbols, you will rarely hear them referred to as "symbols." Most of the time, they are just called buttons and movie clips. Flash designers know intuitively that buttons and movie clips are symbols. Graphic symbols, on the other hand, are often referred to as "graphic symbols" as opposed to just "graphics" because you can also create graphics that are not graphic symbols. So a graphic symbol is the only kind of symbol that needs to be distinguished from a regular graphic.

Graphic symbols are the simplest type of symbols to create in Flash. In this chapter, we will concentrate on the basics of symbols, what they are, and how to use and manage them. Buttons and movie clips are a little more advanced than graphic symbols. Buttons and movie clips often contain graphic symbols, so it's best to study graphic symbols first because they are the most elementary symbol type. Buttons and movie clips are introduced in Chapter 11.

Symbols are objects you create with drawing tools, text tools, imported bitmaps, or vector art, and save in the Library. A major difference between a graphic symbol and a regular graphic element is that a symbol is stored in the Library and can be reused. Symbols dramatically reduce the file size of a movie because they're only saved within the movie once. Multiple uses of this symbol don't increase a file's size. Every time you use a symbol from the Library, it's referred to as an *instance*. You can change the properties of an instance in many different ways. If you revise a symbol, the changes occur globally on all instances. This can minimize production time on large projects where an instance might be used numerous times. It's a good idea to get into the habit of making your graphics into symbols, whether it be a graphic symbol or a movie clip. As we travel along in this chapter, it will become more obvious that symbols are essential in building a well-organized Flash movie.

Create Graphic Symbols

There are two ways to create a graphic symbol in Flash. The first method is to convert an existing graphic to a symbol. The second method is to enter a special editing mode where you can build your symbol. Let's examine how this is done.

Convert a Graphic into a Symbol

Converting an existing object into a graphic symbol is easy. Use this technique if you have an existing object on the stage and, as an afterthought, want to convert it into a symbol. I personally utilize this technique often, especially if I haven't thought out a project as well as I should have from the start.

Use the Convert To Symbol Dialog Box

Convert an object to a symbol by selecting an object on the stage. Click the object. If the object is built from more than one element, hold down the SHIFT key and click each element, or drag a selection marquee around the objects you want to convert. The elements can be grouped, editable, or a combination of both. We covered these selection techniques in Chapter 5. Just like on the main Timeline, the object can exist on a single layer or multiple layers.

With the entire area selected, go to Insert | Convert To Symbol or press F8. When you become accustomed to this special function key, it will help streamline your creation of symbols. In the Convert To Symbol dialog box that appears, give the symbol a name in the corresponding Name box and select a Behavior type. For this chapter, you'll be selecting Graphic for the behavior.

Note that in the bottom right of this dialog box, there is an Advanced button. Clicking this button will expand the dialog box with additional Linkage selections. The Linkage selections enable you to assign an identifier name to a symbol in the movie's Library. A symbol with a linkage identifier can be shared with other movies. Linkage is discussed toward the end of this chapter.

In the Convert To Symbol dialog box, you can also set the registration of a symbol. The registration refers to the reference point on the symbol. You apply a registration by clicking any one of the eight handles that surround the registration thumbnail to the right of the box. For example, let's say I wanted my graphic symbol to be referenced from the center left of the graphic. If I click the handle that's on the center left, a registration mark will appear on the object indicating that this is the new reference point.

If I click the registration of the object on the stage, the Properties Inspector also indicates the exact location (X and Y coordinates) of the object referencing the location from the registration.

As mentioned , movie clips and buttons are the other two behavior types you can select from the Convert To Symbol dialog box. Click OK. Your object is now a graphic symbol. Display the Library window by selecting Window | Library. The symbol you created now appears in the Library.

Create a New Graphic Symbol

Creating a graphic symbol from scratch is just as easy as converting a graphic to a symbol. Create a new symbol by entering Symbol Editing mode. Symbol Editing mode has its own special stage and Timeline that is separate from the main stage and Timeline that we have been working on.

Most everything you can do to an object on the main stage can be done in Symbol Editing mode, too. In this sense, creating a graphic symbol is much like making a regular object. You can have multiple layers, groups of objects, imported bitmaps, and vector art, and add other symbols, among other things. Graphic symbols can be animated, but not on their own timeline. (We discuss

Did you know?

The Free Transform Tool

You can edit a registration point of a symbol with the Free Transform tool. To use this technique, simply select the symbol first, and then select the Free Transform tool. Move the registration to a new point on the graphic. Then, deselect the symbol. The registration point is now changed.

You can also do this in editing mode. To edit the registration in editing mode, perform the following steps:

1. Double-click the symbol in the Library or on the stage, or select symbol and press CTRL-E in Windows/CMD-E on the Mac to enter Symbol Editing mode.

2. In Symbol Editing mode (which we discuss at length in the next section), position the symbol on the registration, in relation to where you want the registration to fall. For example, if you want the registration to be in the upper-left corner of the symbol, move the symbol so that's where the registration falls.

3. Exit editing mode either by clicking the Scene icon in the upper left of the stage or by selecting Edit | Edit Document (CTRL-E/CMD-E) from the menu.

how to animate a symbol in Chapter 8.) Also, sounds and interactivity won't work with graphic symbols. Generally, you'll use graphic symbols to help build buttons and movie clips in Flash.

Create a new symbol from scratch by selecting Insert | New Symbol or pressing CTRL-F8 in Windows/CMD-F8 on the Mac. The Symbol Properties dialog box appears, as outlined in the previous section. As discussed previously, you assign a name, select a behavior, and click OK. You're now in Symbol Editing mode, where symbols are created and modified. Let's further examine this mode and how to work in it.

NOTE   *If you drag an object to the Library, the Symbol Properties dialog box appears, allowing you to make a symbol on the fly. Also, when you import a graphic, sound, video, or bitmaps into a Flash Library, they become symbols. Importing elements into your movie is discussed in Chapter 6*

Use Symbol Editing Mode

Symbol Editing mode looks just like the main Timeline except there is a cross hairs in the center of the editing stage. The only indication you have that you're in this mode are the icons in the upper-left corner of the stage.

Create your graphic directly in Symbol Editing mode. When you're done creating your graphic on the editing stage, exit Symbol Editing mode as outlined in the previous section. This brings you back to the main Timeline and stage.

You may understand Symbol Editing mode better if you compare it to Group Editing mode. A graphic symbol makes an object or group of objects into one element. An object (or objects) that is grouped becomes a single element with other elements contained within it. They can be taken apart, modified, and put back together again in their original state. Both symbols and groups have separate editing stages, and both indicate you're in editing mode in the upper-left corner. You exit both modes the same way—by clicking the Scene icon to return to the main stage and Timeline.

Graphic symbols tend to be more efficient than grouped graphics. Symbols can be used more than once and will not dramatically increase the size of a movie. Certain symbol properties, such as color and alpha, can be modified, whereas this is not possible with grouped objects unless you enter Group Editing mode. As a whole, using symbols gives your movie diversity, structure, and economy when dealing with larger projects.

Edit a Symbol

After you create a symbol, you will often need to edit it to make changes. Edit an existing symbol by reentering Symbol Editing mode, discussed in the previous section. There are a few ways to return to Symbol Editing mode, and personal preference dictates which mode you use.

First, you can double-click an instance that's placed on the stage. You also can double-click a symbol in the Library or select once and choose Edit | Edit Selected from the menu.

When you modify an instance already on the stage, if there are other elements surrounding it, they become dimmed. This makes it easy for you to see your edit in relation to other elements.

When you modify a symbol from the Library, the stage only contains the object being modified on its own Timeline. Both methods will change all instances of this particular symbol.

Exit Symbol Editing mode by either clicking the Scene name in the upper-left corner of the stage or selecting Edit | Edit Movie from the menu. Symbol Editing mode enables you to modify the properties of a symbol as if it were a regular graphic object. For example, you can change the colors in this mode, add an object, or reshape an object.

NOTE   *Editing a symbol causes all instances of that symbol to change.*

Nest a Symbol Within a Symbol

Symbols offer a lot of diversity in the way you can build them. You can place groups of objects in a symbol, and you can edit a group that's within a symbol. When this is done, the Group Editing Mode icon will appear in the upper-left corner of the editing stage, to the right of the Symbol icon and name, as shown in Figure 6-1.

You also can place symbols within symbols, which is referred to as *nesting* or *embedding*. Graphic symbols are often nested in complex graphics, buttons, or movie clip symbols. For example, let's suppose you were designing an animated cartoon of a person's face. An efficient way to plan this cartoon would be to create the different components of the face as graphic symbols—the eyes, nose, mouth, face, and eyebrows—as shown in Figure 6-2.

The graphic symbols of the face would then be nested in movie clip symbols and animated on their own Timeline. The final face movie clip might then be nested in another movie clip symbol on another Timeline. Although the final symbol is a complex movie clip, it's easy to go back to each nested symbol and edit it in Symbol Editing mode for each symbol. Graphic symbols are often the first building block for creating more complex symbols like movie clips.

Hierarchy of a group nested in a group, nested in a group

FIGURE 6-1   When you edit groups within a symbol, the hierarchy of the element appears in the upper-left corner of the stage.

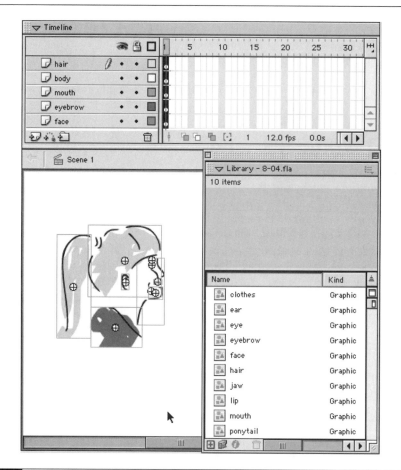

FIGURE 6-2   The components in this graphic symbol were created with existing symbols.

The graphic symbols we have been discussing are static symbols. You also can create an animated graphic symbol on its Timeline and place an instance of it on the main Timeline, as shown in Figure 6-3.

One drawback of this method is that when you place an animated graphic symbol on the main Timeline, in order to see the animation, you have to add frames to the main Timeline. Otherwise, when you play the movie back, it still appears as a static graphic symbol. If animation is required for a symbol, most Flash designers use movie clips instead of the preceding method because animated graphic symbols may seem counterproductive. Movie clip animation is self-contained on its own Timeline. So, when you place an instance of the movie clip on the main Timeline, it appears as one compact keyframe. In addition, if revisions to the animation need to be made, it is much easier to revise a self-contained movie than a symbol spanning the Timeline. (We discuss the specifics of animation in Chapter 8.)

The animated graphic symbol on the main Timeline

The animated graphic symbol in editing mode

FIGURE 6-3   An animated graphic symbol must span several frames on the main Timeline in order for you to see the animation.

Learn to Use Graphic Symbols

Symbols are much more versatile than a regular graphic element. Symbols are stored in the Library, and every time you use one, an instance of that symbol is created. An instance is easy to position, edit, manipulate, and change back into a regular graphic object. You can edit a symbol from the Library easily by re-entering Symbol Editing mode, where you created the original symbol. All these techniques make it easy for you to control symbols in your movie.

Place an Instance

As mentioned before, one of the benefits of using symbols is the ability to generate multiple copies. These are known as *instances*. Create an instance by dragging a symbol from the Library to the stage. Symbols are stored in the Library until you need to use them. To view the symbols in your movie, select Window I Library. Any symbols, sounds, video, fonts, imported bitmaps, or graphics associated with your movie will appear in this Library.

The Library serves as a container for these components, or "assets" as they are referred to in Flash.

In the Library, symbols are depicted as three different icons: graphic, button, and movie clip. This is how you distinguish between symbol types.

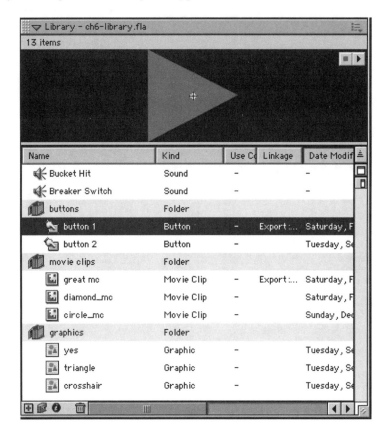

The type of symbol, whether it is a graphic, button, or movie clip, defines the way the symbol will behave. For example, if an instance is a button, it might elicit interactive behavior.

If you click a graphic symbol in the Library, a preview of the symbol displays in the top of the Library. To get the symbol on the stage, drag the symbol icon onto either the stage or the thumbnail preview at the top of the Library panel. As soon as a symbol is on the stage, it becomes an instance.

Transform an Instance

An instance is much like any other object. Just like any other object, you can apply the Transformation tools from the Toolbox, and the Modify | Transform menu. Figure 6-4 shows an instance being skewed from the Transform panel; as you can see, it's treated just like any other objects except there's a registration point on it that identifies it as a symbol. You can use any of the Transformation tools on a symbol.

FIGURE 6-4   Transform a symbol with the Transformation tools.

Break Apart a Graphic

Let's say you created a symbol and then needed one of the instances to return to an editable object state. You can break a link from an instance to a symbol. When a symbol is revised, all instances update, too. An instance that has been broken apart no longer has any association with the symbol. It becomes an independent graphic. Why would you want to break apart an instance? Well, sometimes you may want to reuse an element used to build one symbol on another symbol, without redrawing it. You could break the object apart, extract the part you needed, and create a new symbol from the new illustration without affecting any other elements of the movie. This method provides a quick way to reuse pieces and saves a lot of time in the process.

You can break apart any type of symbol. When you break apart symbols that contain multiple layers, animation, sound, and interactivity, you lose everything but the static object. Objects grouped and nested within the symbol remain intact when the symbol is broken apart.

Modify Instances

Editing instances is a little different than editing a regular graphic or a grouped graphic, because the method of doing so is tied into the fact that it's a copy of a symbol. Because of this, the properties you can change on a single instance are limited.

The most intuitive way to modify an instance is to use the Properties Inspector. Since the Properties Inspector works in context with your selection, when you select a symbol, the properties available on that symbol appear in the Inspector. Let's take a look at how this feature works.

Use the Properties Inspector

When you want to modify the color, alpha, or brightness of an instance, you use the Properties Inspector to do so. The manner in which you modify color on an instance is different from the way you modify color on a regular object. For one thing, it addresses the entire instance. So, if you want to add a red tint to a symbol, it is applied to the entire instance. Color is applied to an instance by selecting the object and then setting the modification in the Properties Inspector, as shown in Figure 6-5.

The difference between modifying an instance using the Properties Inspector and editing a symbol is that the changes you make to a symbol globally update all instances of that symbol. Changing an instance with the Properties Inspector, on the other hand, only affects the selected instance. You can achieve some very powerful effects by changing the properties of an instance—especially in an animated movie, where you can change the opacity or color of an object over time.

Let's take a look at the properties you can edit on an instance. In the Color pop-up menu, you can select from the following options:

- ■ **Brightness**   Select Brightness to make the instance lighter or darker in increments that range from 100% for pure white to –100% for black. Use the vertical slider to select a percentage.

- ■ **Tint**   Set the Tint amount and the RGB percentages of a selected instance with the sliders next to each box. Click and drag the vertical sliders or type a number in the boxes to blend the RGB colors on the instance.

- ■ **Alpha**   Set an Alpha value to modify the opacity of an instance. Use the vertical slider to select a percentage or type a percentage in the box. A 0% setting on an instance makes the object transparent, and a 100% setting is total opacity.

- ■ **Advanced**   The Advanced setting enables you to blend tint and alpha color together on a selected instance. Adjust RGB color and Alpha with the sliders associated with that particular color. To apply advanced settings, click the Settings button to the right of the advanced color setting. This displays the Advanced Effect dialog box. You can alter the intensity of an RGB multiplied by the current color as indicated by the multiplication (×) symbol between entry boxes. The added value appears in the boxes to the right. The numbers in the right boxes can be set with sliders or typed in. Experiment with the sliding bars to create custom color effects.

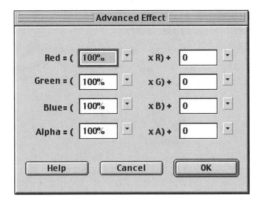

You can achieve some interesting effects using the Properties Inspector to apply color effects to instances. In Chapter 9, when we learn how to create motion tweens, you'll see how you can change the tint or alpha of an instance to create an object with animated color or transparency that changes in time.

Examine Additional Features in the Properties Inspector

In addition to being able to modify the color of an instance in the Properties Inspector, you can also do some other great things from this panel. Just like a regular graphic, you can scale the object here, and track and set the exact location of the instance on stage.

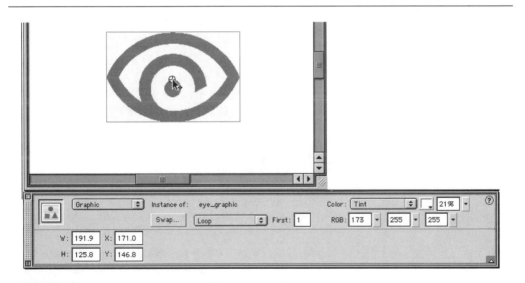

FIGURE 6-5   Use the Properties Inspector to modify color on an instance.

Change the Behavior of a Symbol

You can also change the type of instance you have selected. For example, if you created a graphic symbol and decided you wanted only one instance of this graphic to be a button instance, you can change the behavior in the pop-up menu.

Depending upon which behavior you change in the Properties Inspector, additional selections related to that behavior become available:

- **Behavior: Graphic** If you select Graphic as your behavior type for your symbol, loop options become available. Looping is an action applied to animations and refers to the number of times an animation plays within a movie. The Loop pop-up list gives you three looping options:

  - Loop, which plays as long as the movie is playing

  - Play Once, which plays once and stops

  - Single Frame, which displays only one frame of the animation sequence

  When Single Frame is selected, enter the frame number you want displayed on this instance. Loop and Play Once enable you to indicate a frame number you wanted to play from. In order for the looping options to work properly, you need to use a Stop action on the main Timeline to stop the frames in the main Timeline from controlling the looping.

- **Behavior: Button** If you select Button as the behavior type for your symbol, from the Options portion of the panel, you can select Track As Button or Track As Menu Item. Use Track As Button for a single button and Track As Menu Item for pop-up menus.

  You can also assign an instance name to a button instance. When a button instance has a name, you can apply interactive scripts to it. This technique is discussed in Part IV of this book.

- **Behavior: Movie Clip** When you select Movie Clip as the behavior type on a symbol, an instance name can be indicated in the Name box. As is the case with button instances, movie clip instances with names can be manipulated with ActionScript. Names are generally assigned to movie clips so that you can reference the instance in a script.

You could change any of the three behaviors on an instance. The next logical question is, why would you want to do this? This method offers a quick fix if you need a behavior change on an isolated instance. It means you don't have to go back and build a separate symbol from scratch and assign a different behavior. The downfall is that the new behavior won't have all the functionality you may require for a button or movie clip. But if you need a quick script on a static button or movie clip, this provides an instant change in behavior.

Swap Symbol Instances

With all three types of behaviors, you can swap one symbol instance with another.

You swap an instance by right-clicking (Windows)/CTRL-clicking (Mac) on the symbol instance and selecting Swap Symbol… from the context menu. This displays the Swap Symbol dialog box. You can also access this dialog box from the Properties Inspector. To display the Swap Symbols dialog box from the Properties Inspector, click the Swap button.

6

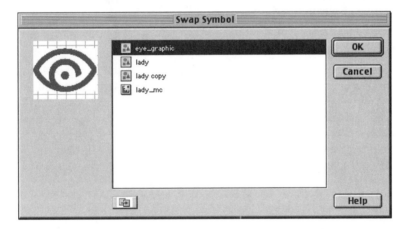

In this dialog box, you can swap one instance with another, even if the behavior is different. So a movie clip can be swapped with a button, a button can be swapped with a graphic symbol, and so on. This is a very convenient feature because the replaced instance remains in the same position as the old instance. So it streamlines the process of switching symbols in some cases. The Swap Symbol dialog box provides a running list of the current symbols you can swap with. To use it, just navigate to the new symbol and click OK.

You can also duplicate a symbol from this box by clicking the Duplicate Symbol button in the bottom left of the dialog box. This displays the Symbol Name dialog box. In this box, you can rename the copy of your new, duplicate symbol.

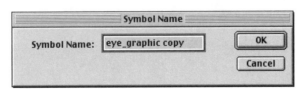

Using this technique to duplicate symbols can be another time saver. This way, you can use a copy of one symbol to create another one that might be very similar. Once you have a copy, you can go back in and edit this symbol. If the symbol is really complex, you don't have to rebuild it from scratch.

Get Information on Symbols and Instances

You often need to get quick information on an instance. Of course, the Properties Inspector is the quickest way to get information about a selected instance, but you can also use the Info panel and the Movie Explorer.

The Info panel gives you the width and the current position of the cursor, among other things. As discussed in Chapter 2, you can display the Info panel from the Window menu.

The Movie Explorer tracks every element in a movie, including the use of symbols, instances, scripts, and many other things. Instances can sometimes be hard to keep track of, and to this extent, the Movie Explorer is a big help.

Use the Movie Explorer

When movies become more complex—with multiple layers, movie clips, and nested symbols with actions on instances and frames—it becomes harder to track different elements and their history. It's particularly hard to track instances because they can take on so many different personas. Multiple instances from one symbol can have different scripts attached to them and can be swapped, duplicated, or changed to a different behavior. Movie clips can be deeply nested, making it hard to figure out that some of them even exist. One way to help keep track of buried scripts and hidden symbols is to use the Movie Explorer to help you find things. The Movie Explorer keeps track of symbols, scripts, every line of text that's typed in, and so on. It even keeps track of the location of everything. You can get a readout of where an element is located at any given moment.

Figure 6-6 shows the Movie Explorer panel of a simple movie. This panel is packed with useful features to help you zone in on any element in the movie. Display the Movie Explorer in the Launcher bar by selecting Window | Movie Explorer or by pressing F4. The Movie Explorer window's default display is docked in a group with the Object/Frame Actions panel.

The Movie Explorer has six Show icons at the top of the window that enable you to customize the way the Movie Explorer displays. So, if you wanted to filter out all elements of a movie except for the symbols, you could click the Show Buttons, Movie Clips, And Graphics icon. From the left, you can select from the following icons:

- ■ Show Text
- ■ Show Buttons, Movie Clips, And Graphics
- ■ Show ActionScripts
- ■ Show Video, Sounds, And Bitmaps
- ■ Show Frames On Layers
- ■ Customize Which Items To Show

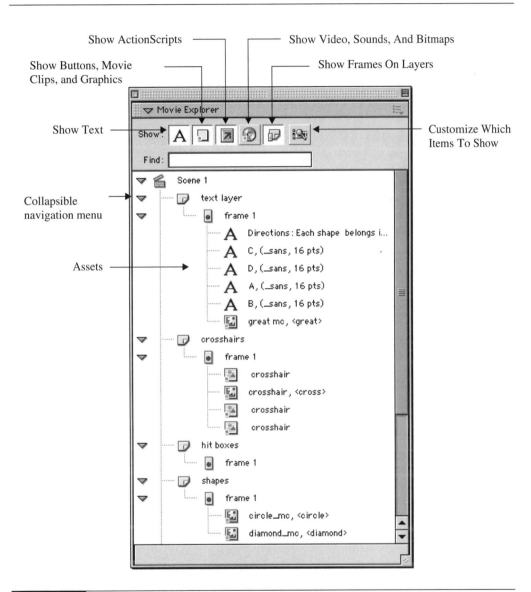

6

FIGURE 6-6   Use the Movie Explorer window to track the history of a movie and get detailed information about symbols and instances.

Clicking the Customize Which Items To Show button displays the Movie Explorer Settings dialog box, in which you can custom select the items you want displayed.

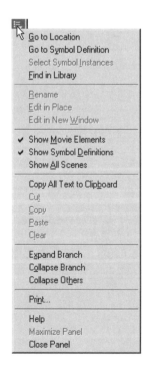

Under the Show icons, there's a Find feature. Type in the name of anything in the movie (instance, frame, symbol, imported video, sound, and so on), and the Movie Explorer will take you to its position in the Movie Explorer Hierarchy.

The Movie Explorer pop-up Options menu can be accessed by either clicking the triangle in the upper-right corner of the Movie Explorer window or right-clicking in Windows/CTRL-clicking on the Mac.

When you click an element in the Movie Explorer window, you can select from the following options in the pop-up menu:

- **Goto Location**   Select to jump quickly to a selected element in the Movie Explorer.

- **Goto Symbol Definition**   Select to jump directly to a symbol definition. Symbol definitions list all the elements used to create the symbol in a collapsible branch folder. In order for this to be selectable, Show Symbol must be selected.

- **Select Symbol Instances**   Select to jump directly to an instance listed under the Symbol Definitions in the Movie Explorer. For this to be selectable, Show Movie Elements must be selected.

- **Find In Library**   Select to jump directly to an item in the Library window.

- **Rename**   Select to give the element a new name.

- **Edit In Place**   Select to edit an object you've selected in the Movie Explorer right on the stage.

- **Edit In New Window**   Select to edit a selected element in a new window.

- **Show Movie Elements**   Select to show elements neatly organized in scenes.

- **Show Symbol Definition**   Select to display all information associated with a selected symbol.

- **Copy Text To Clipboard**   Select to copy selected text to the Clipboard for use in another part of the movie or a text editor.

- **Cut, Copy, Paste, and Clear**   Select these old standbys to reshuffle, duplicate, and eliminate items from the Movie Explorer.

- **Expand Branch, Collapse Branch, and Collapse Others**   Select the name of any element in the Movie Explorer structure that has an expansion arrow to the left of its name. Then, from the pop-up menu, select Expand Branch or Collapse Branch. If you expand a branch by clicking a right-pointing arrow, the structure of that branch is revealed. If you click on a down-pointing arrow, the branch is collapsed. When a branch is collapsed, the contents are contained within a head in the structure. This structure is called "branch" because its organizational structure is like that of a tree, with elements of the movie branching off one another. This navigation technique helps clean up the appearance of the windows in complex movies. Expand Branch and Collapse Branch is the equivalent of physically clicking the right- and down-pointing arrows to accomplish the same task of opening and closing branches of the structure. Collapse Others collapses all open branches in the movie.

- **Print**   Select to print the Movie Explorer.

The Movie Explorer is packed with features to make it easy for you to navigate even the most complicated movie.

Use the Common Libraries

The Common Libraries are separate from the Library you store symbols in. The Common Libraries contain an assortment of ready-made buttons, sounds, and reusable scripts. Access a Common Library by selecting Window | Common Libraries. In the pop-up menu, you can select Buttons, Sounds, and Learning Interactions Libraries. Once you drag an element from the Common Library onstage, the assets become stored in the regular Library. If you drag a Learning Interaction or a component onto the stage, the assets used to create these elements are also stored in the regular Library (see Figure 6-7).

Use the Common Library to grab quick, simplistic buttons and sounds. This can be a time-saving device for creating simple elements. You also can add symbols, sounds, and components to the permanent Library. (We discuss components in Chapter 15.)

Display the Common Library by selecting Window | Common Libraries. A drop-down arrow lists three different types of Libraries you can display:

- **Buttons**   This Library contains a large list of interactive buttons including LED styles, VCR styles, arrows, circles, and bars.

- **Sounds**   This Library contains a broad selection of short sounds that are perfect for attaching to buttons.

- **Learning Interactions**   This Library contains a few ready-made modular scripts with instructions on how to modify them for your purposes. It also contains components, which are easy-to-use interactive elements, like buttons and scroll bars, that can be modified for your projects. These features are for the designer who has limited experience with scripting and is looking for some fill-in-the-blanks recipes for interactivity. You can acquire more components from Macromedia and other third-party developers. In fact, some of them are quite useful, especially for repetitive interactions. They can be easily added to your Library. For more information on components, go to the Macromedia web site, www.macromedia.com.

Navigate the Library Window

As you become a more experienced Flash author, you realize the importance of organization in your movie. A complex movie can have hundreds of elements, including several movie clips all running on their own separate Timelines. Most often, you'll be creating and gathering all the assets of the movie before you begin. A well-organized Library will help you easily find what you're looking for when you build your movie. Flash offers many tools to help you customize and organize your Library just the way you want it.

The Library window is a container for symbols, imported sound, bitmaps, vector drawings, and videos. Display the Library by selecting Window | Library from the menu or by pressing CTRL-L in Windows/CMD-L on the Mac. When you click a Library entry, a thumbnail preview appears in a window at the top of the Library. The scroll-down Library window lists in a horizontal array the name and kind of element, the number of times an instance has been used, links, and the last time it was modified. Customize the window to expand and contract horizontally using

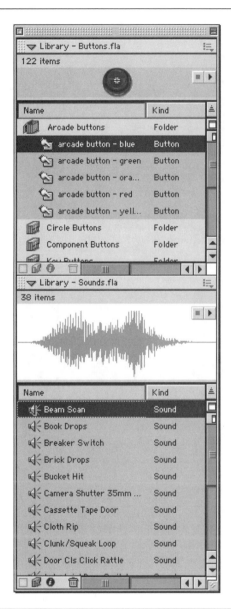

FIGURE 6-7   The Common Libraries for buttons and sounds

the Wide State and Narrow State buttons in the upper-right corner of the window. Reverse the viewing order of elements by clicking the Sort button in the upper-right corner of the window, as shown in Figure 6-8.

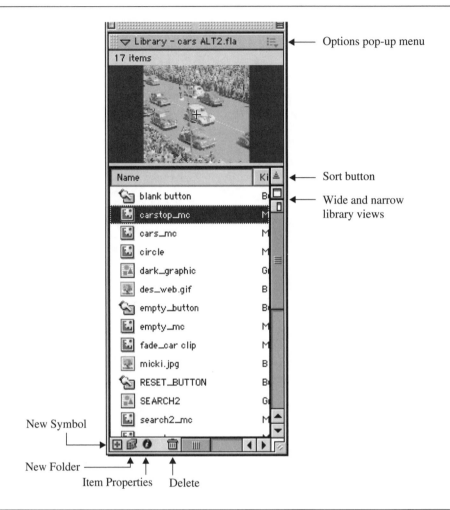

Options pop-up menu

Sort button

Wide and narrow library views

New Symbol

New Folder

Item Properties   Delete

The Library window is where all your movie assets are stored.

When you click an asset in the Library, you can use one of the four buttons on the bottom right. From the left, the following are the four buttons and descriptions of the functions they perform:

■ **New Symbol**   Click the first button to create a new symbol. The Symbol Properties dialog box appears. This is where you select the behavior of the symbol before moving on to Symbol Editing mode. Use this as an optional way of creating a new symbol, as opposed to using the menu selection Insert | New Symbol.

■ **New Folder**   Click this button to create a folder within the Library. Name the folder by clicking and dragging over the name and typing over it. The Library window navigates like a standard window on the Mac and Windows. You can create folders to further subdivide your assets. Click the folder to expand and contract the contents of a folder.

- ■ **Item Properties**   Click a symbol and select the Item Properties button to modify the properties of a symbol. This displays the Symbol Properties dialog box. This is the same dialog box that appears when you double-click a symbol in the Library window, or double-click an instance on the stage, but with the addition of an Edit button. Click another behavior type to change the behavior of the selected symbol. Click the Edit button to enter Symbol Editing mode.

- ■ **Delete**   Click an asset and select the Trash Can to delete it from the Library.

To use a symbol in your movie, click the layer on which you want the asset to appear, select the symbol in the Library, and drag it to the stage to create an instance.

The Options menu in the upper-right corner of the Library window offers even more options to help organize and manage your Library assets. Access the options in the pop-up menu by clicking the triangle in the upper-right corner.

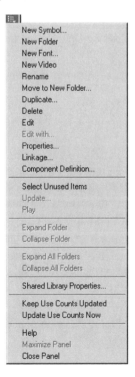

The pop-up options in the Library Options menu are as follows:

- **New Symbol**   Select this to display the Symbol Properties dialog box. This dialog box also can be accessed from the New Symbol button in the bottom left of the window.

- **New Folder**   Select this to create a new folder in the library. A new folder also can be created by clicking the New Folder button in the bottom left of the window.

- **New Font**   This displays the Font Symbol Properties dialog box. Use this dialog box for font symbols. Font symbols are created for shared Library items for fonts to be shared across multiple sites.

- **New Video**   This selection creates a new video object. Any methods or transformations that can be applied to a video object would be available to this symbol.

- **Rename**   Select this option to rename a symbol.

- **Move To New Folder**   This displays the New Folder dialog box, where you can create and name a new folder. This dialog box also can be accessed from the New Folder button in the bottom left of the window.

- **Duplicate**   This option displays the Symbol Properties dialog box and enables you to duplicate and rename an element.

- **Delete**   This deletes an element from the Library. The Delete function also can be accessed from the Trash Can button in the bottom left of the window.

- **Edit**   This option takes you to Symbol Editing mode of a selected symbol.

- **Edit With**   This selection displays an Open dialog box that enables you to edit a bitmap in the program it was created in.

- **Properties**   This option displays the Properties window associated with a selected object in the Library.

  - If a symbol is selected in the Library, the Symbol Properties dialog box will display.

  - If a bitmap is selected in the Library, a Bitmap Properties dialog box appears. The Bitmap Properties dialog box allows you to update a revised bitmap from this location, import another bitmap into the symbol, and choose a compression type. Compression can be GIF, PNG, or JPEG. Check the Allow Smoothing box for antialiasing of the bitmap. In other words, if you want the edges of your bitmap to appear less jagged, check this option.

  - If a sound is selected in the Library, a Sound Properties dialog box appears. In this dialog box, you can import another sound, update the current sound, test the sound to hear it, change the Export settings, and set the Compression Rate. Compression options include Default, ADPCM, MP3, Speech, and Raw, all of which are discussed in Chapter 7.

  - If a font is selected in the Library, the same Font Properties dialog box is displayed as in the New Font selection.

- If a video clip is selected, the Video Properties dialog box appears. Video in Flash can be either embedded as part of the movie or referenced from an external path. You can import QuickTime movies into Flash. In this dialog box, you can import, export, or update the video. In the next chapter, we discuss using video in Flash.

- **Linkage** This displays the Linkage Properties dialog box. Use this dialog box to assign linkage properties to a selected element. You can also assign linkage attributes when you create a new symbol (Insert | New Symbol). Linkage properties enable you to share a Library asset from a source movie with other movies and load assets from other Libraries into your source movie.

Linkage Properties dialog box:

Linkage Properties	
Identifier: fade_car clip	OK
Linkage: ☐ Export for ActionScript	Cancel
☑ Export for runtime sharing	
☐ Import for runtime sharing	Help
☑ Export in first frame	
URL: car_movie.swf	

You can set up symbols so they can be linked to other movies. Use the Linkage Properties dialog box by first giving the element an Identifier name. An Identifier name is like an instance name in that it enables you to reference a particular asset in a script using this name. After assigning a name, select one of the following Linkage buttons:

- **Export For ActionScript** Considered an author-time shared asset, select this option if you want to use a source symbol in a local destination movie. For example, if you wanted to attach a movie clip from a source movie to a movie clip in a destination movie using attachMovie, you would use this command. Linkage is discussed in Chapter 13.

- **Export For Runtime Sharing and Import For Runtime Sharing** Use these selections for run-time sharing. Run-time sharing loads linked assets from an external source when a movie plays (at run time). Selecting one of these requires the assignment of the URL to the source symbol so the destination movie can load the symbol from that URL.

The ability to assign linkage names is a very powerful feature in Flash. It provides another way to keep your file sizes smaller by sharing Library items.

- **Component Definition** If you click a component in the Library, you can choose this option. This displays the Component Definitions dialog box. Here, you can change the various parameters of your component. Chapter 15 discusses components in more detail.

- **Select Unused Items** This highlights and identifies elements not yet used in your movie.

- **Update** Use this feature to update any imported graphics that have been revised in an outside program.

- **Play** This selection plays any interactive or animated element in Flash, such as sound, buttons, and movie clips. Use this to test an interactive or animated element. You also can test an interactive or animated element by clicking the Play triangle in the upper-right corner of the Preview window in the Library.

- **Expand And Collapse Folders** This opens and closes selected Library folders. You also can double-click the folder in the Library to expand or collapse the folder.

- **Expand And Collapse All Folders** This feature opens or closes all folders in the Library.

- **Shared Library Properties** This displays the Shared Library Properties dialog box, where you can indicate a URL you want to share a library with.

- **Keep Use Counts Updates and Update Use Counts Now** These selections update the number of times an instance from the Library has been used in the movie. The total is indicated in the Use Count in the Library window.

The Library window is used frequently when creating multimedia movies. Because it contains a multitude of ways to display, manage, and customize your Library, it's a big help when it comes to organizing your project.

In the next chapter, we will expand upon elements we can add to the Library and manipulate in Flash—namely, bitmaps, sounds, and video. As you will see, the ability to import multiple types of elements into Flash allows you much diversity in building Flash movies.

Chapter 7

Add Pictures, Video, and Sound to Your Flash Movies

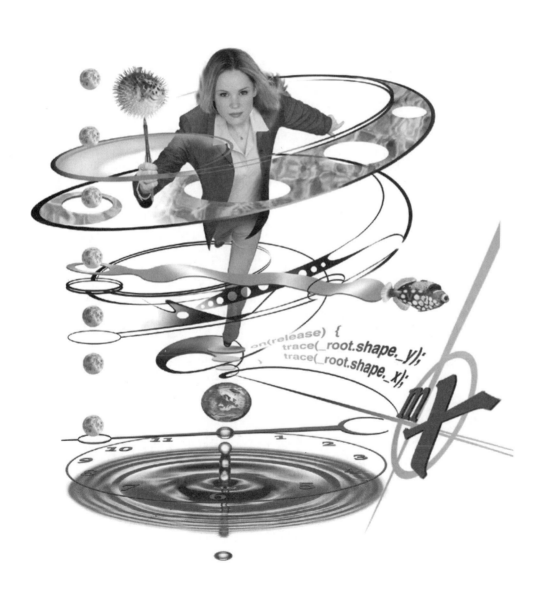

How to...

- Understand vector and raster graphics
- Import graphics into your Flash movie
- Import file sequences
- Use vector graphics
- Use bitmapped images
- Import video
- Import and assign sounds
- Link sounds

By now, you know that Flash is packed with an impressive array of drawing tools. But what about using graphics and other elements you created in other programs? Flash can import formats from many different sources. You can import both vector and raster images into a Flash movie. In addition, you can import video and sound in many different formats into Flash.

To take full advantage of the import features and be able to further manipulate those images, it's important to understand the difference between vector- and raster-based graphics.

Understand Vector Graphics

Vector graphics are defined with mathematical precision. An object created in a vector-based program is described with a series of lines and curves that move from point to point to create a shape. Vector objects have properties that can be modified. You can group, move, scale, rotate, duplicate, change the color, and much more with vector art. You also can assign a stacking order to objects and change this order at will. Unlike bitmaps, vector graphics maintain their quality at any scale, as shown in Figure 7-1. They are resolution independent, giving them consistent quality in print or in multimedia. The drawing features of Flash are vector based, as are programs like Macromedia FreeHand and Adobe Illustrator. Use vector graphics for logos, technical drawings, or any art where precision is important.

Understand Raster Graphics

Raster graphics are *bitmaps*. Bitmaps are created from pixels arranged on a grid. Each pixel is assigned an RGB color value, and the juxtaposition of pixels creates the illusion of an object. Zoom in on a bitmapped image in its native program, or even in Flash, to see how the pixels are arranged in a grid-like order. The larger you zoom the image, the more the pixels appear as a group of squares. Zoom in enough and the image no longer resembles the original art; it will look more like an abstract painting. Zooming in on a bitmap provides a good idea of how a bitmap is made. Programs such as Adobe PhotoShop are raster-based applications.

FIGURE 7-1   A vector illustration maintains quality when it's enlarged three times the original size.

Bitmaps are very different from vector art. When you modify a bitmap, you change the properties of each pixel within the selected area. If you reduce or enlarge a selected bitmap, the pixels reduce or enlarge within the scheme of the pixel grid. Enlargement of a bitmap can cause a *pixelated* effect (see Figure 7-2) and seriously downgrades the quality of the original image. Bitmaps have resolution issues, too. *Resolution* is a mathematical calculation relating to the way images display their final output, which could be various forms of print or multimedia (Web, video, and slides). The higher the resolution of the image, the clearer the image will display or output.

At higher resolutions, pixels become more densely populated and, as a result, display a better quality picture. The image size increases, too. This might not be a problem if the final output is for print. If the bitmap is being put up on the Web, bigger files mean longer download times and, on some systems, crashes. The standard resolution for a bitmapped image being prepared for the Web is 72 dpi (dots per inch). When creating bitmaps in a paint program, plan to make the art either the same size or larger than the final output. This helps eliminate some of the pixelated, or jagged, edges.

FIGURE 7-2   When this vector drawing is transformed into a bitmap and enlarged, pixels become visible.

Paint programs enable you to smooth out the edges of pixels. This is a technique known as *antialiasing*. Antialiasing creates extra pixels around an object that provide a more gradual transition of color from the object to the background. Antialiasing can create problems if the background in the paint program is not the same color as the background in your Flash movie. For example, if you save antialiased art as a transparent GIF, a halo of the remains of the background color can appear around the edges of the image. Fortunately, bitmap editing programs like Fireworks and Photoshop programs provide ways to eliminate this effect.

If you plan to use bitmaps in Flash, you need to familiarize yourself with file export formats for Web media to ensure a smooth transition into Flash.

Import Graphics into Your Flash Movie

When you create graphics in other programs for use in Flash, they must be saved in a file format that Flash recognizes. Flash imports many different file formats from raster editing, drawing, and animation programs, plus many more applications. Systems with QuickTime 4 and later installed give you additional file format capabilities and cross-platform compatibility on Macintosh and Windows-based systems.

To import a file into Flash, you select File | Import or press CTRL-R in Windows/CMD-R on the Mac. From the Import dialog box, you can navigate to the file you want to import, select it, and click the Open button.

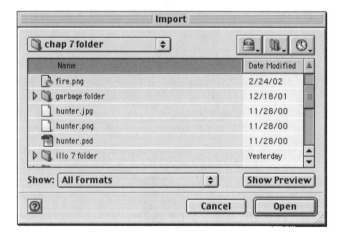

The file appears on the stage as well as in the Library. Sometimes, importing a file can be annoying because it may fall on top of an editable object or in an undesirable area. In this case, Flash offers an alternative command so the file will store directly in the Library. This way, you can control when an instance is placed onstage.

To import a file directly into the Library, select File | Import To Library. Navigate and select the file in the Import dialog box as just outlined.

Although it's easy to import art into Flash, there are some rules and issues you should familiarize yourself with to ensure that your import works to your advantage. In the following section, we will take a look at various methods of importing graphics from some popular graphics applications and the file formats you can import from.

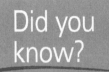

Export Vector Graphics

In addition to being able to import vector graphics into Flash, you can export vector graphics.

To export an image, select File | Export Image. In the File Export dialog box in Windows, name the file and indicate a Save As Type from the pop-up menu. The export formats (and their file extensions) are as follows:

- **Flash Player (.swf)**   The native format for Flash.

- **FutureSplash Player (.spl)**   An older Player version.

- **Enhanced Metafile (.emf) and Windows Metafile (.wmf)**   These formats are exclusive to Windows.

- **EPS 3.0 (.eps)**   Encapsulated Postscript. Flash can only be exported to older EPS formats.

- **Adobe Illustrator (.ai)**   Native file format for Adobe Illustrator.

- **AutoCAD DXF (.dxf)**   This is a format used in AutoCAD 2-D and 3-D.

- **Bitmap (.bmp)**   Bitmaps are used for Windows applications and are similar to PICT files on the Mac.

- **JPEG Image (.jpg)**   Joint Photographic Experts Group. Creates 24-bit continuous tone art, if the system is capable of viewing 24-bit color. This format doesn't support Alpha channels. JPEG is lossy compression (which creates image deterioration).

- **GIF Image (.gif)**   Graphics Interchange File. This supports indexed color (256-color palette) and produces medium- to low-quality export.

- **PNG Image (.png)**   Portable Network Graphic Format. This is the native file format for Fireworks and supports 8-bit, 24-bit color, and Alpha channels.

SWF and AI file formats will export as editable vectors. Export to an SWF format if you're using FreeHand 8+ or Illustrator 9+. This gives you a clean export with color, path, and layer support. The other formats will export as bitmaps. In the Mac Export dialog box, type a name in the Save As box and select a Format from the pop-up menu. The format types on the Mac are the same as for Windows with the following exceptions: Mac exports to a PICT (.pict, .pct) format instead of a bitmap (.bmp). Enhanced Metafile and Windows Metafile formats are only available on the PC.

7

Import from Fireworks and Freehand

FreeHand and Fireworks are Macromedia's drawing and image manipulation software programs. Flash is very forgiving when importing from Fireworks and FreeHand, and many different import options are available.

When exporting art from Fireworks to be placed in a Flash file, you can use any of the following formats:

- **PNG** This is Fireworks' native format.

- **SWF** Flash's native format and also imports flawlessly into Flash.

- **Illustrator 6** When saved in this format, the file assumes an extension of .ai, the Adobe Illustrator file format. Certain elements, such as gradients in vector drawings, will be lost in this conversion.

- **GIF** An indexed color (256) file format. Although you can import a GIF format into Flash from Fireworks, the SWF format is so comprehensive, there would be little reason to do so.

The preferred import format for Fireworks to Flash is the SWF format because SWF is a vector format. When you import a PNG format from Fireworks into Flash, the Fireworks PNG Import Setup dialog box appears in Flash, as shown in Figure 7-3. Use this dialog box to further streamline the importing of the image. Here, you can select various import options relating to layers, rasterizing, and text.

You also can copy and paste a graphic from Fireworks into Flash by clicking the object and selecting Edit | Copy from the Fireworks menu (CTRL-C in Windows/CMD-C on the Mac). Select Edit | Paste (CTRL-V/CMD-V) from the Flash menu to paste the graphic on the Flash stage. This

Fireworks PNG Import Settings

File Structure: ● Import as movie clip and retain layers
○ Import into new layer in current scene

Objects: ● Rasterize if necessary to maintain appearance
○ Keep all paths editable

Text: ● Rasterize if necessary to maintain appearance
○ Keep all text editable

☐ Import as a single flattened bitmap

[Cancel] [OK]

FIGURE 7-3 When you import a PNG file from Fireworks into Flash, a settings dialog box appears.

copies the object into Flash as a bitmap with an opaque background. Keep in mind that when you use the copy-and-paste method, it imports as a flattened, single-layer image.

FreeHand files (7.0 or later) import seamlessly into Flash. Although FreeHand files can be imported in many different formats into Flash, most often you'll import files from FreeHand in an *FH* format (.fh). FH is the native file format for FreeHand. This format offers more options than other methods for retaining the integrity of FreeHand art in Flash. When you select an FH format for import, the FreeHand Import dialog box displays.

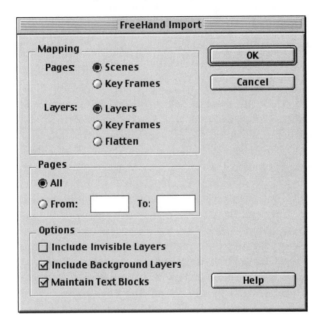

You can custom select several settings from this dialog box:

- Mapping refers to the way FreeHand pages translate onto the Flash stage. You can map a FreeHand page to a scene or a keyframe in Flash.

- Mapping to Scenes places all pages in the FreeHand document in a separate scene.

- Mapping to Key Frames places every page in the FreeHand document in separate keyframes.

- FreeHand layers can be mapped to Flash layers, too, by selecting the Layers option. Select Key Frames if you want your FreeHand layers to be mapped into individual keyframes in Flash. You also can select Flatten as an option if you want the FreeHand document to be one frame, one layer. The other convenient feature in this dialog box is the ability to specify a particular page or pages for import from FreeHand to Flash (in FreeHand, you can create multiple pages).

Additional options at the bottom of the dialog box areas include the following:

- **Include Invisible Layers** This option imports invisible layers along with your layers containing objects. Use this feature for files that have certain layers made invisible in FreeHand that you need to view in Flash to complete a picture.

- **Include Background Layer** If your FreeHand file contains an intricate or hard-to-replicate background layer, you might choose to bring it with you. Or perhaps there is some guide on the background layer that you need as a guide in Flash. In either case, it might be essential for you to retain the background layer.

- **Maintain Text Blocks** This option keeps the width of text blocks intact from one program to the other. The text is then editable in Flash.

You can copy and paste graphics from FreeHand to Flash by selecting the object and choosing Edit I Copy from the Fireworks menu, and then selecting Edit I Paste from the Flash menu. This copies the objects into Flash as editable objects. This works quite well for quick simple things and can be a time-saver if you don't need to save your FreeHand art or retain layers. You can display both programs, create art in FreeHand, copy it, and paste it into Flash, albeit without all the customized options. Objects on multiple layers will appear stacked on one layer.

There are other issues to keep in mind when importing from FreeHand to Flash. If you select Layers under Mapping, each object will appear on a separate layer in Flash. If you copy and paste objects on multiple layers from FreeHand to Flash, they will appear on the same layer and in the stacking order they were created in.

Gradient objects can carry up to eight colors from FreeHand to Flash. If you're going to import a gradient from FreeHand to Flash, it's best to try to stick with eight colors. Otherwise, Flash has to create clipping paths to simulate the gradation. Clipping paths could mean trouble because the file size can increase dramatically. Blends from FreeHand to Flash also are interpreted as separate paths, which also increases the file size. When imported in an SWF format, FreeHand 8 and over, gradients are converted to Flash gradients.

NOTE *If, for some reason, you opt to import a FreeHand file into Flash as an EPS (or perhaps you receive one from another source and you have to make use of it), you need to click Convert Editable EPS in the FreeHand Export dialog box. Otherwise, it won't appear on your Flash stage.*

Import from Other Applications

Although Flash is most friendly to programs in the Macromedia family, there are other popular programs and formats you can import from. Adobe Illustrator is a vector-based application like FreeHand. Flash does a nice job of importing and exporting Illustrator 8 and earlier files. The preferred Illustrator format for importing into Flash is the AI format. However, in Illustrator 9 and over, you can now import to the SWF format. The same features that apply to FreeHand when imported in the SWF format apply to Illustrator. Gradients aren't supported in versions of Illustrator before version 5. Bitmaps are supported in version 6 and over. You also can copy and paste between Illustrator and Flash.

You can import and export solid and gradient color palettes between Flash and Fireworks and Photoshop and Fireworks

When art is imported from Illustrator, the elements used to make the objects are grouped together and the stacking order is maintained in Flash. Layers created in Illustrator are also recognized in Flash.

Files generated from Adobe Photoshop, ImageReady, and other popular graphics programs can be imported into Flash using any of the appropriate extensions listed in Table 7-1. See this table for a listing of file extensions you can use with Flash MX.

File Type	Extension	Windows	Macintosh
Adobe Illustrator (version 8.0 or earlier)	.eps/.ai	Yes	Yes
AutoCAD DXF	.dxf	Yes	Yes
Bitmap	.bmp	Yes	No
Enhanced Windows Metafile	.emf	Yes	No
FreeHand	.fh7–.fh10	Yes	Yes

TABLE 7-1 File Formats That Can Be Imported into Flash

File Type	Extension	Windows	Macintosh
FutureSplash Player (older version of Flash)	.spl	Yes	Yes
GIF	.gif	Yes	Yes
JPEG	.jpg	Yes	Yes
PICT	.pct/.pic	No	Yes
PNG	.png	Yes	Yes
Flash Player (Flash native format)	.swf	Yes	Yes
Windows Metafile	.wmf	Yes	No
WAV Audio	.wav	Yes	No
AIFF Audio	.aif	No	Yes
Photoshop*	.psd	Yes	Yes
WAV Audio*	.wav	Yes	Yes
AIFF Audio*	.aif	Yes	Yes
Silicon Graphics*	.sai	Yes	Yes
TGA*	.tgf	Yes	Yes
PICT*	.pct/.pic	Yes	Yes
QuickTime Image*	.qtif	Yes	Yes
QuickTime Movie*	.mov	Yes	Yes
Digital Video*	.dv	Yes	Yes
Macromedia Flash Video*	.flv	Yes	Yes
Motion Picture Experts Group*	mpg, .mpeg	Yes	Yes
Audio Video Interleaved	.avi	Yes	Yes

*For QuickTime 4.0 or over

TABLE 7-1   File Formats That Can Be Imported into Flash *(continued)*

NOTE   *When you import a Photoshop file into Flash, a message appears alerting you that Flash doesn't recognize the format. It asks you whether you want to import via QuickTime. Click Yes to import.*

Import File Sequences

You also can import file sequences generated from other programs such as Bryce, Adobe Dimensions, Poser, Strata 3D, Lightwave, Maya, Premiere, AfterEffects, FinalCut Pro, AutoCAD, and many more. A file sequence is a series of files that, if viewed together, would give the illusion of a flipbook or a frame-by-frame animation. Flash recognizes a group of files as sequential if the files have the same names but end in sequential numbers.

To import sequential files, go to File | Import. Navigate to the folder containing the files you want to import. Click the first file in the numerical file sequence. On a PC, click the Open button. On a Mac, click the Add button and Import button. An alert displays: "This file appears to be part of a sequence of images. Do you want to import all the images in the sequence?" Click Yes. The sequence will import into Flash. The files appear on a single layer and sequentially occupy the frames on that layer. The total number of frames equates to the number of sequential files you imported.

When you import a sequence, you create a frame-by-frame animation in Flash. You can easily create animated 3-D effects using sequences from programs such as 3-D applications, as shown in Figure 7-4. Using sequential files to create a frame-by-frame animation (especially sequential files from 3-D programs) can add some interesting frame-by-frame animation effects

7

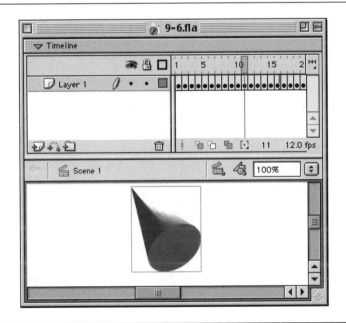

FIGURE 7-4   A sequential file format imported into Flash

to your Flash movie. A word of caution about file size: Files from 3-D programs, depending on how they're rendered, can be big. Careful attention should be paid to keeping the file sizes low. Even the most spectacular Flash Movie is anticlimactic when you have to wait too long for it to play.

With a multiframe movie in Flash, you also can export a file sequence to another program. Do this by selecting File | Export Movie. The Movie Export dialog box appears. In Windows, type in a filename and select Save As Type in the pop-up menu. You can export a file sequence to the following formats:

- PICT (Mac) or BMP (Windows)
- EPS 3.0
- AI (Adobe Illustrator, 8.0 and under)
- DXF
- JPEG
- GIF
- PNG

Once you export a file sequence from Flash, you can then import your sequence back into another application, like Premiere to enhance a video or Fireworks to make a GIF animation. This method works well for projects with multiple pieces. It makes it easy to use parts of a Flash animation in other support materials for print and web applications.

Import SWF Animation from Other Applications

The SWF file format has become so universal that many other applications besides vector applications offer it as an export option. The SWF format generates such beautiful, low-bandwidth images on the Web, it's no wonder more and more software developers are embracing this technology. Not all applications that support the SWF format enable you to import the SWF file back into Flash and have full functionality, like layers and symbols. However, there are at least a couple of applications worth mentioning because they address a special niche in the developer market.

Toon Boom Studio is a 2-D vector-based application for cartoon animation. It includes features important to cartoon animation developers such as lip synching, smoothing of animations, and perspective tools. Toon Boom animation can be exported to SWF format. You can also import your cartoon animations into Flash using the Toon Boom Studio Importer plug-in for Flash MX. Once the animation is in Flash, you can add interactivity to your cartoon animations. You can download a free evaluation copy of Toon Boom, as well as download the full application for purchase, at www.toonboom.com (see Figure 7-5). Also, a trial copy is located on your Flash application CD in the Goodies folder.

FIGURE 7-5   The Toon Boom user interface on the Mac

Swift3D by Electric Rain is a vector-based 3-D animation application that offers an easy-to-use set of tools that enable you to extrude, rotate, and lathe vector objects, among other things. If you're accustomed to working in a 3-D environment, the tools will look very familiar (see Figure 7-6). Another benefit to this program is that it's relatively inexpensive considering all of its useful features. You can export to SWF format or you can import into Flash as an SWF. From here, you can add interactivity. For example, if you wanted a user-controlled object like a car or a robot, this would be the perfect solution. On the product site, www.swift3d.com, you can download a tryout version of the application and also see some very cool examples of 3-D Flash animation.

There are many other applications that export to SWF format, like LiveMotion and Corel R.A.V.E. However, the applications previously mentioned are the most interesting in terms of producing special graphics animation beyond the capabilities of basic Flash. Also, they are more niche specific.

FIGURE 7-6 Swift3D by Electric Rain (www.devlab.swift3d.com)

Import Video into Flash

There are many interesting effects you can achieve by importing video into Flash. In MX, you can easily use video as a design element in your Flash movies, and you have more options than ever before. Once you import the video into Flash, you can layer Flash animation over it and add interactivity. In Chapter 15, we'll be examining the process of adding interactivity to video in Flash. In a time when video clips are so accessible and digital video is virtually plug and play, this is an extremely powerful Flash design tool.

There are two different ways you can import video into Flash: embedded video and linked video. Let's examine these two methods.

Import Embedded Video into Flash

When video is embedded in a Flash file, it actually becomes part of your movie. Earlier versions of Flash did not enable you to do this. You could only link a video file to a Flash file, creating a

Did you know?

Video Formats

You can import videos saved in all the most popular formats, such as QuickTime (MOV), digital video (DV), MPG, MPEG, and AVI. These formats, however, require QuickTime 4.0 or over installed on your PC or Mac. If you're working in Windows and DirectX 7 or over is installed, you can import AVI, MPG, MPEG, and WMV. This selection is far less limiting than the previous version of Flash, which only enabled the export of QuickTime movies.

path between the Flash file and the video file. You can still link video to a Flash file, and we will discuss that process in the next section. Before importing embedded video into Flash, you have to understand a little about the compression process, since this is an important element of embedded video.

Since digital video files are inherently enormous in size (full-screen compressed video is approximately 1MB per frame), video usually is compressed to be more portable and efficient. When video is compressed for export, on playback, the video is decompressed. File compression is an entire science unto itself and is far beyond the scope of this book.

Flash uses the Sorenson Spark codec ("codec" stands for compression/decompression) as an import and export standard. This codec makes a tremendous difference in the final file size, and is truly amazing technology. Video in Flash is more versatile than ever. Because of technology like this codec, and the advent of reasonably priced digital video camcorders and FireWire connectivity, you can expect to encounter more video all over the Web very soon.

Like JPEG compression, video compression is always a trade-off between file size and output quality. Through the Sorenson codec, you can balance these settings to customize the movie for your particular output goal. For example, if your Flash movie with embedded video is bound for the Web, and you're delivering to a low-bandwidth audience, quality will take a backseat to file size. You will notice that, frequently, video-driven web sites will offer alternative links for low-bandwidth users. This way, both ends of the spectrum are addressed, so the designer doesn't have to globally compromise the quality of his/her project for one specific group.

To import embedded video into Flash:

1. Select File | Import, and in the Import dialog box, navigate to the folder where your video is located.

2. If you know what the file type is and you want to select it specifically, you can click the Format box to select a format type from the pop-up list. This can help speed up your

search by isolating specific file types. You can also choose the All Formats option if you're not certain of the file type.

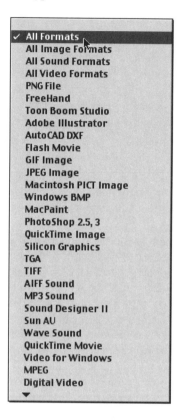

3. Select the file type and click Open. You will then need to make some decisions about your imported video. In the Import Video dialog box, under Import options, you have two selections:

    ■ Embed Video In Macromedia Flash Document

    ■ Link To External Video File (video will only be visible when imported as a QuickTime file)

4. After you select the Embed Video In Macromedia Flash Document option and click OK, the Import Video Settings dialog box appears with many settings. These settings are essential to the quality and size of your final video output in Flash. Let's cover the various functions in this window (see Figure 7-7):

    ■ **Thumbnail preview**   At the top of the window is a thumbnail preview of the video you are about to import. To the right, the size and length of the source video are indicated.

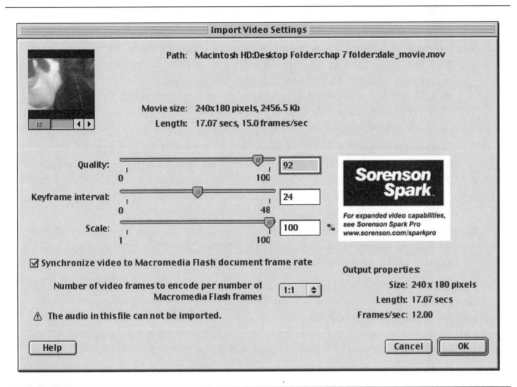

FIGURE 7-7   The Import Video Settings dialog box

■ **Quality slider**   Use this slider to set the quality of the movie. The farther you slide the Quality slider toward 100 percent, the larger the file size and the better the output quality. The following illustration represents the difference in quality between a video on a low-quality setting and a video at 100 percent quality.

15 percent quality

100 percent quality

■ **Keyframe Interval slider**   Use this slider to pick the frame interval of keyframes in the video. Keyframes store total data for a frame. In-between frames store only data that differs from the keyframes. The more distance between keyframes, the smaller the movie size.

- **Scale slide**   Use this slider to change the size of the video. As you slide, the new size is indicated in the Output properties listed to the right.

- **Synchronize Video To Macromedia Flash Document Frame Rate**   Select this check box if you want to synchronize frame rate of both the imported video and your movies' frame rate. To synchronize frame playback, Flash may drop frames or duplicate them, depending upon the ratio between frame rates. If the embedded video has a lower frame rate than the Flash movie, frames will not drop if this option is selected. Rather, they will duplicate.

- **Number Of Video Frames To Encode Per Number Of Flash Frames**   Select from this pull-down list to pick the ratio of video frames played versus the number of Flash frames played. This provides you with another tool to scale down the size of the file by dropping frames. You can achieve some interesting video effects by experimenting with these settings. The default frame rate ratio is 1:1.

- **Output settings**   The settings (to the right) provide you with current data on the size, length, and frames per second of your embedded video. This information will help you adjust the other settings.

Once you adjust all your settings and click OK, an alert box appears telling you that the embedded video contains more frames than will fit in just one Flash keyframe. You then have the option of extending the span of frames to the last video frame. If you click No, you can manually adjust the frame span. The video object is not self-contained in Flash. Rather, you must specify the span of frames in the Flash Timeline to see them all. If you select No, and you want to add more frames in the Timeline later, click the first keyframe (the black circle) and select Insert | Frame or press F5. Each time you press F5, another frame will be added to the Timeline.

If you add more frames to the Timeline than are in the video, blank frames will begin to appear.

 *You can drag frames by turning on Span Based Selection in the Edit | Preferences dialog box. However, this makes individual frame selection difficult. With this turned on, to select an individual frame in Windows, press CTRL-click. To select an individual frame on the Mac, press CMD-click.*

You can preview your video in one of four ways:

- Drag the Playhead in the Timeline over the frames, as shown next.

- Press the ENTER/RETURN key.
- Display the Controller (Window | Controller) and click the Controller's right arrow.

7

- Select Control | Test Movie to see the video in a Flash Player file.

To assign an instance name to an embedded video instance on the stage, select the object, and, in the Properties Inspector, type in a name in the upper-left corner. With an instance name, you can refer to this video in a script to add interactivity.

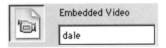

Update and Replace Embedded Video Files

Often, you may need to return to the source video and edit it. If you have already built most of your Flash movie and it includes interactivity relating to the video, this could cause a real problem. Fortunately, you can edit a source video and update it easily in Flash, keeping it intact.

To update a video:

1. Select it in the Library and, from the pop-up menu, select Properties.
2. In the Embedded Video Properties dialog box, select the Update button.
3. In the Open dialog box that pops up, navigate to the updated movie and click Open.
4. The movie imports again and is updated in the Library as well as instances onstage.

In the Embed Video Properties dialog box, you can replace a video by clicking the Import button. To do so, select a video in the Library first and follow the preceding procedure, but this time, click Import.

To export a selected video from Flash, follow the same procedure, but click the Export button. In the Save dialog box, enter a name and navigate to the folder you wish to save the file in. The video will export in a Flash Video format, the extension for which is .flv. You can then import the FLA file back into another Flash file.

Import Linked Video into Flash

Importing linked video into Flash behaves differently than embedded video. With embedded video, you can only link a QuickTime format video to a Flash file and you can only export the file to a QuickTime format. Once you publish the movie to a QuickTime format (MOV), you can't edit the QuickTime version in Flash. You can, however, edit the movie in QuickTime, if you happen to own QuickTime Pro, an inexpensive application you can purchase from Apple (www.apple.com). QuickTime 4 (and over) contains a Flash track, which enables you to perform minor edits on the Flash-based portion of the new QuickTime movie.

Publishing to QuickTime is not right for every project. If your movie is dependent upon advanced interactivity, it won't work in QuickTime format. Simple behaviors like buttons that start and stop the main Timeline work fine. However, anything that involves multiple Timelines (movie clip interactivity) is out of commission in QuickTime format because it only recognizes simple interactivity on the main Timeline.

The other element that's different about linked video is that it serves as a placeholder in Flash for a video file that resides elsewhere. So, when you import linked video into Flash, you are indicating a path to the video, much like you would do in an HTML file.

There's another issue you need to be aware of with linked video. Although you can test the movie in the Timeline (drag the Playhead, use the Controller, or press the ENTER/RETURN key) to preview the linked video as you do with embedded video, you cannot test the movie in Flash Test Movie mode. When you drag the Playhead over frames to test the movie in Flash, you also will not be able to hear audio, if the linked movie contains it.

 You cannot test your linked video in Test Movie mode because you must export this movie to a QuickTime format first, before you can see it.

To import linked video into Flash:

1. Select File | Import, navigate to the video file you want to import, and click Open.

2. An alert box appears telling you that the embedded video contains more frames than will fit in just one Flash keyframe. Just like with embedded video, you can extend the span of frames to the last video frame or click No to manually adjust the frame span.

3. The movie now appears onstage.

Just as with embedded video, you have the option of selecting File | Import To Library if you only want the video to be stored in the Library.

Modify a Linked Video

Although the video only exists as a link, there are a few additional features you can use to streamline your production and avoid unnecessary extra steps. This is especially relevant if the source video has been edited and you need to replace it.

To swap a video instance with another linked video that is imported in your video:

1. Select the instance you want to swap.

2. Click the Swap button in the Properties Inspector.

3. In the Swap Linked Video dialog box, click the new video. The new instance replaces the old. You can also swap an embedded video instance with another embedded video in the same way as previously outlined.

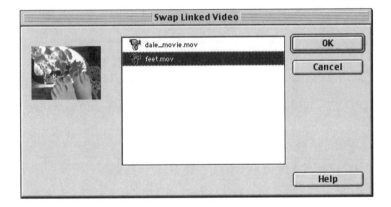

To change the path of a linked video:

1. Select the video in the Library and, in the pop-up options menu, select Properties.

2. In the Properties dialog box, click the Set Path button.

3. Navigate to the new location of the video and click OK.

NOTE *You can also swap, import, export, and update an embedded video object.*

A linkage name allows you to share a linked video from the Library in multiple Flash movies. To add a linkage identifier to a video:

1. Select the video in the Library and, in the pop-up options menu, select Linkage.

2. In the Linkage Properties dialog box, there are two additional linkage options: Import For Runtime Sharing and Export For Runtime Sharing. These two options allow you to specify the URL for the movie where the linked video is stored. The linked video will download and play (as per script instructions) when the file loads on the user's computer. This URL can reside remotely on another server. To export the video for sharing the video with remote Flash files, click the Export option, provide a linkage name, and provide a URL where the video is located in order to facilitate the sharing between Flash Player files.

Linkage Properties		
Identifier: dale_movie		OK
Linkage: ☐ Export for ActionScript		Cancel
☑ Export for runtime sharing		
☐ Import for runtime sharing		Help
☑ Export in first frame		
URL: http:www.analog.com/images/foot.swf		

To import a video from another Library, click the Import button and follow the same procedure as outlined.

Use Vector Graphics in Your Flash Movie

As mentioned in the previous section, vector graphics are made in drawing programs such as FreeHand and Adobe Illustrator. Although Flash is a vector-based program, some artists like to take advantage of features in other drawing programs. FreeHand has a perspective grid to help shape an object into a 3-D shape. It also contains all sorts of interesting fill textures. Illustrator is packed with filters that enable you to distort paths. Some people are so accustomed to drawing in one package, they don't care to learn a new one. Fortunately, Flash makes it easy to import vector drawings.

Drawing programs were originally intended for print, although the latest releases of FreeHand and Illustrator address the increasing need for Web features in vector programs. RGB color should always be used when making art for Flash because CMYK color doesn't translate well into RGB. If you can import in an SWF format, your color and art will always translate well when brought into Flash.

Although vector art in general tends to be smaller than bitmaps, using many complex paths can increase file size. When creating vector art for import into Flash, make certain you use the program's utilities for minimizing points on a path, or plan in advance to eliminate unnecessary paths.

Use Bitmapped Images

Bitmapped images, or raster images, are associated with paint or photo-editing programs. Some artists turn vector art from illustration programs such as FreeHand and Illustrator into bitmaps to take advantage of filters and techniques that can be applied to raster images.

You import a bitmap into Flash the same way you import a vector image. Select File | Import, select the file(s) you want to import, and click the Import button. In Windows, select the file in the Import dialog box. Select from the Files Of Type list at the bottom of the dialog box. Your bitmap will appear on the current layer.

If you want the bitmap to be imported, stored in the Library, and not appear on the stage, select File | Import To Library. The image won't appear on the stage until you drag it from the Library.

NOTE   *The bitmap formats you can import from are listed in Table 7-1.*

Set or Modify the Properties of a Bitmap

Just like any other graphic element, there are properties you can change in a bitmap image. Although the properties you can change are limited, there are still some interesting effects you can achieve with bitmaps if you're a creative designer.

When you import a bitmap into Flash, it appears in the Library. One way you can change a bitmap is to use the Bitmap Properties dialog box. To display this dialog box, select the bitmap in the Library, and then display the pop-up options menu. In this menu, select Properties. You can also right-click (in Windows/CTRL-click on the Mac) the image in the Library to access this dialog box.

In the Bitmap Properties dialog box, there are several options to choose from, as shown in Figure 7-8. The top of the box provides you with file information: when it was created, the size, and a thumbnail preview. The following options are also available:

- Select Allow Smoothing for an antialias effect. This will smooth any rough edges.

- Choose a Compression format. You can select from Photo (JPEG) or Lossless (PNG/GIF). If color and image detail are important, JPEG is the best choice. Selecting the Use Document Default Quality check box enables you to either keep the previous setting or re-enter a new value of quality between 1 and 100 in the Quality box that appears when this option is deselected. You cannot change the image quality of a JPEG image in the Publish Settings dialog box. If you need to modify the quality setting, it must be done in the native program or in the Bitmap Properties dialog box.

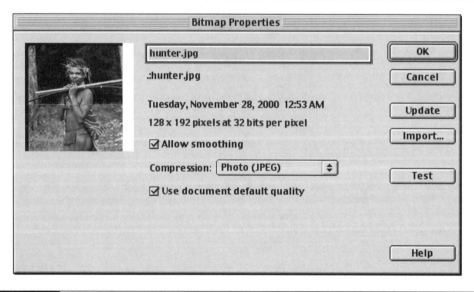

FIGURE 7-8 The Bitmap Properties dialog box allows you to modify elements of a bitmap.

■ The Update, Import, and Test buttons enable you to update the file throughout the movie, import it to another format, and test the quality of your new settings. The new settings ratio appears at the bottom of the dialog box when you test the settings.

Bitmaps can be transformed just like any graphic element you create in Flash. You can scale the bitmap, rotate, skew, and flip it, and change its position on the stage. Transformations are performed on bitmaps as outlined in Chapter 6. You can also use the Properties Inspector to modify the bitmap. Here you can type in a new size and new position, and you can also swap the image with another graphic.

To swap this image with another image in the Library, select the bitmap instance on the stage and click the Swap button in the Properties Inspector. In the Swap Bitmap dialog box, select the graphic you're swapping with and click OK. The instances will then be swapped on the stage.

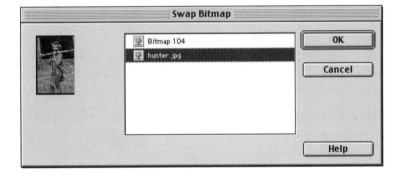

Edit a Bitmap

If you need to modify a bitmap in its native program, you can launch the program in Flash. To do this, select the bitmap in the Library. From the Options menu, click Edit With (or right-click in Windows/CTRL-click on the Mac to display the context menu). In the Select External Editor dialog box, navigate your hard drive to find the application the bitmap was created in. When you select the application, it will appear in the File Name box. Once you locate the program, click OK. The file opens in the program it was created in. Make your changes and resave the document. When you return to Flash, the edited version will now be in the Library. If you have an instance of this bitmap on the stage, the change will be reflected in that also.

You can also launch the editing program on a bitmap instance on the stage by clicking the Edit button in the Properties Inspector.

Trace a Bitmap

Being able to trace a bitmap serves many purposes. If the correct settings are chosen, you can substantially reduce your movie file size. If it's not done the right way, it can increase the size of the file beyond belief. You also can create some cool effects using this technique. When you trace a bitmap, Flash paints over it and renders it as vector art—your bitmap is gone. Sometimes it adds a great effect; sometimes it can make your bitmap look like an unrecognizable blob. Because the results can be unpredictable, you need to experiment with the settings to get just the right effect.

To use this technique, select a bitmap on the stage. Choose Modify | Trace Bitmap. The Trace Bitmap dialog box appears, as shown in Figure 7-9. You can customize tracing options in this dialog box to achieve a variety of results. From the top, your options are as follows:

- **Color Threshold** The default is 100. Choose between 1–500. Increasing the threshold decreases the number of colors used to trace the image.

- **Minimum Area** The default setting is 8 pixels. You can enter a value between 1 and 1000 pixels. This sets the number of neighboring pixels surrounding a dominant color. A low number gives you more areas of color because fewer pixels are surrounding a color.

- **Curve Fit** From the pop-up menu, select from the following:

  - **Normal** This is the default setting.
  - **Pixels, Very Tight, Tight, Smooth, and Very Smooth** These options determine the smoothness of an outline. Pixels have many points for detail and Very Smooth has fewer points between curves.

- **Corner Threshold** From the pop-up menu, select from the following options to determine the way edges will look:

- **Normal** The default setting.
- **Many Corners** Gives the resulting trace more detail.
- **Few Corners** Gives the resulting trace less detail.

In some cases, these settings might cause the file size to become too large. Check the resulting file size before settling on the image.

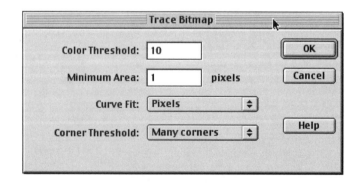

FIGURE 7-9 Use the Trace Bitmap dialog box to automatically trace.

Flash recommends the following settings for a decent-looking trace:

- Color Threshold of 10
- Minimum Area of 1 pixel
- Curve Fit with Pixels
- Corner Threshold of Many Corners

A trace can only look as good as the original. If the quality of the bitmap is substandard, the trace will be too. Also, certain bitmaps with a lot of detail or dark colors don't lend themselves to being traced. I've had much success tracing clip art objects with transparent backgrounds from stock photo collections. They come out looking very clean and almost not recognizable from the original bitmap. This tracing uses the Flash recommended settings for tracing a bitmap.

Break Apart a Bitmap

Breaking apart a bitmap is another way to achieve some creative effects in Flash. When you break apart a bitmap, the selected picture becomes broken up into an editable object. These objects can be modified by filling them with color and applying transformations like scale, rotate, and skew. You also can make the bitmap the current color in the Color Options pop-up menu or in the Color Panel. With this option, you can actually fill any object using the broken-apart bitmap as the color fill.

To be able to paint with the broken-apart bitmap, select the bitmap and choose Modify | Break Apart. After the bitmap is broken apart and sampled with the Eyedropper tool, the bitmap's content will reflect the Fill Color option. You can now fill objects with it. If you deselect the object and want to use it as a fill again, select the Eyedropper in the Toolbox. The Fill Color option will change back to the selected bitmap that's been broken apart. Use this technique to create mask-like effects with the Paintbrush or to fill objects with bitmap background effects such as clouds or a landscape.

To break apart a bitmap and modify the fill colors:

1.   Select a bitmap on the stage and choose Modify | Break Apart.

2.   In the Toolbox, select the Lasso tool. The Options portion of the Toolbox now displays the Magic Wand tool, Magic Wand Properties icon, and the Polygon Mode tool.

The Magic Wand tool enables you to select an area within the image to modify its properties. To customize the selected area, you can set the properties of the Magic Wand tool by clicking the Magic Wand Properties icon. This displays the Magic Wand Settings dialog box.

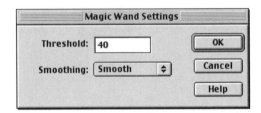

In this dialog box, you can set Threshold and Smoothing:

■   The Threshold can be set between 1–200 pixels. The Threshold number determines how close the colors have to be in hue to be included in the selection. A low setting indicates a more exact selection, picking only colors similar to the few pixels you have selected. A higher number gives you a broader and more diverse selection of pixels.

■   The Smoothing options are Pixels, Rough, Normal, and Smooth. The Pixels option gives you a pretty rough edge selection. Smooth evens out the pixels on the edge of your selection. The middle selections of Rough and Normal fall somewhere in the middle in edge smoothness.

TIP   *Pictures with contrasting colors or broad areas of color are easier to select from.*

To use the Magic Wand tool, set the properties if needed. Then, click the Magic Wand icon and click the broken apart bitmap. Your selection is now editable with the Paint Bucket or any of the Transformation tools. To color the selected object, with the object selected, click the Paint Bucket. You can apply a fill or gradient as you would to any editable object in Flash.

To transform the object, click the part of the object you want to transform using the Magic Wand tool, and then select it with the Arrow tool.

Use the Free Transform tool in the Toolbox to scale, rotate, or skew, as outlined in Chapter 6. Since the object is editable once you break it apart, you can also make a selection by drawing an invisible marquee around a portion of the object. Once you've made a selection, it can be transformed.

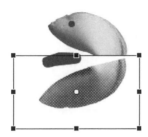

You can also make a selection with the Polygon Lasso tool. Use this tool by following these steps to select a piece of a broken apart bitmap:

1. With the editable bitmap selected, click the Lasso tool.

2. Click and drag in the editable object to make a freeform selection.

3. To make a polygon selection, click the Polygon tool in the Options section of the Toolbox.

4. Press and depress the pointer to create a point-to-point polygon.

5. To end your selection, double-click the last point.

You selection will now appear as an editable object. Any modification you can make to a regular editable object can be made on this element, too.

Import and Assign Sounds

The ability to import sound into Flash is another feature that makes Flash a full-featured multimedia authoring program. To understand sound in Flash, it's important to understand how sound works on a computer.

Because sound on your computer is digital, you can modify it. Sound is depicted in the form of sound waves.

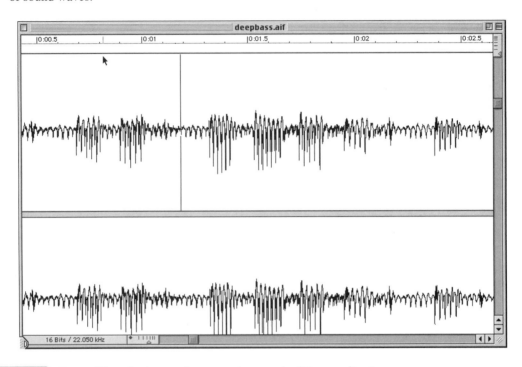

To modify and mix sound, you need a sound-editing application.

You can modify the properties of a sound wave in many ways: you can change the tempo, insert and delete tracks, delete part of the sound, remix it, and make many other changes. Sound can be digitized from a number of sources including CDs, recordings, cassettes, or live audio. Many audio-editing programs are available on Windows and Mac platforms to enable you to make modifications to this digitized sound. On the Windows platform, there are programs such as Cool Edit 2001, Sonic Foundry, Cakewalk, and Goldwave, to name a few. On the Mac, there are Beatnik, Cakewalk, Cubase, mEdit, PEAK, and many more. Web sites such as askjeeves.com and zdnet.com offer a plethora of information on Windows and Mac audio-editing programs, including features, reviews, demo versions, and freeware editing programs.

Understand How Digital Sound Works

Digital sound is known as *sampled* sound. It's recorded by taking samples of a sound every fraction of a second and storing the sound in bits and bytes. The sample rate indicates the number of times the samples are stored, and the sample size is information stored on the sound. A high sample rate and sample size equates to better sound resolution. Sample frequencies are measured in hertz (Hz) or kilohertz (KHz).

The most common frequency settings are the following:

- **44.1 KHz**   This produces the cleanest sample and is the standard CD quality.
- **22.05 KHz**   Usually a good choice for music for the Web. Produces acceptable quality.
- **11.025 KHz**   This is voice quality or AM radio quality.

The bit resolution is the number of bits used to describe a sound sample. An 8-bit sample size uses 256 units of data to describe the current sound level. A 16-bit sample size uses approximately 65,000 units of data to describe the current sound. The higher the bit rate, the clearer the sound and the larger the file. Stereo sound makes for file sizes twice the size of the original.

The formula for determining the final bit size of a stereo recording is the following:

```
rate sample × recording × (bit resolution ÷ 8) × 2 = sample size
```

The formula for determining the final bit size of a mono recording is identical to that of stereo, except it is multiplied by 1 because it has a single audio track.

Because this formula might seem a little obscure, the following are some sample rates that will give you a better idea of how frequency, resolution, and length of recording work in conjunction with one another and what kind of results they yield:

- A 60-second sound with a 44.1 KHz sample rate that's 16-bit stereo is 10.5MB in size. This produces superior-quality sound. The same file in mono and in 8-bit is approximately half the size.
- A 60-second sound with a 22.1 KHz sample rate that's 16-bit stereo is 5.25MB in size. This produces average-quality sound, but the size is large. The same file in mono is approximately half the size.
- A 60-second sound with a 22.1 KHz sample rate that's 8-bit mono is 1.3MB in size. This is probably the best bet for the Web in terms of balancing quality with file size.
- A 60-second sound with a 11 KHz sample rate that's 8-bit stereo will be 1.3MB in size, so low, stereo is barely recognizable. Good for voice recordings on the Web, the mono version of this equation is approximately half the size.

The trick to keeping the sound file size down while not sacrificing too much quality is to sample the sound as a loop. *Looping* a sound means you extract a tiny piece of a sound and visually match the beginning of the sound wave to the end of the sound wave so that when it plays back, it sounds like one continuous sound. You can program the looping of a sound in Flash, too. In fact, looping is an action in Flash that's automatic. You have to tell Flash how, when, the number of times, or on what event you want the sound to loop, or whether you want it to loop at all. Assigning simple sound to buttons and movie clips is discussed in Chapter 11, and working with the sound object is discussed in the Chapter 15.

7

Import a Sound File

When sound is imported into Flash, just like a picture file, it must be compressed and saved in a format that's recognizable to Flash. The following sound file formats can be imported into Flash:

- **AIFF (.aif)**   This format is the standard Mac sound format. Windows with QuickTime 4 can read AIFF files.
- **WAV (.wav)**   This format is the standard sound format for Windows. Macs with QuickTime 4 can read WAV files.
- **MP3 (.mp3)**   MP3 format is becoming an increasingly popular file format because of its impressive compression capabilities. It can reduce the size of an audio file considerably and still retain good sound quality. It is both Mac and Windows compatible.

The following additional file formats can be imported into Flash with QuickTime 4 or higher installed on your system:

- Sound Designer II (Mac)
- Sound Only QuickTime Movies (Windows and Mac)
- Sun AU (Mac)
- System 7 Sounds (Mac)

Importing a sound into a Flash file is as easy as importing a graphic. From the main menu, choose File | Import to display the Import dialog box. Navigate to the sound file and click it. Click Open in Windows or click Import on the Mac. Nothing appears on your stage because you're importing a sound. Although digital sound is represented graphically as sound waves, Flash does not depict the sound this way on the stage. Rather, it is displayed as a sound wave in the Timeline and in the Library.

Like bitmaps and video, imported sound is stored in the Library. To see the sound you import, choose Window | Library. Sound is depicted with a loudspeaker icon. When you click a sound in the Library, the graphical representation of the sound wave is shown in the top of the Library, as shown in Figure 7-10. Sample the sound by clicking the control arrow in the top right of the sound wave. Stop the sound by clicking the square Stop button. Adding sound to a Flash movie is discussed in the next section.

Export a Sound File

To edit the properties of a sound in the Library, you need to access the Sound Properties dialog box. To do this, either double-click the Sound icon in the Library and select Properties, or right-click in Windows/CTRL-click on the Mac to display a pop-up context menu and select Properties. In the Sound Properties dialog box, you can compress or recompress your sound in another format. For example, if you've imported a WAV file and want to recompress it in an MP3 format to reduce file size, this is where it can be done in Flash. You also can change a sound and test the quality results of several different compression ratios.

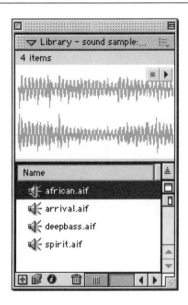

FIGURE 7-10   When you click a sound in the Library, a thumbnail preview displays.

Figure 7-11 shows the Sound Properties dialog box displayed on a sound residing in the Library named deepbass.aif. This dialog box is used to specify the export settings of the sound. The name of the sound file appears at the top of the dialog box. Under the name, the file path, date, and specs on the sound file in its current state are displayed. In the Compression box, you can experiment with different compression formats and ratios. Test your sound by clicking the Test button. Generally, the MP3 setting will balance size and quality well in Flash.

NOTE   *You also can set export settings for sound in the Publish Settings dialog box, which is discussed in Chapter 16. If you didn't select export settings in the Sound Properties dialog box, you can assign export settings to sounds in the Publish dialog box. You also can ignore the export settings in the Sound Properties dialog box. Do this by selecting Override. Use Override if you want to retain two sets of files to be used for different purposes, with different audio export settings.*

The Compression pop-up menu offers the following compression formats: MP3, ADPCM, and Raw. When you select from one of these three compression formats, additional menu selections become available relating to the format you selected:

■   If you select MP3 as your compression, you can also set the Bit Rate and Quality of the sound file from pop-up menus to the right of the selection. The Bit Rates range from 8 KBps (kilobytes per second) on the low end of the sound spectrum to 160 KBps on the

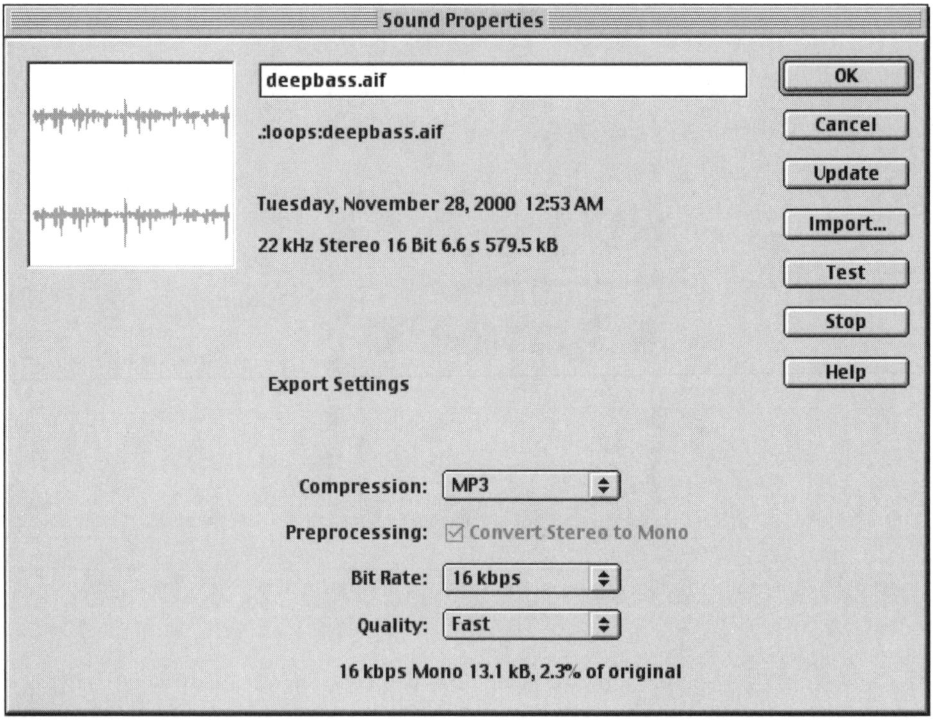

┌───┐
│ ▦▦▦▦▦▦▦▦▦▦▦▦▦ **Sound Properties** ▦▦▦▦▦▦▦▦▦▦▦▦▦ │
│   │
│ ┌──────────┐ **deepbass.aif**   ┌──────────┐   │
│ │ ╱╲╱╲╱╲╱╲ │   │   OK   │   │
│ │   │ .:loops:deepbass.aif   └──────────┘   │
│ │   │   ┌──────────┐   │
│ │ ╱╲╱╲╱╲╱╲ │ Tuesday, November 28, 2000   │ Cancel │   │
│ └──────────┘ 12:53 AM   └──────────┘   │
│   22 kHz Stereo 16 Bit 6.6 s   ┌──────────┐   │
│   579.5 kB   │ Update │   │
│   └──────────┘   │
│   ┌──────────┐   │
│   │ Import...│   │
│   └──────────┘   │
│   ┌──────────┐   │
│   │   Test   │   │
│   └──────────┘   │
│   **Export Settings**   ┌──────────┐   │
│   │   Stop   │   │
│   └──────────┘   │
│   ┌──────────┐   │
│   │   Help   │   │
│   └──────────┘   │
│   │
│   **Compression:** [MP3   ▣]   │
│   **Preprocessing:** ☑ Convert Stereo to Mono   │
│   **Bit Rate:** [16 kbps   ▣]   │
│   **Quality:** [Fast   ▣]   │
│   │
│   16 kbps Mono 13.1 kB, 2.3% of original   │
└───┘

FIGURE 7-11   The Sound Properties dialog box enables you to compress, test, and update a sound.

high end. From Quality, you can select Fast, Medium, or Best. Fast Quality is smaller in size than Best Quality. When you select different bit rates, the resulting file information appears underneath the Quality setting. Experiment with different settings by clicking the Test button in this dialog box. Notice the difference in sound quality between a file with a bit rate of 8 KBps versus a file with a bit rate of 48 KBps.

■ If you select Adaptive Differential Pulse-Code Modulation (ADPCM) as your compression, you can select a Sample Rate from the pop-up menu that gives you a range from 5 KHz–44 KHz. You also can select the number of ADPCM Bits in a pop-up menu. Mono or stereo settings can be checked also. ADPCM is commonly used in voice technologies and digital phone networks. ADPCM compresses well (although not as well as MP3), and as such is a viable choice for keeping file sizes on the low side. This compression format was the default setting on older versions of Flash and is useful for short sounds you might use on button events.

■ Raw enables you to export uncompressed sound. With Raw compression selected, you can change the sample rate from 5 KHz–44 KHz, as well as choose mono or stereo settings. Raw audio offers big file sizes and lossless compression. This wouldn't be an option you would choose for movies being put up on the Web. There might be some special circumstance where you might need to use this format. As a general rule for beginners and intermediate Flash users, just ignore it.

NOTE   *MP3 sound requires the Flash Player version 4 and above to be heard.*

Use the Import button to assign another sound to the currently selected one. The currently selected sound will become the newly selected sound. This is a useful technique if you need to globally update instances of sound. Select Update if a sound has been changed in another program. Click Update, and the sound will automatically update.

Assign Sounds to Your Flash Movies

You've probably noticed that Flash technology on the Web is chock-full of sounds these days. With the new MP3 compression standard and streaming capabilities, sound is easier to use and to hear on the Web than ever before. Getting sound from its original source into your movie is pretty easy to do.

You can do some interesting things with sound in Flash. You can determine how the sound will load into the movie when it's played by choosing a sync type. There are also tools with which you can edit the balance and the volume of the sound. Additionally, you can assign an identifier to a sound, thereby creating a sound object, and also share this sound with other Flash movies. With the sound object, you can assign ActionScript to the object to allow your user to interactively control sound. We discuss how to use the sound object in Chapter 15. Once you import your sounds, they become stored in the Library. To make the sound work, you need to put it in your movie. You can add sounds to layers, buttons, and movie clips.

Add a Sound to a Layer

Assigning a sound to a layer is simple. Multiple sounds can be added to more than one layer, too. To add sound to a layer, do the following:

1. Create a keyframe (press F6 or select Insert | Keyframe) or select an existing keyframe.

2. From the Library, drag a sound to the stage. The sound wave appears in the frames on the layer. In other words, you won't see the sound on the stage.

TIP   *If you want to see the sound waveform in the Timeline, add frames to the sound. Do this by clicking the sound frame in the Timeline and then inserting as many frames as you want (F5 or Insert | Frame). As you insert frames, you will see the visual of the waveform appear.*

Edit Sounds

If there are many sounds built into your movie, you can edit them by selecting the sound from the Sound pop-up list in the Properties Inspector. When a sound is selected here, you can further modify it in the Properties Inspector. Instances of the sound in the movie will reflect these changes. These settings are discussed next.

If you test the movie at this point, the sound loops only once. You can modify the properties of the selected sound and sync the sound to the frames in the movie from the Properties Inspector. Going back to the stage, select the sound wave on the layer and look at the Properties Inspector. The Inspector enables you to do minimal editing on the selected sound. It's convenient to be able to do this, especially if you don't have access to an audio-editing program.

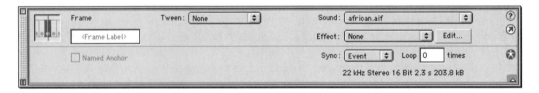

In the Effect pop-up list, you can set the balance of the sound and the volume. The following settings are available to do so:

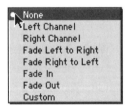

- ■ **None**   This is the default for no application of effects. It also removes previously applied effects.
- ■ **Left Channel and Right Channel**   Use one of these options to play in one of the selected channels.
- ■ **Fade Left To Right or Fade Right To Left**   Use one of these options to fade a sound from one channel to another.
- ■ **Fade In or Fade Out**   Select one of these options to gradually fade in or out the loudness of a sound.

■ **Custom**   Displays the Edit Envelope dialog box where you can customize your effect. This dialog box is discussed in the next section.

The Sync option has a pop-up list that enables you to synchronize your sound with your movie. This is an important feature because, if your movie is dependent on sounds playing in conjunction with graphics, you want to make sure the sound doesn't skip or appear to play at the wrong time. The options in this pop-up menu are as follows:

■ **Event**   When you sync on an event, the sound will synchronize to an event that elicits an action. For example, a sound might play on a layer when a button is clicked.

■ **Start**   A sound with a start and stop sync starts playing when the movie loads.

■ **Stop**   Select Stop if you don't want the sound to play when the movie loads. Stop is commonly used if you want the sound to play on an event such as a mouse click.

■ **Stream**   This option makes sound keep up with the animation in the movie, so the sound doesn't fall out of sync with the animation. The number of frames determines the length of a streaming sound. MP3 sounds synchronized for streaming must be recompressed in the Sound Properties dialog box.

To the right of the Sync selections, you can set a loop. Loops indicate how many times a sound will repeat a play action. If you want the sound to play throughout an animation, enter a number larger for looping than the duration time of the animation. Flash designers often enter a loop of 999 if they believe their audience may be hanging around their Flash site for a long time. This number is large enough to ensure the sound will play for quite some time.

Looping doesn't work well with streaming sounds. When a sound is streamed, frames are added to the movie to keep up with the animation. Looping can conflict with streaming because each time the sound loops, the file size increases unnecessarily. Looping, however, is one of the best ways to keep a file size down in a movie that incorporates local sound. Since long sounds mean bigger file sizes, if you can create loops and use compression schemes like MP3, your Flash movie will be more accessible to a lower-bandwidth audience.

Use the Edit Envelope Dialog Box

The Edit Envelope dialog box becomes available when you select Custom from the Effect pop-up menu. This dialog box enables you to further customize the predefined effects. In fact, if you select an effect like Stop, Start, Fade Right To Left, or Fade Left To Right, and then click the Edit button, the Edit Envelope dialog box will graphically display the results of that effect. If you alter the sound envelope on a predefined effect, when you click OK, the effect returns to Custom because you've now created a new effect (see Figure 7-12).

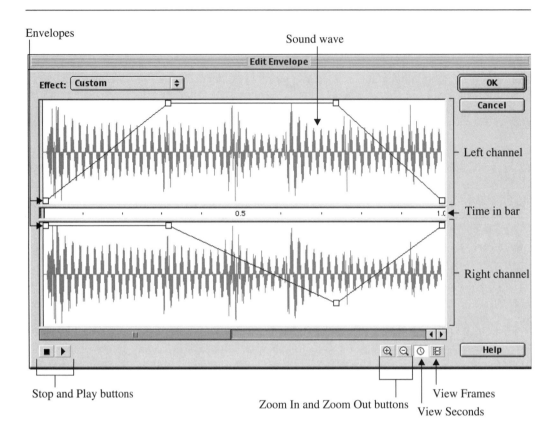

FIGURE 7-12 You can customize the balance and volume of a sound in this dialog box.

The Edit Envelope dialog box displays the selected effect in the top left of the box. This is your starting ground for modifying the sound. The sound waves are displayed one on top of another, the top representing the left channel and the bottom representing the right channel. The Envelope Handles are the little squares attached to the Envelope lines. Click and drag these square handles to change the amplitude of the sound's volume. Add handles to the envelope by clicking anywhere on the envelope line. Notice that when you add a handle, a mirror handle appears in the other channel. When you drag up and down on a handle, this action is not mirrored in the other channel. However, horizontal dragging of the handle is reflected on both channels.

In between the left and right channels are the Time In and Time Out controls. These enable you to control where sound starts and stops. If you want to loop the sound and need to tweek In and Out points, you can do it with these tools. To use the Time In and Time Out controls, click and drag them to the new points where you want the sound to begin and end. Toggle between Frames and Seconds in the bottom-right corner of the window to help select your In and Out points.

In the bottom right of the box, you can select the Zoom In and Zoom Out icons to magnify the sound waves for pinpoint precision when setting the options in this dialog box. The bottom of the dialog box offers a scroll bar so that if the magnified sound wave exceeds the size of the box, you can scroll left and right. The bottom left of the box offers sound controls to test the state of the current sound. Use these to experiment with envelope settings and test them.

Link a Sound

As mentioned previously, you can assign an identifier name to a sound in the Library, making it accessible to other Flash movies. When you do this, you are, in effect, sharing Libraries between movies. The obvious benefit of doing this is the file size issue, especially for size-intensive objects like sound. If there is just one Library and multiple movies can share common instances, your movie will perform a lot more efficiently.

To assign a linkage name to a sound, perform the following tasks:

1. Select the sound you want to link from the Library.

2. From the Options pop-up menu, select Linkage. The Symbol Linkage dialog box appears.

3. In the Symbol Linkage dialog box, assign an identifier name and select Export For ActionScript or Export For Runtime Sharing. Export For ActionScript is for links contained locally, so you don't need to supply a URL. If you select the second option (Export For Runtime Sharing), you must supply a URL where the movie with the linked object resides. This can reside on a remote server and will load when the movie plays.

Now this sound can be used in another movie's Library or used as a sound object.

You can share linked sounds from one Library to another by opening up only the Library of a movie. Do this by selecting File | Open As Library. Then, drag the linked sounds into your new movie. You will notice in the Linkage column of the new Library the status of the linked sound, or other linked elements.

If you display the Linkage dialog box on a linked sound in the new movie, you will notice the information carries over from the original Library.

The ability to link sounds and graphics to other Libraries as well as other Flash movies is a tremendous feature. If you're still a beginner, the technology here may not strike you as innovative. But it can really help streamline big projects with multiple uses of sounds, video, and graphics. It helps you organize your project better, keeps the file sizes down, and cuts down on a lot of duplication of objects.

Add Sound to Button and Movie Clip Symbols

Sounds can be added to layers, and sound objects can be created that can be controlled interactively. You can also add sounds to buttons and movie clips. You do this by entering Symbol Editing mode. In Chapter 6, we examined various components of this mode as it relates to graphic symbols. Since movie clips and buttons are a little more involved, Chapter 11 covers the process of making them in detail.

Since sound is often a component of your buttons and movie clips, let's take a brief look at what this involves.

Add Sound to a Button

When you add a sound to a button, you add it in Button Editing mode, as shown in Figure 7-13. Buttons are created on their own custom Timeline. Sound for buttons is often placed on a separate layer from the button layer to make it easy to distinguish between the two.

Button sounds are usually short because they often serve as button events. For example, when you click a mouse, which would signify an event, you may use a short sound as an alert that something is about to happen. You also can add a sound to a button so that when the user moves their mouse over the button, it elicits a sound. Sounds from the Common Sound Library are often used on button states because they are quick, small, and easy to apply. You're not limited to these, though. Short sounds can easily be made or acquired from many places on the Web for free and for purchase. Consult Appendix B for some sound resources. See Chapter 11 for more information on buttons and sound.

Add Sound to a Movie Clip

Movie clip symbols are self-contained movies that run independently on their own Timeline (see Figure 7-14). Sounds can be added to movie clips on their own layer in the movie clip editing mode the same way they're added to the main Timeline.

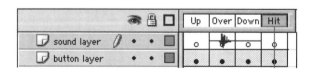

FIGURE 7-13   Add sound to button states on a separate layer.

FIGURE 7-14   In movie clip editing mode, you can add sound to a movie clip.

Sounds on a movie clip Timeline can be controlled with simple actions. For example, you could have a button that, when clicked, stops a movie clip that has sound on the Timeline. Another button could start the sound in the movie clip when clicked. Sound and movie clips are a much more versatile duo when sound exists in the form of a sound object. But there are still some fun things you can do with simple actions and a little creativity applied.

In the next chapter, we will explore animation in Flash. Flash was born as an animation application, and animation still remains an important part of the interface.

Part III

Lay the Groundwork for Flash Interactivity

Chapter 8

Learn the Basics of Flash Animation

```
on(release) {
    trace(_root.shape._y);
    trace(_root.shape._x);
}
```

How to...

- Think like an animator
- Plan your movie
- Animate on different time sequences
- Animate on different layers
- Make keyframes
- Create frame-by-frame animations
- Test your animation
- Set Onion Skins

Animation has always been a major feature of the Flash authoring environment; and in Flash, you can create beautiful, complex, and stunning animation. One of the reasons Flash animation is so widely used on the Web is that it's a vector-based application, and as such, it is capable of generating smaller size files.

Years ago, animation was created on stand-alone systems with proprietary software. Animators were highly skilled technicians who had both the technical expertise and artistic know-how to conceptualize and create linear animation by hand. The last decade brought professional animation and video-editing capabilities to the desktop, an achievement we never thought possible many years ago. With computers getting bigger and better every day, animation is no longer the mystery it used to be. Animation is accessible to you on your desktop, and it's relatively easy to create in Flash.

Think Like an Animator

Animation in its most simplistic terms is graphics in motion. To understand the way an animator thinks, let's consider animation in its most primitive state.

First, let's consider flip books. You've probably seen a flip book, where each page in the book represents a slight movement or change, so that when the book is flipped quickly, the elements on the page appear in motion. Then remember the old animated Disney movies. Armies of artists were recruited to create hand-drawn, individually rendered frames. Artists would create keyframes where major shifts in movement occurred within the animation and then sculpt the rest of the secondary frames around them. The in-between frames were the interpolation of movement between one keyframe to another. This is where the term "tween" comes from, referring to the frames "in between" the keyframes of the animation.

With this old technique, a substantial number of frames needed to be hand-rendered to create the illusion of fluid movement. Thirty seconds of animation might require up to 700 frames. As you can imagine, this required a large staff and a lot of time. Tricks were devised to make hand-drawn animation a little more streamlined. Animators painted their animation on cells, the transparent celluloid sheets used to render each frame. Because cells were transparent, parts of the cell animation that didn't change over a span of frames could be reused by placing them over or under new cells, thus creating a layer effect. This way, the artist didn't have to duplicate drawings in other cells.

You've probably noticed in old animations where a character may be running against a backdrop of some sort, like mountains or a field. If you've ever examined the animation closely, you would notice that the background loops and repeats itself at some point. It's the same moving backdrop being repeated again and again to create the illusion of a running character.

Computer animation today is more streamlined than the hand-drawn animation of yesterday, but many of the basic rules still apply. Animators always strive for consistency in their animation, as well as economizing on visual elements just like in the old days of animation, when the cell technique was used.

Flash offers many ways in which you can economize on the creation of objects. Not only can you reuse parts of already-drawn objects with symbols from the library, you also can automatically create the "in between" frames of an animation using tweening animation, which is discussed further in the next chapter. In addition, Flash has layers, which in ways could be viewed as a modern-day equivalent to cell animation.

Understand Animation in Relation to Static Graphic Design

Animation is a species apart from static graphics. Static graphics broadcast a message unto themselves. Animated movies combine the passing of time in a limited, linear space to relay the message. Both static and motion graphics need to be designed, but the thought process and method are different. Images displayed in the passing of time create a rhythm regardless of whether sound is added. The frames in an animation can have a beat that can be measured by controlling the delivery time of your frames, much the same way a composer measures the beat of a song. A rock-and-roll, jazz, or Latin beat is measured in four beats to a measure.

In Flash, the frame rate is 12 frames per second. The frame rate can be altered or duplicate images can span more than one frame to redefine the rhythm and mood of the movie. By nature, motion graphics are more entertaining than static graphics, increasing their ability to deliver a subliminal message. People will stare at something moving much longer than a printed piece because they don't have to work as hard as with a printed piece. Hypnotic in its methods, moving graphics can have more impact than print if presented in an engaging way. Motion is a universal language that everyone understands.

Plan Your Movie Before You Begin

It's easy to animate in Flash, but it's not always easy to create a successful animation. It's all too easy for a new animator to create a movie that quickly becomes confusing, busy, or noisy. What's more, professional animators don't become professionals overnight. On large projects, just like in the days of the old Disney movies, professionals work in large teams on a project, the less experienced animators acting as protégés to their more seasoned counterparts.

You don't have to create a full-length feature animation to make a Flash movie. Your animation may last just a few seconds, bringing the viewer to a static page. The beauty of Flash animation is that it can be used for small or large movies, games, e-commerce, or just to add accent to a simple web page. On either end of the spectrum, you must think like an animator to create a successful animation.

Whether a movie is small or large, video or animation, movies of any sort are generally born in storyboard form, often in conjunction with a written script. Storyboards are much like the cells of a cartoon strip, depicting key movements in the animation sequence and indicating the planned length of time and the mood of the animation. They can be presented to your client on the computer, in print, or both.

Two of the most widely used drawing programs on both Mac and PC platforms, Macromedia FreeHand and Adobe Illustrator, make it easy to export whole storyboards (or parts of a storyboard) into Flash. FreeHand and Illustrator have addressed the need for artists to realize keyframes of their Flash movie on paper before it ever gets to Flash. Both programs enable you to export images and layers into the Flash native format, so art created in these programs can be incorporated into your movie.

TIP   *If you're planning to import art from a drawing program into Flash, make certain the document size in the drawing program is reflected in the Movie Properties dialog box of Flash. The latest versions of FreeHand and Illustrator enable you to measure your page in pixels, and the Flash measurement system includes inches and picas. If publishing to the Web or multimedia, it's best to measure in pixels, because the measurement system on the Web is pixels.*

Animate on Different Time Sequences

The default frame rate for Flash animation is 12 fps, about half that for a movie. A small Flash animation can appear pretty smooth in its blending from frame to frame on the Web at 12 fps if your intention was to make the animation appear smooth. You can adjust the frame rate in Flash if you want to slow it down or speed up your animation. The frame rate you set is global throughout the Flash movie. There are tricks you can use to give the illusion of slowing down or speeding up certain frames in the animation sequence, like adding extra frames or easing in or out on tweening. These methods are covered in the next chapter.

There are two ways to change the frame rate in Flash. Select Modify | Movie from the menu. In the Movie Properties dialog box, highlight the frame rate and type a new rate. You also can double-click the Frame Rate at the bottom of the Timeline to access the Movie Properties dialog box (see Figure 8-1).

Changing the frame rate should be done with caution if your file is being published to the Web. Your cyberspace audience uses a mélange of different configurations, including old, slow, and fast modems and processors. Not everyone will be able to view the new frame rate the way you intended it to look. If you do intend to change the frame rate setting for a movie to be published on the Web, it's not a bad idea to test the movie on a wide range of configurations and browsers after it's put up, to eliminate the prospect of undesirable results.

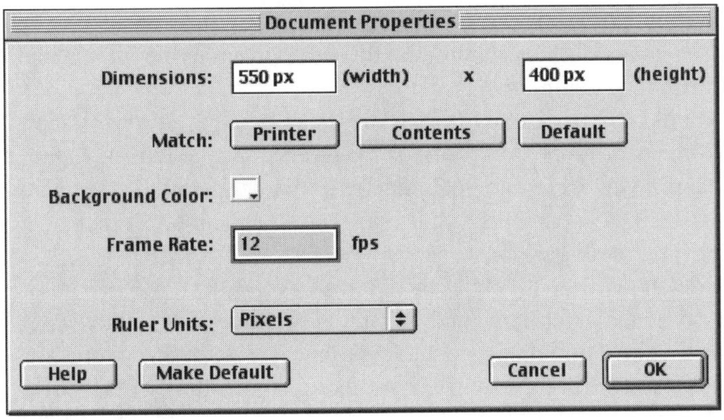

FIGURE 8-1   Change the frame rate of the movie in the Movie Properties dialog box.

8

Animate on Different Layers

Layers are an integral part of moving graphics. If you were directing a real-world movie on a stage, there could be many scenes going on simultaneously. For example, say you were shooting a scene where two people were talking against a bustling city landscape and the conversation they were engaged in was the main focus of the scene. The layers of events occurring simultaneously create a rhythm that balances the main focus of the movie. In effect, the background events, although subliminal to the viewer, augment the two people talking.

Our perceptions of the real world tell us that movement and events occur in the passing of time, as well as simultaneously. Film and video have a sense of real-world spatial relationship on a two-dimensional plane. The equivalent of the real-world spatial relationship in Flash is layers. Layers enable you to have more than one object moving behind and/or in front of one another simultaneously. Layers give a kind of stacking order to animation.

In the previous section, "Think Like an Animator," we discussed the cell sheets used in hand-drawn animation. Because cells were transparent, to save time, certain cells were reused in places where the elements were identical. Flash uses this same concept of a cell as a layer. Layers not only act as a stacking order to other layers, they also can extend objects or backgrounds on a layer in linear time to display one layer while something else is going on in another layer.

Let's examine the previous example where a movie was being created with two people chatting against a bustling city backdrop. If this were a Flash animation, the moving cars in the background could continue looping on one layer, and a moving crowd in the background could coexist on another layer while the main scene was running. The ability to layer your animation expands your creative possibilities.

Layers also are useful when making movie clips. Movie clips are reusable symbols that run independently on their own timeline. Flash is so compact, you can have movie clips with their own self-contained layers and frames running on different layers in the main Timeline. This allows for endless creative possibilities.

Complex animations in Flash usually have more than one layer. It's not uncommon to create a movie with 35–40 layers or more. A monstrous project requires extensive organization up front to ensure success. Naming layers in a logical manner in the preplanning stage is important, too. Like members of a cast, all the elements of your Flash movie should know their place and purpose before production begins (see Figure 8-2).

Layers in Flash default consecutively to the names Layer 1, Layer 2, and so on. To name a layer, click and drag over the layer name and type the new name. Change the stacking order of the layer by clicking the layer and dragging the layer up or down in the layer row.

Create a new layer by clicking the Insert Layer icon at the bottom of the Layer section of the Timeline. Delete a layer by selecting the layer and clicking the Trash Can icon at the bottom of the Layer section.

In Flash MX, you can organize layers in layer folders. Layer folders enable you to store related layers in a folder. If your Timeline has many layers, you have to vertically scroll the Timeline to see all the layers. Layer folders allow you to expand and collapse the contents of a folder, making it easier for you to navigate vertically through layers.

Create a new layer folder by clicking the Layer Folder button in the bottom left of the Timeline. Add to the contents of a layer folder by dragging and dropping layers in it. Open a layer folder just like any operating system folder by double-clicking it. This feature helps you keep house in your movie.

Layers are one of the main ingredients in creating basic animation. Beginners often make the mistake of relying on a single layer to do most of their animation. Just like in traditional animation, it's easier to delete a cell—or in this case, a layer—than it is to trash a file because it wasn't planned out properly. The other problem you could run into in a one-layer animation is objects

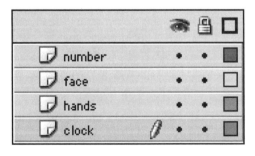

FIGURE 8-2   Name the layers on a Timeline by selecting the layer name and typing a new name.

erasing one another or connecting when you didn't intend them to. Making use of multiple layers for objects and backdrops is a wise design decision.

Frames in Animation

If layers are a cart, frames are the wheels that make the cart move. Frames reside on layers in the Timeline, and this is where your animation comes alive. There are two major types of frames used to create an animation: the keyframe and the frame. Keyframes indicate key moments in your animation, where the properties of an object change. Keyframes are depicted with black circles in the frame placeholder boxes on the Timeline. Frames are a duplicate of the previous keyframe (see Figure 8-3) and are depicted as gray boxes that reside in the placeholder boxes on the Timeline. There are also blank frames and blank keyframes, both of which are used to display a blank frame. For example, if you wanted an object to appear and disappear in a frame sequence, you may use a blank keyframe to do so. There are other variations on frames used when you create a tweening animation, which are discussed in Chapter 9.

Use the Timeline to Add Keyframes

Although a static graphic can call the Timeline its home, timelines are designed to accommodate all facets of animation. Keyframes and frames on selected layers occupy frame placeholders in the Timeline, as depicted in Figure 8-3. Frame numbers depicted in increments of five above the layers act as a time ruler for your frames. Manually play back the animation (or scrub through) by clicking and dragging on the Playhead. Because it's hard to tell which frame your Playhead is sitting on, the current frame is indicated at the bottom of the Timeline, too. Because timelines become the framework of your animation structure, it's important to have a well–planned-out Timeline.

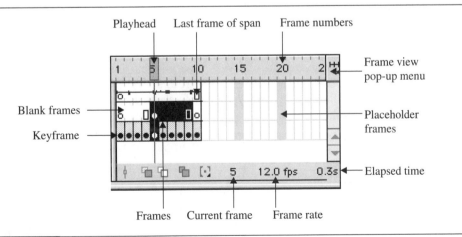

FIGURE 8-3   A Timeline with frames and keyframes

Frame-by-Frame Animation

When learning animation, it's important to understand frame-by-frame animation. Frame-by-frame animation relies on keyframes to indicate changes in the animation sequence. The change in the frame can include a different image or the same image with the properties of the image changed. This change in frames is known as a "keyframe."

Create a frame-by-frame animation on a new layer by doing the following:

1. Select a frame in the layer and draw the object you want to animate. A keyframe indicated by a black circle will be generated in the first frame of the layer you selected.

2. Create the next frame of the layer by clicking the blank placeholder frame to the right of the keyframe and selecting Insert | Keyframe (F6) from the menu. When you do this, the content of the previous frame duplicates.

3. After the keyframe is created, either modify the properties of the object on the new keyframe or draw another image.

4. Continue the process of inserting as many keyframes as is sufficient for your frame-by-frame animation. Properties include, but are not limited to, X and Y position, scale, skew, color, transparency, or a combination of these elements. You can alter each keyframe whenever and as often as you like, each time resulting in a modification of that frame in the animation sequence. The end of an animation sequence is indicated with a white rectangle.

Figure 8-4 depicts a frame-by-frame animation of a clock. On each keyframe, the hand of the clock moves clockwise to the next point on the clock. The clock face, hands, and numbers are all on separate layers. The gray frames represent regular frames, which we will discuss in the next section.

The importance of layers becomes obvious when creating a frame-by-frame animation. If you have more than one object on a layer but you only want to animate one of the objects, each time you select a keyframe, all objects on the layer become selected, even if this was not your intention. You must deselect all other objects to animate the one object. This is easy if you're only animating a few frames. If there are a lot of frames, it becomes confusing and inaccurate to have to deselect all items on each frame to alter the properties of one object. Consequently, making use of layers to draw different parts of your animation becomes very important to avert a potentially disastrous animation.

To delete a keyframe, click a keyframe to select it. From the menu, select Insert | Clear Keyframe (SHIFT-F6). If the keyframe is between several frames, this will remove the keyframe and connect the previous frames with the remaining frames, making the animation continuous.

To move an individual keyframe to another place in the Timeline, select the keyframe and drag it to its new location. To move a set of keyframes, hold down the SHIFT key while clicking each keyframe. This creates a movable frameset. Drag the selected set to its new location on the Timeline. You also can move an individual keyframe and a frameset to a new layer by dragging them onto the desired layer.

Frame-by-frame animation is relatively easy once you get the feel for it, and it serves as a great technique for animations where rhythm is emphasized.

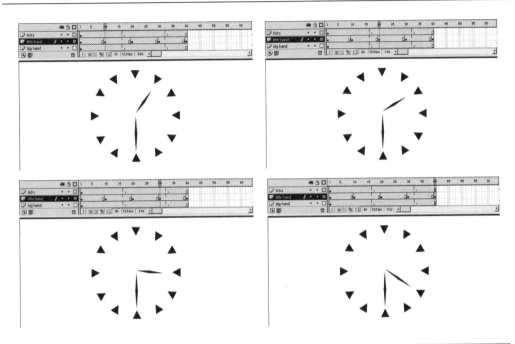

FIGURE 8-4   Four sample keyframes from an animation of a clock demonstrate a frame-by-frame animation.

Insert In-Between Frames in a Frame-by-Frame Animation

Not every frame has to be a keyframe in a frame-by-frame animation, as is evident in the illustration of the clock in Figure 8-4. You can insert regular frames next to the keyframes to extend the length of time a keyframe is displayed in an animation. Because changing the frames per second in the movie alters the entire Timeline, this enables you to change the length of time on individual elements. To insert a frame between two keyframes, select the first keyframe, and from the menu select Insert | Frame (F5). A gray rectangle appears in the frame placeholder, representing a regular frame.

To add more frames, repeat the process. Adding more frames extends the animation time of the keyframe to the left even more. If your movie is 12 fps and you add 11 frames to the keyframe to bring the frame count to 12 in the Timeline, theoretically, this set of frames will last for one second. In animation time, one second is a considerable amount of time, and you don't always want your animation to move fast. The ability to control the display of frames over time gives the artist more creative flexibility in Flash.

To delete a frame, click an individual frame while holding down CTRL in Windows/CMD on the Mac to select it. From the menu, select Insert | Remove Frames (SHIFT-F5).

To move an individual frame to another place in the Timeline, select the frame while holding down CTRL/CMD, and drag it to its new location. To move a set of frames, hold down

SHIFT-CTRL/SHIFT-CMD while clicking the frames you want to move. This creates a movable frameset. Drag the selected set to its new location on the Timeline. You also can move an individual frame or a frameset to a new layer by dragging it onto the desired layer. Move an already-created frameset by clicking the frameset and dragging it to its new position.

Copy and paste frames onto another layer or on the same layer in a different frameset by holding down SHIFT-CTRL/SHIFT-CMD to select a frameset. Select Edit | Copy Frames or press CTRL-ALT-C/ OPTION-CMD-C. Click the starting frame in the new location. Select Edit | Paste Frames or press CTRL-ALT-V/OPT-CMD-V. A copy of the frames will now reside in the new frames. Frames also can be cut from their location and pasted into a new location using the same method, by selecting Cut instead of Paste from the Edit menu. Selecting Cut or Copy places a copy in the Clipboard, so multiple copies of the frameset can be pasted in the Timeline if so desired.

The properties of frames also can be altered by right-clicking/CTRL-clicking on the frame(s) to display the pop-up context menu.

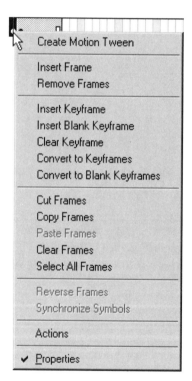

Frame Manipulation

You can change the way you manipulate frames. To do so, go to the Edit | Preferences menu and select Span-based Selection. When this is turned on, you can easily select entire spans of frames, as well as extend and reduce frame spans in a layer.

The options available are the same as in the Insert and Edit menus. You can insert and remove frames and keyframes, cut and copy frames, select all, and display the Actions window and the Frame and Sound panels quickly by using this method.

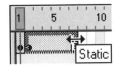

8

Test Your Movie

Previewing a static graphic in a paint or drawing program is a lot easier than previewing a motion graphic. With static art, you only need to look at what's on your screen. Graphics with motion are a different story. To test a motion graphic, you have to periodically preview it while it's moving. Unless you're psychic, it's impossible to know exactly how long objects should play and when other objects should be introduced on the stage, and animation involves a lot of tweaking before it reaches the ultimate state of perfection. Flash offers many ways to preview your animation, all of which are outlined here.

The quickest way to test your animation is either by manually scrubbing the frames with the Playhead in the Timeline, or by selecting Window | Toolbars | Controller from the menu.

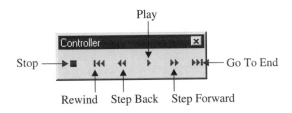

In Windows, the Controller window can either float independently, or dock on the bottom of the toolbar or under the menu. On the Mac, display the Controller window by selecting Window | Controller from the menu. The Controller window is used to play back, rewind, and scrub through your animation on the Flash stage. To rewind your animation, click the second button. To play the animation, click the fourth button.

The movie also can be tested as a Flash Player file format (SWF) by selecting Control | Test Movie or pressing CTRL-ENTER/CMD-ENTER. This method creates and displays an SWF file of the movie. The SWF file will be saved in the same folder as your movie. Test the movie as an SWF file when you need to get a better idea of how the movie will appear in its finished state. Sometimes the SWF version will look different from what you expected. One example may be a rectangle used as a background that is intended to bleed off the stage. It may appear as if it bleeds on the Flash stage. However, when you view it as an SWF file, the background may appear chopped off. In a case like this, previewing the SWF file will give you a better idea of what the movie will look like on the Web as opposed to only testing the movie in Flash. A Flash Player (SWF) version of the movie also can be generated by selecting File | Publish Preview | Flash.

You also may want to get an idea of what your movie would look like in a browser. To do this, select File | Publish Preview | HTML. This will generate and embed your SWF file in an HTML page, as well as give you an instant preview of the file. This is a wonderful feature because it shows you exactly what your movie looks like when embedded in an HTML document on the particular browser and platform. Flash automatically generates an HTML page and an SWF file, and names them and embeds the SWF file in the HTML page. Both files are automatically saved in the folder that holds the Flash movie you're previewing.

When you preview an animated file, the default action is a looping action. This means the animation plays until you close the file. In Chapter 12, you'll learn how to apply a simple stop action to a frame to make the movie play only once. This is a very simple form of interactivity.

If you happen to be importing your HTML preview into Macromedia Dreamweaver for further tweaking, Dreamweaver enables you to automatically code options available to embedded Flash Player files. The AutoPlay looping action can be overridden in HTML by deselecting the AutoPlay button in the Properties window. This makes the play of the animation false in the HTML code. In the Properties window, you can change the quality of the Flash file as well as the X and Y positions and the scale; you also can add a border and alter the alignment, all of which are generated automatically in HTML (see Figure 8-5).

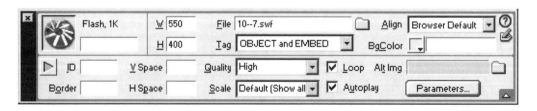

FIGURE 8-5 Information on a Flash object in the Properties Inspector in Dreamweaver with a Flash object selected

If your viewer doesn't have the correct Flash Player version loaded, he or she will not be able to view the movie on the Web. The latest version of the Flash Player can be downloaded for free from the Macromedia site, www.macromedia.com/software/downloads. It's not a bad idea to put a link on your page to this URL so viewers can easily get the version 6 Player if they don't have it. Your other option is to include a Flash version 6 Player detection script directing visitors to an alternative HTML URL if they can't view the Flash file. Your other alternative would be to publish your SWF file in a format that would be compatible with older versions of the Flash plug-in. Be aware, though, that earlier versions may not support some of the new MX features. We'll discuss the specifics of exporting and publishing your Flash movie in the last chapter.

Set Onion Skins

When you create a frame-by-frame animation, or any animation for that matter, sometimes it's hard to determine where you want to move the next keyframe in relation to the previous frames. Because you can only see one frame at a time while you're composing the animation, it's impossible to see where the animation has come from to determine where it's going in time. Tweaking an animation by randomly altering objects and playing them back could take hours. Onion Skins come to the rescue and resolve the problem in Flash. The Onion Skin technique is used in animation packages to give you a glimpse of the path of existing frames in your animation. It allows you to see a preview of as many frames as you want at your discretion. This technique is especially useful if you've created a frame-by-frame animation and all your keyframes are identical as a result of pressing F6 too many times.

Onion Skins display a selected portion of the animation as translucent ghost images of the original. The term "Onion Skin" comes from the concept of onion-skin paper, a thin, see-through paper artists use to trace over images. How do you move an object from one end of the stage to another in a frame-by-frame animation if the next keyframe keeps jumping back to the original position of the object in the first keyframe? Onion Skins to the rescue.

When you click any of the Onion Skin buttons at the bottom of the Timeline, an Onion Skin Marker appears as a translucent rounded-corner rectangle over the Frame Numbers in the Timeline. The Onion Skin Marker enables you to customize the span of frames you want previewed. Adjust the Marker by clicking and dragging the round handles at the beginning and end of the marker. Pick up and move the entire marker by dragging the Playhead to a new location.

The Onion Skin buttons reside at the bottom of the Timeline, and there are four in total. From the left, the following are the Onion Skin buttons and a description of the tasks they perform when clicked:

- **Onion Skin**   Click this to view the animation path as a dimmed image. This option does not enable you to modify the Onion Skins on previous frames, as it serves the purpose of indicating the path. Only the current frame can be modified (see Figure 8-6).

- **Onion Skin Outlines**   Click this to display the Onion Skins in outline form (see Figure 8-7). Only the current frame can be modified with this selection.

- **Edit Multiple Frames**   This displays the Onion Skins as opaque art and enables you to edit all frames within the confines of the Onion Skin Marker. You can also use Edit

Onion Skin button

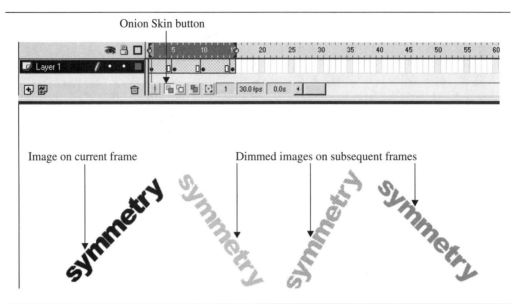

Image on current frame

Dimmed images on subsequent frames

FIGURE 8-6 The Onion Skin button is turned on—notice the Onion Skin Marker spanning a frameset at the top of the Timeline.

Onion Skin Outlines button

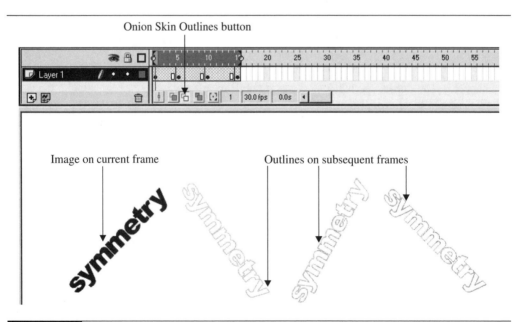

Image on current frame

Outlines on subsequent frames

FIGURE 8-7 The Onion Skin Outlines button is turned on to depict the path of an animation in outline form.

Multiple Frames to move a frame sequence or frame sequences on several layers. To move multiple layers to another position on the Timeline, follow these steps:

1. Lock or hide layers you don't want to move.

2. Click the Edit Multiple Frames button.

3. Drag the Onion Skin over frames in the group you want to move.

4. Select Edit | Select All Frames (CTRL-ALT-A/OPT-CMD-A).

5. Drag the timeline animation somewhere else (see Figure 8-8).

■ **Modify Onion Markers**   Click this button to display the Onion Skin Modification pop-up menu. The selections from the menu are as follows:

■ **Always Show Markers**   Displays a hollowed-out Marker even when Onion Skinning is turned off.

■ **Anchor Onion**   Locks the Onion Skin Marker in its current position. Select this to prevent the Onion Skin Marker from moving when you move your Playhead throughout the frames. In regular mode, the Onion Skin Marker follows the path of the Playhead position.

■ **Onion 2**   Displays two frames on either side of the selected frame.

■ **Onion 5**   Displays five frames on either side of the selected frame.

■ **Onion All**   Displays all frames on either side of the selected frame.

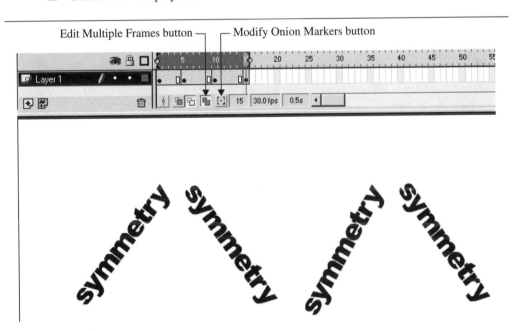

FIGURE 8-8   The Edit Multiple Frames button enables you to edit objects on multiple frames.

Turn off Onion Skinning by clicking the buttons again. The buttons act as a click on/click off toggle switch.

 *Locked layers do not display Onion Skinning. The Onion Skin feature in Flash enables you to pinpoint the path of your animation. This is an important and time-saving tool in the creation of animation.*

In the next chapter, we will expand upon our knowledge of simple animation and take a look at tweening.

Chapter 9

Incorporate Motion Tweening into Your Design

How to…

- Make a simple motion tween
- Tween with multiple keyframes
- Change size, rotation, skew, and color on a motion tween
- Tween symbols on multiple layers
- Control frames and frame sequences in a motion tween
- Adjust tweened objects with the Properties Inspector
- Create a motion guide
- Use a mask layer with a motion tween

As discussed in Chapter 8, frame-by-frame animation occurs when objects are manually changed on each frame of a movie. Sometimes frame-by-frame animation may be time-consuming and inaccurate for certain animations that require smooth movement between keyframes. In this case, tweening animation may be more appropriate. When you tween an object in Flash, the software mathematically generates a sequence of frames between two keyframes. The farther apart the keyframes sit, the smoother the movement. In contrast to frame-by-frame animation, tweening takes the guesswork out of the gradual transition of an object between two keyframes. In Flash, you can choose either frame-by-frame or tweening animation, depending upon the requirements of your project.

Motion Versus Shape Tweening

Tweening in Flash is a standard animation technique, and it comes in two forms: motion and shape. Although both methods of tweening are based on the same concept, their applications and purposes are very different. In fact, Flash beginners sometimes become puzzled as to which one to use in a movie. In a very simple animation, it may not matter whether you use motion or shape tweening.

However, when animations become more sophisticated, your selection will indeed matter. This is why it's important to understand the similarities and differences between the two. This way, you'll know exactly which one to use to optimize the performance of your movie. This chapter focuses on all aspects of motion tweening, and Chapter 10 examines shape tweening.

Understand Motion Tweening

Before learning to make a motion tween, you need to understand some basic rules. A motion tween can only be used on grouped objects, symbols, and text. Shape tweens can only be used on editable objects. Both shape and motion tweens can be used to change the position of an object and the object's color, scale, rotation, and skew. However, to tween color and opacity in a motion tween, the object must be a symbol. Graphic symbols are reviewed in Chapter 6, and buttons and movie clip symbols are discussed in Chapter 11.

Make a Simple Motion Tween

Motion tweening basically involves four steps: creating and selecting a grouped object or symbol; inserting an end keyframe in the Timeline; changing the object on the last frame; and creating the motion tween by selecting a frame in between the two keyframes. Figure 9-1 displays a motion tween created on a grouped object.

The procedure used in Figure 9-1 is detailed here:

1. Create a simple object on the first frame of the main Timeline, and either group the object or make it into a graphic symbol or movie clip. By default, a keyframe will appear on Frame 1, Layer 1. This will serve as the first point in the animation you are about to create.

2. Click a new frame on Layer 1 farther on down the Timeline layer where you want the next keyframe to occur. In Figure 9-1, keyframe 6 was selected. Add a keyframe on this

9

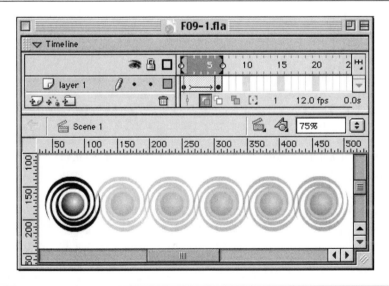

FIGURE 9-1   A simple motion tween that spans six frames

frame by selecting Insert | Keyframe or pressing F6. A span of frames will now appear in between the keyframes.

3. With any in-between frame selected, right-click in Windows/CTRL-click (or click and hold) on the Mac and select Create Motion Tween from the pop-up context menu. When you do this, frames are automatically generated between Frames 1 and 5, and are depicted with a light-gray fill. A right-pointing arrow appears on a light-blue background on the in-between frames to indicate a motion tween. You can also add a motion tween to this selection by selecting Tween in the Motion pop-up list in the Properties Inspector.

4. With the last keyframe selected, drag the object to another location on the stage to change its position.

5. Test the movie in the Timeline to see the gradual transition of the object between the two keyframes.

To make an existing object into a symbol for using in a motion tween, click the object and select Insert | Convert To Symbol (F8). Select the Behavior of the new symbol (Movie Clip or Graphic) and click OK. The object is now a symbol, stored in the Library. A symbol can be tweened in the same way that you tween a grouped object. The only difference is the motion tweening of one color to another. With symbols, you can change the tint on an instance to do a motion tween from one color to another. Group objects, on the other hand, cannot motion tween the color property of an object.

Insert, Remove, and Select Keyframes and Frames

Even motion tweens that look simple can be very time-intensive. For example, if you were tweening a word and wanted each separate letter of the word to move onto the screen at different intervals, you would need to make the word, break the letters apart, symbolize the letters, place each one on a separate layer, and tween them all individually. Because there sometimes is a lot of work to be done, it helps to know how to insert and remove frames and keyframes expeditiously. Let's review some shortcuts for inserting frames and keyframes, and selecting frames and keyframes:

■ To insert a frame, press F5; to insert a keyframe, press F6.

■ To remove a frame, press SHIFT-F5; to remove a keyframe, press SHIFT-F6.

- To select a keyframe or keyframes, click the frame or keyframe.

- To insert a blank keyframe, press F7.

- To move a keyframe or a frame sequence to a new position in a layer, select it and click and drag it to the new position.

- To convert a keyframe to a frame, right-click /CTRL-click on the keyframe and, in the context menu, select Clear Keyframe.

- To increase or remove a span of frames from the end of a frame sequence (when the last frame is a placeholder), press CTRL/CMD and drag the last frame. The pointer will turn into a double-headed arrow. If Span Based Selection is checked in Preferences, this will be the default setting.

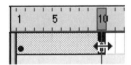

- To select a span of frames on the same layer as well as several layers, hold down the SHIFT key and click to select them.

- To select a span of frames between keyframes, double-click a frame in a frame sequence.

- To select all frames in a Timeline, select Edit | Select All Frames or press CTRL-ALT-A/ OPT-CMD-A.

- To clear a span of selected frames, select Edit | Clear All Frames or press ALT-BACKSPACE/ OPT-BACKSPACE. You can also select a span of frames and press SHIFT-F5.

- To turn a selected sequence of frames into keyframes, select Modify | Frames | Convert To Keyframes.

- To turn a selected sequence of frames into blank frames, select Modify | Frames | Convert To Blank Keyframes.

- To duplicate a keyframe, ALT-drag/OPT-click | drag on a keyframe.

Learning shortcut keys will help you speed through the process of making complex, multilayer animations.

Add Frames on a Motion Tween

If you play back a movie with six frames, such as the movie we looked at previously in Figure 9-1, you will notice it's a little choppy and moves quickly. It appears this way because only four in-between frames were generated to interpolate the tween, and, at 12 frames per second, this animation lasts for less than half a second. This is fine if it's the effect you want to achieve. But

9

let's say you wanted a smoother and longer transition between keyframes. If you add more in-between frames, the movement will appear less choppy because the animation will be longer.

To add more in-between frames, click a frame in your motion tween. If Span Based Selection is turned on in the Preference menu, press CTRL/CMD to select a frame in the middle of the tweened keyframes. Once an individual frame is selected, click F5. Each time you click F5, another frame will be added.

In the case of Figure 9-1, if you added frames up to Frame 24, the animation sequence would last about two seconds, creating a much smoother animation. Smoothness comes with a hitch, though. The movie will display slower. Also, the more frames, the larger the file. This is not something to worry about in a simple movie. But, as your movie grows with layers and complex movement, you will need to economize on the movie's growing size. The number of tweened frames may need to be trimmed down to decrease the size of the movie.

Motion Tween with Multiple Keyframes

In Figure 9-1, the object travels in a single line, from one keyframe to another. This creates limited movement and really isn't very interesting. You can give the object a livelier path by creating additional keyframes on a layer and changing the direction of the object on each keyframe.

In Figure 9-2, the position of an object has been changed several times by adding additional keyframes to the frame sequence. To add a keyframe to an existing frame sequence, select an in-between frame (hold down CTRL/CMD if Span Based Frames is turned on), and then click F6 to add the keyframe. To add a keyframe to frame placeholders beyond a frame sequence, select a frame outside the frame sequence and click F6. This extends the length of the current frame sequence. You also can extend the length of an existing frame sequence by clicking the last keyframe and pressing CTRL/CMD and dragging it to its new position. When you do this, the selection tool turns into a double-headed arrow.

Figure 9-2 is actually an alternate version of Figure 9-1, whose last keyframe stops on Frame 6. In the new version, additional keyframes were added (F6) to frames. After the frames were added, the tweening process was repeated in between some frames. Once the tweening was set in between the frames, the object on each keyframe was moved to a different position to give the illusion of the ball bouncing up and down. Turning on an Onion Skin button makes it easy to go back and change the object on any keyframe because you can preview the path of the object. When you're using Onion Skins for the purpose of viewing an entire path, as was done in Figure 9-2, it's important to drag the Onion Skin Markers over the entire frame sequence. Otherwise, you'll only see part of the path.

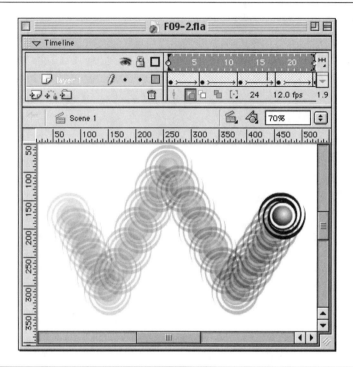

FIGURE 9-2   The object on the stage is tweened between multiple frames (with Onion Skins turned on).

Change Size, Rotation, Skew, and Color on a Motion Tween

In the previous examples, only the position of the object changes. You also can apply any of the other transformation tools to your object, and tween the size, rotation, and skew of an object using the Free Transform tool from the Toolbox or from the menu (Modify | Transform). To apply a transformation to a motion tween, select a keyframe in the tween. With the object selected, modify it using one of the transformation tools as outlined in Chapter 5.

Figure 9-3 shows a star object whose position and size are modified in motion. Onion Skins is turned on to make it easy to preview the path. On Frame 6, the scale is changed to 50 percent of the original. On Frame 18, the scale is changed to 25 percent of the original. To scale an object in between keyframes, click the keyframe you wish to perform the transformation on. Scale the object in that keyframe, and then apply a tween. The object gradually changes size between keyframes.

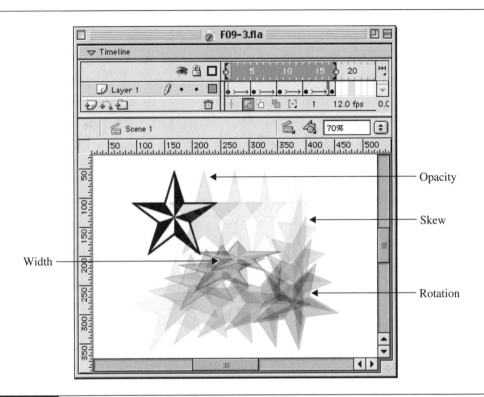

FIGURE 9-3   A graphic symbol with a motion tween applied; the position, width, rotation, skew, height, and opacity transform between keyframes.

Change the Color of a Tweened Symbol

When an object is made into any kind of a symbol, you can tween the color and opacity of the object. In Figure 9-3, the opacity changes from solid color to partially transparent color and back again. The opacity of a symbol (alpha), as well as the color settings on a symbol, is changed using the Properties Inspector.

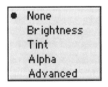

To make this feature become active, a symbol must be selected in the desired keyframe where you want the color/opacity change to take place. So you can change one symbol color to another using the Tint or Advanced settings.

To change the alpha of an object, select Alpha from the pop-up list. You can either use the vertical slider to pick an Alpha percentage or type in a new number in the Alpha percentage box.

Refer to Chapter 6 for a detailed description of color settings for symbols in the Properties Inspector. These features in the Properties Inspector enable you to tween some interesting color effects using symbols.

Motion Tween Graphic Symbols on Multiple Layers

The possibilities for tweening animation are endless considering that just a few tools give you so many different ways to animate an object. Figure 9-4 is an example of a motion tween on multiple layers, with the position and size of a bus and car symbol transformed. There are five graphic symbols on the stage, and each object resides on its own layer. Layers stack upon each other in order of display. For example, the street layer is under the bus and car layer. Examining the movie step by step will help you learn the process of creating a tween animation on multiple layers.

It's important to understand that the following example of a tween is strictly Flash beginner animation. When you become a little more experienced with the drawing and animation tools, you will find that the most efficient way to work is to symbol as many elements as possible in a movie. In fact, containing symbols within symbols is the most prudent form of production. Also, many of your tweened animations will be contained within movie clips, on their own Timeline, which makes it easy to edit every aspect of the symbol. Before you learn how to do this, though, you have to understand how to tween in the main Timeline first.

Deconstruct a Multilayer Movie That Uses Motion Tweens

1. First, you should always plan your symbols, layers, and layer stacking order, as was done in the movie we're about to deconstruct. It's a good idea to name layers and symbols to reflect the nature of the object that resides on the layer. For example, in Figure 9-4, the car symbol is called "car," as is the layer. When you name symbols and layers in a logical manner, there's no mistaking the purpose of each layer or its objects. The layers in Figure 9-4 are named in the following order:

- Bus
- Car
- Street
- Sidewalk
- Sky

2. After the layers were created, the first frame in the sidewalk layer was selected and the sidewalk symbol was dragged from the Library onto the stage. The symbol is a rectangle with a fill and no stroke.

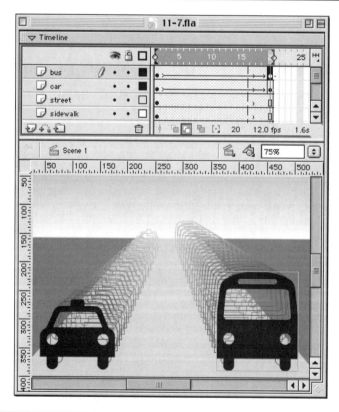

FIGURE 9-4   The positions and sizes of the car and the bus are tweened on multiple layers.

3. After the sidewalk was in place, Frame 1 of the street layer was selected and the street symbol was dragged from the Library onto the stage. The street was created with a polygon fill.

4. Once the street was created, Frame 1 of the sky was selected and the sky symbol was put in place. The sky is a simple rectangle with a gradient fill.

5. Frame 1 of the bus layer was selected and the bus symbol was dragged from the Library onto the stage. The bus and the car were drawn with the Pen tool. The process was repeated and the car symbol was positioned on the car layer. The car and the bus symbols are the only objects that animate. The goal was to make the bus and the car appear as if they've moved forward in perspective, on the road. This involved changing the position and the scale of the bus and car symbols.

6. With all the elements in place, the bus and car were motion tweened. The bus symbol was tweened first. With the bus object selected, a keyframe was inserted in Frame 20. This created the keyframe where the end movement occurs. The process was repeated on the car layer.

7. To create the tweened frames, the in-between keyframes were selected by right-clicking in Windows/CMD-clicking on the Mac and selecting Create Motion Tween from the pop-up menu. A black arrow with a blue backdrop appears within the frame sequence to indicate a motion tween.

8. Finally, the bus and car symbols were changed in Frame 20 on their respective layers. With the bus selected in Frame 20, the bus was moved to the bottom of the stage onto the street. The process was repeated with the car. The paths of the bus and car conform to the forward perspective of the street. Enlarging the scale of the two objects creates the illusion of objects moving forward in space. In Frame 20, the scale of the car and bus symbols was enlarged to approximately 400 percent in the last keyframe of both the bus and car layers. If you were to play back the movie with the Controller, the bus and car appear to move forward in space and time.

Motion tweening on different layers also can be used to make objects appear behind or in front of one another. If you were to transpose the position of the bus and car in Frame 1 of their respective layers (placing the car to the right and the bus to the left), they would cross paths somewhere in the middle of where they tween. Layering also can be used for hiding objects underneath one another during the span of a tween.

Control Frames and Frame Sequences in a Motion Tween

Once you've created a movie with several layers and tweens, there's always a possibility that the movie will need revising. Even the smallest revision can create a domino effect, which could change the entire flow of the movie. This, of course, is the reason that creating symbols is more

Editable Objects and Tweens

You can't apply a motion tween to an editable object. You can only apply a shape tween to an editable object. If you try to motion tween an editable object, or if the last keyframe in the frame sequence is missing, a dashed line will appear instead of the arrow in the tweened frames. This is a warning to let you know the tween won't work. Likewise, you can't apply a shape tween to a grouped object or a symbol. The exception to this rule is if you create a shape tween on the Timeline of a movie clip.

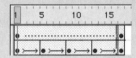

prudent. It's a lot easier to edit tweened symbols than it is to edit complex tweens on the main Timeline. We discuss this more in Chapter 11; but for now, let's consider a tweened animation on the main Timeline that needs revising.

Flash offers several techniques to modify frame sequences and move keyframes around. This is helpful because, as often as objects in a movie need to be changed, the actual frames themselves may need to be moved. Sometimes the timing of tweened objects on different layers may need to be revised, too.

Let's return to the previous example of the tweened car and bus movie in Figure 9-4. There are many ways to modify this movie. For starters, let's suppose your client believes the timing of the animation is wrong, and they want the car to move a split second after the bus. Instead of redoing the entire animation, you could experiment with moving the car frame sequence up a bit on the Timeline so the car is introduced after the bus. Figure 9-5 shows the revised Timeline of this animation with the car frame sequence moved on its layer to begin at Frame 10. Ironically, if you played the movie back at this point, all the other elements would disappear from the stage in Frame 21, and the client wouldn't be happy with that outcome.

To prevent objects from disappearing on the playback when it wasn't intended, you can add frames to all other layers up to Frame 30, where the car frame sequence now ends. To do so, click Frame 30 of each layer and press F5. This fills in the frames to the last frame on the selected layer. If the last frame is a regular frame, you can also use the CTRL/CMD drag method to increase or reduce the frame span. When you use either one of these techniques on the top tweened layer called "bus," it only adds blank keyframes. On a tweened layer, CTRL-click/CMD-click on the tween and press F5 until you reach Frame 30. This will enable you to control the frames in a tween.

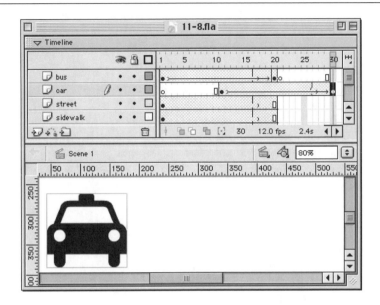

FIGURE 9-5   When a frame sequence is moved on a layer, it changes the playback of the movie.

To delete tweened frames, blank frames, or regular frames, CTRL-click–SHIFT/CMD-click-SHIFT and press F5.

CTRL-dragging/CMD-dragging the last keyframe of a tweened frame sequence to another point in the Timeline also can extend/reduce the tween. If the frame sequence is tweened, dragging the keyframe to another position will break the tween. Remedy this by redoing the tween.

Copy and Paste Frames

If you need to copy a keyframe, frame, or frame sequence to another layer, you can do so easily in Flash. Copying frames leaves the selected frames in place and makes a copy of the frames in the Clipboard. A copy of the frame sequence can be pasted at any time while in the program (until you exit the program or copy/cut another object).

You can copy a frame sequence or an individual frame by selecting the frame (or frame sequence) and right-clicking/CMD-clicking to display the context pop-up menu. Select Edit | Copy Frames or press CTRL-ALT-C/OPT-CMD-C. Click the first frame you want to paste to, and again right-click/CMD-click to display the context pop-up menu. Then select Edit | Paste Frames or press CTRL-ALT-V/OPT-CMD-V. A duplicate of the frame sequence will appear. If you're selecting a tweened frame sequence, make certain the last keyframe is in the selection. Otherwise, a dashed line will appear, indicating the tween is broken.

Copying Keyframes

You can also copy keyframes in the same frame sequence by selecting a keyframe and ALT-dragging in Windows/OPT-dragging on the Mac. This makes a duplicate keyframe. In addition, objects can be copied and pasted into place on the object's current layer as well as another layer. To do this, select the object and select Edit | Copy (CTRL-C/CMD-C). Then select a new frame, and select Edit | Paste In Place (CTRL-SHIFT-V/CMD-SHIFT-V). This tip can be a real time saver if you place a frame sequence on a layer and then decide later you need to move it or replicate it.

Frames can be cut as well as copied using the same method as Copy, by selecting Cut instead of Copy in the Edit menu. Cutting frames removes the frames and places a copy in the Clipboard. The frames can then be pasted, as with the Copy Frame command.

Reverse a Frame Sequence

When you reverse a tweened frame sequence, it goes in the opposite direction. Figure 9-6 is an illustration of a simple bouncing ball that has one frame sequence that makes the ball appear to go up and a reverse frame sequence that makes the ball appear to go down. So it creates a continuous, flowing motion of a bouncing ball. This simple ball animation provides a good example of how you can save time with repetitive tasks by using the copy technique and then reversing the frames to move in a direction that's opposite the original tweened frame sequence.

Here's how you can do a simple reversal of tweened frames:

1. Create a tween on an object using the steps outlined previously.

2. Select a tweened frame sequence, copy a tweened frame sequence (Edit | Copy Frames), and paste the frames (Edit | Paste Frames) right next to the last frame in the layer where you just copied them from.

TIP *To easily select a frame sequence, double-click the frame sequence.*

3. If you scrub the Playhead over the frames, the movement of the object will seem strange because the motion abruptly returns to the beginning of the loop when it reaches the end. We can easily fix that by reversing the second frame sequence.

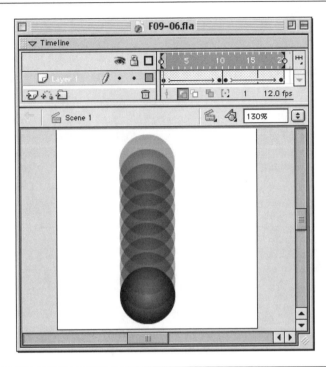

FIGURE 9-6   This tweened animation was reversed on the last set of frames.

4. Select the new frame sequence, and right-click/CTRL-click to display the context menu. Select Reverse Frames. This reverses the selected tweened frame sequence. Now, when you test the movie, the object that you tweened and reversed frames on appears to move back and forth.

Convert to Keyframes

Reversing frames on a tween can be a little quirky. Sometimes, reversing tweened frames on more complex objects actually disengages the tween, and the reversed playback can appear as if there is no tween at all. To avoid any problems, you can convert your copied tween frames into keyframes *before* you reverse the order of the frame sequence. Do this by selecting the entire span and right-clicking/CTRL-clicking and, in the context menu, selecting Convert To Keyframes. You can also select Modify | Frames | Convert To Keyframes from the menu. Once you've converted the tweened frames into keyframes, select all the keyframes and right-click/CTRL-click. In the context menu, select Reverse Frames. The frames in the selected frame sequence now reverse. This is a foolproof method and always causes the frames to reverse their order correctly.

9

You can use this technique not only to reverse movement, but also to reverse tweened transformations and the color effects on a tweened symbol. Figure 9-7 shows a cartoon of a chicken whose wings are flapping back and forth. The wings flapping back and forth were created using the methods outlined in the previous paragraph. As you can see in the right wing and left wing layers in the Timeline, the keyframes after Frame 15 are the reverse of the tween on Frames 1 through 15.

The size, rotation, skew, or color can't be reversed on a motion tween; only the position. However, you can reverse the size, rotation, skew, and color properties between two objects using a shape tween instead of a motion tween. Although the preparation of objects is a little different for a shape tween, the frame reversal method is the same for a shape tween as it is for a motion tween. Shape tweening is discussed in Chapter 12.

FIGURE 9-7 The wings on this animated chicken flap back and forth and were created using copy and paste frames, Convert to Keyframes, and Reverse Frames.

Convert to Blank Keyframes

Sometimes in your animation, you want a keyframe to appear and disappear to achieve a certain effect. Intermittent display of keyframes can create a strobe or a blinking effect. In Figure 9-8, on the layer named "sequence," the frame sequence starts out with a tweened alpha. The next part of the animation is a frame-by-frame animation with blank keyframes interspersed among the frames. What this technique does is create blank keyframes in a frame sequence. In the playback of this Flash movie, it creates a disjointed motion by causing a flickering effect. There are many other reasons to use blank keyframes. For example, you may want an object to appear in one part of an animation and disappear in another. To create blank keyframes within a set, follow this procedure:

1. Select a frame or frames in a frame sequence that is not tweened. If you try to create a blank keyframe in a tweened frame sequence, it will break the tween.

2. Right-click (Windows)/CTRL-click (Mac) the frame you want to be blank, and, from the context menu, select Insert Convert To Blank Keyframes

3. The frames you selected become blank placeholders in the frame sequence.

Converting regular frames to blank keyframes this way maintains the original length of the animation.

9

FIGURE 9-8 A Flash file that uses blank keyframes in the Timeline

Adjust Tweened Objects with the Properties Inspector

There are additional effects that can be applied to a tween using the settings in the Properties Inspector. Grouped graphics and symbols can further be customized with rotation effects and easing in and out effects. Rotate in the Properties Inspector enables you to create special effects like the spinning of an object, and Ease lets you control the speed of an object in the beginning or end of a tween.

Rotate a Graphic in the Properties Inspector

When you motion tween a rotating object using the Free Transform Rotation tool, its capabilities are somewhat limited. If you want an object to spin once and end in the place where it began, or spin continuously, the Rotation tool won't work. In the Properties Inspector, you can adjust the rotation of a tweened object to create some very cool effects (see Figure 9-9). You can automatically set and customize the rotation of an object so it will appear as if it were spinning. An object can be oriented to a specified path, which is discussed in the next section. This option is only available for motion tweens.

Let's consider an example of how you might put this feature to use. In Figure 9-10, the little hand of the clock graphic spins counterclockwise in position when the movie is tested. A tweened rotation is applied to the little hand. Let's quickly review the process of how to create this effect.

The clock in Figure 9-10 was created on three layers: the "ticks" layer, the "little hand" layer, and the "big hand" layer. The only element that is animated is the little hand graphic symbol on the little hand layer. This symbol was created with a reference point of bottom center; so when the rotation is applied to the symbol, the registration remains static while the tip of the hand spins around.

The little hand tweens to Frame 40. With a frame in the tween selected on the little hand layer, in the Properties Inspector, for Rotate, CW was selected and the number 3 was typed in for the Times setting.

This makes the object rotate clockwise three times each time the frame sequence loops. The higher the number you type in for the Rotate Times setting, the faster the movie will appear to rotate. Counterclockwise also can be selected as a rotation direction. If you modify an object in a keyframe with the Rotation tool, when the Properties Inspector is displayed, Rotate will be indicated as Auto.

FIGURE 9-9 You can easily add custom rotations to an object on a tweened frame sequence.

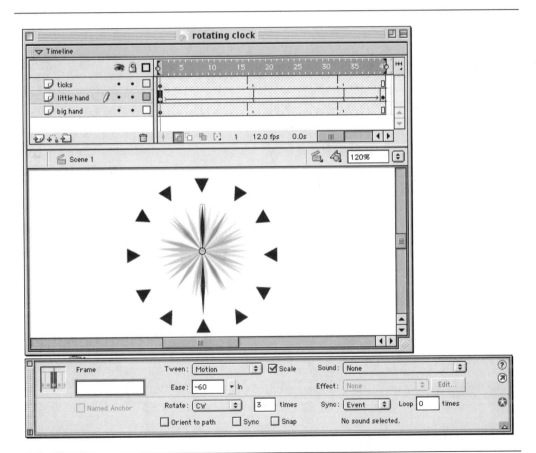

FIGURE 9-10 A clock with a spinning hand created with the Rotate and Ease options in the Properties Inspector

Ease In and Out

Tweening from one keyframe to another doesn't give you much control over the speed of an object as it begins or ends its transformation. Easing in and out by adjusting this setting in the Properties Inspector gives you more control over the speed of the rotating object. The Ease box is a sliding arrow that goes from −100 at the bottom to +100 at the top.

To make the tween appear as if it starts slowly and speeds up at the end, select an increment between −1 and −100. To make the tween appear as if it begins fast and slows down toward the end, select an easing increment between 1 and 100.

Animate on a Guided Path

For the most part, regular tweening involves a linear movement. Sometimes, you may need an object to follow a complex path. You can't accomplish this with a regular motion tween, but you can have an object follow a predefined path that you create. You can do this by creating a path on a guide layer, and then creating a tweened object on another layer that follows this path.

Figure 9-11 is an example of an object tweened on a motion guide. The little planet is tweened and follows a motion guide to revolve around the bigger planet. If the little planet was tweened with a frame-by-frame animation, it could take hundreds of keyframes to accomplish this. This would be very time consuming and you probably have better things to do with your time.

The perfect solution to an object moving around a curved path is tweening on a motion guide. The little planet in the example in Figure 9-11 was attached to a circular motion guide to create the illusion of the little planet rotating around the big planet. Let's take a look at how you can create a tweened element that follows a path on a guide layer.

 Motion guides are invisible on playback of the movie.

Create a Motion Guide

A motion guide consists of a path that's drawn on a guide layer. The path can be drawn with the Pen, Pencil, Line, Brush, Circle, or Rectangle tool. To create a motion guide, follow these steps:

1. In our example (Figure 9-11), the small planet resides on its own layer, as does the big planet. They are on different layers, so they don't cause confusion when the tween takes

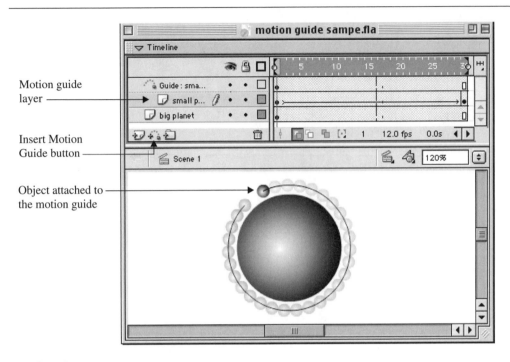

FIGURE 9-9   Tweening with a motion guide allows you flexibility in the object's movement.

place. Assuming all your layers and graphics are in place for the tween you are about to create, the motion guide is ready to be made. Select the object that the motion guide will be tweened around, and click the Add Guide Layer button at the bottom of the Layer section of the Timeline. A Motion Guide icon will appear on the new layer along with the name of the layer that the guide is attached to. Note that this layer is beneath the motion guide layer and indented slightly to the right of the guide layer.

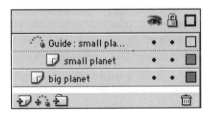

2.   Select the motion guide layer and prepare to draw the guide. In the planet example in Figure 9-11, the Oval tool was selected for this purpose with a Stroke of blue and a Fill of none. A motion guide can be any stroke color. In fact, you might want to use a contrasting color to make it easy to distinguish. An editable oval was drawn as a guide to extend the parameters of the big planet. A motion guide has to have a beginning and an end so the guided object can attach itself on the keyframes. To make the oval work as a motion guide, a small piece of the guide circle needs to be erased using the Eraser tool. Now the oval guide has a beginning and end (see Figure 9-12).

3. It's a good idea to lock the motion guide layer so you don't accidentally grab it while adjusting the small planet to the ends of the guide. Lock the guide by clicking the Lock button on the motion guide layer.

4. Extend the motion guide and big planet layers to Frame 30. This way, none of the elements on the layers disappear while attaching the small planet to the motion guide, when you go past Frame 1.

5. When you have all the components in place, attach the small planet to the partial circle on the motion guide layer. Then, select the first keyframe on the small planet layer. With the small planet selected toward the center of the object, drag it to the beginning of the circle guide. A hollow circle will appear in the small planet, and it snaps to the start of the circle.

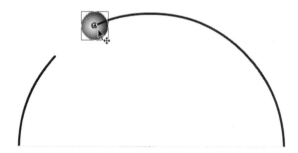

6. Make a keyframe in Frame 30, the last frame, and move the small planet to the end of the oval guide. Notice the planet easily snaps to the end of the motion guide.

7. Select the new frame sequence on the small planet layer, and create a motion tween on the small planet.

Depending on where you grab the object, the object will snap-to the motion guide from that very point. For example, if you selected the object at its middle left, a hollow circle would appear while you dragged the object, declaring the hollow circle as the current reference point while dragging.

When you play the movie (Control | Test Movie), the motion guide at that point is invisible. You can test the movie without seeing the motion guide by turning off its visibility on the motion guide layer.

If your motion guide path is very complex, you have to place additional keyframes for your object along the path. To do so, follow the same procedure as previously outlined, except create the keyframes and snap the object on those keyframes along the guide.

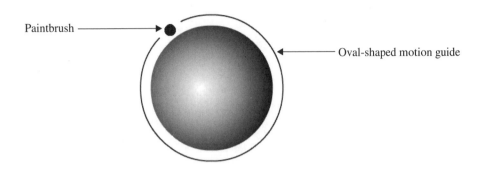

Paintbrush

Oval-shaped motion guide

FIGURE 9-10   A small portion of the circle motion guide was erased, so the object that's following it can lock to a beginning point and an endpoint.

Orient Objects to the Path of a Motion Guide

Sometimes, when an object follows a motion guide, the object needs to bend and turn in the direction of the path in order for it to appear properly. For example, if you created a car and it was following along a windy road, the car would look fake if the front of the car didn't turn in the direction of the path. In Flash, you can easily guide an object along a path in a specified direction of the object. Accomplish this by using the Orient To Path option in the Properties Inspector.

In Figure 9-13, there is now an arrow rotating around the big planet in the opposite direction of the little planet. In the first and last keyframes of the tween, the arrow has been rotated in the direction of the motion guide.

To orient a tweened object along a motion guide, click the tween frames and, in the Properties Inspector, check the Orient To Path box. Other options include Sync (synchronize) and Snap. Select Sync if you're using an animated graphic symbol and the total number of frames within the symbol doesn't equal the number of frames it will occupy on the Timeline. Checking the Snap box ensures the object will snap to its reference point. Select this option if your object appears to be veering off the path while in motion.

As mentioned previously, if your guide is complex and long, the object may not follow the path correctly at certain points. In this case, you can add more keyframes at certain intervals on the motion guide path to help the object along in following the path. To do so, click a frame within the frame sequence where you want to add the new keyframe. Reposition the object on the new keyframe. When the movie plays, the object is reoriented to the path.

To unlink a layer from a motion guide path, drag the layer above the motion guide. It then returns to a regular layer.

9

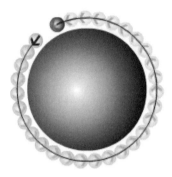

FIGURE 9-11   The arrow rotating around the planet is oriented to the path of the circle motion guide.

Use a Mask Layer with a Motion Tween: A Tutorial

The number of effects you can create with tweened objects is endless. In addition to the techniques discussed in this chapter, other effects that have been covered in previous chapters can be combined with motion tweening. In this tutorial, a mask is tweened. This basic recipe can be applied to other projects, generating many interesting results.

TIP   *In Flash, you can make interactive masks with the setMask method. This is discussed in Chapter 15.*

In Figure 9-14, an animated, moving mask is used to create the illusion of running water through a word. The word "water" is static on the top layer, which is named text, and a bitmap picture of water moves in a continuous loop from left to right in the background, giving the illusion of flowing water. A mask in this sense is like looking through a porthole, and the porthole creates the shape of the mask. The process for creating a motion tween under a mask such as in the sample is as follows:

1. As always, plan out the movie before you begin. Plan objects, layers, and names. Determine how large you want the movie to be.

2. Create and name the first layer, and type out a word. This will become the mask layer. In the water example, the word "water" was typed in and made editable by breaking it apart (select Modify | Break Apart from the menu or press CTRL-B in Windows/CMD-B on the Mac). The text would still work as a mask if you didn't break it apart. However, breaking apart display text that you know won't be further edited is a good idea. That way, there won't be any font conflicts with your audience and you know what it is they are seeing.

3. Create a second layer as in the example, and name it. Make sure the second layer is under the text. Import an image onto this new layer. This will be the masked layer, or

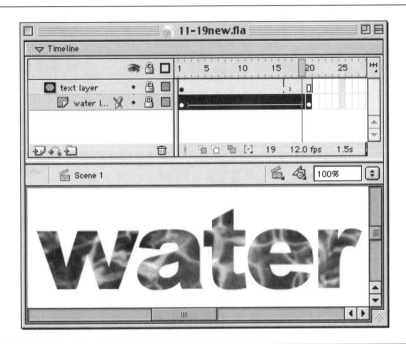

FIGURE 9-12 A graphic object is used as a mask over a layer with a bitmap image of water to create an effect of water running behind the word "water."

the layer that is masked out. This water image is a PICT file, but Flash imports many other formats. (Consult Chapter 7, Table 7-1, for a complete list of supported formats.)

4. Convert the imported picture to a bitmap by clicking the image and breaking it apart. In most cases, this should help reduce the size of the image.

5. Convert the image into a graphic symbol by selecting Insert | Convert To Symbol (F8) from the menu. Now, multiple uses of the symbol will also economize on file size.

> **TIP**
>
> *There are many custom backgrounds you can create right in Flash instead of importing a background from another program. An effect in Flash, such as a gradation that moves or pulsates, creates a nice masked effect, too.*

6. The water image on the water layer was duplicated three times, and all copies were butted up against one another; and made into a graphic (F8). When the masked image loops, it looks like the water is flowing continuously behind the word. To create this long series of duplicated bitmaps, drag the long instance of the masked symbol to the masked layer (in this case, it's called the "water" layer). For the tile effect to work properly, the left side of the bitmap must mirror the right side so that the images begin and end in the same place, and the sum of the tiles should be long enough to accommodate the entire word. Note that the water tile bleeds off the right edge of the stage so that a break won't occur in the masked image (water) during the tweening (see Figure 9-15).

7. To apply the mask, right-click/CTRL-click the page icon in the text layer to display the context pop-up menu.

8. Select Mask from the menu. The page icon now turns into an oval-shaped, checkered background icon, indicating the layer containing the mask. Conversely, the water layer

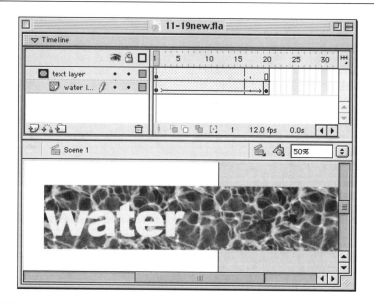

FIGURE 9-13 The water image has been tiled to create a masked effect of continuous water flowing.

page icon turns into a checkered pattern background with a turned-up corner. The masked layer must always reside under the mask layer.

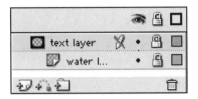

9. The masked layer (water image) now needs to be tweened. Remember: the word stays static while the water bitmap moves. Click a frame in the masked layer to create the second keyframe (F6). In our example, Frame 20 is selected. On the text layer, even the frames out to Frame 20 by clicking this frame and pressing F5 (Insert I Frame). That way, the mask won't disappear while the water layer is still running.

10. Reposition the water image in the first and last keyframes so the water appears to move from left to right. You may have to go back and tweak the position of the water after playing back the movie to obtain the desired result. Click the in-between frames and right-click/CMD-click to display the context menu. Select Motion Tween from the menu.

If you play the movie on the Timeline, you won't see anything happen. By default, masks don't display in the Flash Timeline. To test the movie, do one of two things:

- Select Control I Test Movie.
- Click the Lock button at the top of the layer section of the Timeline to lock all layers.

Locking the layers enables you to see and test the mask in the Timeline. Remember to unlock the layers again to move the objects.

Once you get the feel for it, motion tweening can produce some wonderful results. In the next chapter, shape tweening is discussed. With frame-by-frame, motion, and shape tweening, you'll possess a powerful array of tools to produce a multitude of animation effects.

9

Chapter 10

Use Shape Tweening to Animate

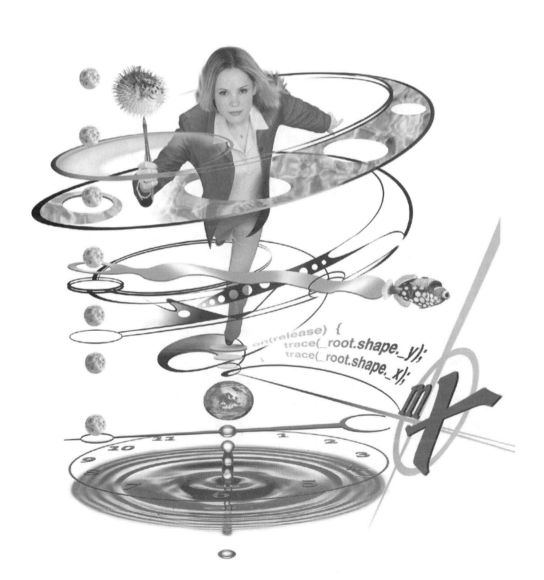

How to...

- Create a shape tween
- Use a shape tween with multiple keyframes
- Modify properties of a shape tween
- Tween on a multilayer movie
- Morph between objects
- Apply shape hints
- Set shape tween properties
- Organize your Timeline

As discussed in Chapter 9, motion tweening only works on objects that are grouped or symbols. In fact, the very name "motion tween" implies that its primary use is to change the motion of an object over time. In contrast, shape tweening can only be applied on editable objects.

You can change the size, skew, rotation, color, and position of an object with a motion tween. The same properties can be altered with a shape tween, and often with a different and unexpected outcome. The reason a difference exists between a motion tween and a shape tween is that when you change the rotation and skew of an object with a motion tween, the object is addressed as a whole entity; whereas when you change the rotation and skew of an object with a shape tween, the object is perceived as an editable shape instead of a whole entity. Thus, with a shape tween, the individual edges of the editable shape can transform separately from the object as a whole, causing a shape tween to yield different results from a motion tween. Motion and shape tweening can perform similar functions, but they serve different purposes.

Because of the malleable nature of editable objects, shape tweening is used for morphing objects. Morphing occurs when one shape transforms into another shape. In addition, color can be tweened easily on an editable object. This effect won't work with a motion tween unless, of course, the tweened object is a symbol.

Both motion and shape tweening can generate different results. Once you get the feel for tweening, you will better understand when it's appropriate and effective to use a particular method.

Create a Shape Tween

You can create a shape tween to change the position of an object. However, the method you use to create a shape tween is slightly different from the method you use to create a motion tween. Not only that, but if you only wanted to tween the position of an object, you probably wouldn't use a shape tween. With that in mind, let's consider how to make a simple shape tween where the position and color change over time.

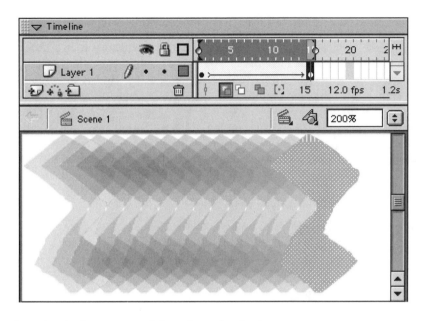

To make a simple shape tween, follow these simple steps:

1. Draw or import an editable object onto a keyframe in the Timeline.
2. Make another keyframe for the end frame.
3. Click the last keyframe and move the object to another position on the stage.
4. Make the object another color.
5. Click the frames in between the two keyframes and select Shape from the Tween pop-up list in the Properties Inspector.

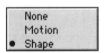

6. Notice that the frame sequence now has a green tint with a right-pointing arrow in it.

7. When you play the movie back, the shape changes position and color over time.

At face value, shape tweening doesn't look much different from motion tweening, other than the fact that you create a shape tween from the Properties Inspector and it displays differently in the Timeline. But as we move through this chapter, you will begin to see how you might use shape tweening for some interesting effects you can't achieve with motion tweening.

Let's take a look at the following example. Figure 10-1 is an animated gradient background. The gradient colors transform from one to another, creating a pulsating color effect. This technique can only be done with a shape tween because the colors have to be editable in order to change in time.

To create a shape tween gradient object, follow this procedure:

1. Create a rectangle over the area you want the gradient to appear on a frame in the Timeline. (Gradients are discussed in Chapter 5.)

2. Create additional keyframes. Make as many as you want depending on how many times you want the colors to cycle through new colors.

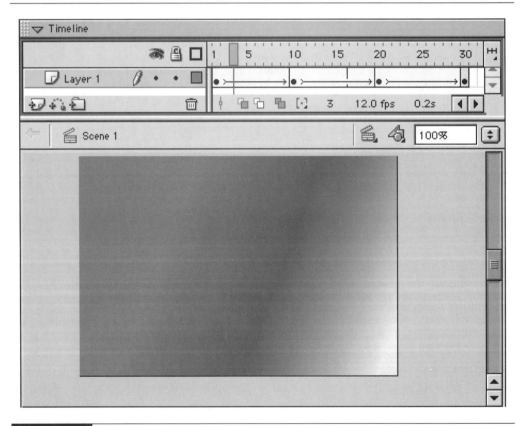

FIGURE 10-1   A shape tween whose gradient color, position, and angle change over time

3. Return to each keyframe and change the gradient. You can also change the angle, size, and position of the gradient on each keyframe.

4. Click a frame between the first set of keyframes and select Shape from the pop-up list in the Properties Inspector. Repeat this process between each set of keyframes.

5. Test the movie and you'll see the color gradually transform like a kaleidoscope.

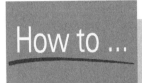 **Make a Simple Stop Action in the Main Timeline**

If the continuous looping of a movie is driving you crazy, you can put a stop action on the last frame in the Timeline. To do so, follow these steps:

1. Create a new layer, and name it **action**. Although you don't have to place this action on a separate layer, it's much easier to see it if it's separate, so it's a good idea to get into the habit of putting frame actions on their own layer. More information on this issue is provided in Chapter 12.

2. Press F2 to display the Actions panel. In the top right of the panel, in the Options pop-up menu, select Expert. This allows you to type in your own script. In the right portion of the panel (the Actions list), type **Stop();** exactly the way you see it here:

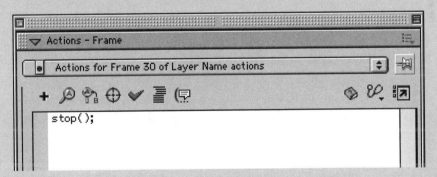

3. When you do this, a little letter *a* appears on the first frame in the layer along with a blank keyframe. Drag this keyframe to the last frame that your animation in the other layer appears on.

When you test your movie, the animation stops when it reaches the last frame. In Chapter 12, you will learn how to control the playback of frames on the main Timeline.

10

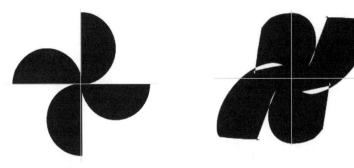

Shape tween on Frame 1   Shape tween on Frame 7

FIGURE 10-2   An object that shape tweens with a rotation and skew can distort in an unpredictable manner.

Modify Properties in a Shape Tween

As mentioned previously, you can use the Free Transform tools on a shape tween just like you do on a motion tween. The difference between a shape and motion tween becomes obvious when you add rotation and skewing to a shape tween.

Figure 10-2 shows a shape tween of an object with three keyframes. The beginning and ending keyframes are identical, but the middle keyframe has a rotation and skew applied to it. When played back, the object appears to distort in the in-between frames. In fact, around Frame 7, the object appears as a shapeless blob, momentarily loosing all visual connection to the original object.

The same skewed and rotated object with a motion tween applied to it appears to maintain its basic shape, as shown in Figure 10-3. In a motion tween, the object is treated as a whole entity. No matter what properties are changed, the motion tween always maintains the integrity of the original object. In a shape tween, the same object transforms into another object and sometimes separates into pieces of the original object when a rotation and/or skew is applied.

Shape Tween vs. Motion Tween on a Multilayer Movie

Grouped or symbol objects are easy to edit in a motion tween, but you can't take advantage of the techniques available to shape tweens, like morphing. Placing objects on separate layers can easily resolve the difficulty of editable objects in shape tweens. These elements can be easily edited by going to the appropriate layer the object resides on. Let's compare the same multilayer, tweened graphic as a shape tween and as a motion tween and see what kind of different results they yield.

Figure 10-4 represents a four-layer shape tween. When the in-between frames are examined, shape tweening causes radical transformations on each layer, returning to its original state on the last keyframe.

Motion tween on Frame 1   Motion tween on Frame 7

| FIGURE 10-3 | The same object that motion tweens with a rotation and skew appears as a whole object. |

There are several changes taking place over the course of the shape tween in Figure 10-4. The word "eye" resides on the top layer. The alpha, rotation, and width are changed throughout the tween. Because the word is editable, when paths of the object cross during rotation, it causes the text to almost appear as if it's inside out, as it looks in Frame 27.

10

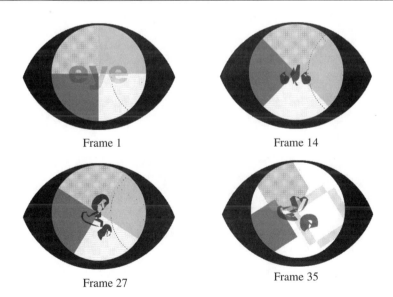

Frame 1   Frame 14

Frame 27   Frame 35

| FIGURE 10-4 | The editing of a tweened object can be made easier by placing elements on separate layers. |

The same word rotated in a motion tween with almost the identical settings would appear to rotate on a center axis, as shown in Figure 10-5.

In the motion tween, the four sections of the masked background rotate from a center axis, unlike on the identical shape tween, where the sections separate and distort like the center of a kaleidoscope.

Both movies were created with the same objects, but in Figure 10-4 (shape tween), the moving objects are editable shape tweens, and in Figure 10-5 (motion tween), the moving objects are grouped motion tweens. Because the tweening methods are different, the animation in both cases plays back differently.

It's interesting and helpful to compare the two types of tweening to understand the depth of each method. Both methods have their special applications. You also can combine both methods of tweening on different layers in a movie to reap the benefits of both shape and motion tweening.

Deconstruct a Multilayer Shape Tween

To better understand shape tweening and the significance of a multilayer tween, it's helpful to dissect a multilayer movie in which only shape tweens are used. Figure 10-6 represents a multilayer movie on which two of the layers are assigned a shape tween. We looked at this movie previously, but now let's consider how it was made. There is also a mask used in this movie, and the masked object is tweened and conforms to the shape of an eye.

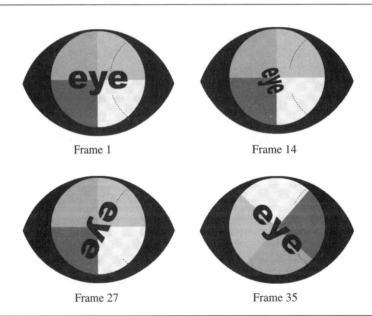

Frame 1   Frame 14

Frame 27   Frame 35

FIGURE 10-5   The motion tween equivalent of the shape tween in Figure 10-4

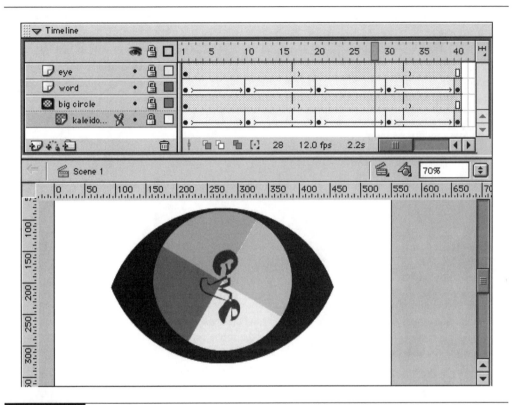

FIGURE 10-6   The Timeline of a complex shape tween

Use the following steps to create this movie or re-create a similar effect on another movie:

1. The names and order of the layers in that movie are as follows:

- Eye
- Word
- Big circle
- Kaleidoscope

2. Select the eye layer and create an object that resembles the shape of an eye. The eye provides a framework with a hollowed-out pupil, for two overlapping tweens.

3. Select the word layer, type **eye**, set the properties of the text, and center it within the pupil part of the eye on its own layer. Because these objects reside on separate layers, the editable objects won't get tangled up in one another. The text also needs to be editable to work as a shape tween. So to do this, select the text and break it apart (Modify | Break Apart).

4. Select the big circle layer. This layer contains a circle the size of the pupil in the center of the eye, and it acts as the mask for the last layer, called kaleidoscope. If the mask didn't exist, the kaleidoscope animation in the background of the pupil would just appear as four rectangles sitting on a layer behind the eye, and as such, would not connect to the pupil. So, to create this effect, make a colored circle and use the edge of the pupil on the eye layer to determine the approximate circumference of this circle.

5. The masked layer, kaleidoscope, consists of four identical boxes framed together in the shape of a big rectangle.

Each rectangle has a different color, so the movement resembles big pieces of confetti in a kaleidoscope, shifting as the center twirls. Make these boxes with a rectangle shape. You can easily duplicate the rectangle three additional times with CTRL-SHIFT (Windows)/ OPT-SHIFT (Mac). Once all four rectangles are aligned together (the sum of which creates one big rectangle), center this new big rectangle over the mask (big circle).

6. Going back to the big circle layer, select the page icon to the left of the layer to apply a mask to this layer. Apply a mask by right-clicking/CTRL-clicking and selecting Mask from the pop-up context menu. When a mask is applied to a layer, the page icon turns into a black icon with an oval checked pattern. The layer beneath becomes the masked layer. Masked layer icons are represented in the Timeline with an indented page, filled with a checked pattern. The result of this masking effect can be previewed on the stage by clicking the lock at the top of the Timeline in the Layer column.

7. Place a keyframe (F6) on Frame 40 of the word and kaleidoscope layers, and place a regular frame (F5) on Frame 40 of the eye layer and the big circle layer.

8. The word and kaleidoscope layers are all set for tweening. Select an in-between frame on the word layer and, in the Properties Inspector, choose Shape for the Tween type. Repeat this for the kaleidoscope layer.

9. After the shape tweens are established, add keyframes to the word and kaleidoscope layers on Frames 10, 20, and 30. Display guides (View | Rulers-View | Guides) to help align elements with the center stage.

10. With keyframe 10 selected on the word layer, reduce the width of the word to approximately 50 percent and move it back to its center reference point from Frame 1 using the guides.

11. Select keyframe 20. Because the keyframes were created before any changes were made to the Timeline, the word object still looks as it originally did on keyframe 1. Rotate the word object 180 degrees in keyframe 20 using the Rotation tool. On keyframe 30, rotate the word object again 90 degrees clockwise.

12. Select the four rectangles on the kaleidoscope layer (with the other layers temporarily locked and made invisible in the Timeline to make the kaleidoscope layer easy to manipulate), and rotate the four rectangles together at different degrees on keyframes 10, 20, 30, and 40. The movie is now complete.

When the movie is played back (Control | Test Movie), instead of the words "object" and "kaleidoscope" rotating as objects on their own layers, individual pieces of each shape transform into different shapes while rotating. Some shapes intersect their own paths during the course of the animation, causing an outline effect. The resulting movie (refer to Figure 10-4) looks completely different from its motion tween counterpart (refer to Figure 10-5). The only difference in producing these movies is that the objects in the shape tween are editable, whereas in the motion tween they aren't.

This comparison should help you understand the difference between shape and motion tweening. When used together on separate layers, you have an impressive range of alternative tweening effects.

Morph Between Objects

Shape tweening is often used to create a morphing effect in an animation. Unlike motion tweens, which treat an object as a whole entity, shape tweens enable you to transform from one object into another.

When you morph an object, it gradually transforms into another object based on what the first and last objects look like and the properties and settings you change in the in-between frames. Morphing in Flash enables you to tween two entirely separate objects located on different keyframes. What's more, size, rotation, and skew of an object can be added to further distort the morph effect.

Figure 10-7 displays a rectangle outline that morphs into a triangle, then into a circle, then into a swirl on Frame 40, and finally disappears—leaving a blank scene for a brief second. On Frame 41, the shapes gradually reappear on stage from left to right. On Frame 41, the editable objects are replaced by graphic symbols, and they are motion tweened in steps of five framesets

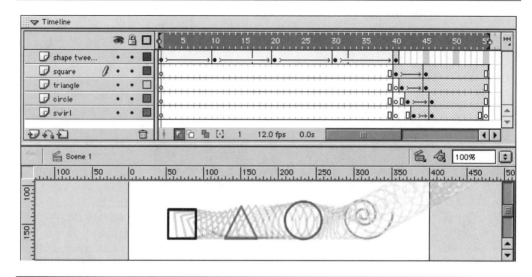

FIGURE 10-7 The morphing of an object goes through three incarnations before ending up a swirl.

each, one frame apart. This movie plays for about four seconds, but packs a powerful impression on its viewer in a short period of time. It's a very simple movie and a good example of how simple images are often more effective than complex images in morphing.

Morphing does involve planning and discretion to work successfully. Otherwise, this technique can produce ugly results when not used correctly.

Deconstruct a Movie Using a Morph Effect

The process of morphing is different from that of an everyday shape or motion tween. A regular tween involves gradually changing the properties of an object from one keyframe to another. Morphing is different because it involves gradually changing one object into another object from one keyframe to another. The position, size, color, rotation, and skew also can vary from one object to a completely different object. In Figure 10-7, the object changes as well as the position and color of the object on keyframes up to keyframe 30, when the swirl flies off the stage. To thoroughly understand the process of morphing an object with a shape tween, let's examine the steps required to create Figure 10-7:

1. Create five layers and name them in the following order:
   - Shape tweens
   - Square
   - Triangle
   - Circle
   - Swirl

2. The first layer, shape tweens, contains the majority of the contents of the movie. On keyframe 1, you can set up all four shapes (rectangle, triangle, circle, and swirl), put them into place, and align them. You can turn on the Snap To Grid to make it easy to align and distribute the rest of the shapes on the stage (View | Grid | Snap To Grid). Make a simple triangle outline shape with a stroke of three pixels, and place it to the right of the first shape. Repeat the process with the creation of a circle outline and a swirl shape sequentially falling to the right of each other.

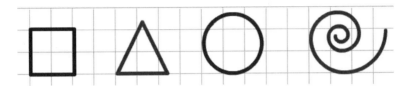

You can also use the Align panel if you want to distribute the objects evenly. Display this panel by selecting Windows | Align. To use this panel, select all objects and click one of the horizontal Align options (the bottom, center, or top icon) and one of the horizontal Distribute icons to distribute each object evenly between one another.

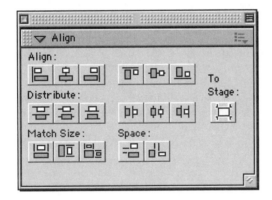

10

3. With all four shapes in place, add a keyframe to Frame 40 in the shape tweens layer and add a shape tween using the methods outlined in the section "Create a Shape Tween."

4. Add keyframes (F6) to Frames 10, 20, and 30. With all the tweening and elements in place, the movie will begin to take shape when objects are systematically eliminated from each keyframe, creating the illusion of one object morphing into another.

5. Working backward, select keyframe 40 on the shape tweens layer and drag the swirl object off the stage to the upper-right corner. This makes the object fly off the stage after the circle transforms into the swirl. With Frame 40 selected, delete the other three objects to the left (square, triangle, and circle).

6. With keyframe 30 selected, leave the swirl in place and delete the square, triangle, and circle.

7. With keyframe 20 selected, delete the square, triangle, and swirl, leaving this keyframe to highlight the circle, as shown in Figure 10-8.

8. Repeat the process on keyframe 10 by deleting the swirl, circle, and square and again on keyframe 1, with all objects to the right of the square being deleted.

9. At this point, when the movie is played back, each simple shape transforms into another, and between keyframes 30 and 40, the swirl flies off the stage.

In the balance of the movie from Frame 40 on, the shapes from layer 1 are eliminated completely. They are replaced by a graphic symbol of a square, triangle, circle, and swirl on their subsequent layers. These graphic symbols were copied from the previously created editable shapes that were used on the first layer to create the morph. By Frame 55, all the objects gradually reappear in the identical position from which they were originally morphed from in Frames 1–30, as shown in the Timeline in Figure 10-7.

Apply Shape Hints to Your Morph

When you morph from one object to another, the in-between frames often transform in an unpredictable way. If you were to scrub over each in-between frame, the object would appear to gradually take shape from the first frame to the last. The manner in which objects morph is a default setting in Flash. Shape hints on a morph identify key points on the beginning state of one object and the end state of another object. The shape hints on each object correspond to one another by having an identical letter assigned on each object.

The position of these shape hints as key tweening points is crucial to the outcome of the morph. They serve as a roadmap for the morph, determining what direction the points will travel to arrive at the shapes' final destination. Just like a road map, there are many different ways to get to your destination. Shape hints provide markers to help you get there and, on the way, provide different scenery, depending on which path they take.

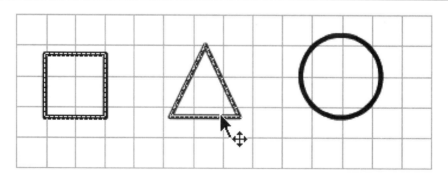

FIGURE 10-8   Objects are being systematically deleted backward from keyframe 40 to create a morphing effect.

You, the designer, can control shape hints. If you don't like the way your shape is morphing in Flash, you can go back in and move the hints until the morph meets your expectations. Shape hints are an important feature when doing serious morphing. The ability to control the hints can mean the difference between frames appearing as shapeless blobs or as a transformation with a clear direction.

Hints are indicated as letters (from *a* to *z*) contained in small circles. You can place up to 26 shape hints on an object. To control the hints on a shape tween, click an object in a keyframe and select Modify | Shape | Add Shape Hint (CTRL-SHIFT-H in Windows/CMD-SHIFT-H on the Mac). A hint letter appears on the stage, and the first hint letter is always the letter *a*. Drag the hint to a point on the first object. To add more hints, repeat the previous process. In Figure 10-9, three additional hints were added and positioned on the circle.

You will notice that as you add and manipulate hints on various keyframes, they change color. Hints are yellow in the first frame and red in the last frame. Red hints are hints that don't reside on a curve.

Shape hints are most successful if placed in a logical, clockwise order, starting from the top left of the object as a reference point. Otherwise, unpredictable results will occur. In Figure 10-10, a star transforms into a rectangle. The shape hints on the star (a, b, c, and d) rotate clockwise from the left around four points of the star.

The corresponding shape hints on the rectangle in the last keyframe (a, b, c, and d) also rotate clockwise from the upper-left corner, making the star flawlessly morph into a rectangle in the last keyframe.

TIP	*When you move the hints from different points on your object, if Onion Skin Outlines are turned on, you can preview the path of the shape hints within the tween.*

10

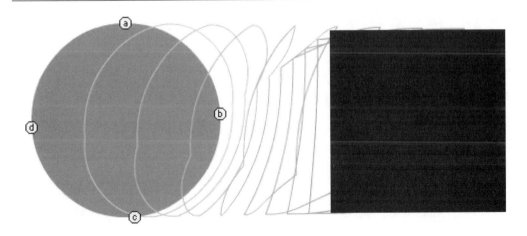

FIGURE 10-9   Additional hints are added to an object in the first keyframe of this movie.

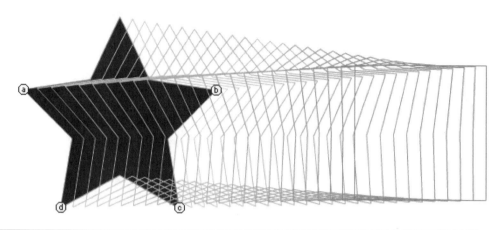

FIGURE 10-10   When shape hints are applied in a logical, clockwise order, the shape tween movement is generally more successful.

Hints also can be removed from an object. To do so, click the object and select Modify | Shape | Remove Shape Hint. All shape hints will disappear.

Shape hints are easy to tweak if they don't meet your expectations. It's simple to go back to the first and last keyframe and reposition the hints. Each time this is done, the morph changes shape. Do this as many times as is necessary to achieve the desired effect. Using simple discretion, like placing the hints in a logical way, helps maintain the integrity of the morph.

Set Shape Tween Properties

Like motion tweens, shape tweens can be assigned parameters. When the in-between frames of a shape tween are selected, the Ease and Blend settings become available in the Properties Inspector.

The Ease setting is based on the same premise as easing on a motion tween. Tweening from one keyframe to another doesn't give you much control over the speed of an object as it begins or ends its transformation. Easing in and out gives you control over the speed of the object. The Ease box is a sliding arrow that goes from −100 at the bottom to +100 at the top, as shown in Figure 10-11.

To make the tween appear as if it starts slow and speeds up at the end, select an increment between −1 and −100. To make the shape tween appear as if it begins fast and slows down toward the end, select an easing increment between 1 and 100.

The Blend settings become available when a Shape Tween is selected in the Properties Inspector. Select Distributive or Angular from the pop-up Blend menu. When Distributive is chosen, the shape tween will smooth out edges in a tween. When Angular is selected, hard, straight edges and

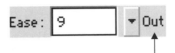

Pop-up sliding arrow with Ease settings

FIGURE 10-11   The Ease slider in the Properties Inspector

lines will maintain their integrity throughout a tween. Like the Ease parameters, the Blend settings are applied to the in-between frames of a shape tween.

Shape tweening also can be combined with other types of animation to create dynamic effects. Good planning always remains a key ingredient with a shape tween. Shape tweens can cause unpredictable results, so planning before you begin will ensure a successful animation.

Organize Your Timeline

10

Once you know how to create complex, multilayer animations, you will appreciate the tools Flash offers to help organize your Timeline. In Flash, you can create labels and comments on layers in the Timeline, as well as named anchors. None of these features actually appear in the movie on playback. They are simply tools to help you identify certain elements in a Timeline. They are particularly useful if your Flash file is being worked on by multiple users. They give you a chance to explain to another worker what is going on in your movie. Tools like this are vital in multilevel, time-based applications.

Let's take look at each one specifically to see what they do and how you apply them:

■ **Labels**   These are little messages you type in the Properties Inspector on a frame.

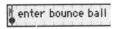

Labels in frames help you remember what it was you did on a group of frames. In addition, you can refer to labels when you apply frame actions with ActionScript. We will cover this in Chapter 12. To create a frame label, do the following:

1. Click a keyframe in a frame sequence, and in the Properties Inspector, click in the Frame box.

2. Type in a name. The name appears next to the keyframe you selected, to the right of a red flag icon in the Timeline.

■ **Comments**   These are descriptive text notations you can add to a frame sequence. These are often used when an element or condition enters a frame in the Timeline. In a complex movie with multiple developers, comments on a Timeline are a common sight. You can also use comments in the ActionScript panel. More information on comments and using them in the Actions panel is provided in Chapter 12 on ActionScript. To make a comment on a keyframe in the Timeline, follow these steps:

1. Click a keyframe and, in the Frame box, type **//**. These slash marks tell Flash that you're about to make a comment.

2. To the right of the //, type the comment. That's all there is to it.

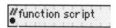

■ **Named anchors**   These provide an easy way for a viewer to use the forward and backward buttons in their browser to navigate your movie. To make a named frame into a named anchor, simply select the Named Anchor check box under the Frame label.

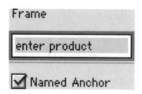

This feature will only work for viewers whose browser is equipped with Flash Player version 6 plug-in.

In the next chapter, we will jump right into buttons and movie clips. Once you master the movie clips, the Flash interface will really start to fall into place for you.

Chapter 11

Grasp the Concept Behind Buttons and Movie Clips

How to…

- Make a button
- Test a button
- Add sound to a button
- Add simple effects to a button
- Change the behavior of a symbol
- Understand movie clips in Flash
- Create an animated movie clip
- Make an animated button from a movie clip

Symbols are self-contained elements in Flash that are stored in the current movie's Library. Symbols help bring order to the chaos of movie creation, and using symbol instances can greatly help reduce your movie's file size.

As discussed in previous chapters, symbols come in three types: graphic, button, and movie clip. Graphic symbols, the simplest kinds of symbols, were discussed in Chapter 6. In fact, many of the rules that apply to all symbols were discussed in Chapter 6. For example, storing symbols in the Library and using multiple instances also holds true for buttons and movie clips. In addition, all movie clips can be reused many times in a movie without compromising the file size.

Explore the Power of Buttons and Movie Clips

Buttons and movie clips are often used in conjunction with the more advanced applications of Flash. Although buttons are important, movie clips are probably one of the most powerful and important aspects of Flash. Both buttons and movie clips are considered objects and, as such, can be assigned both properties and methods. The *properties* of a button or movie clip instance are the characteristics of the object, like color, height, and so forth. The *methods* of an object are what an object is supposed to do, like play or drag. *Event handlers* can also be attached to both buttons and movie clip instances. Event handlers, literally, handle an event (press, release, roll over, roll out, and so on) that is taking place in a movie.

Objects, methods, and events are all part of the framework of ActionScript, the Flash scripting language. ActionScript, which is quite extensive and complex, is discussed in Chapters 12–15. ActionScript is a study all unto itself, and this book's four chapters barely skim the surface of this language. For now, we will concentrate on the basics of making buttons and movie clips. You need a solid understanding of these objects before you pursue any advanced studies in ActionScript (see Figure 11-1).

A movie is defined as *interactive* when a viewer can respond to the movie and make choices that change the viewing experience. Interactivity not only makes a web site more engaging, it

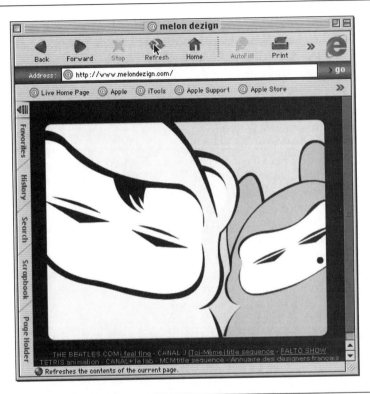

FIGURE 11-1   A beautifully architected site, melondezign.com, combines colorful animated movie clips with interactive buttons.

encourages the viewer to participate in the ongoing process, thereby keeping him or her on your site longer.

A good example of simple interactivity are hyperlinks. Hyperlinks in an HTML document are interactivity in its simplest form. The process of clicking an object or text and having it take you to another location demands that the viewer interact to experience the site. Although links to HTML documents and SWF files are easy to make, the Flash interface enables you to create far more sophisticated types of interactivity. In Flash, interactivity on an object generally involves buttons, movie clips, or both in some capacity. Therefore, before understanding ActionScript and interactivity, one must have a solid base in buttons and movie clips.

When it comes to interactivity, buttons and movie clips are very powerful. With the click of a button, your viewer can control the properties of a movie clip or any Timeline in the movie— even Timelines nested in movie clips. For example, on a button event such as press, a movie clip can change its properties, such as size, position, rotation, or color. It can perform certain methods, like start and stop, or become invisible, as well as many other actions. Buttons also

11

can be nested in movie clips to create special effects for games, e-commerce applications, and interactive web sites.

Before you begin scripting, let's explore how to make and control buttons and movie clips.

Make a Button

Buttons in Flash can range from simple to ultra complex, and they are only limited to your imagination. They don't all have to look like the classic push buttons seen on so many web sites and in the Flash Button Common Library. In fact, many buttons in Flash don't look like buttons at all. The rollover and clicking capabilities of buttons make it a viable choice for custom-designed navigation menus that have elements popping out in the movie wherever you want. You can also use bitmaps, sounds, and movie clips on your button Timeline. You can also make buttons with no contents that only exist to take advantage of the scripting available on a button object. But starting with the basics is always best in the learning process. Making a simple button in Flash is relatively easy and helps you understand the concept behind all buttons.

Buttons are essentially little interactive movies on their own simple Timelines. A button Timeline doesn't look the same as the main Timeline or a movie clip Timeline. Rather, buttons are created on their own four-frame Timeline. The first three frames on the button Timeline enable you to define a button state (Up, Over, Down). The last frame is the Hit frame where the boundaries of the active area within the button are determined.

To create a simple button, select Insert | New Symbol or press CTRL-F8 (Windows)/CMD-F8 (Mac). In the Symbol Properties dialog box, select Button for the symbol type, name the button in the Name box, and click OK.

You will now enter Button Editing mode where buttons can be created or edited. Figure 11-2 represents the building of a simple button, named my_button. When in button editing mode, the name of the button and the button icon appear in the upper-left corner of the stage, next to the scene icon. The Timeline in Button Editing mode looks different from the Timeline in the main movie, but has some similar features. For example, you can create multiple layers, just like on the main Timeline. But, unlike the main Timeline, the frames are no longer displayed in numbers. Rather, they are represented in four states: Up, Over, Down, and Hit.

When you first enter editing mode for the button you're about to create, the first object you draw will appear on the Up state. When the movie loads in the viewer's browser, the button will appear the way it does on the Up state. When in Button Editing mode, there is a cross hairs in the

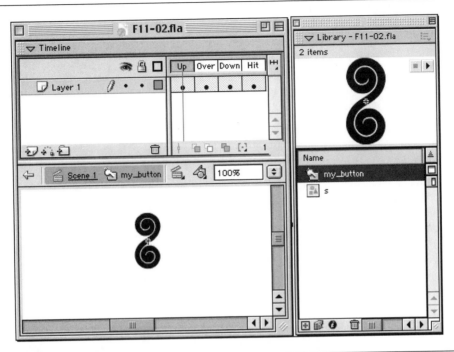

FIGURE 11-2   A graphic symbol was dragged from the Library and placed on the Up state of this button.

center of the stage that indicates where the center of the symbol will be. Use this cross hairs as a reference to determine where your button elements will appear on each state. This same cross hairs appears in the editing mode for a graphic symbol and a movie clip.

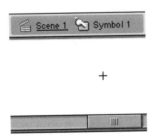

In Figure 11-2, a graphic symbol was added on the Up state, and the center reference point of that symbol was aligned to the cross hairs in Button Editing mode. The graphics you use to create your button can be assembled right on the stage in Button Editing mode, in the main Timeline, or outside the Flash application. You can make your button from grouped graphics, editable objects, or another type of symbol.

To make a button similar to the button in Figure 11-2, follow these steps:

1. As discussed previously, add a graphic to the Up state. A keyframe will appear here.

2. Add a keyframe to the Over state. The Over state is the way the button will look on this frame when the user rolls over the button with their mouse. On the Over state in our example, the color of the object changes, so when the user mouses over the button, the button changes color. The color of the object was changed on the Over state.

3. On the Down state, add another keyframe (F6). The Down state is activated when the user clicks a button. Rotate the button on the Down state 45 degrees, and then change the color of the object in the Effects panel.

4. Add a keyframe (F6) to the Hit state. On the Hit state, draw a rectangle over the area where the user will mouse over the button. Any color or shape can be used to indicate the hit area. Shapes drawn on the Hit state will not be visible on movie playback. The purpose of a Hit state is to declare a certain area surrounding the button as active. It is not absolutely necessary for you to indicate a hit area. If you elect not to do so, Flash assumes the object on the Up state represents the hit area of the button. Indicating a hit area is a good idea when making buttons with unusual shapes or animated movie clips where it might be hard for the viewer to select it.

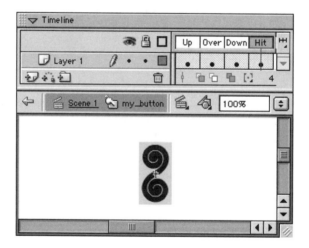

5. To exit Button Editing mode, click the Scene icon in the upper-left corner of the menu or select Edit I Edit Movie (CTRL-E in Windows/CMD-E on the Mac). To see the button, open the Library (Window I Library or CTRL-L/CMD-L). The button can be tested in the Library, as shown in Figure 11-3. If the button selected in the Library is interactive, an arrow will appear in the bottom-right corner of the Library thumbnail preview. Click this button to see the changes on the different button states. If you have included a graphic on the Hit state, the graphic will appear in the Library preview. In the next section, you'll learn how to test the button without seeing the Hit state.

FIGURE 11-3   Test a button by selecting it in the Library and clicking the right arrow in the Library preview.

Delete the button from the Library by clicking the button and selecting the Trash Can icon at the bottom of the window. A dialog box will alert you that the symbol is about to be deleted. Choose Delete to get rid of the symbol, or Cancel if you change your mind and want to keep it. The delete action is undoable. A symbol also can be deleted from the Options pop-up menu in the Library. To delete the button with the Options menu, click the button in the Library, click the Options menu, and select Delete. All Library items, including graphics, movie clips, sounds, and bitmaps, can be deleted with this option.

TIP   *When you delete a button, your movie size will remain the same unless you do a File | Save As. When you save an existing project with the File | Save command—as opposed to File | Save As—additional data is generated within the file, and, as a result, the file size is increased.*

Create a Very Simple Button

This button is an example of just one of the many kinds of buttons you can create in Flash. A button doesn't have to change on the Over and Down states. Often, you don't need the actual button to be interactive on the Over and Down states. You might just need a clickable button to perform an action on a frame or a movie clip. In a case where you don't want your button to do fancy things, the process would be as follows:

1.   Select Insert | New Symbol (CTRL-F8/CMD-F8).

2. Select the Button option, give the button a name, and click OK. On the Up state, add or make a graphic. A keyframe will automatically be generated on the Up state when you draw the object. If you want to define the active area, click the Hit state, add a frame (F6), and place a graphic on this frame.

3. Exit Button Editing mode by either clicking the Scene in the upper-left corner, or selecting Edit | Edit Movie or pressing CTRL-E/CMD-E.

With a simple button, you don't have to add frames to the states that are not in use (over and down). An image occupying the Up state is sufficient to make a button work. Use this simple method if you only need a button to handle a script event.

Make an Invisible Button

Sometimes you might want to create an invisible button if you want an area of the stage to be clickable, but you don't need the actual graphic representation of a button. When a button is clickable, you can assign actions to it, even if there is no visible button. To make an invisible button, create the button as you would a regular button, but leave all states blank except for the Hit state. The Hit state is necessary because the clickable area must be defined for it to work.

To make an invisible button, simply create a button and don't place any objects on the Hit state.

Test a Button

If you drag an instance of a button onto the stage from the Library and click or mouse over it, nothing will happen even if it's supposed to change in the different states. The button probably works, but you can't preview it while in Movie mode. So far, you've only been able to test the interactivity of your button in the Library. Although the Library is good for quickly catching mistakes on a button, you still need to examine the button further in case it needs adjusting of some sort. Buttons can be further tested in the stage environment.

There are a few ways to test buttons. In addition to being able to test buttons in the Library thumbnail preview, buttons can be tested on the stage. To do this, select Control | Enable Simple Buttons or press CTRL-ALT-B/OPT-CMD-B (see Figure 11-4). Now when you mouse over and/or click the button, if the button is interactive, it will be displayed on the stage. This menu selection acts as a toggle switch and also disables buttons. When you've finished testing the buttons and want to bring them back to an editable state, select Control | Enable Simple Buttons or press CTRL-ALT-B/OPT-CMD-B again.

When buttons are enabled, your pointer responds to mouse events assigned to that button. This means you can't move or modify the button the way you ordinarily would if you wanted to edit a movie.

1. To select the button while in Button Editing mode, click the Arrow tool and drag an invisible marquee around the boundaries of the button to select it without touching it with the pointer.

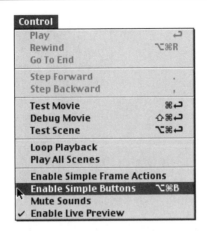

FIGURE 11-4   The Enable Simple Buttons command allows you to test buttons on the stage.

2. To move the button, use the arrow keys. A button also can become selectable using CTRL-ALT-right-click/CTRL-double-click.

3. Transform the properties of a button by selecting any of the Transformation options from the menu (Modify | Transform). For example, if you wanted to scale and rotate the button while the button is enabled and selected, display the Scale And Rotate dialog box from the Modify | Transform menu, or press CTRL-ALT-S/OPT-CMD-S. Type in the new size or rotation and click OK. The button will reflect these modifications.

> NOTE *Although you can edit a button while it's enabled on the stage, it's much easier to edit when buttons are not enabled.*

Enabling a button might not work on all buttons. If the button is complex, or has movie clips or animation on frames or layers, it will need to be tested in Test Movie or Preview mode, which we will discuss next.

Another way to test a button is to select Control | Test Movie. This creates an SWF version of the file and stores it in the same folder as your movie. The buttons will be fully active in this mode. The movie can be previewed in a browser by selecting File | Preview | HTML. This also generates an HTML page and an SWF file with the SWF file embedded in the HTML document. The file also is stored in the folder with your movie. Use either one of these options to preview the movie in a manner closer to what the user will experience.

11

Create More Complex Buttons

You're probably used to looking at the same old kind of radio-like buttons that change color and shape slightly when you position your cursor over an object or when you click an object. But in Flash, buttons don't have to be limited to the same old object transforming on different states. Buttons can be as creative as your imagination allows. Different objects can occupy the button on different states, and you can add sounds, add additional layers, and even incorporate movie clips to add animation to a button. Let's explore some techniques you can apply to buttons to make them stand out from the crowd.

Change Objects on Button Hit States

If you're thinking out of the box, there's no reason a button always has to be the same old picture when you roll over it or click it. Changing the object on different button states is easy in Flash. Figure 11-5 shows a button in the Up, Over, and Down states and the different shape it takes in each state. The three different objects used on this button are astrology pictures that were made into graphic symbols before being used on the button states. When the movie loads, the button appears as an image of two fish. When the viewer mouses over the fish, the button turns into a goat. When the viewer mouses down on the button, it turns into a man pouring water.

This button was created much like the others, by placing different images on the Up, Over, and Down states in Button Editing mode. Nothing was added to the Hit state on this button, so the live area of the button is defined by the image on the Up state. When the button is tested, the image is swapped on the Over and Down states.

This technique exhibits a simple form of interactivity because the button responds to mouse events. You can use this technique of switching images to add some interesting effects to your button. Although our sample might seem like an unremarkable button in its present state, we

Down

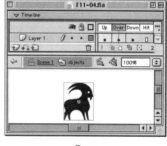
Over

Up

FIGURE 11-5   The image on this button is swapped with other images on the Over and Down states.

expound upon this technique in the next section and substitute animated movie clips for the static objects on the Over and Down states. And then, your buttons do become exciting.

Add Sound to a Button

As you would probably agree, making buttons in Flash is pretty easy. Equally as easy is adding sounds to buttons that elicit a sound on a button event. You can import your own sound for a button or use a wide selection of short sounds offered in the Flash Common Library.

Adding a sound can increase the chances of your audience paying attention to your movie. You can make the button sound like a real click, a beep, or anything your imagination can conjure up. Button sounds should be short and small in file size. Since sound plays all the way through, a long sound may intermingle with another sound that's just firing, causing sounds to get all mixed up with one another like the Tower of Babel. So, with that in mind, let's discuss how to add sound to a button.

Add Sound to a Button from the Sound Library

Flash comes with a library full of short sounds that are perfect for buttons. The Sound Library, shown in Figure 11-6, can be found in the menu under Window | Common Libraries | Sounds.

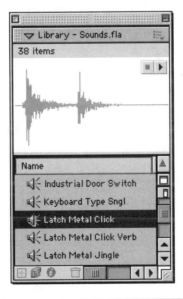

11

FIGURE 11-6   The Sound Library contains short sounds that are perfect for buttons.

When you add a sound to the movie from the Sound Library, a copy of the sound appears in your Library panel. Just like any instance, you can use the sound multiple times without compromising the file size.

To add sound to a button on the Over and Down states, complete the following steps:

1. Create a button following the steps outlined previously. Make sure you have a keyframe on the Over and Down buttons where we will be adding sounds. In this example, we will use the astrology button again and expand on it by adding sounds from the Common Library.

2. While still in Button Editing mode, open the Common Libraries panel and the Library panel. Notice that both of these panels become docked with one another.

   You can add a sound to any of the three states on your button (Hit only defines the clickable area), but the most logical states to use sounds on would be the Over and Down states. If you place a sound on the Up state, it will fire when the user mouses over the button, the same as it would do if you placed the sound on the Over state.

3. Preview the sounds in the Sound Library by clicking a sound and testing it in the thumbnail preview at the top of the Library panel.

4. Select the Over keyframe and drag a sound to the stage. Select the Down keyframe and drag the other sound to the stage.

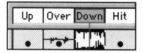

5. Test the button by using the Control | Enable Simple Buttons or Control | Test Movie method.

Place Sound on Its Own Layer in Button Editing Mode

You can also make a new layer in Button Editing mode and place the sound on that layer instead of on the keyframe with the layer. Sound on its own layer is sometimes easier to keep track of. You don't have the distraction of a gray frame and black keyframe to contend with, so it's easy to see the sound wave.

To place a sound in its own layer in Button Editing mode, do the following:

1. In Button Editing mode (assuming you have already created a button), create a new layer by clicking the Insert Layer button in the Button Editing mode Timeline.

2. The new layer will appear on the top of the Timeline. Name the new layer.

3. On the sound layer, place a keyframe (F6) on the state(s) you want the sound to occur on.

4. Drag a sound from the Sound Library to the stage. In the following illustration, sound was again placed on the Over and Down states on the sound layer.

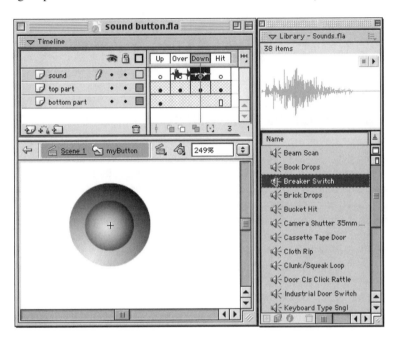

5. Test the button.

TIP

If you don't find a sound that's appropriate in the Sounds Library, you can add your own. It's easy to find short sound effects and loops on the Internet for free or purchase them. See Appendix A for audio resources. If you utilize an audio-editing program, you can make your own sounds. Either way, if you're looking for a special sound and you can't find it in the Flash Library, it's easy to add it yourself.

Add Sound to a Button from an Imported Sound

There are a couple of issues to keep in mind if you plan to import your own sounds for buttons. The sound effects in the Common Sounds Library last about a fraction of a second; so when a user rolls over or mouses down on a button, the sound is quick. Depending on how long it is, your imported sound will play through until it reaches the end of the audio clip. The user can be long finished mousing over or clicking the button and that sound will keep on going. What's more, if you put a sound on the Over and Down states, if they're not short enough, they can sound like they're tangled up in one another while the user moves over and clicks, spoiling the whole sound experience altogether.

The point is that you need to plan carefully when using custom imported sounds on buttons. It's okay for a sound to be longer than a fraction of a second, as long as you anticipate the ramifications of this design decision in every possible scenario.

To import a sound into Flash and apply it to a button, select File | Import or press CTRL-R (Windows)/CMD-R (Mac). In the Navigate dialog box, navigate to the sound you want to import and then import it. The sound will now appear in your Library. Add the sound to a button the same way you add a sound from the Common Library, as was covered in the previous section.

Change the Behavior of a Symbol

One of the many cool features in Flash is the ability to change the behavior of a symbol on-the-fly. You can actually change the behavior of a button instance to a graphic or a movie clip on the click of a button. By changing the behavior of one instance to another, that instance can have limited access to the properties associated with the new symbol. For example, by changing the behavior of a button to a graphic symbol, the button instance is no longer clickable. It behaves just like a regular graphic symbol. By changing a button instance to a movie clip, the button can now be scripted as if it were a movie clip. Of course, it can't contain animation on its own Timeline, but you can talk to it as if it were a movie clip. And, as you would expect, changing a graphic or a movie clip to a button makes the object clickable. You won't be able to change the button instance in Button Editing mode with the four states, but you can treat this instance as a button in a script.

To change the behavior of a symbol, do the following:

1. Select an instance of a symbol on the stage.

2. In the Properties Inspector pop-up list, select an alternative behavior.

Now, when you select the object, the behavior will have changed in the Properties Inspector. If you're changing an instance to a button, additional selections become available for this behavior type. For a button, there are two selections:

- ■ **Track As Button** This selection is used for a standard, single button, and is the default.
- ■ **Track As Menu Item** This selection is used if you're creating pop-up navigational menus that have several selections within a defined area that can have the option of having mouse events attached to them.

At the bottom right of the menu is a Swap button. This is a cool little button that enables you to swap one instance of a symbol with another. For more information on swapping symbols, refer to Chapter 6.

In the Properties Inspector, you can also assign an instance name to a button. An instance name is a special name you give an instance so you can manipulate the object in a script. Button instances can have button events assigned to them, too. Assign an instance name to a button if you intend to talk to it via a script. To give a button an instance name, select the button and, in the Properties Inspector under the Behavior type, type in a name for the button.

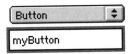

The subject of button objects is discussed further in Chapter 15. Movie clips can also be assigned instance names. We discuss movie clips later, in the section "Understand Movie Clips in Flash."

Add Simple Effects to a Button

There are many cool things you can do with the Button object. In Chapter 12, we will return to the subject of buttons in a different context—that is, assigning ActionScript to buttons.

The following is an example of how you might construct a simple navigational menu in Flash. The buttons in this menu aren't used or constructed as typical buttons on a web page. Since buttons are objects on their own Timelines with simple event scripts attached to them, let's see how we can be creative with these tools.

Figure 11-7 shows a linear navigation bar. When the user positions their pointer over a topic, "what's new," "archives," "glossary," or "resources," a highlight effect that looks like a paintbrush stroke appears in the background. When the user positions their pointer over a topic, the previous topic drops the highlight, and the highlight then appears on the current topic. This effect is created with a button that is empty on the Up state. The highlight only shows when the topics are moused over. Empty button states are often used for various effects like this. Buttons that are empty on all four states (blank buttons) are often nested within movie clips and assigned scripts that give orders to other movie clips. We learn how to make interactive buttons in Chapter 12. The following is an account of how to create a navigation bar similar to the one in Figure 11-7:

1. The assets were gathered before the navigation bar was created. This also means planning before you build the file. The maze was imported from Illustrator. The curly bracket was created in Flash as was the navigation bar structure. Lastly, all elements were converted into symbols. In this case, graphic symbols were used. However, if you wanted to include additional interactivity on the maze or other elements, you would use movie clip symbols instead of graphic symbols.

11

FIGURE 11-7   This navigation bar done in Flash works just like a JavaScript navigation bar typically used in web pages.

2. With all the assets organized in the Library, the layers were then constructed. The layers in the main Timeline were set up and named in the following order:

    ■ topics

    ■ static_art

    ■ buttons

3. On the static_art layer, the navigation bar was built. With the Library displayed, an instance of the curly_bracket, graphic_line, and maze were dragged to the stage on the static_art layer. The maze and the graphic_line were positioned as shown in Figure 11-7, and the first curly bracket was butted against the graphic_line instance toward the left where the first topic (what's new) sits. The curly_bracket instance was duplicated three more times by clicking the object and pressing SHIFT-CTRL/SHIFT-OPT. A reasonable distance was approximated between these duplicate curly_bracket instances, and then they were all aligned and spaced evenly apart using the Align panel (Window I Align). The purpose of holding down the SHIFT key is to constrain the horizontal position of the curly_bracket instance while duplicating it.

4. On the topics layer, the Text tool was selected. On this layer, the words that sit on top of the curly_bracket instances were typed in as separate text blocks (**what's new**, **archives**, **glossary**, **resources**). The text was then dragged into position within the curly bracket and centered horizontally.

5. Everything is now in place except for the button that responds to the user's mouse-over. This button was created next. If you recall, when the user mouses over the navigational text, a paintbrush stroke (swish) appears and disappears when the user mouses off of it. The paintbrush stroke was made as a graphic symbol before making the paintbrush (swish) symbol.

6. To make the paintbrush (swish) button, enter Button Symbol Editing mode (Insert I New Symbol). This symbol was named *swish*. In Editing mode, the Up state is left blank so that when the movie loads, you don't see the paintbrush stroke.

7. A keyframe was added to the Over state, and an instance of the paintbrush stroke symbol (swish) was dragged onto the stage from the Library and centered over the cross hairs.

Another keyframe was added to the Hit state. On the Hit state, a rectangle was drawn over the area to indicate the active area of the button. The Editing mode was exited. The button was then stored in the Library.

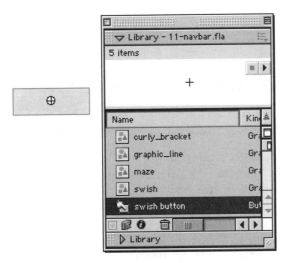

8. With the button layer selected, an instance of the button was dragged onto the stage and centered over the first topic. Because nothing was in the Up state within the button symbol, the button appears on the stage as a light-blue rectangle. This blue rectangle indicates the Hit area on a button with a blank Up state. When the button loads, it will not show in the movie. The button instance was duplicated on all four topics on the navigation bar.

On testing the navigation bar, if you mouse over the topics, the swish button instance (whose layer is under the topic layer) displays on the Over state. As the movie stands now, nothing occurs on the Down state other than the swish symbol disappearing.

Generally, a navigation bar button will navigate to another HTML page, another SWF file, or another frame in the current Timeline or another Timeline. In fact, there are many things you can do with button events.

Next, let's apply a simple script to the first button ("what's new") that will open up another SWF movie on top of the current movie when the mouse is clicked. Here's how to do it:

1. On the button layer, click the first button instance and display the Actions panel (F2 or Window I Actions). We are going to apply a simple script directly on this button. The script will instruct the button to open a file named new.swf when the button is clicked. You can reference any SWF file that might happen to be conveniently located; but if you want to follow along, the files for this example are located on the Osborne site (www.osborne.com) in the Chapter 11 source files folder for this book.

11

2. In the left column of the Actions panel (Actions toolbox), click the first folder, Actions, to expand it and see its contents. Click Browser/Network to expand that folder, too. Double-click loadMovie. In the right column, the following will appear:

```
on (release) {
    loadMovieNum("", 0);
}
```

In the next chapter, we will discuss the specifics of the Actions panel and how it works. For now, let's start getting accustomed to using this tool.

> **NOTE**   *Make sure you are displaying the Actions panel in Normal mode by clicking the options pop-up menu in the upper-right corner and making certain Normal is checked.*

3. Click the first line of code, on (release) {; at the top of the panel, for Event, click the Press button and deselect the Release button. Press corresponds to the Down state on a button. Now that line of code will read like this:

```
on (press) {
```

4. Click the second line of code; at the top of the panel, for URL, type the name of an SWF file that is in the same directory as the current file you are working on (which you will be exporting as an SWF file). In this script, I typed **new.swf**, a SWF file in the same folder. The Level indicates what level the new movie will load into. Level 0 is the top level, so this movie will load on the top level. The script on the first button now reads

```
on (press) {
    loadMovieNum("new.swf", 0);
}
```

5. Save the file and test it (Control | Test Movie). When you click the what's new button, the new movie loads on top of the current movie. Pretty easy, isn't it?

The loadMovie action is a commonly used action in Flash. You can also load SWF files and JPEG files into targeted movie clips on multiple Timelines. The loadMovie action helps keep the file size down on a complex Flash file because you can link to external files that can play on top of your movie or within your movie. Plus, movies loaded into Flash files don't have the refresh issues you have with browsers. In other words, the loadMovie action helps maintain an even flow between movies without interruption. We discuss loadMovie more in Chapter 15.

Understand Movie Clips in Flash

As mentioned many times throughout this book, movie clips are independent movies that run on their own Timelines. Because they are symbols, movie clips possess many of the attributes common to all symbols. For example, movie clip instances can be used as many times as needed in a movie without affecting the file size.

Just because movie clips are self-contained movies, it doesn't mean that a movie clip must contain animation. A movie clip can be a static graphic and occupy one frame, or it can be a full-fledged animation, just like you would create on the main Timeline.

Movie clips can be controlled by buttons, frame actions, and other movie clips, and vice versa. They can talk to each other and live inside one another on different levels. Movie clips can be simple or very complex, but they always serve as one of the most scriptable elements in a Flash movie. In this section, the basics of making movie clips are covered. Once you understand how to make movie clips, you can move onto more advanced applications—controlling movie clips with interactivity.

Animate Movie Clips Versus Graphic Symbols

Movie clips only occupy one frame on the main Timeline, even if the movie clip contains animation. Animated graphic symbols, on the other hand, need to occupy the same number of frames on the main Timeline as they occupy on the Timeline in Symbol Editing mode in order to play the whole animation. For example, with movie clips, an animation that uses 15 frames on its own Timeline would occupy only one frame on the main Timeline. In contrast, the same animation created as an animated graphic symbol would need to occupy 15 frames on the main Timeline (see Figure 11-8). From this example, you can see how compact a movie clip can be, even if it contains extensive animation.

Plan Your Movie Clip

Throughout the book, organization is stressed as a key element in a successful Flash movie. More than any other element, movie clips demand extra planning and attention for movies of a medium-to-complex nature. As you will see when you start adding actions to movie clips, they can become very confusing.

Instances of movie clips take on a unique role in Flash. You can refer to them in a script if you give the instance a name. You name an instance the same way you name a button instance, in the Properties Inspector.

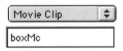

Movie clip instances are identified in a script by their instance name and their location in your movie. Since movie clips can be nested in other movie clips, you can communicate with movie clips on multiple Timelines within Timelines. In Flash, the path of a movie clip can be either absolute or relative. An *absolute* path is the complete path to an instance, which includes the level it is located on. There are ways you can refer to these levels in ActionScript, including _level, _root, and _parent. A *relative* path refers to an instance in relation to the instance it's talking to. If you're familiar with HTML, this will all seem familiar to you. In other words, when multiple Timelines are being used in your movie and communicating with one another, in a

11

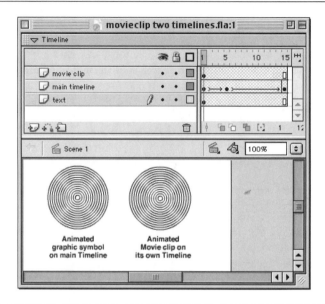

FIGURE 11-8 The frames on an animated graphic symbol must be re-created on the Timeline on which it's being placed, as opposed to an animated movie clip whose frames are self-contained on its own Timeline.

script, you can use not only the name of the instance, but also its location in either absolute or relative terms.

It can be called from any level in any Timeline in the current movie or other movies, if a movie is being loaded into Flash. For now, let's address the "how tos" of making a movie clip.

Examine the Main Timeline Versus the Movie Clip Timeline

To understand how Timelines and movie clips function, let's consider the following example. Figure 11-9 shows two animated pictures that appear identical. The picture on the left is a static graphic symbol that has been animated on the main Timeline. The identical picture on the right is animated on its own Timeline as a movie clip. The Timeline on this movie clip is identical to the animated graphic on the main Timeline.

Notice in the main Timeline that you can see the animated frames on the animated graphic layer. On the layer with the movie clip (animated movie clip layer), only one frame is occupied on the main Timeline because the animation takes place on the Timeline of the movie clip. So the movie clip is a self-contained movie on the main Timeline. You can have many movies existing simultaneously because of the movie clip architecture. Now let's take a look at how to construct an animated movie clip.

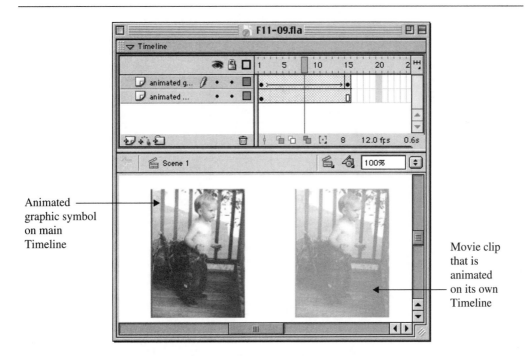

FIGURE 11-9   Although they look different on the stage, the graphic symbol animation on the main Timeline is identical to the corresponding movie clip, which was animated on its own Timeline.

Animated graphic symbol on main Timeline

Movie clip that is animated on its own Timeline

Create an Animated Movie Clip

Animating movie clips is just like making an animation on the main Timeline. You can achieve some very interesting design effects utilizing them.

The following example, shown in Figure 11-10, is a simple multilayer animated movie clip of the words "movie clip." This figure demonstrates how important it is to organize your movie clip Timeline and assets before building an animated movie clip. Sometimes, the building of the clip is simple. It's the organization and gathering of all the components beforehand that can become complex.

Let's talk about what this movie clip does. First, it only lasts a couple of seconds. It appears to type the words "movie clip." When it's done, the animation stops because there is a Stop action on the last frame of the movie clip. Also, on a layer beneath the typed words is the shadow of the words "movie clip." This shadow is, in fact, another animated movie clip that is nested inside the other movie clip's Timeline. Since both movie clips are on a different Timeline, they can be scripted to talk to one another.

11

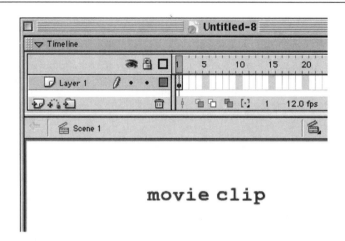

FIGURE 11-10   This movie clip was animated on individual layers using the Distribute To Layers command.

Where do you begin when making a multilayer animated movie clip with a lot of pieces? Let's review the process that was used to make this movie clip to give you a better idea of where to begin:

1. Enter Movie Clip Editing mode (Insert | New Symbol or CTRL-F8 in Windows/CMD-F8 on the Mac).

2. Give your symbol a name and select Movieclip for its behavior.

3. Type a word or words. In this case, the words "movie clip" were typed.

4. Break the words apart (Modify | Break Apart).

5. One by one, symbol each letter as a graphic (F8) and name it while still in Movie Clip Editing mode.

6. Select all the letters and then select Distribute To Layers. This takes everything selected on one layer and redistributes it to separate layers. When we animate the movie clip, you will see why creating instant layers allows you to do some creative things.

7. Now to animate the layers. Add keyframes to all frames on Frame 5. An easy way to select all of them is to hold down SHIFT, select the first layer on Frame 5, and then select the last layer on Frame 5. Press F6 and keyframes will appear on all layers on Frame 5.

8. Repeat this process by adding keyframes to all layers on Frame 10. The resulting Timeline should look like the following illustration:

9. Return to the letter symbols on Frames 1 and 5, and jumble the letters around a little as shown in the following illustration:

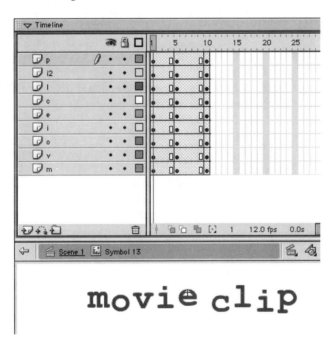

10. If you scrub the Playhead over the Timeline, you'll notice everything happens at the same time. We wanted to create an effect where each letter would be laid down separately in time, almost like a typewriter typing. In the final movie clip, the frames are staggered so the letter animation builds in time. To drag each frame sequence forward in time, it's easier to turn the Span Frames feature on from the Preferences dialog box (Edit | Preferences | Span Based Selection). Click the entire second layer frame set (o) and drag it forward in time. Repeat this process on each layer until each frame sequence is dragged forward a few frames more in time than the previous frameset. If the Span Based Selection annoys you, you can easily deselect it in the Preferences dialog box.

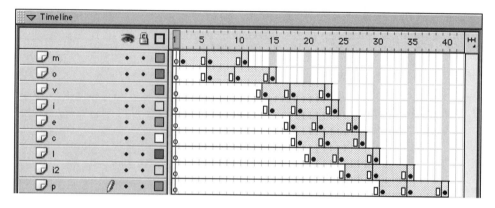

11. To get all the letters to remain on the stage at the end, add frames on all layers to the longest frame in the Timeline. To do so, click a frame and press F5 to fill in the blank frames.

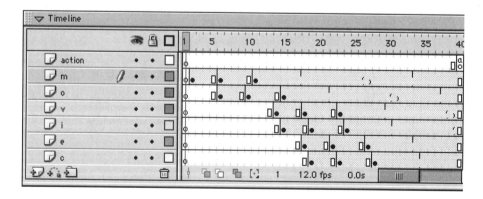

12. Exit Movie Clip Editing mode, drag an instance of this movie clip onto the stage, and test it. You'll notice it loops continuously. To make the movie clip only loop once, we can add a Stop action to the movie clip Timeline. Since this is a common procedure, we'll review the process.

13. Return to Movie Clip Editing mode by double-clicking either the icon in the Library or the movie clip on the stage.

14. Add a new layer to the top of the movie clip Timeline and name it **action**.

15. Open the Actions panel (F2 or Window | Actions); from the pop-up menu, select Expert. In Expert mode, you create your own script, with no assistance from Flash.

16. In the Actions window, enter the following exactly as you see it:

```
stop();
```

17. Close the Actions panel; and on the actions layer, drag the "a" to the last frame in the Timeline. Now, when the movie clip plays, it will stop on the last frame.

The other movie clip, mc blur, is on the Timeline of the movie clip named movieclipWord. This movie clip is an animated tween that changes slightly in alpha and position. If you display the Library and double-click this movie clip, you can see how it is constructed (see Figure 11-11). You can also double-click the movie clip in the movieclipWord Timeline to edit it.

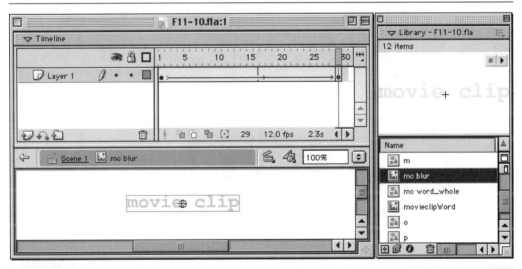

FIGURE 11-11   The movie clip named mc blur is nested in the Timeline of another movie clip.

You can also assign a button on any Timeline to control either of these movie clips. We will discuss that process further in Chapter 12.

Make an Animated Button from a Movie Clip

Buttons can be made from vector art, bitmaps, and photos, as well as movie clips. A movie clip instance can be nested on the Up, Over, or Down states in Button Editing mode. You can nest movie clips in buttons, and vice versa.

Figure 11-12 depicts a button that has an animated JPEG sequence on the Over state. When you position the mouse over the picture, the animated JPEG sequence begins to play. When you position the mouse off the picture, the animation stops. When you click the picture, a still JPEG image replaces the picture on the Up position.

With a little creativity, there are many interesting effects you can achieve by combining buttons and movie clips. Let's review the process that was used to make this button:

1. The still pictures were exported as a JPEG sequence from a video-editing program and imported into Flash.

2. The JPEGs were all symboled and named individually, in sequence, as movie clips (walk1, walk2, walk3, and so on). Although the JPEG sequences don't have to be movie clips, it's easier to go back in later and apply effects if they are already turned into movie clips.

3. Another movie clip was created and named walk_mc. In Movie Clip Editing mode, the movie clip JPEG sequence was reconstructed, frame by frame, on the first layer. To do so, a keyframe was added to each frame, and each movie clip of the JPEG sequence was dragged onto a frame until the whole movie clip sequence was completed. When the frame-by-frame JPEG sequence animation was completed in the movie clip Timeline, Movie Clip Editing mode was exited (see Figure 11-13).

FIGURE 11-12   This button has an animated movie clip on the Up state.

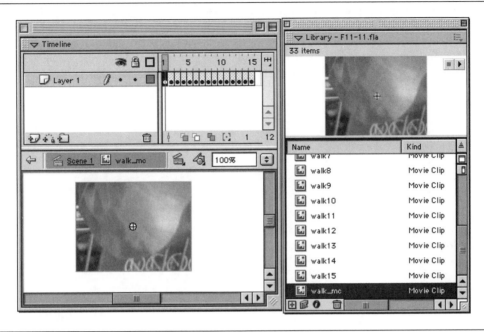

FIGURE 11-13   Movie Clip Editing mode for an animated JPEG sequence

11

4. Next, a button was created and named (Insert | New Symbol... | Button).

5. On the button Timeline, keyframes were added to all four states.

6. On the Up and Down states, two of the JPEG sequence still movie clips were added to the appropriate keyframes.

7. On the Over state, the movie clip named walk_mc was added to the keyframe.

8. Nothing is on the Hit state in this button. You could put a rectangle here to designate the hit area, but it's not necessary because the shape of the button in the Up state also can define the hit area.

9. Exit Button Editing mode, and drag an instance of the button onto the stage in the main Timeline. Test the movie. Rolling over the button plays the JPEG sequence, and rolling off stops it.

So, with these static JPEG pictures, some movie clips, buttons, and a little imagination, you can create an interactive button that a user can control. You can also easily add sound to either a button state or the JPEG movie clip sequence. If you want to practice re-creating this effect, the JPEG files used to create this button are located on the Osborne site for this book (www.osborne.com).

In the next chapter, interactivity on buttons and movie clips is explored further. We will assign ActionScript to buttons and movie clips to give the user control over the way a movie plays. We also examine ActionScript in terms of what it is and how it works.

Part IV

Lay the Groundwork for Flash Interactivity

Chapter 12

Use ActionScript to Create Simple Interactivity

How to...

- Understand the basics of object-oriented programming
- Understand objects, classes, methods, and properties
- Use the Actions panel
- Understand the Actions Toolbox
- Get up and running with ActionScript
- Assign actions to a frame
- Create button events
- Use variables
- Understand the scope of variables, strings, and expressions
- Use operators to change the value of variables
- Manipulate strings with operators and escape sequences

The depth of Flash ActionScript is immense and far-reaching, and in this chapter, we will begin to examine the basic structure of ActionScript as a language. As you will see, ActionScript is a very powerful scripting language. A scripting language is designed to function within a specific application, the way JavaScript allows web browsers to do many things it couldn't do by processing HTML alone. Many Flash developers use ActionScript to create games, informational kiosk-type movies, shopping carts, special applications, and even full educational courses. If you have never programmed before, especially in JavaScript, you will likely find that basic ActionScript is fairly easy to learn.

Luckily, the Flash software gives beginners and even intermediate users a bit of help, because, like any new language, the syntax is sometimes hard to wrap your mind around. To create simple interactivity in Flash, you really don't need to memorize a large number of cryptic commands. Flash provides all the commands you will ever need in a special Actions Toolbox, and you can select from these commands (providing you have some idea of what they are and where they are located in the Toolbox) in a menu-style manner. Once you become accustomed to the contents of the Actions Toolbox, you may want to venture out on your own and write scripts (in Expert mode) without any assistance from the Toolbox.

The ActionScript panel accommodates both "newbies" and experienced Flash scripters alike. So, as your knowledge of ActionScript grows, so will your confidence in writing your own scripts. We will discuss the architecture of the ActionScript panel in this chapter, and you will get to take it for a test drive. In the meantime, let's concentrate on some scripting basics.

For those who have programmed before, you will find that ActionScript is structured like many other languages. If you are familiar with JavaScript, you will find many similarities between JavaScript and ActionScript. If you are familiar with a previous edition of ActionScript, you will be pleased to know that although the language has been upgraded and new features have been added, you will be able to get up to speed very quickly on ActionScript in Flash MX.

Did you know?

The Origins of the First Scripting Language

Many attribute the first scripting language—a programming language designed to work within a specific application—to Apple Computer's popular '80s program Hypercard. Not only did Hypercard allow authors to create an interactive experience for users through scripting, but it also was one of the first programs to use hyperlinks, now so popular on the World Wide Web.

Before jumping in and scripting, it is best to review some basic concepts of object-oriented programming (OOP). Since ActionScript is an OOP language, understanding the basics of OOP language will provide you with a framework from which to produce more solid, error-free code in less time.

Interactivity and ActionScript

When a movie is interactive, the users control the flow or direction of the movie through their choices and selections. There can be many different outcomes of an interactive movie, depending on the options that users select. Each user can have a unique experience with a Flash movie, due to the choices they make. This is the core to interactivity and the genius behind ActionScript.

Traditionally, media runs in a linear fashion. Movies run from beginning to end. Television programs run in a linear fashion as well. Interactive media is different. There is no specified order in which the user will experience the media. Web sites are a great example of interactive media. Users don't typically read every word on a web site, starting at the beginning and reading to the end. Instead, users make selections that are based on the web site's menus and executed through hyperlinks. If one user goes to a web site about Major League Baseball, he or she may seek out scores or news about a favorite team. Another user going to the same baseball web site may skip the scores and go directly to a story about a favorite player. The user is in charge of their experience in interactive media.

The Basics of Object-Oriented Programming

Before jumping into ActionScript, it is beneficial to examine the framework of object-oriented programming languages. Object orientation is a relatively new idea in programming, and understanding the basic concepts is critical to understanding how ActionScript functions.

Perhaps the best way to explain what OOP is, is to explain what OOP is not. Years ago, before OOP was popularized, programmers used a method known as *structural* or *procedural* programming. In structural programming, the code was executed in a specific order, designated by the programmer. By contrast, OOP languages do not execute commands in a specific order.

12

Different modules of code are triggered by different events. For example, clicking a button causes the click event associated with that button to execute.

ActionScript is an object-oriented scripting language, based on the concepts of OOP. In ActionScript, as in all OOP languages, there is a heavy emphasis on code structure and organization. ActionScript code is organized into objects or modules. ActionScript code is very similar to JavaScript code. In fact, ActionScript is based on the same ECMA-262 specifications as JavaScript. ECMA-262 (European Computer Manufacturers Association) is a document that defines the rules and parameters of the JavaScript language. This means that if you are already familiar with JavaScript, learning ActionScript will be a breeze.

Classes, Objects, Methods, and Properties

Objects, classes, methods, and properties are the building blocks of OOP. These terms are all related, and you will find that understanding their hierarchy is one of the keys to understanding ActionScript.

People new to ActionScript are often surprised to discover they have been creating objects since they first began using Flash. In fact, everything created in a movie is an object. Rectangles, imported bitmaps, and text entities in a Flash movie are all individual objects. In fact, each individual frame and layer, and the movie itself, can be considered individual objects. You can use ActionScript to create your own objects right in the code.

Objects are identified by unique names and are also referenced by their location on a particular level. Objects exist within a hierarchy in a movie and are called on not only by their established unique name, but also by their location within the hierarchy. Objects may remain static through one part of the movie but later change. Also, objects in Flash movies exist within other objects. A symbol may exist within a frame or several frame objects. All objects in a movie exist within the larger movie object. The Movie Explorer feature presents a representation of the movie hierarchy, as shown in Figure 12-1. You can access it by clicking Window | Movie Explorer or by using the keyboard shortcut F4.

Objects have properties. Properties describe objects. Think of properties as elements that make an object unique. For example, text objects have many properties that you set through the context-sensitive property panel within Flash. When creating a text box, you can set the font face property, controlling style of the font, or the text color property. Many of these properties are accessible through ActionScript code. For example, you can position an object within the movie by modifying the _x and _y properties, or change the height of an object by modifying the _height property. Changing elements such as the frame rate within a movie changes the properties of the predefined movie object.

A *class* describes everything there is to know about an object. You can think of a class as code that defines an object's properties, methods, and event handlers. Properties such as height, width, and position can be included in a class. The methods describe what an object is capable of. The object may move or explode. The event handlers describe when the methods occur. If the object is dragged, it moves; but if it is dragged out of the movie, it explodes.

A class can be thought of as an object that makes other objects. When a class creates an object, that object is known as an *instance* of the class. This is all getting a bit esoteric, so let's try to relate this directly to a Flash movie. Let's say a Flash movie contains an illustration of a tennis ball. The properties of the ball can change from instance to instance—some instances of

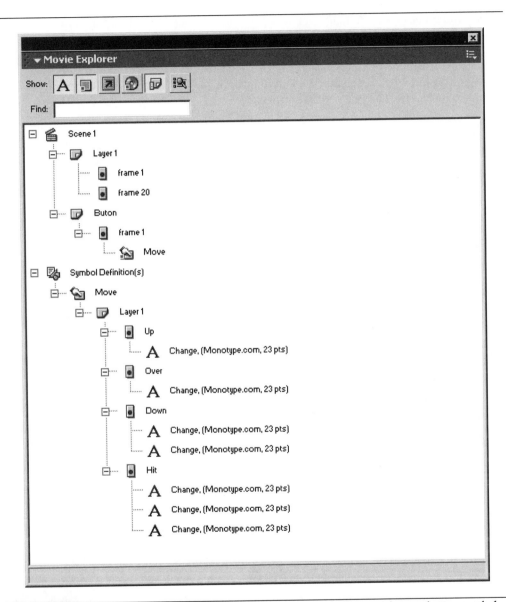

FIGURE 12-1   The Movie Explorer hierarchy for a short movie that contains one button symbol

the ball may be green, while others may be yellow. Its methods can change as well. Some instances of the tennis ball might be allowed to move, while others just sit there. Event handlers may vary as well, as some instances of the tennis balls will respond when clicked, while others will remain static.

The basic actions within ActionScript have not changed much from Flash 5 to Flash MX. However, there are new actions and a few new commands. A few older methods have been deprecated, and a few methods that have been previously deprecated are no longer available. If you are an experienced ActionScript user, you will probably agree that this version is the most intuitive and powerful yet. If you are new to ActionScript, you are learning it at a time when it has matured into a robust and easy-to-learn language.

Using the Actions Panel

The Actions panel allows you to create ActionScript that is attached to several types of objects (as discussed at the beginning of this chapter). Scripts are written in the Actions panel and attached to frames or movie objects such as buttons or images. The Actions panel interface is perfect for beginners because, in Normal mode, actions can be entered using the simplicity of point and click. More advanced users may prefer to use Expert mode, which allows them to directly type script into the window.

By default, the Actions panel appears directly below the stage. However, it can be moved and docked elsewhere or be allowed to float freely within the Flash window. The Actions panel can be accessed through several methods:

- Choose Window | Actions.

- Press F9.

- If the panel title bar appears, but the panel itself is closed, click the right-facing triangle to the left of the word "Actions." This will expand the panel. You can expand and collapse the panel to give you more room on your screen. In a small-screen environment, this can be quite helpful. Double-clicking anywhere on the Actions panel title bar will expand the panel also.

- Right-click (Windows)/CMD-click (Mac) an object in a movie, and choose Actions from the context pop-up menu.

Figure 12-2 shows the Actions panel with a simple script in it set in Normal mode. Notice the title bar is labeled Actions – Frame, indicating that the actions being coded will occur when the movie frame is displayed. Since actions can be associated with just about any object, the title bar will often change to reflect the target of the actions being coded. As you write a script, you assign both frame and object actions. Therefore, it's important to make sure your code is being generated in the right place. In Expert mode, there will be additional functions in the Actions panel. We will play around with these in Chapter 15.

 *Not all actions are available for all types of objects. When it is not possible to associate a specific action with a selected object, that action will appear grayed out in the Actions panel.*

As mentioned before, ActionScript may be written in either Expert or Normal mode. To switch between the two modes, click the Panel Options button, and, in the pop-up menu, make the appropriate selection. If you click the View Options button, you may also switch between Normal and Expert mode, as well as display the line numbers for code in the code window.

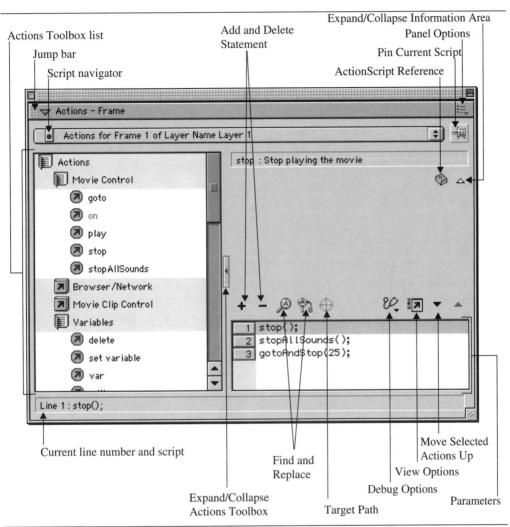

FIGURE 12-2 The Actions panel with important components labeled

Clicking the Panel Options button reveals several utilities that may make coding more convenient. The options are as follows:

- **Normal Mode** Switches to Normal mode, which is discussed after this list.
- **Expert Mode** Switches to Expert mode, also discussed after this list.
- **Go To Line** Quickly navigates to an indicated line number in the code. This can be especially useful for very long code snippets.
- **Find** Finds a particular string in the code listing. Again, this is useful in long passages of code to find particular variables or commands.

- **Find Again**   Finds the next instance of the indicated string of characters.
- **Replace**   Finds a particular string and then replaces it with another string entered by the user. Can be used to replace variable names within code or specific passages of text. If the case-sensitive option is selected, the text must have the same case to be replaced.
- **Check Syntax**   Checks the code for errors and lists any errors found so that they may be corrected.
- **Autoformat**   When this is selected, the code will be formatted according to the Autoformat Options utility, the next selection in the Panel Options menu.
- **Autoformat Options**   Allows the user to select preferences to change how code is spaced and how nested commands are displayed.
- **Import From File**   Takes an external text file and imports it into the code window.
- **Export As File**   Exports the code as a text file. This feature is useful for archiving code that you may want to examine, use again later, or easily transport between machines.
- **Print**   Outputs only the code in the code window to the printer.
- **View Line Numbers**   Toggles the line numbers on and off in the code window. The line numbers have no function in the code. They are a visual aid for the writer.
- **View Esc Shortcut Keys**   When this is selected, the ESC key combinations for commands will be displayed next to the actual commands when displaying the commands through the Add Statement button.
- **Preferences**   Allows the user to set preferences for the Actions panel, such as fonts, font colors, font size, and text indentations.
- **Help**   Displays Flash MX help.
- **Maximize Panel**   Displays the Actions panel at maximum size.
- **Close Panel**   Closes the Actions panel.

If you're using ActionScript to talk to an object, the object to which the code is being attached must be referred to in the script. This is actually quite logical because it's like talking to one person about another. The person you are talking to wouldn't know who you were talking about unless you referred to the other person by name. To add script to a particular frame as opposed to an object, click the desired frame and verify that the panel title bar says Actions – Frame. You will also notice that the script navigator indicates the appropriate frame as well. This is very helpful for orienting you to where you are at a given moment in a script. It's also very common to have multiple scripts within one Flash movie, and the script navigator is also helpful for rapidly moving between both frame and object scripts.

TIP
You may notice that when you are writing a frame script, if a different frame is selected on the Timeline, the script disappears from the Actions panel. If you want the script you are working on to remain visible in the Actions panel when other frames are displayed, click the Pin Current Script icon. To unpin the script so you can see other scripts in other frames, simply click again.

Script in Normal Mode

Normal mode is for users new to Flash. In Normal mode, statements may be added to a script in two ways. Clicking the Add Statement button will expose a pop-up menu through which all the ActionScript commands may be accessed. They are categorized in submenus to make it easier to find the command that you are looking for. When a command is selected, it is automatically added to the code. Statements may also be added to the script by clicking through the command hierarchy in the Actions Toolbox, expanding and collapsing folders until you find the right action, and then either double-clicking the desired statement or dragging it into the code window. In Expert mode, code may also be typed directly into the code window. Many find it easiest to work in Normal mode until they are familiar with the ActionScript syntax.

NOTE
Actions in ActionScript are organized into many different categories. Some actions are called "methods," some are called "functions," some are called "conditionals," and the list goes on. All of these actions in the Actions panel constitute various tools you will use to build scripts. It is not uncommon to hear all the selections in the Toolbox referred to as "actions." When you become more experienced, you will be able to discern the differences between all categories in ActionScript.

As code is written in Normal mode, it is generally added to the code window in the order that commands are selected. You can change the order of your script quite easily. To change the order in which statements execute in the Actions panel, use the Move Actions Up and Move Actions Down arrows. Note that these arrows, like many other elements in Flash, are context-sensitive and only appear when germane to your selection. The order in which statements are executed may also be rearranged by dragging a statement upward or downward in the code window.

12

Looking at the Actions Toolbox

The Actions Toolbox contains a list of all the available actions, operators, functions, and properties available in Flash MX. They are listed in convenient, collapsible navigation folders. A folder that contains nested actions is represented in the Actions panel by a box icon with a diagonal arrow pointed toward the right. To see the contents of that Actions folder, simply click the icon and the folder will expand. Within each folder are several subfolders, which contain more subfolders or commands. A command is represented by a circle with the same diagonal arrow that is found on the folders. This is the Flash ActionScript way of being neat and organized.

On-The-Fly Command Reference

Flash MX comes with a complete and easy-to-use ActionScript reference. If you need assistance with a particular command (and believe me, you will), select the command in your code and click the reference icon, which looks like a book. The reference window will open and give you the correct syntax for and an explanation of the selected command. Once you are in the reference window, you may navigate through the command hierarchy to see information about any command. This is an incredibly useful tool for the beginner and advanced user. It is impossible to remember what each and every action does, and sometimes you need a refresher on-the-fly. This saves you the time-consuming task of trying to find the information in the reference manual

SHORTCUT   *If you are accustomed to the locations of actions in the Actions Toolbox from Flash 5, you will be a little disoriented in MX. Like an overzealous cleaning person that comes into your home and rearranges all of your belongings, Macromedia has relocated almost all old actions into new folders and subfolders. The good news is that Macromedia has included a code index at the end of the Actions Toolbox list. So, if you remember the name of an action, you can also select it from the code index folder, where all actions are listed alphabetically. Also if you right-click (Windows)/CTRL-click (Mac) an action in the Index, you can select Show original from the pop-up context menu. This will take you to the location of the action in the Toolbox.*

The folders are organized in a hierarchy by the type of code. Flash MX also adds a code index, which is the bottom item in the Toolbox. The index lists all the available ActionScript commands alphabetically. This new index feature is useful for those who want rapid access to the comprehensive list of actions, operators, functions, and properties.

In addition to the code index, the following folders are available in the Actions Toolbox:

- **Actions**   Actions are commands that make something happen within the movie. Some are simple events that can be assigned to frames, such as `stop`, which stops the progress of the movie, or `Stop All Sounds`, which stops any sounds that are being played. Other actions can allow the assignment of values to variables or even print the current frame on a printer.

- **Operators**   Operators are used for performing calculations or comparing objects. Some of these operators include +, −, =, >=, *, as well as many other symbols.

■ **Functions**   Functions receive values, evaluate the values, and return some sort of result. Often, these are referred to as *methods*. A typical function is the `getVersion()` function, which returns the version of the Flash player that the viewer is using. Other common functions include `getProperty()` and `getTimer()`.

■ **Constants**   Constants are values that can be used in just about any expression. `True` and `False` are common constants that are used with Boolean expressions. The `newline` constant moves to a new line when it is encountered. Constants are a convenience for the ActionScript user.

■ **Properties**   Every object has properties, and you can access the properties through ActionScript using this section of the Actions Toolbox. Some properties refer to the entire movie, while other properties refer to a single object. Properties are easy to recognize because they are always preceded by an underscore character. Common properties include `_x`, `_y`, `_visible`, `_rotation`, and `_alpha`.

■ **Objects**   Objects represent instances of a class that have their own predefined methods. Some of the more commonly used objects include Numbers, Movie Clip, Color, Date, and Mouse. Each object has a subset of actions in the Actions Toolbox relating to that particular object.

■ **Deprecated**   In case they are needed for old Flash files with scripts that reference them, actions, operators, functions, and properties that are no longer part of ActionScript are listed here.

■ **Flash UI Components**   Methods associated with instances of the new Flash components Interface Objects are listed here. These methods allow you to do such things as see whether a check box or option button has been selected by the user, or disable or enable scrolling within a scrolling text box.

Get Up and Running with ActionScript

ActionScript is easy to learn if approached in a logical manner. The remainder of this chapter and Chapter 13 will discuss the basics of ActionScript. The idea is to get you up and running with some basic techniques, as well as provide you with the framework for understanding and using the most widely used ActionScript properties. This book does not cover all the actions associated with ActionScript—the topic is simply too broad and would probably take another couple of books to thoroughly explain it. However, most of the commonly used actions and techniques are covered in Chapters 12 through 15, and this will serve as a solid springboard to your future studies of the language.

Assign an Action to a Frame

Frame actions are generally designed to control the flow of the movie. Typical frame actions can stop a movie or go to a designated frame. You may have even worked with frame actions and not even known it if you've ever played around in HTML authoring programs like Macromedia

12

Dreamweaver or Adobe GoLive. In these programs, you can create simple frame actions on timelines that allow a user to control the play of a timeline. In these programs, you select actions from a menu, and a JavaScript is generated in the background while you work.

Assigning an action to a frame in Flash is a surprisingly simple process. As illustrated next, when a frame contains an action, a small cursive letter *a* is placed in the appropriate frame in the Timeline. It is possible to put contradictory frame actions in the different layers, yielding unpredictable results. For this reason, many designers put an Actions layer on their Timeline for all frame actions.

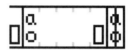

To assign an action to a frame, click the desired frame and make sure the Actions panel is visible. Then, to add the actual action to the frame script, find the desired action in the Actions Toolbox and click it. Many of the actions that will be used as frame actions are found in the Actions Toolbox under Actions | Movie Control.

NOTE   *The* Goto *action performs two separate actions. If* GotoAndPlay *is selected, the action will move the movie to the frame specified in the action properties and continue playing the movie. If* GotoAndStop *is selected, the specified frame will be displayed, but the movie will stop at that point.*

Frame actions occur as soon as the movie reaches the frame that contains the action. The user has no control over whether the frame actions are executed or not. A more complex level of interactivity would be to allow the user to select when an action is being executed. Most users won't know that they are executing ActionScript code—they will think they are simply causing the movie to move forward, backward, or in whatever manner the designer allows. This more complex level of interaction requires the use of object actions.

Make Things Happen: Events on Buttons

As discussed in Chapter 11, buttons have a type of interactivity of their own and they are actually like primitive little movie clips with their own Timelines. A button can change its properties when a user clicks or rolls over it. In addition to the preassigned events associated with buttons (on (press), on (release), and so forth), actions can be attached to buttons that are associated with button events. That ActionScript will be executed when a predetermined event occurs. For example, when entering an elevator, there are several buttons. You could point at the button or talk to the button—both of which could be considered (odd) events. However, it is not until you press the button that the action—the elevator moving to the desired floor—will occur.

There are several standard events that can be associated with buttons in ActionScript. Events can be defined using the `on()` command, which is found in the Actions Toolbox, by clicking Actions | Movie Control | on. The `on()` command says, quite simply,

```
on (some event){
Do all this stuff
}
```

The standard events are listed in the Parameters section of the Actions panel. The following are the standard events:

- **Press**   This refers to clicking a button.

- **Release**   The event occurs when the mouse button is released. If the user drags off the object and releases the mouse button, the event will not occur.

- **Release Outside**   The event will occur if the user points at the object, clicks the mouse button, drags off the object, and releases the mouse button.

- **KeyPress**   If the KeyPress event is selected, the event occurs when a key specified in the parameters is pressed. This event allows designers to make keyboard shortcuts for different buttons within the Flash movie.

- **Roll Over**   The user moves the mouse over the object without pressing the mouse button.

- **Roll Out**   Similar to Roll Over, this event occurs when the user rolls over and then off a button with the mouse.

- **Drag Over**   Similar to Roll Over as well, but the mouse button must be depressed.

- **Drag Out**   Similar to Roll Out, but the mouse button must be depressed.

As depicted in Figure 12-3, you may elect to have multiple events associated with a single action. In the figure, the event `play()` will occur if the user either clicks the specified button or presses the letter G. Notice the check marks by both the Release and KeyPress events in the Parameters area. Also notice that the `on` action has two arguments.

```
on (release, keyPress "G") {
    play();
}
```

NOTE   *"Arguments" are parameters (in this case, the parameters of the event) that help define exactly what it is you want to happen to make the action (`play`) happen.*

12

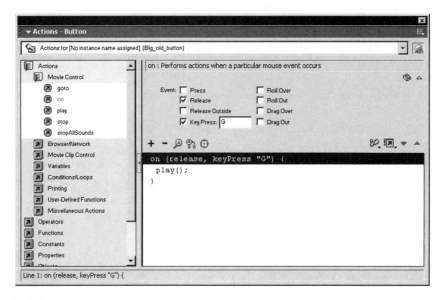

FIGURE 12-3   The Actions panel after two events have been associated with the `on` action

Someone with little knowledge of ActionScript should be able to determine what this class does. When the Release event occurs or the KeyPress "G" event occurs, the `play()` action will be executed, moving the movie to the next frame. The actions that will be executed when the specified event(s) occurs are always surrounded by French brackets.

Keep Track of Things: Variables and Operators

Variables are a common element in all programming languages. Variables are pieces of information that are temporarily stored in memory. These pieces of information, which you define, can be called by an event in the movie. Variables can be numerals, text, or even movie clips. Variables are assigned two different ways in Flash. Earlier in this book, you created a text input box, which was assigned a variable name. Later, that variable name was assigned to another text box. The text typed into the original input box was automatically generated in the text box with the same variable name. This is an example of how a variable works. The text displayed in the second text box would change, depending upon who typed in the information. This kind of variable is displayed "dynamically." In other words, it changes on-the-fly.

The second method of assigning a variable name is to assign the parameters of this variable in ActionScript. For example, the following code assigns the value 3 to the global variable `apples`:

```
apples = 3;
```

How to ... Create a User-Controlled Movie

Using just a few simple events, you can allow your movie viewers to occupy the driver's seat as they interact with the movie and determine when to move from one frame to another. At this point, the actual content of the frames is irrelevant. What is relevant is that the user will control when the movie moves on to the next frame. This example allows the user to move through a series of quotes at his or her own pace. This is accomplished through two buttons:

- Button one (First Quote) moves back to the first frame of the movie, regardless of the current frame number.

- The second button (Next Quote) allows the user to move to the next frame.

No man is an island

FIRST QUOTE   NEXT QUOTE

Here are all the steps:

1. Create a new Flash movie by clicking File | New. Right-click/CRTL-click the stage and select Document Properties. In the Document Properties dialog box, change the size of the movie to 400 pixels wide × 200 pixels high. Leave the other settings at their defaults and click OK.

2. Create three layers. Call the top layer **Actions**, the middle layer **Quotes**, and the bottom layer **Control Buttons**.

3. On the Actions layer, create keyframes (F6) at Frames 5, 10, 15, 20, 25, and 30.

4. In Frame 1 on the Quotes layer, create a text box, and, toward the top of the frame, enter your favorite quote. Make sure that Static Text is selected in the Properties panel. On this layer, also create keyframes at Frames 5, 10, 15, 20, 25, and 30.

12

| Actions | · | · | □ |
| Quotes | 🖉 | · | ■ |

5. On the Quotes layer, click Frame 5 to highlight the text in the text box you just created (the quote), and enter another quote so that a different quote appears in each frame. Repeat the process for Frames 10, 15, 20, 25, and 30.

6. Next, create the first button (Insert | Symbol) residing on the Control Buttons layer in Frame 1. Name this button **First Quote**. In Button Editing mode for this button, create two layers, the top one for text, the bottom one for the actual button. Use the rectangle tool to make the button on the bottom layer. On the top layer, use the Text tool to label the button **First Quote**. Exit Editing mode and put a keyframe on Frame 1 of the Control Buttons layer. Drag a copy of this button from the Library to Frame 1, Control buttons layer.

7. Click the First Quote button in the Library, and, in the Library options pop-up menu, select Duplicate. This will make a duplicate button. This is a great command because it does not duplicate the instance; it duplicates the button. Name the new duplicate **Next Quote**.

8. Double click the "Next Quote" button in the Library and change the text on this from "First Quote" to "Next Quote" to reflect the name of the new button. Now we have a totally different button generated from a duplicate. Drag a copy of this onto the stage on the Control buttons layer and align it to the right of the First Quote button. Your stage should look like this:

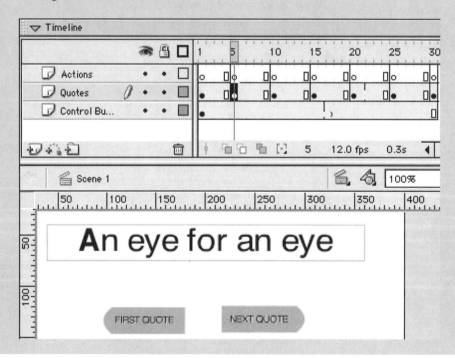

9. Now all the pieces are in place, and we're ready to assign the actions. On the Actions layer, click Frame 1, and, in the Actions panel Toolbox (Normal Mode), click Actions | Movie Control, and double-click `stop`. A `stop` action appears in the Actions list. Your script is being generated to the right of the Toolbox. Repeat this process in the Actions layer for Frames 5, 10, 15, 20, 25, and 30.

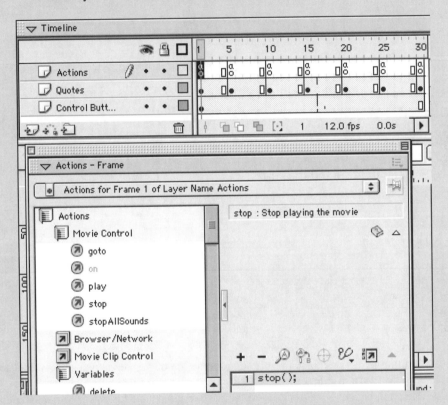

10. Now we will script the buttons. Click the Next Quote button, and, in the Actions panel Toolbox, click Actions | Movie Control, and double-click `play`. Click line 1 of the script, click Press, and deselect Release. The only difference between Press and Release is the Press event fires the action a little quicker than Release.

11. Now click the First Quote button, and, in the Actions Toolbox click Actions | Movie Control, and double-click `goto`. Make sure Go To And Play is checked at the top of the panel, and that Frame 1 is selected for frame. When the user presses this button it returns the framehead to Frame 1.

12. Test your movie. When you press the Next Quote button, the movie plays, but the stop action in the frames causes it to stop. It's actually a pretty simple concept, but ActionScript gets a lot more complex than this, as you will see in the next few chapters.

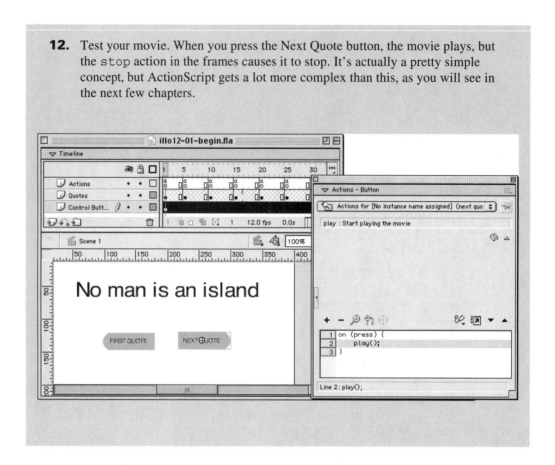

The value 3 will remain stored in apples throughout the life of the movie unless manipulated or changed later in the movie itself (see Figure 12-4)

The values stored in variables are designed to change over time, and this is why variables can be a very powerful tool in ActionScript. Think of playing a computer game that keeps score of your keystrokes. Your score varies depending upon how you interact with the game. Variables can be used for all sorts of interesting things in a script. For example, you could track the position of the mouse pointer and display the exact position in a text field, as you drag the mouse.

Naming variables within Flash is fairly simple. Variable names are not case sensitive, meaning APPLE and apple can be used interchangeably and are understood to be the same variable in Flash. However, it is recommended that you are consistent with capitalization as you assign and use variable names throughout ActionScript. Variable names must be one

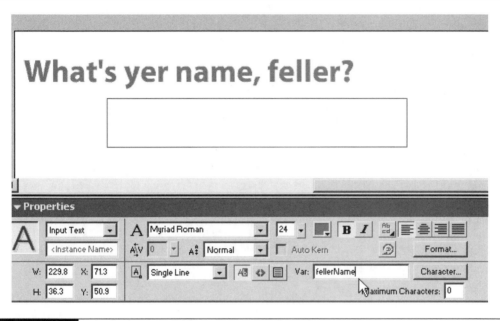

What's yer name, feller?

FIGURE 12-4   Assigning a variable name to a text input box

uninterrupted string, and reserved words—predefined ActionScript commands—cannot be used as variable names.

> **TIP** *It is a good idea to give your variables meaningful, easily recognizable names in your movie. Years ago, some programming languages forced programmers to use one- or two-letter combinations as variables. If you can recognize what the purpose of a variable is simply by looking at its name, it will make it easier to track down problems within the code later.*

Scope of a Variable

Variables can be local or global in scope. As you might guess, global variables are available throughout the life of the movie. You can access them in Frame 1 and Frame 1000. Local variables are recognized only within one statement in ActionScript. They are enclosed in the curly brackets you have seen generated in the code window. Outside of that statement, the local variable cannot be accessed.

To set a global variable in the Actions panel, in Normal mode, in the Actions Toolbox, click Actions | Variables | Set Variable. As shown in Figure 12-5, the parameters panel gives you two options. In the text box labeled Variable, type the variable name. In the Value box, type the value you want that variable to hold. Notice that next to both the Variable and Value text boxes is the Expression option. To determine whether or not the Expression check box needs to be selected, you need to understand the difference between strings and expressions.

Understanding Strings and Expressions

When you declare a variable in ActionScript, you are prompted to provide a variable name and value and indicate whether or not the variable is an expression. Incorrectly declaring variables is a major source of errors in ActionScript, since strings and expressions are processed differently in the code.

When left unselected, a variable is considered to be a text string. Strings in Flash refer to data comprised of text characters, numbers, quotation marks—anything that exists as pure text. For example, a name of a person or thing may be considered a string. String literals are distinguished from expressions by quotation marks surrounding the string. For example, the number "33" with quotes would be a string literal. One reason you might create a string would be to store information, such as a user's name and address if they are prompted to enter them while browsing your movie. The following code would assign a string to the variable Name:

```
Name="Millard Fillmore";
```

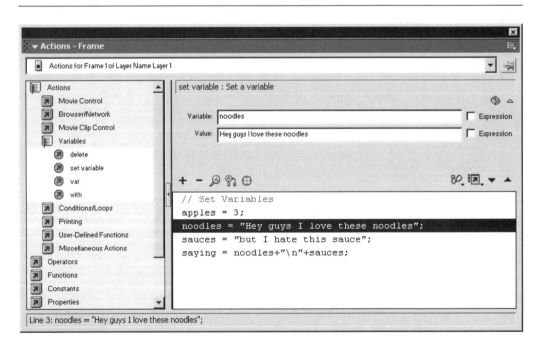

FIGURE 12-5   Assigning a global variable

Expressions serve a different purpose in ActionScript. Expressions can be a simple numerical value, or several elements connected by operators, which will be discussed at length next. The following are all variable assignment expressions:

```
//Expression sets the value of Apples to 3
Apples=3;
//Expression sets the PlayerScore to 27000
PlayerScore=27000;
//Expression sets the variable HighScore = to PlayerScore variable
HighScore=PlayerScore;
//Variable dinner is equivalent to the text in
Dinner= Spaghetti + Sauce;
```

NOTE *When you see "//" with text following it in ActionScript, the text following the slashes is a comment that is ignored by ActionScript and is there simply to document and make the code more understandable.*

NOTE *Even if it is string variables that are being manipulated by operators such as + or −, the variable declaration is still considered an expression. The only time it is not an expression is when a single test string is being assigned to a variable name, as in* `Name=Baba O'Reilly`*.*

Using Operators to Manipulate Values

You have already seen several examples of operators at work. Operators tie variable names and values together. The most common operator is =, which is often called as *assignment* operator because it assigns a value to a variable name. What makes variables powerful is the way they can be manipulated with operators. Other common operators include +, the addition operator; *, the multiplication operator; −, the subtraction operator; and /, the division operator. Some ActionScript users also frequently use ++ and − −, the increment and decrement operators, respectively. Here is an example of several operators in action:

```
//Take the value of Apples and add it to itself. Doubles the value of Apples
Apples=Apples+Apples;
//Divides the value of Apples by 15
Apples=Apples/15;
//Subtracts one from the value of Apples
Apples--;
```

In the next script, which also uses operators, the multiplication operator (*) is used. The * operator in this script is used to help define a variable. The variable z is multiplied with x by the number 2. In addition, a Trace action is added to the end of the script to test the results of adding two of the defined variables together. The Trace action helps you test a script to make certain it's working correctly. This is particularly helpful if you cannot see the results of your script when

12

you test the movie, as is the case in the following script. Let's see what the results are if we actually create the following script in Expert mode:

1. Display the Actions panel in Expert mode by going to the pop-up Options menu and selecting Expert.

2. Click the first frame of the Timeline, and then click in the Actions panel.

3. Type in the following script exactly as you see it:

```
x=3;
y=4;
z=x*2;
trace(x+z)
trace(z)
```

The Trace action is a quick way to test your script that couldn't otherwise be seen when you test the movie. If you want to see the results of the previous multiplication script from the Trace action, do the following:

4. Test the movie (CTRL-ENTER in Windows/CMD-ENTER on the Mac). An output window will display with the correct calculation. In this case, the calculation yields a number of 9 based upon the preceding script.

Although the preceding script is just a small sampling of how variables and operators can work together in a script, you can begin to see what powerful tools variables and operators are in ActionScript. Now let's take a look at some other basic concepts.

Manipulating Text with Operators and Escape Sequences

Text manipulation is one of the trickier tasks in any programming language. If you understand the difference between strings and expressions, it will help you when you try to manipulate text in ActionScript.

Often, you may need to take the value of two strings and add them together. For example, if users enter their first and last names in separate text boxes, represented by separate values, you may wish to connect the two values to make one variable that contains both the first and last names. This is known as *string concatenation*. It is accomplished through fairly simple code—the two variables would be added together using the + operator, which not only is the addition operator but also is the concatenation operator. In the following code, the value of `FullName` would be "General Tom Thumb." To test this script, display the Actions panel in Expert mode as we did in the previous section. Click the first frame in the Timeline and type the following code in the Actions panel:

```
Title="General";
First="Tom";
Last="Thumb";
FullName=Title + " " + First + " " + Last;
trace(FullName)
```

Notice the empty quotes that are added between Title, First, and Last. The purpose of these quotes is to add spaces in the string so that the text is not displayed as "GeneralTomThumb."

There are some characters that are not reproducible within a string. For example, a string can include a carriage return, but you can't type a carriage return between the quotes in the variable declaration. Instead, you must use an *escape* sequence. Escape sequences allow you to insert characters that you otherwise could not use in a string. Escape sequences are preceded by a backslash character. Some common escape codes include the following:

- ■ \f   Inserts a form feed.
- ■ \r   Inserts a carriage return.
- ■ \"   Inserts double quotes. This is necessary because if you typed the quote directly, it would be considered part of the string declaration syntax.
- ■ \t   Inserts a tab character.

Any escape sequence can be included in a string through concatenation. In the following example,

```
TopEightiesBands= "Journey" + "\r" + "Flock of Seagulls" + "\r" +
"Mister Mister";
```

a carriage return would be placed between Journey, Flock of Seagulls, and Mister Mister, displaying each on a separate line.

How to ... Call a Variable on a Frame and a Button Event

Variables are incredibly flexible, and you can use them in many different ways. You can set single or multiple variables on a button or a frame. You can use them to define a custom-made function and call that function at a later date. User-defined functions allow you to define a task (the function) and then call it any time you want in a script. In this section, we will set variables on the main Timeline and also on a button event.

Figure 12-6 displays a simple two-frame movie. When the movie loads, the user is asked to enter his or her name. This name is stored, and on the next frame (which is entered on a button event), the person's name is remembered. The user clicks a button to navigate to the next frame. The dynamic text field in this frame recalls the name the user typed in. In addition, there are two variables in this frame on a button event that calculate the variables scripted on the button in two dynamic text fields. Each time the user clicks the button to select the number of marbles he/she wants to buy, the Price text field calculates the price of the marbles. This is a simple movie, but it will help reinforce your understanding of variables.

To create a movie with variables on the main Timeline as well as on a button event, follow these steps:

1. Set up two layers. Name one layer **actions** and the other one **variables/buttons**.

2. On the variables/buttons layer, create some static text to explain how the movie functions. Type a line of text that says **Please enter your name**. In addition, place some static text on the left side of the screen showing where and what to input. In Figure 12-6, the top text says "First Name" and the bottom text says "Last Name."

3. Create two new text fields to the right of the labels. For both text fields, select Input as Text Type in the Properties Inspector. Input text allows the user to input text. In addition, select Single Line for Line type, since the user will only need to use one line for his/her first and last name (unless it's a very long name). Position one text field on top of the other. In the Properties Inspector, give the top text field a variable name of **first** and the bottom text field a variable name of **last**.

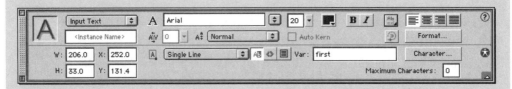

4. Place a button arrow in the bottom right of the stage; to the right of the button, place some static text to the left explaining what the button does. In Figure 12-6 (shown after this exercise), the text instructs the user to "Press the arrow to enter the site."

5. Now let's create the second frame. Put a keyframe in the second frame of the variables/buttons layer (F6).

6. On the top of Frame 2, layer 6, type a static **hello**. Continue to type the remainder of static text that instructs the user what to do as per the second frame in Figure 12-6. This includes **How many marbles would you like to buy today?**, **Click the button to select a number**, **Price @ $3.00 each**, **$**, and **Return**.

7. Drop a button to the right of the text that says "Click the button to select a number." Drop a button to the left of the word "Return."

8. Create a dynamic text field to the right of "Hello," and give it a variable name of **wholename**. Create another dynamic text field next to the "Click the button to select a number" button. Give it a variable name of **total**, Create a third dynamic text field to the right of "Price @ $3.00 each." Give it a variable name of **price**.

9. Now that all the pieces are in place, we can add the scripts. Click Frame 1, Actions layer; add a keyframe (F6), and display the Actions panel (F9) in Normal mode. In the Actions Toolbox, click the Actions folder and Movie Control folder, and then double-click `stop`. In the right of the Actions panel, the script will now read `stop();`. This will stop the frame from going to Frame 2

10. Put a keyframe on the Actions layer, Frame 2. Display the Actions panel in Normal mode and repeat the process outlined in the preceding step to add the `stop` action to this frame, too. With Line 1 of the script selected, in the Actions Toolbox, click the Actions Folder, click the Variables folder, and double-click `set variable`. In the Variable box, type **wholename**. This is the name of the text field we created at the top of this frame. For Value, type **first + " " + last**. Select the Expression check box. This defines the value of `wholename`, which is the sum of the two dynamic text fields on the first frame. Notice this is a concantenated string expression because it's two names being joined together. The " " will create a space between the sum of the two values. Don't forget to put a space between the " ".

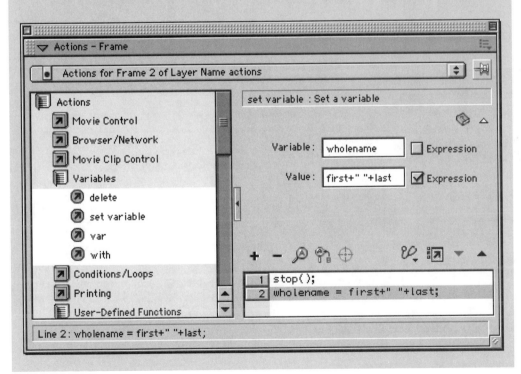

12

11. Now let's create the script on the button in the second frame. Click the button to the right of the "Click the button..." text and display the Actions panel in Normal mode. In the Actions Toolbox, click the Actions folder and the Variables folder, and double-click set variable two times. Click Line 2 of the script. For Variable, type **total**. For Value, type **total +1**. Select the Expression check box. Click Line 2 of the script. For Variable, type **price**. For Value, type **total *3**. Select the Expression check box. The Actions panel should look like this:

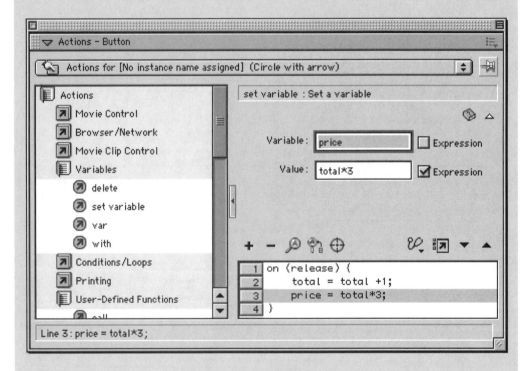

Let's review how this movie works so far. When the user clicks the arrow button ("Click the button..."), the text field variable, total, equals total plus the number 1. This variable keeps on counting each time the user presses the button and the result displays in the total text field. The price text field is the value of total * 3. The + and the * (multiplication) are operators that perform a mathematical function in this script. The calculation of the price variable (whose value is defined on the click of the mouse) is displayed in the price text field.

Now let's complete the script on the remaining two buttons in the movie.

12. Click the button in the bottom-right corner (Return) and display the Actions panel in Normal mode. In the Actions Toolbox, click Actions | Movie Control, and double-click `goto`. In the Actions panel, make sure the Go To And Play button is selected at the top of the panel. In the Frame box, type **1**. When this button is selected the framehead returns to Frame 1.

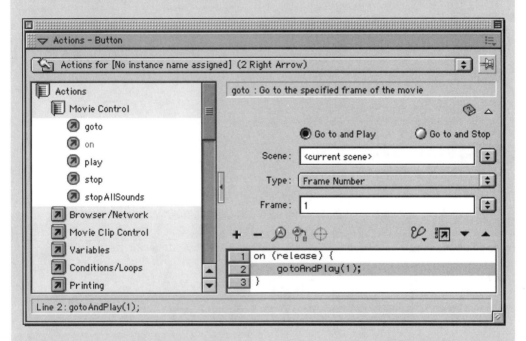

13. Click Frame 1 and select the button in the bottom right ("Press the arrow…"). Repeat the process in step 12, except for Frame, type **2**. When this button is clicked, the framehead will go to Frame 2.

12

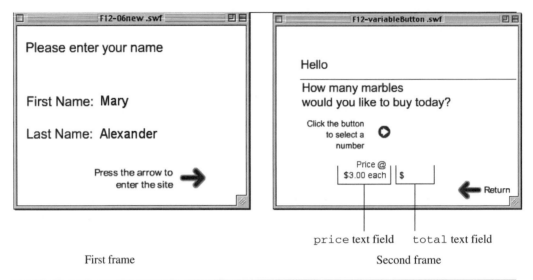

First frame

Second frame

FIGURE 12-6   A new variable has been added to a button to return the price of the total marbles the user selects.

In the next two chapters, we will take what we've learned in this chapter, expand on it, and start scripting frames and objects in Flash. Although this introduction to ActionScript barely touches the surface, it has prepared you with important concepts that will make it easier to understand more complex ActionScript syntax when you are ready to tackle it.

Chapter 13

ActionScript in Complex Interactions

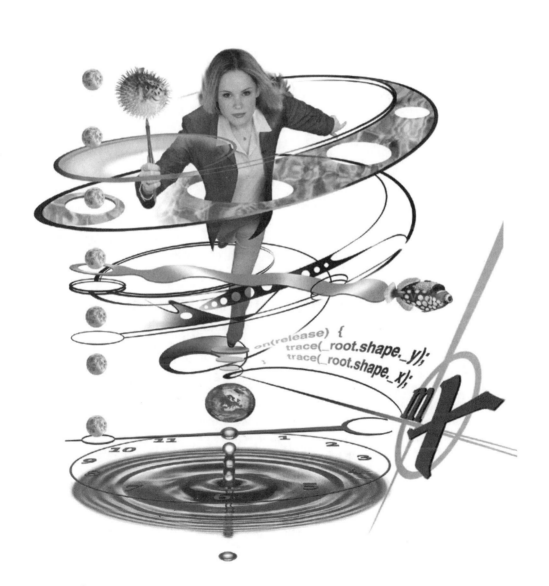

```
on(release) {
    trace(_root.shape._y);
    trace(_root.shape._x);
}
```

How to...

- Understand and use conditionals
- Create complex conditionals
- Use loops to repeat actions
- Store several data items in one variable with arrays
- Change the properties of objects
- Understand nested symbols
- Use the `with` action

The basics of ActionScript were covered in Chapter 12. The basic commands covered enable Flash movie producers to add quite a bit of interesting interactivity to their movies. However, there is so much more to ActionScript than just the few concepts covered so far.

In this chapter, we continue to develop our knowledge of programming structures in ActionScript.

We also examine how to access objects outside of the main movie Timeline. So far, we have looked only at objects in the main Timeline and attached scripting. Frame scripting allows control over movement between frames. Button scripting creates responses when a particular event occurs on a button symbol. Accessing symbols external to the main Timeline allows Flash authors complete control over their movies. So let's take our knowledge of ActionScript a step further and expand on it by studying some additional programming concepts.

More Programming Concepts with ActionScript

When learning to program, many find that no matter what particular language they are trying to master, there are always some basic concepts that need to be understood. One concept that exists across almost all programming languages is that of variables, which you will find mentioned and used many times throughout Parts III, IV, and V. Also among those universal programming concepts are conditionals, loops, and arrays, which we put to use in the last two parts of the book. All are powerful and necessary tools that will add versatility to your ActionScript bag of tricks.

Conditionals allow testing of logical conditions within a movie and react based on the result. For example, in a Flash movie game, if a player has reached a certain score, they may go to the next level of the game. If not, they continue on the same level. Loops allow repetition of code. If your movie calls for the same actions to be repeated ten times, it is not necessary to repeat the code ten times in a row. A simpler solution is to create a loop that executes the code ten separate times. Arrays are another important universal programming concept. Arrays allow the storage of multiple pieces of related information in one variable. As we explore these basic concepts in ActionScript, common examples of their usage will be explained and demonstrated.

Understand and Use Conditionals

The main purpose of conditional statements is to test for a logical condition, and then react based on whether that condition is found to be true or false. There are many examples of when the use of a conditional is necessary. Conditionals are used to evaluate users' input into a text box. Conditionals can be used to decide which path a movie should take, based on a user's preferences. Conditionals are also often used to test whether or not a user's inputs are within some predefined boundaries. The basic code for basic conditional statements looks like this:

```
If (condition in here is true){
    Do All this stuff};
```

Let's say that you have a text box in which you want the user to type his or her ZIP code. To keep things simple, we'll use the old-style five-digit ZIP codes only. There are several logical tests that can be applied to the numbers entered to see if the result is a legitimate ZIP code. Let's take a look at some plain-English pseudo-code:

```
If ZipCode (Does not Contain 5 Digits)
    {It's Not a Zip Code}
If ZipCode (Contains Letters)
    {It's Not a Zip Code}
If ZipCode (Contains punctuation)
    {It's Not a Zip Code}
```

NOTE   *Pseudo-code is a plain-English version of code that shows the logical steps that the code will execute, but does not represent the syntax of the actual programming language. Most people who read pseudo-code should be able to understand the logic, even if they do not know the actual programming language. Pseudo-code is commonly used as a preparation and planning step before actually writing code.*

In this example, if the user-entered ZIP code does not contain five digits, contains letters, or contains punctuation, logically, we know the user made some kind of error and the It's Not a Zip Code routine will be executed, which tells the user they made an error and need to reenter the information.

It's important to note that the conditionals test for a logical condition—a condition that can be either true or false. There is no gray area in conditions! These conditions usually come in the form of comparisons. For example, the most common type of comparison is to test whether the value of one variable is equivalent to the value of another. Comparison operators are different than mathematical operators, so you have to be aware of which one to use. The most common comparison operators are defined in Table 13-1.

In the Actions panel, the conditional statements are found either in the Toolbox or by selecting Actions | Conditions/Loops and then clicking the Add New Item button (see Figure 13-1). In this section, we're going to use the simple `if` command in the Conditions/Loops menu to create a simple guessing game. As you go through the example, carefully note how the conditional `if` statement is used to control the outcome of the game.

13

Comparison Operators	Results
Apples = = Oranges	Tests equality. The value of Apples is equivalent to the value of Oranges.
Apples != Oranges	Tests inequality. The value of Apples is not equivalent to the value of Oranges. ! is the logical NOT operator.
Apples > Oranges	The value of Apples is greater than the value of Oranges.
Apples >= Oranges	The value of Apples is greater than or equal to the value of Oranges.
Apples < Oranges	The value of Apples is less than the value of Oranges.
Apples <= Oranges	The value of Apples is less than or equal to the value of Oranges.

TABLE 13-1   Common Comparison Operators Used in ActionScript

So far, with simple conditionals, we can only test for one logical condition. If that condition is true, one thing happens. If the condition is not true, something else happens. In the next section, we'll create conditionals that will allow testing for several conditions.

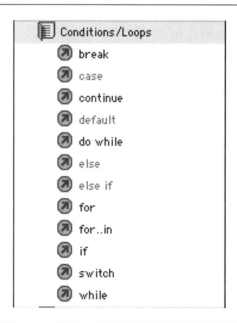

FIGURE 13-1   The Conditions/Loops in the Actions panel can be used to create simple or more complex conditionals.

Create a Simple Guessing Game Using a Conditional

This simple guessing game prompts the user to guess a number from 1 to 10 and enter it into the provided input text box. This little game will provide you with a quick introduction on how to use conditionals. We will use them again in Chapter 14 to do another type of game that's a little more sophisticated.

Let's examine how this game works. There are only two frames in this movie, and this next illustration depicts the first frame.

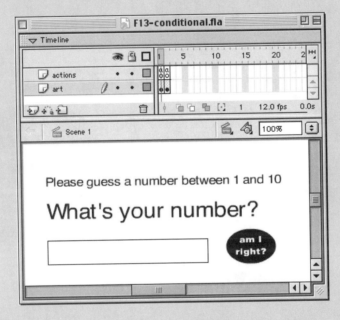

When the first frame loads, the user is prompted to enter his or her special number between 1 and 10 in the text input field provided. When the user clicks the button, if he or she guesses the right number (which is 5), the playhead goes to the next frame and displays a message that says "That's Right!" If the user guesses the wrong number, the playhead goes to Frame 2 and the message reads "Wrong Answer." Also, if the user guesses wrong, he or she can click Guess Again on the second frame to return to the beginning of the game.

The input text box on Frame 1 is assigned the variable name of "guess." The value of guess is then compared to the correct result, which is the number 5. The playhead then moves to Frame 2 and the dynamic text field, and the variable will either reflect the right or wrong answer by displaying the appropriate text.

In this file, conditionals and variables are used, as well as the setProperty action, which is used on a button script. The setProperty action allows you to change the property on an object. You can change properties like width, height, and X and Y coordinates. In this script, the visibility of the button on the second frame disappears if the condition returns true. Let's walk through the steps involved in making this game:

1. Create a new Flash File and make the document size 400 width × 200 pixels in the Document Properties dialog box. Make two layers in the Timeline and name the first one **actions** and the second one **art**.

2. Now, make the assets for the movie. Make two buttons. In the Button Editing mode of the first button (which will go on the first frame), type **am I Right?** On the other button, type **Guess Again** (which will go on the second frame) on the top of the button.

3. On the art layer, let's begin to build the movie. Type in some static text as per the first illustration. The first line should read "Please guess a number between 1 and 10." The second static text box should read "What's your number?" This static text is strictly for the purpose of instructing the user what to do.

4. To finish up the first frame, on the art layer, make an Input text box under the instructions "What's your number?" Click this Input text field and, in the Properties Inspector, give this Input text field a Variable name of **guess**. Now, drop an instance of the Am I Right? button to the right of the stage on the first frame, so the user can click this to find out if he or she guessed the right answer.

5. On the art layer, insert a keyframe on Frame 2 (F6). Now we'll build a second frame. In Frame 2, create a Dynamic text field in the middle of the stage. In the Properties Inspector, set the font, text size, and alignment, and select Dynamic from the Text type pop-up. Drag an instance of the Guess Again button underneath it. Give the Dynamic text field a Variable name of **answer**.

6. In Frame 2, click the Guess Again button; and in the Properties Inspector, give this button an instance name of **guessButton**. Since buttons are objects, if they have instance names, you can talk to them just like you can talk to movie clips.

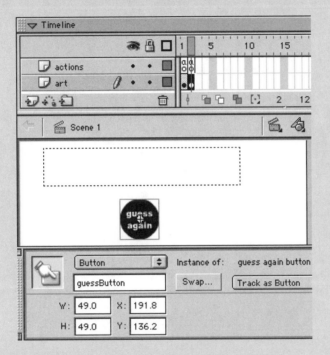

7. Return to the first frame, Actions layer, and display the Actions panel. Add a keyframe to this frame (F6). In the Actions Toolbox, click Actions I Movie Control, and double-click `stop`. Click Frame 2 of the actions layer and repeat the process so there are two stop actions on both frames.

8. Now let's script the buttons. On Frame 1, click the Am I Right? button. In the Actions panel Toolbox, select Actions I Movie Control, and double-click `goto`. Click line 2 of the script; and for Frame, type **2**. Make sure the Go To And Play button is selected. This will send the playhead to Frame 2 when the button is clicked. Now for the conditional statements. Click line 2 of the script; and in the Actions

Toolbox, select Actions | Conditions/Loops and double-click if. For Condition, type
guess==5. With line 3 selected, in the Actions Toolbox, click Actions | Variables,
and double-click set variable. For Variable, type **answer**. For Value, type
That's Right!. With line 4 selected, in the Actions Toolbox, select Actions | Movie
Clip Control, and double-click setProperty. For Property, select _visible.
For Target, type **guessButton**. For Value, type **False**. Select the Expression check
box for both Variable and Value. With line 5 selected, in the Actions Toolbox, select
Actions | Conditions/Loops, and double-click else. With line 6 selected, in the
Actions Toolbox, select Actions | Variables, and double-click set variable. For
Variable, type **answer**. For Value, type **Wrong Answer!** The Expression check
boxes are not selected here. The finished script for the Am I Right? button should
look like this:

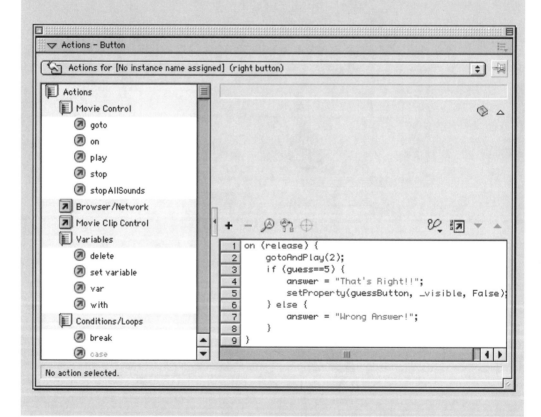

9. Now we need to script the Guess Again! button on Frame 2. Go to Frame 2 and select this button. In the Actions panel Toolbox | Actions | Movie Control, double-click `goto`. Select line 2; and for Frame, type **1**. Make sure Go To And Play is selected at the top of this box. Click line 1, click the Press button, and deselect the Release button. You are now done.

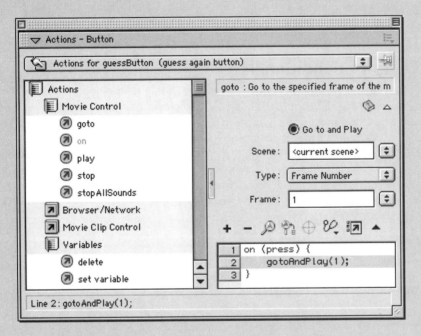

Test the movie to make sure it works. The bulk of the script is on the Am I Right? button in Frame 1. In this script, the first conditional (`if`) declares that if the Input text field variable, "guess" (on Frame 1), is equal to the number 5, then the Dynamic text field (whose variable is named "answer") will say "That's Right!" Also, the button you gave an instance name of "guessButton" to becomes invisible. With a `setProperty` action, the visibility is declared `false`.

13

10. The `else` statement gives an alternative solution. When the `if` statement returns false, the Dynamic text field whose variable name is "answer" (Frame 2) has a value of "Wrong Answer!" This text string is returned in the text field. As you can see, this is an easy exercise, and it gives you a solid demonstration of how you can use conditionals. In addition, it introduces the `setProperty` action, which allows you to alter the properties of objects.

Create Complex Conditionals

Frequently, Flash movies are complex enough to require testing for multiple conditions. That's where the `else` and `else if` commands come in. Complex conditional statements require a bit more planning to get the correct result. Once you get the knack of using them, however, you will find that they are an absolute necessity in any programmer's toolkit.

Complex conditionals are similar to simple conditionals. They test for logical conditions and use comparison operators. It is often a good idea to map out the logical path that complex conditions follow to avoid improper nesting, which occurs when programmers lose track of which conditions refer to specific results within a complex conditional statement.

Consider this code example:

```
on (release) {
 {
        gotoAndPlay(5);
    } else if (grade >= 80) {
        gotoAndPlay(10);
    } else if (grade >= 70) {
        gotoAndPlay(15);
    } else if (grade >=60) {
        gotoAndPlay(20);
    } else if (grade >0 and grade <60){
        gotoAndPlay(25);}
    else {
        gotoAndPlay(30);}
}
```

Upon examining the code, you can see that there is a logical path that the statements follow. In this script, the first `if` statement (`if (grade <= 100 and grade >= 90)`) tests to see if the grade is both less than or equal to 100 and greater than or equal to 90. If both of those conditions are met, the movie moves to Frame 5 (gotoAndPlay(5);), which, in this example, informs the user that they received a grade of "A." The logical path of the statements continues as the conditions for a grade of "B," "C," "D," and "F" are tested. (See Figure 13-2 for an example.) The statement is completed by the `else` statement, which states that if none of the above conditions are met, the movie should move to Frame 30, which informs the user that they made an error and need to enter a numerical grade between 0 and 100. This `if` series works because

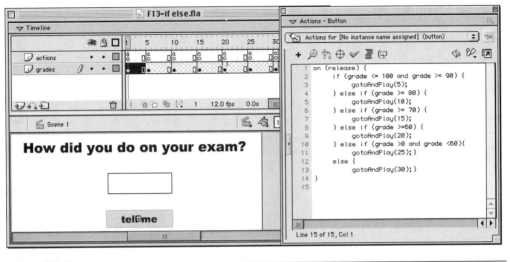

The following is an approximation of the code shown in the Actions panel in the figure:

```
on (release) {
    if (grade <= 100 and grade >= 90) {
        gotoAndPlay(5);
    } else if (grade >= 80) {
        gotoAndPlay(10);
    } else if (grade >= 70) {
        gotoAndPlay(15);
    } else if (grade >=60) {
        gotoAndPlay(20);
    } else if (grade >0 and grade <60){
        gotoAndPlay(25); }
    else {
        gotoAndPlay(30); }
}
```

FIGURE 13-2 This movie uses nested if statements on a button event to determine the letter grade earned based on a numerical entry.

every possible condition for receiving a grade is anticipated. Also, in this example, if the user types anything other than a numerical grade between 0–100, an error will be displayed.

TIP *One of the more difficult things to anticipate is the type of errors that a user may make. It is best to always provide code that tests what users type into a text input box to ensure that the entry is valid.*

Use Loops to Repeat Actions

Loops are commonly used by programmers to repeat an action or series of actions a finite and predetermined number of times. Loops have hundreds of uses in programming. Loops can be used to load a series of variables with values; to repeat an action a number of times; or, in Flash, to repeat animations. There are four basic kinds of loops in Flash, but they all have the same function:

- `while` loops
- `do...while` loops
- `for` loops
- `for...in` loops

Although all the loops have the same function, it's often best to plan which type is best for the individual situation in which it's being put to use.

Examine while Loops

while loops do something while a certain condition is true. The general syntax looks like this:

```
while (some condition is true){
Do all this stuff
}
```

while loops are usually set up with a local counter variable, which is used for the purpose of determining how many iterations the loop should execute. Typically, this variable is set to the upper limit of the count, and then the count is incremented within the loop itself.

Open a new file and display the Actions panel in Expert mode. Add a keyframe to the first frame, and then type the following code:

```
var X=0;
 while (x<101){
     airplane._alpha=x;
     x=x+1;
      trace(x);
}
```

When you're done typing this, test the movie and see what happens in the Output box, as shown in Figure 13-3. You can actually see the while loop in action. The variable x is used as a counter. It is first initialized (when the movie enters the first frame) at zero. The while statement will continue to execute until x is greater than or equal to 101. When that occurs, the loop will stop executing. With each iteration, the _alpha property of the symbol airplane is set to the value of the current iteration and the value of the counter is increased by one.

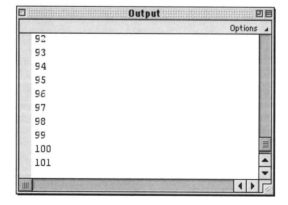

FIGURE 13-3   The Output window results from a script using a while loop

do...while Loops

do...while loops are very similar to `while` loops. The difference between the two, besides syntax, is that the statements within the loop structure must be executed at least once. The general syntax places the condition after the statements that are executed in each iteration of the loop:

```
do{
    All this stuff}
while (this is true);
```

Notice that the do statements occur before the `while` condition. This ensures that the do statements are executed at least once, unlike the `while` loop.

If we take the script from Figure 13-3 and adjust it slightly, we can use a do...while loop and achieve almost identical results. Open another new file and display the Actions panel in Expert mode. Add a keyframe to the first frame and type the following code:

```
var X=0;
 do{
     airplane._alpha=x;
     x=x+1;
        trace(x);
}while (x<101);
```

When you're done typing this, test the movie and see what happens in the Output box. You will notice that the results of this script are identical to the results of the other script using just the `while` action. The only difference between the two is the manner in which the code is executed. In other words, in a do...while loop, the `while` is checked at the end of the script instead of the beginning of the script, as opposed to the `while` action, where it's checked in the beginning of the script. Although the do...while action is equally as useful as the `while` action, most programmers tend to use the `while` action because it's common to other programming languages. The do...while action, on the other hand, is exclusive to ActionScript. As a result, it's easier for them to remember the more commonly used `while` action.

for Loops and for...in Loops

The `for` loop is a compact loop structure. The `for` loop only requires one action, instead of two or three as is found in other loop structures. While it is a little harder to learn at first, the `for` loop is frequently chosen by ActionScript developers because it's easy to make changes to and, if necessary, debug.

The general structure of the `for` loop is as follows:

```
for (initialization, condition, increment){
    this stuff occurs until the condition in the for loop is met
};
```

13

The initialization declares and sets a beginning value for the counter variable. The condition is the logical statement that determines how many iterations the loop goes through. The increment increases the counter.

 It is possible to create a loop that never meets the condition for stopping the loop iterations. Known as an "endless loop," this type of error can cause the Flash Projector to lock up.

The `for...in` loop is the most complex type. It allows you to create a loop that executes until a certain property within an object has a particular value.

Store Multiple Data Items in One Variable with Arrays

Another important ActionScript concept are arrays. Arrays allow related lists of information to be stored within one variable. So far, the code we've used stores one value in a single variable name. The value can change over time, but it is designed so only a single value is stored. Employing arrays is efficient and allows access to the methods of the array object, which can be useful for manipulating the individual data points stored within the array object.

The code to declare an array is fairly straightforward. The array object must be used, and the list of values stored within the array must be declared. The following code is an example of storing values in an array. Try typing this code in the Actions panel in Expert mode and test the movie. The `trace` action allows you to test the movie by displaying the results in an output window:

```
var oldTelevision = new Array ("Facts of Life", "Growing Pains", "Magnum
PI", "Punky Brewster");
trace(oldTelevision);
```

The output window will display the following:

```
Facts of Life, Growing Pains, Magnum PI, Punky Brewster
```

Each item in the array is accessed by its position. The first item in the array is in position zero. The first item is always zero. In the above code, "Punky Brewster" has an index position of three, since it's the third entry. The value of the third index position in the array could be changed without disturbing the other values, by using the following code:

```
oldTelevision[3]= "Different Strokes";
```

There are two different ways you can display an array. When you display the position of the array in between brackets, as is done in the above code example, it allows you to treat the array almost as if it were in a table or a spreadsheet (`oldTelevision = new Array ("Facts of Life", "Growing Pains", "Magnum PI", "Punky Brewster") ;`).

Let's take a look at another example of how the previous code could be executed. Try to type it in the Actions panel in Expert mode and test it in the browser:

```
var OldTelevision=new Array
OldTelevision [0]=" Facts of Life";
OldTelevision [1]=" Growing Pains";
OldTelevision [2]=" Magnum PI";
OldTelevision [3]=" Punky Brewster";
trace(oldTelevision);
```

As you can see, the trace results outcome is identical to the first method.

Arrays are often used in games or on sites that require extensive storage of multiple values that will ultimately yield an outcome of some sort (see Figure 13-4).

Tracing is a cool way to test a script, but it does nothing more than check your script to see if it's working correctly. The trace does not actually become part of the movie. It merely serves as a testing device that programmers use during the development stage. We have just been experimenting with bits and pieces of scripts. There comes a time, though, when you

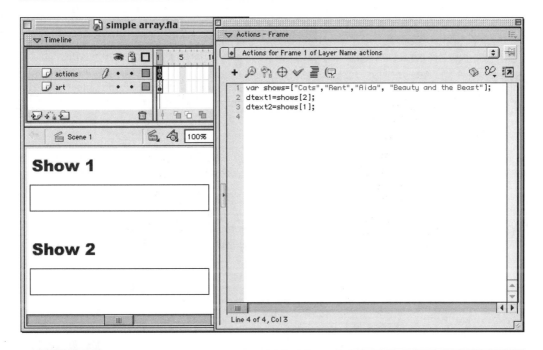

FIGURE 13-4   Code that loads several values into an array and then displays two specific items for the array in Dynamic text boxes

eventually have to build a functional movie using movie clips and text fields. In Chapter 14, we will actually build an array to create a menu that can be easily modified, simply by changing the elements stored in the array. Then all the pieces of the ActionScript puzzle will start falling into place for you.

Controlling Movie Clips

Movie clips are perhaps one of the most versatile objects in ActionScript. Imagine the ability to control another movie clip within a movie clip, and so on, with any number of actions. If you're familiar with HTML, you probably know about "absolute" versus "relative" addressing. Addressing in HTML simply relates to where things (other HTML pages, graphics, and plug-ins) are located in relation to one another both locally and on a remote server. In other words, the path of a page must be clearly defined before a page can display. Otherwise, you get one of those messages we have all seen that the page can't be found. In the case of a graphic, you see a blank space with an "x." This can be very embarrassing for the web designer if this occurs.

In ActionScript, movie clips have a hierarchy just like in HTML. If you tell a nested movie clip to do something, the action won't work if the movie clip can't be located. So Flash, like HTML, uses absolute and relative addressing (or paths) to solve the problem of locating the path of an instance within a movie.

With an absolute path, the path always goes to the root level of the movie. Absolute paths in Flash go all the way up to the root and work their way down. As in HTML, absolute paths spell out the complete path of an object. Where HTML uses a slash syntax to define paths, Flash uses a dot syntax. An absolute path in ActionScript looks like this:

```
_root.Mainmov.face.eye
```

The first structure, `_root`, refers to the very top level of the movie. The remainder of the path follows the movie's hierarchy to get to the instance of the symbol eye within the instance of the symbol face, in the Mainmov instance.

 When creating absolute paths, be careful that you do not change the movie hierarchy, once the paths are established. If changes are made, the paths could become invalid, causing errors. Similarly, if you gave someone directions to your car and then moved your car, the directions would be invalid.

A relative path has a particular starting point within the movie, identified by the `this` statement. When you see the `this` statement, the relative path refers to the object on which the script is written.

```
onClipEvent (load)
this.startDrag(lockCenter, 100,100,200 500) ();
```

Control Nested Movie Clips in ActionScript

In Chapter 6, we discussed the concept of nesting symbols within symbols to create a more compact type of symbol. Let's take a look at controlling movie clips nested in movie clips. In the clock represented in Figure 13-5, we are able to control the Timeline of a movie clip that is on the Timeline of another movie clip from a button on the main Timeline. Sounds confusing, doesn't it? Actually when you examine the script, it's really quite simple. Nesting and controlling movie clips just involves a little organization.

In the clock movie, the Stop and Go buttons control the stop and play of the littlehand_mc instance called "little." The littlehand_mc is nested in the ticks_mc movie clip. Nesting is an important concept in Flash because it demonstrates how powerful movie clips can be when they can be addressed from a part in a movie. Let's examine how to create this movie (see Figure 13-6).

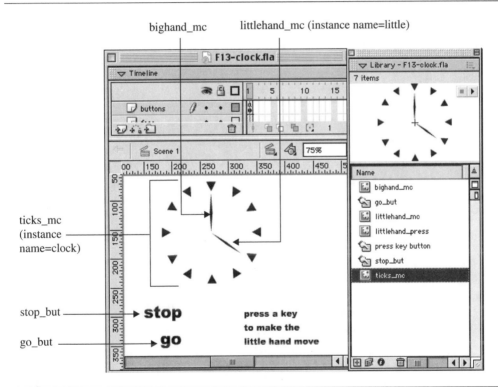

FIGURE 13-5   A clock movie clip that's passing time is controlled on a button event

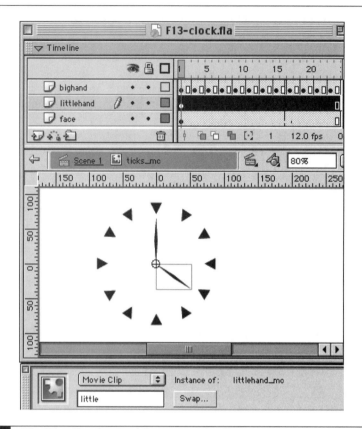

FIGURE 13-6   The Timeline for the ticks_mc movie clip

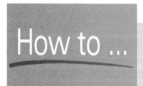 **Control a Nested Movie Clip with a Button Event**

In a movie such as Figure 13-5, where you have a lot of assets, you need to plan and create the assets up front.

1. First, build the ticks_mc movie clip. Insert a new movie clip symbol, and in movie clip editing mode, create three layers in the following order: bighand, littlehand, and face. On the face layer, make the tick marks for the clock and arrange them in a circle as per Figure 13-6. Then exit editing mode.

2. On the main Timeline, make three buttons. One needs to say "stop," another needs to say "go," and the third button should say "press a key to make the little hand move." (You can guess what these buttons do by the names they have been assigned.) Drag these buttons from the Library onto the buttons layer in the main Timeline. Drag an instance of the ticks_mc movie clip onto the face layer in the main Timeline, too.

3. In the Library or in the main Timeline, double-click the ticks_mc movie clip to enter the clips editing mode. On the littlehand layer, make an object that looks like a little hand of a clock on Frame 1 and group it. On the bighand layer, Frame 1, make an object that looks like the big hand of a clock and group it. Click the little hand in Frame 1 and click F8. In the Convert To Symbol dialog box, select Movie Clip, and give the little hand a name of **littlehand_mc** and a registration of top center. Repeat the process for the big hand, naming it **bighand_mc**. Now you can see the movie clip begin to take shape.

4. Now that the two movie clips are nested in the ticks_mc movie clip, we will animate the littlehand_mc on its own Timeline. In the Library, double-click the littlehand_mc. In movie clips editing mode, create an additional layer and name it **actions**. Make sure the head of the hand is touching the cross hairs in editing mode, as in the following illustration. This way, when the hand rotates around the tick marks, it will rotate around the clock from the top of the hand instead of the middle of the hand. We need to animate the hand so it appears to fall on the ticks on the ticks_mc movie clip just like a real clock. Exit the editing mode of littlehand_mc and return to Timeline of ticks_mc.

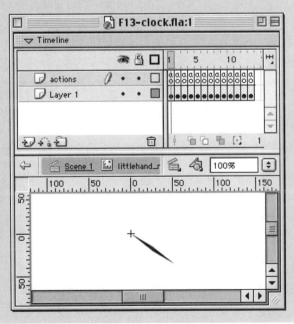

13

5. In the ticks_mc Timeline, double-click the littlehand_mc to enter the editing mode of this hand. Why did we exit littlehand_mc editing mode before when we intended to edit more? Because we couldn't see the ghost of the ticks_mc movie clip in the background as we can now. When you double-click an instance to enter its editing mode, whatever is already on the stage acts as an onion skin to help guide you when you animate. We need to see the ticks so that when we rotate the little hand, we know how far to rotate it, as shown here.

6. On Layer 1 in the littlehand_mc Timeline, insert keyframes on Frames 2 through 13. Now return to each frame and rotate the littlehand_mc so it stops on each one of the tick marks whose ghost image you can see on the parent movie clip, ticks_mc. You can use either the Free Transform Rotate tool to do so, or the (Modify | Transform) Scale And Rotate dialog box and type rotation percentages in the dialog box.

7. On the actions layer in littlehand_mc editing mode, click Frame 1 and display the Actions panel in Normal mode. Insert a keyframe on Frame 1; and in the Actions panel Toolbox; click Actions | Movie Control, and then double-click Stop. Repeat this on each frame until Frame 12. On the last frame (Frame 13), add a keyframe, click the Actions Toolbox, Actions | Movie Control, and double-click `goto`. For Frame, type **1**. On the top right of the panel, click Go To And Stop. The second line of code on this movie clip will now read `gotoAndStop(1);`. Now, all frames in the littlehand_mc have a stop action. The frames on this movie clip can only play if they are instructed to do so in a script, which we will add on a button event in a later step. Exit editing mode for the littlehand_mc by clicking to the left on the ticks_mc icon in the top of the stage. You will now be in ticks_mc editing mode. In ticks_mc editing mode, make certain the registration point on the little hand is in the middle of the ticks_mc clock. As mentioned previously, it will appear as if the hand is ticking around the clock when it rotates.

8. In ticks_mc editing mode, double-click bighand_mc. In editing mode for this movie clip, make sure the head of the hand is on the registration cross hairs in editing mode. Exit editing mode for bighand_mc by clicking the ticks_ mc icon in the top left of the stage; and in ticks_mc editing mode, place the big hand so the head and the registration point is in the middle of the ticks_mc movie clip.

9. On the bighand layer in ticks_mc editing mode, insert keyframes on frames 3, 5, 7, 9, 11, 13, 15, 17, 19, 21, and 23, and place a regular frame of Frame 24 (F5). Insert a frame (F5) on Frame 24 on both the face layer and the littlehand layer. Now, click Frame 1 in the bighand layer and use the Free Transform Rotate tool to rotate the big hand to Frame 3. Repeat this process for all the keyframes you created on this layer. Turn on onion skinning so you can see where your rotation is going. Note that we are rotating the bighand_mc in the ticks_mc Timeline. The littlehand_mc, on the other hand, was rotated on its own Timeline.

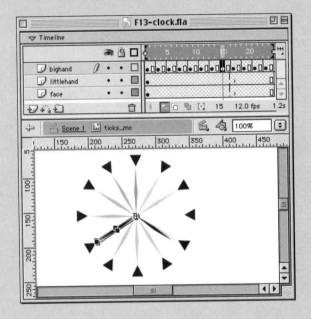

10. To finish up the ticks_mc movie clip while still in ticks_mc editing mode, click littlehand_mc and, in the Properties Inspector, give the movie clip an instance name of **little**. Exit ticks_mc editing mode. Since littlehand_mc now has an instance name, we can control its Timeline from anywhere in this movie.

11. On the main Timeline, click the ticks_mc movie clip; in the Properties Inspector, give it an instance name of **clock**.

12. On the main Timeline, we can now script the three buttons that will control this movie. Click the Stop button and display the Actions panel in Normal mode. In the Actions Toolbox, click Actions | Variables, and double-click with. Click the Object box and click the Insert Target Path button. In the Insert Target Path dialog box, click Relative mode, select clock as the object, and click OK, as shown next. The with action allows you to instruct an instance to perform multiple tasks without having to repeatedly refer to the name of the instance. With line 2 selected, in the Actions Toolbox, select Actions | Movie Control and double-click stop. This instructs

13

the clock instance to stop when this button is clicked. The script on this button is now complete.

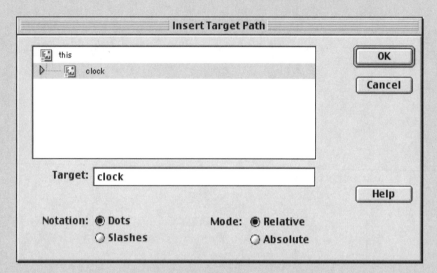

13. Click the Go button and, in the Actions panel Toolbox, select Actions | Variables, and double-click with. Click in the Object box, and repeat the process from step 12 to get the name of the object (Insert Target Path button). Click line 2; and in the Actions Toolbox, click Actions | Movie Control, and double-click play. When this button is clicked, the clock instance will play.

14. Click the Press A Key To Make The Little Hand Move button; and in the Actions Toolbox, select Actions | Variables, and double-click with. Click in the Object box again, and click the Insert Target Path button. In the Insert Target path dialog box, select Absolute for Mode, click the expanding arrow, and click Little. The Target box will now read "_root.clock.little." Click OK. This is the path of the little instance from the main Timeline. With line 2 selected, in the Actions panel Toolbox, select Actions | Movie Control and double-click goto. For Type, select Next Frame. Select line 1, click Key Press, and deselect Release. Click in the box to the right of Keypress, and press the RIGHT ARROW key. The code <Right> will now appear in the box and in the script. When the user presses the RIGHT ARROW, he or she can now control the little hand of the clock. The finished script on this button looks like the next illustration.

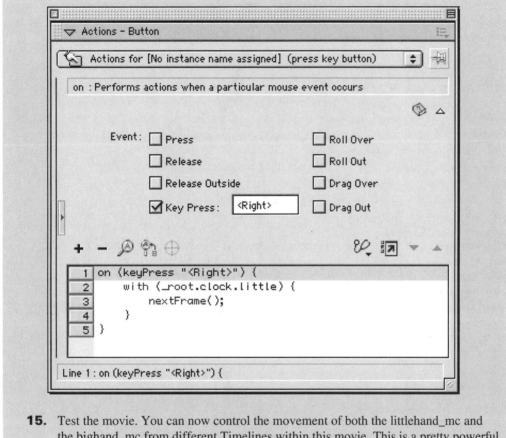

15. Test the movie. You can now control the movement of both the littlehand_mc and the bighand_mc from different Timelines within this movie. This is a pretty powerful concept in ActionScript. With this knowledge, you can create extremely complex interactivity in Flash.

13

Changing the Properties of Objects

As discussed in the preceding chapter, every object in a Flash movie has properties. Many of these properties can be set in the Properties panel as the object moves through various frames in the movie. Frequently, the properties of objects change as the movie progresses. A motion tween on an object changes the X and Y position properties, and possibly the rotation property.

Changing the properties of an object (movie clip instance) using ActionScript allows the use of variables and user input to define the properties of objects. This is most often done using the `setProperty()` method. The `setProperty()` method has a standard syntax:

```
setProperty(Property, Target, Value);
```

The first argument, or parameter, that appears within the parenthesis, `Property`, requires that you select which property is to be changed. Table 13-2 contains a list of commonly used properties. The second parameter, `Target`, allows you to select the object that the property will be applied to. The third parameter, `Value`, is either the numerical value or the variable containing the value that the property will be set to.

In Figure 13-7, the `setProperty()` method is used to position a ball. The instance of the ball being moved is named `ball`. The `_x` and `_y` in each of the `setProperty()` methods are the properties being adjusted. When the movie is tested and the button is clicked, the ball moves to the `_x` and `_y` parameters indicated within the parenthesis of the `setProperty()` method. In addition, the `xpos` and `ypos` are the variable names of two Dynamic text fields that display the exact `_x` and `_y` positions of the ball after it moves on the button event. The cross hairs on the stage represents the X and Y position that the ball will relocate to after the button event occurs.

Another important method that addresses the properties of an object is the `getProperty()` method. Similar to the `setProperty()` method, it returns the value of the selected property

Propherty	Function
`_alpha`	Transparency of an object. A 0 value means the object is completely transparent; 100 refers to a completely opaque object.
`_currentframe`	Current frame of a movie clip.
`_framesloaded`	Number of frames currently loaded in a movie clip. Used commonly for preloaders.
`_height`	Height of an object.
`_width`	Width of an object.
`_x`	Horizontal position of an object.
`_y`	Vertical position of an object.
`_xmouse`	Horizontal position of the mouse.
`_ymouse`	Vertical position of the mouse.

TABLE 13-2   Commonly Used Properties Accessible Through the `setProperty()` Method

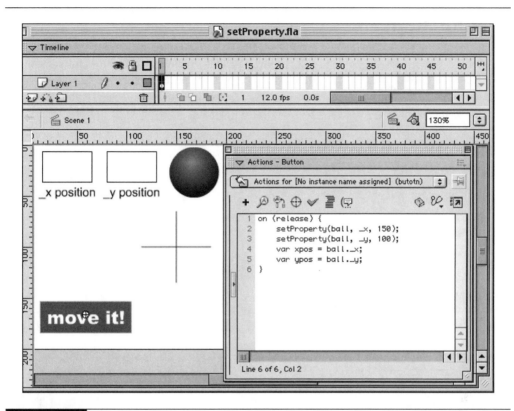

FIGURE 13-7   The setProperty() method used to change the position of a target object

for the target object. When using this method, it is necessary to define the object and property that are to be displayed. The general syntax is as follows:

```
getProperty(target,property);
```

To get the _alpha value of an object called happyFace, you would use the following syntax:

```
getProperty(happyFace,_alpha);
```

which would return a value between 1 and 100 because the _alpha property can be set on a movie clip in between that span of numbers.

The getProperty() and setProperty() methods are invaluable in making instances within a movie dynamic. We will be using both of these methods several times in Chapters 14 and 15.

Detect a Collision

Detecting a collision refers to a movie clip either colliding with another object or ending up in a position on the stage indicated as a hit test. The `hitTest()` method is often used for games. For example, you have probably seen games—like asteroids or Space Invaders—where you shoot at something, and when a bomb hits a target, the asteroid or alien blows up. The hit target in this case would be an asteroid or an alien, and the bomb is the object that hits the target, causing something else to occur.

The syntax for the `hitTest()` method is as follows:

```
MovieclipName.hitTest(target);
```

You can also configure the `hitTest` to hit an X and Y coordinate instead of colliding with a hit target. The syntax for that would be as follows:

```
MovieClipName.hitTest(x, y, shapeFlag)
```

The `_x` and `_y` properties refer to the registration point of object to object. The `ShapeFlag` is a value that returns `True` or `False`. `True` refers to the two objects intersecting at their registration point (X and Y coordinate) based on their true shapes. `False` refers to the shapes intersecting based on their bounding boxes. In other words, if you were to picture an invisible rectangle around the objects (their bounds), the hit test would be based upon the boundaries of this object.

The `hitTest` method is almost always used with conditional statements. In the next How To, we will examine a movie that combines some of the Actions | conditions, and methods we have covered in this chapter so far, in addition to a couple of new tricks.

Let's examine how the movie works before we take a look at how to make it. Figure 13-8 displays a checkerboard highway background with a pink car in the upper-left corner. This is a game of sorts. The object is to move the car in the upper-left corner to the bottom-right corner without getting a flat tire. Buried within the checkered background are little movie clip instances named "mines." When the car collides with one of the mines, the movie clip instance of mines plays. The mines consist of a little animated circle and a noise like a blowout that sounds when the car collides with one. In other words, when the car makes contact with a mine, the mine appears to explode.

FIGURE 13-8   This movie uses the `hitTest` method to create a collision between the car and invisible mines within the movie.

Let's take a look at how to make this movie in the following How To. The source file for this movie is located in the Chapter 13 folder for this book on the Osborne site (www.osborne.com).

As you have evidenced first-hand, there is a lot of script on these buttons, and much of it is repetitious in nature. There are other ways to write scripts to make them more streamline. In the next chapter, we'll take a closer look at making custom functions and arrays. Functions and arrays can help simplify repetitious tasks to make your scripting faster and easier.

13

Create a hitTest and Change the Properties of a Movie Clip

Since this movie has so many things going on in it, we will hone in on the topics we have been discussing in this chapter so you can get an idea of how you might be able to put them all to work. Specifically, we will be using `hitTest`, `setProperty`, `getProperty`, and the `if` action.

Looking at the finished movie and Timeline, you will see that there are nine layers; the last layer (highway) serves as the background.

Let's first examine the elements we need to know about in order to change the properties of the car and perform the hitTest. We can start with the movie clips we have to make.

1. Make a movie clip that will be the object that collides. In our car game example, it's the `car` object. The `car` instance in this case has an instance name of "car."

2. Now make a movie clip that the car will collide with. In the car game example, the object that the car collides with is a movie clip named `mine`. Let's take a look at this movie clip on its own Timeline and use this Timeline as a model for the way yours should look.

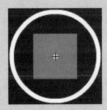

3. To view the movie clip on its own Timeline, double-click the mine movie clip in the Library. This movie clip is a multilayer clip with a `stop` action on the first frame and the 14th frame in the Action layer. If you drag the playhead over the Timeline in the movie clip, you will see an animated circle appear to grow, blink, and fade out.

4. You will also notice that the first frame of the movie is blank, so when you drag an instance of this movie clip onto the stage, the user won't see it. Exit Movie Clip Editing mode, and now let's return to the main Timeline.

13

5. Assuming you have created a movie clip like the mine movie clip, drag several instances of it onto the stage to a layer that is beneath the layer the car movie clip will reside on. In other words, you want the object that will collide with the car to be on a lower layer. In the car game example, the mines are located on the realchecks layer. Name each one of the instances because, in order to create the collision, we need to address the mines by their instance names. In this movie, there are six instances of the mine movie clip hidden in the background. They have instance names of mine1 through mine6.

TIP   *If you display the Movie Explorer for this movie, you can double-click elements listed in the Movie Explorer (Window | Movie Explorer). The Movie Explorer can help you locate various elements like text, scripts, and objects.*

Let's also identify a movie clip that will serve as the object that moves. In this case, the moving object is a bitmap of a car, and it has an instance name of car. Drag a movie clip instance, or the car instance, from the Library over to the top (car) layer and give it an instance name.

6. Now let's create the arrow buttons that will move the car instance up, down, left, and right, across the highway checkerboard background. The script residing on these buttons controls the X and Y position of the car on a button event. Drag one arrow button to the stage from the Common Button Library (Windows | Common Libraries | Buttons.Fla); duplicate it four times; and rotate the copies so one points east, one points west, one points north, and one points south.

7. There are two more buttons we need to create. These are the buttons that reduce and enlarge the car instance on a button event. Make two buttons; label one **GROW** and the other one **SHRINK**.

8. There are also two Dynamic text fields to the right of the stage. These text fields display the values of the X and Y coordinates of the car dynamically as it moves. The variable names of these text fields are xv (for X value) and yv (for Y value). Create two Dynamic text fields and use the variable names from the preceding sentence (xv, yv).

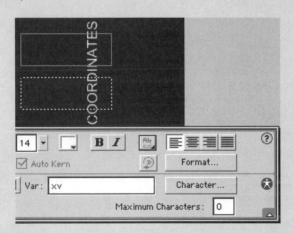

9. Now all the major pieces are in place on the stage, and we can begin scripting. Most of the script is on the arrow buttons and on the Grow and Shrink buttons, so the bulk of action is fired by mouse events. Let's begin by scripting the arrow button that points

13

upward (North). Since this is a long script, we'll type this in Expert mode. Later, in Chapter 15, we will exclusively be using Expert mode. Now is a good time to start getting our feet wet. Click the button; and in the Actions pane options pop-up window, select Expert mode. Click in the Actions panel and type the following code:

> TIP   *Notice there are several comments in this script. Comments, as mentioned in Chapter 12, are indicated with two slashes (//) at the beginning of a script. Their sole purpose is to help you understand what is going on in the script. Comments are used here to indicate what the proceeding line of code means. You don't have to include the comment code when you type the script. However, you may want to use this as a reference later.*

```
//set the _y property of the car instance
on (release) {
        setProperty(car, _y, getProperty(car, _y)-27.5);
        //declare the values of the two dynamic text fields.  Use the
math.floor method to return a whole number in the text field.
        xv = Math.floor (getProperty(car, _x)*0.9);
        yv = Math.floor (getProperty(car, _y)*0.9);
        //Use a conditional (if) statement to define the collision parameters.
If the car instance hits the mine instance, the second frame of the mine
movie clip plays.  This repeats through all six instances.
        if (_root.car.hitTest(_root.mine)) {
            _root.mine.gotoAndPlay(2);
        }
        if (_root.car.hitTest(_root.mine2)) {
            _root.mine2.gotoAndPlay(2);
        }
        if (_root.car.hitTest(_root.green_home)) {
            _root.home_safe.gotoAndPlay(2);
        }
        if (_root.car.hitTest(_root.mine3)) {
            _root.mine3.gotoAndPlay(2);
        }
        if (_root.car.hitTest(_root.mine4)) {
            _root.mine4.gotoAndPlay(2);        }
        if (_root.car.hitTest(_root.mine5)) {
            _root.mine5.gotoAndPlay(2);
        }
        if (_root.car.hitTest(_root.mine6)) {
            _root.mine5.gotoAndPlay(2);
```

```
        }
    }
```

In the preceding script, we used `setProperty`, `getProperty`, the `Math` `.floor` method, and the `if` statement. If you examine the script, you will see that much of the script is repetitious.

10. Let's script the button that is pointing to the west. Follow the same procedure as on the preceding button and type the following script. Notice that this script is almost identical, except the button moves the X position as opposed to the script on the previous button, which moved the Y position:

```
on (release) {
        setProperty(car, _x, getProperty(car, _x)-27.5);
        xv = Math.floor (getProperty(car, _x)*0.9);
        yv = Math.floor (getProperty(car, _y)*0.9);
        if (_root.car.hitTest(_root.mine)) {
            _root.mine.gotoAndPlay(2);
        }
        if (_root.car.hitTest(_root.mine2)) {
            _root.mine2.gotoAndPlay(2);
        }
        if (_root.car.hitTest(_root.green_home)) {
            _root.home_safe.gotoAndPlay(2);
        }
        if (_root.car.hitTest(_root.mine3)) {
            _root.mine3.gotoAndPlay(2);
        }
        if (_root.car.hitTest(_root.mine4)) {
            _root.mine4.gotoAndPlay(2);
        }
        if (_root.car.hitTest(_root.mine5)) {
            _root.mine5.gotoAndPlay(2);
        }
        if (_root.car.hitTest(_root.mine6)) {
            _root.mine5.gotoAndPlay(2);
        }
    }
```

11. Now let's script the button that points south—note again that it's almost identical to the other scripts except the Y position is now moving down instead of up:

```
on (release) {
        setProperty(car, _y, getProperty(car, _y)+27.5);
        xv = Math.floor (getProperty(car, _x)*0.9);
```

13

```
        yv = Math.floor (getProperty(car, _y)*0.9);
        if (_root.car.hitTest(_root.mine)) {
            _root.car.gotoAndPlay(2);
        }
        if (_root.car.hitTest(_root.mine2)) {
            _root.mine2.gotoAndPlay(2);
        }
        if (_root.car.hitTest(_root.green_home)) {
            _root.home_safe.gotoAndPlay(2);
        }
        if (_root.car.hitTest(_root.mine3)) {
            _root.mine3.gotoAndPlay(2);
        }
        if (_root.car.hitTest(_root.mine4)) {
            _root.mine4.gotoAndPlay(2);
        }
        if (_root.car.hitTest(_root.mine5)) {
            _root.mine5.gotoAndPlay(2);
        }
        if (_root.car.hitTest(_root.mine6)) {
            _root.mine5.gotoAndPlay(2);
        }
    }
```

12. To complete the arrow buttons, let's add the script on the button that points east. Here's the script:

```
on (release) {
        setProperty(car, _x, getProperty(car, _x)+27.5);
        xv = Math.floor (getProperty(car, _x)*0.9);
        yv = Math.floor (getProperty(car, _y)*0.9);
        if (_root.car.hitTest(_root.mine)) {
            _root.mine.gotoAndPlay(2);
        }
        if (_root.car.hitTest(_root.mine2)) {
            _root.mine2.gotoAndPlay(2);
        }
        if (_root.car.hitTest(_root.green_home)) {
            _root.home_safe.gotoAndPlay(2);
        }
        if (_root.car.hitTest(_root.mine3)) {
```

```
                _root.mine3.gotoAndPlay(2);
        }
        if (_root.car.hitTest(_root.mine4)) {
                _root.mine4.gotoAndPlay(2);
        }
        if (_root.car.hitTest(_root.mine5)) {
                _root.mine5.gotoAndPlay(2);          }
        if (_root.car.hitTest(_root.mine6))
    {
                _root.mine5.gotoAndPlay(2);
        }
}
```

13. Click the Shrink button, and display the Actions panel again in Expert mode. In the panel, type the following script:

```
//Declare the values of the x_sv and the y_sv variables, which includes
getting the _Xscale and _yscale properties of the car instance and
multiplying them by 0.9
on (release) {
        x_sv = getProperty(car, _xscale)*0.9;
        y_sv = getProperty(car, _yscale)*0.9;
        //sets  _xscale and _yscale properties of the car instance and the
x_sv and y_sv values
        setProperty(car, _xscale, x_sv);
        setProperty(car, _yscale, y_sv);
        //declares the values of hv and wv variables
        hv = x_sv;
        wv = y_sv;
}
```

14. Click the Grow button and type the following script. Note that it is almost identical to the script on the Grow button:

```
on (release) {
        x_sv = getProperty(car, _xscale)*1.1;
        y_sv = getProperty(car, _yscale)*1.1;
        setProperty(car, _xscale, x_sv);
        setProperty(car, _yscale, y_sv);
        hv = x_sv;
        wv = y_sv;
}
```

13

15. The only other script in this movie is the script on the button in the upper-left corner, the Start button. This is just a regular button.

When the user clicks this button, the car returns to the top left of the stage and the size of the car is reset to the way it was when the movie first loaded. Place a button in this position, and click it; and in the Actions panel Expert mode, type the following:

```
//Return the _x and _y position of the car instance to its original size and
position when the movie loads
on (release) {
        setProperty(car, _x, 52);
        setProperty(car, _y, 37);
        setProperty(car, _width, 46.5);
        setProperty(car, _height, 20.9);
}
```

Test the movie to see what happens. You can shrink and grow the size of the car, as well as change the position, by clicking on the arrows. Notice that as you click the arrows, the X and Y position is displayed in whole numbers because we used the `Math.floor` method to round the number out to the nearest whole number. Otherwise, the number would have displayed with decimals in minute increments.

As you can see, some aspects of ActionScript are fairly easy to understand, but it is also not for the weak at heart. In the next couple of chapters, we start putting together some of the pieces of the ActionScript puzzle so you can begin to perform more complex interactive tasks.

Part V

Move Full-Throttle Into ActionScript

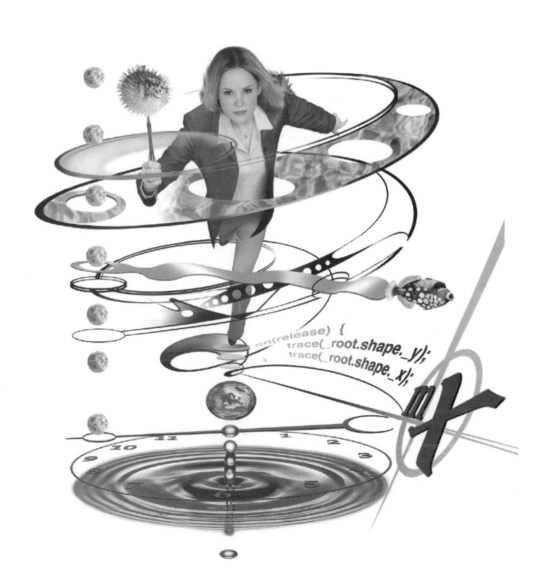

Chapter 14

Creative Programming in ActionScript

How To...

- Create a game using conditionals
- Build an array that sorts and retrieves data
- Create a date object
- Make functions
- Create a drag-and-drop movie clip
- Hide a mouse

Once you become comfortable with the basic concepts in ActionScript, you will probably want to know more. Little by little, you will find yourself absorbing information here and there, and before you know it, you will be adding onto those core concepts. If you're a designer or artist, feeling comfortable with ActionScript can be a very empowering experience.

In this chapter, we will expand upon some of the concepts learned in the last couple of chapters. You will start to understand how ActionScript fits into the scheme of Flash. You will also begin to envision how you can make your own movies interactive, as well as how you can assimilate this knowledge into your own projects.

Create a Simple Game Using Conditionals

In the previous chapter, we played a game that tested a single condition. This was quite simple to do. Often, your movies will be a bit more complex than just testing for a single condition. Let's see what happens if we work with multiple conditionals. Figure 14-1 depicts a game that behaves like a test. The purpose of the game is to test your reading comprehension based upon your memory of the information in the first paragraph. This is how it works:

1. When the first frame loads, the user is presented with a simple paragraph of information that they need to read. When they have finished reading it, they click the right-pointing arrow to continue.

2. The next frame is a question with three multiple-choice answers. If the user clicks the right answer, a status message appears, telling them they are correct and to proceed to the next frame. If they choose the wrong answer, the other answers go away and they are told to click the arrow to go to the next question. This repeats through three more questions. On the last question, the user clicks the arrow to find out the final results and replay the game again if they like.

Although there are other ways to make this game, and the game involves a lot of repetitive code, it serves as a good demonstration of how to use multiple conditionals in a game-like

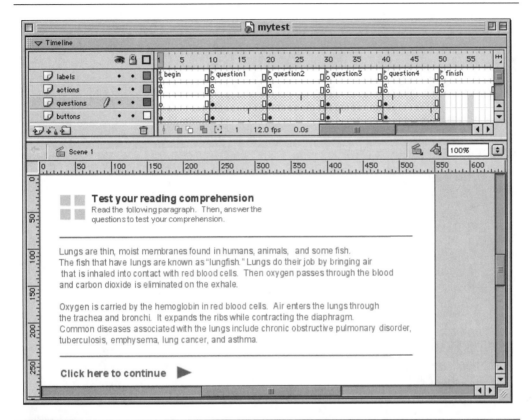

A multiple-choice game that evaluates the user's score on the last frame

movie. Specifically, the script uses `if` and `else if` actions, and variables on button events that display information based upon the condition. The `if` statement tests to see if a condition is met, and then proceeds to the next instruction. The `else if` action comes into play when there is more than one possible outcome to the condition declared in the `if` action. Numerical variables are stored when the user clicks the correct answer button, and in the last frame section, the score is evaluated with the help of the `if` and `else if` actions. There are many variations to this simple script, but for now, we'll stick with the basics.

NOTE   *In the Actions panel Options pop-up menu, select View Line Numbers so you can reference lines by number. This makes it easier to organize your script when your scripts become more complex.*

14

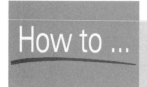

Make a Multiple-Choice Game That Tests Your Memory

Now that you understand the concept of conditionals, let's apply your knowledge to an actual project. We will now walk through the steps of creating a game where conditionals are used to determine the outcome of the game. Here are the steps:

1. First, create the layers. The layers are as follows:

   ■ labels

   ■ actions

   ■ questions

   ■ buttons

   ■ intro

   ■ finish

2. You will notice in Figure 14-1 that there are labels on the frames. These labels are used to flag which frames the questions are located on. The labels are also used in the button script for the button that tells the user to click to continue to the next question. Now we will set up the labels in the frames. To add a label to a keyframe, insert keyframes on Frames 1, 10, 20, 30, 40, and 50. Click each new keyframe, and in the Properties Inspector, add the corresponding labels:

   ■ 1—begin

   ■ 10—question1

   ■ 20—question2

   ■ 30—question3

   ■ 40—question4

   ■ 50—finish

3. Since this is a game and the user will need to control the frames on a button event, let's add stop actions to each frame where we want to pause the playhead. Display the Actions panel in Normal mode. In the actions layer, add a keyframe to Frame 1. In the Actions Toolbox, click Actions | Movie Control and double-click `stop`. Repeat this process on Frames 10, 20, 30, 40, 50, and 60.

4. Click the intro layer. This is the frame the user see when the movie loads. Here you will explain the game, display the text that needs to be read by the user to play the

game, and create the button that will send the user to the first question in the game. In Figure 14-1, there is an instruction and then some text that explains the purpose of lungs. You can use a static text box to make the instruction text. There is also a line of text to the left of the button that tells the user to "Click here to continue."

5. Add a keyframe to the buttons layer, Frame 1, and place a button to the right of the "Click here..." text. In Figure 14-1, an arrow button is used. Click this arrow button and, in the Actions panel Toolbox, click Actions | Movie Control and double-click `gotoAndPlay`. Click line 1 and select Press for the Event. Click line 2 and, for Type, select Frame Label. For Frame, type **question1**.

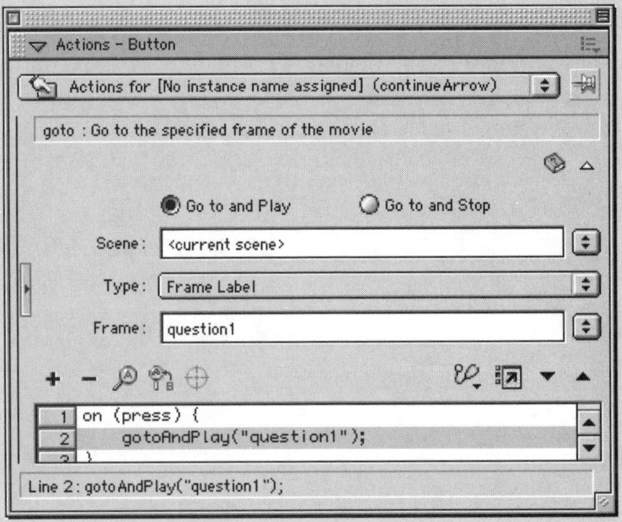

6. Set up the first answer on the questions layer (Frame 10) and the buttons that correspond to the questions. In the following illustration, you can see how the questions and buttons are set up. Create static text fields for Lungfish, Lungers, and Lungfulls, and for the question itself. In addition, place buttons on the same frames (button layer) to the left of the questions. For this question, the first choice is the right answer and the other two choices are wrong answers.

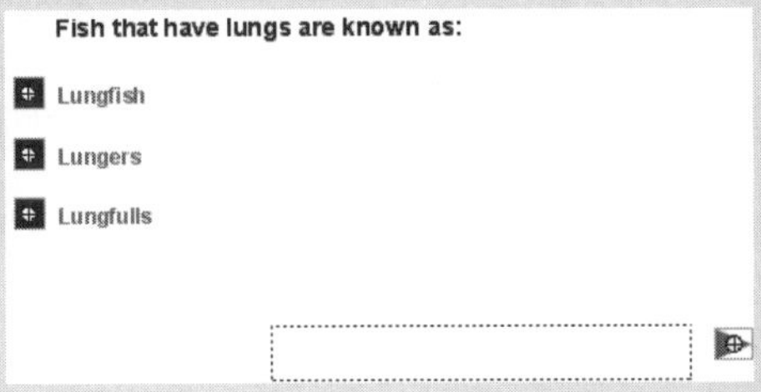

14

7. Set up the status message text field on the bottom right of Frame 10. To do this, create a text field, and, in the Properties Inspector, make this field dynamic and give it a Variable name of **status**.

8. Add to the bottom right of this window the arrow button that will navigate the user to the next frame.

9. Add the script to the various elements in this frame, starting with all the buttons. The first button (Lungfish) is the right answer in this question. Click this button and, in the Actions panel Toolbox, click Actions, Variables and double-click set variable. For Variable, type **q1**. For Value, type **q1+1**. With line 2 selected, click Actions, Variables and double-click set variable again. For Variable, type **status**. For Value, type **Correct. Click here.** Make sure the Expressions check boxes are not selected. When this button is clicked, the variable q1 will add 1. This will allow us to keep score each time the user selects q1, the correct answer. Also, a status message will appear in the dynamic text box we named status: "Correct. Click here."

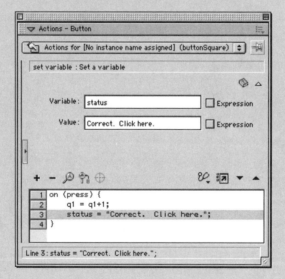

10. Because the remaining boxes, which are the wrong choices, are identical in score (0), they have the same script. Click the second button (Lungers), and, in the Actions Toolbox, select Actions | Variables and double-click set variable. For Variable, type **status**. For Value, type **Wrong. Click here.** Repeat this process for the last wrong button.

```
Actions - Button
  Actions for [No instance name assigned] (buttonSquar: ▼)

  set variable : Set a variable

         Variable:  status                    ☐ Expression
            Value:  Wrong. Click here.          ☐ Expression


  +  -  🔍 🐍 ⊕                      ℓℓ 🗗 ▼ ▲

  1  on (press) {
  2      status = "Wrong.  Click here.";
  3  }

  Line 2: status = "Wrong. Click here.";
```

11. On Frame 10, click the arrow button at the bottom right of the frame, and, in the Actions Toolbox, click Actions | Movie Control and double-click `goto`. For Type, select Frame Label. For Frame, type **question2**. Make sure the Play button is chosen on the top. Click line 2 and, in the Actions Toolbox, click Actions | Variables | set variable. For Variable, type **status**. Leave the Value blank. Now when the user clicks this button to go to the next frame, the status text field will be blank. You can also type ""''. Quotation marks will hold a place in the script, even if the value is blank. This frame is done.

```
Actions - Button
  Actions for [No instance name assigned] (continueArro: ▼)

  set variable : Set a variable

         Variable:  message                   ☐ Expression
            Value:  ""                          ☑ Expression


  +  -  🔍 🐍 ⊕                      ℓℓ 🗗 ▼ ▲

  1  on (press) {
  2      gotoAndPlay("question2");
  3      message = "";
  4      status = "";
  5  }

  Line 3: message = "";
```

14

12. On both the questions and buttons layers, click Frame 20 and insert keyframes on both layers. Repeat this process for Frames 30 and 40. If you navigate to the next frame, you will notice that it has replicated the frame before. If you click a button and look in the Actions panel, you will notice it also replicated the code. This may be a little confusing because we have to go back in and make minor adjustments to the script on the buttons. But these objects can work in our favor if we use them as placeholders for the new information, so we can revise the existing text on the questions layer in Frames 20, 30, 40, and 50. The script on the button in the bottom-right corner is correct. We just have to adjust the script on the buttons so that the correct button corresponds to the right one. Start on Frame 20, buttons layer. If the button clicked is the right answer, follow the instructions for Step 8. If the button clicked is the wrong answer, follow the instructions for Step 9.

The oxygen in your lungs is carried by hemoglobin in:

■ Carbon monoxide

■ Red blood cells

■ Bronchi

You may not have to change the script on a button if the frame duplicated from the last set of frames was the same (either right or wrong). For example, if the script was already in place for a right button, then you can leave it intact because the scripts are all the same for the right button and all the same for the wrong button. The only difference is that the right answers are adding up each time you click one, and the results are being stored until the last frame.

13. Repeat the script on the question buttons on Frames 30 and 40 along with revising the static text on the page. Also, add a frame (F5) to the questions and buttons layers on Frame 49 to extend the frame sequence nine frames.

14. Navigate to Frame 40 and click the Continue button in the bottom right. From before, there is already a script on this button. We are going to delete this script and add a new one. This script is a bit repetitious and may be a little hard to follow, so I will itemize it here:

■ Delete the script by clicking it and clicking the Delete A Script button (–).

■ In the Actions Toolbox, click Actions | Movie Control and double-click `goto`. For Type, select Frame Label. For Frame, type **finish**. Make sure Play is selected at the top of the panel.

■ With line 2 selected, go to Actions | Conditions | Loops, and double-click `if`. For Condition, type **q1>=4**.

■ With line 3 selected, in the Actions Toolbox, click Actions | Variables and double-click set variable. For Variable, type **finalScore**. For Value, type **Congratulations! You got a perfect score!**

■ With line 4 selected, in the Actions Toolbox, click Actions | Conditions/Loops and double-click `else if`. In the Conditions box, type **q1= 3**.

■ With line 5 selected, in the Actions Toolbox, click Actions | Variables and double-click set variable. For Variable, type **finalScore**. For Value, type **Not bad. Only 1 wrong**.

■ Double-click line 6, and again click Actions | Conditions/Loops and double-click `else if`. For Conditions, type **q1= =2**.

■ With line 7 selected, in the Actions Toolbox, click Actions | Variables and double-click set variable. For Value, type **finalScore**. For Values, type **You only got half of the questions right**.

■ With line 8 selected, in the Actions Toolbox, click Actions | Conditions/Loops and double-click `else if`. For Condition, type **q1<=1**.

■ With line 9 selected, in the Actions Toolbox, click Actions | Variables and double-click set variable. For Variable, type **finalScore**. For Value, type **Not very good. Try again.** The final script will look like this:

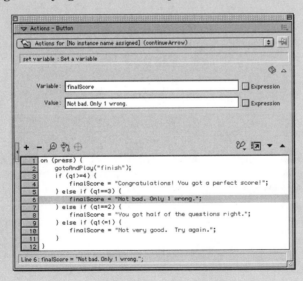

14

15. Now we are ready to make the last frame. Add a keyframe on Frame 50 of the finish layer. Place a static text box that says **Final Results**. Also create a static text box that says **Score**. Place a dynamic text field underneath the Final Results text box. Give this dynamic text box a Variable name of **finalScore**. To the right of the Score text, put another dynamic text field. Give this text field a variable name of **q1**. Also, add a frame (F5) to Frame 59 to stretch the frame sequence to Frame 59.

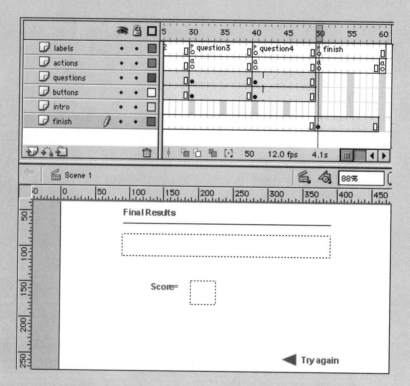

16. Place a back button in the bottom-right corner of this frame. Make a static label to the right of this button that says **Try again**. Click this new button and, in the Actions panel Toolbox, click Actions | Movie Control and double-click goto. Click line 1 and select Play. Click line 2 and, for Type, select Frame Label. For Frame, type **begin**. With line 2 selected, in the Toolbox, click Actions | Variables and double-click set variables. For Variable, type **q1**. For Value, type **0**. With line 3 selected, in the Toolbox, click Actions | Variables and double-click set variables. For Variable, type **status**. For Value, don't type anything.

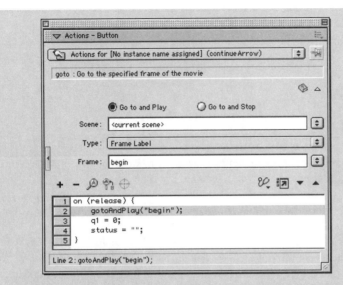

Play the movie to see how it works. If you have any problems, you can always refer to the source file for Chapter 14 on the Osborne site (www.osborne.com).

As you can see firsthand, there is a lot of repetition involved in this script. You can see how, after repeated use of certain actions, you become familiar with the syntax. You can also begin to understand why programmers use functions and arrays. Functions and arrays take repetitive tasks, group them together, and help streamline the scripting process. Now let's use an array to create a simple navigation menu.

Build an Array to Store and Retrieve Data

In the previous chapter, we discussed the basics of arrays. To refresh your memory, arrays provide a way for large lists of data to be contained in a particular sequence, stored, and retrieved later. Arrays can contain number data, string data, or both. Arrays are very powerful because they can include either single or multiple data values.

There are many different ways to create arrays, and sometimes they can become quite complex, especially if you're working on a game with multiple chunks of information or a complex shopping cart for an e-commerce site.

In this section, we are going to create part of a simple navigation menu and use an array to do so. We are also going to look at two different ways to create arrays. The concept here is that if you have an element in something like a navigation bar that needs daily updates, and the data you want displayed is part of a list, creating an array is a simple way to perform this task. In addition, one of the navigation text fields gives the date on a button event, so we can also take a brief glimpse at how to utilize the date object in Flash. Are you ready? Let's begin.

Figure 14-2 displays this simple navigation menu. The top row of the menu (Today's Weather, and so on) includes buttons. Underneath the buttons are dynamic text fields that display data when the button is clicked. It doesn't look like much, but picture the same sort of menu with

14

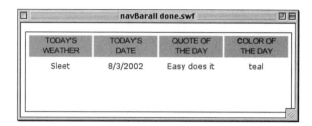

FIGURE 14-2 A navigational menu that uses an array to store the information returned on a button event

1000 items with multiple criteria that need to be dynamically changed every day. Creating this list in an array would make it easier to revise.

The array in this menu has been set up on the first frame of the main Timeline. Once the data is set up, you can easily change it. In Figure 14-2, when the user clicks the buttons (Today's Weather, Today's Date, and so on), the indexed data associated with that button is displayed underneath the button. The concept here is that if you needed to quickly update data that frequently changes, you could streamline the update process by building the movie using arrays.

First, we'll walk through the process of creating an array for Today's Weather. Before we continue, you will need to create two layers on the main Timeline and name them **actions** and **main**.

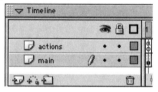

On the main layer, make a button with the label text **Today's Weather**. Place a dynamic text field underneath the button so that the information will appear under the button after you click it. Duplicate the text field and the button (Library Options | Duplicate) three more times, as shown in Figure 14-2. Name the new buttons **today**, **quote**, and **color**. Change the text on the new buttons in each button's editing mode (**Today's Date**, **Quote of the Day**, and **Color of the Day**). Now that the whole movie is set up, let's define the array.

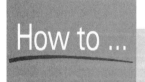

Make a Navigational Menu Using an Array

Now that you have an understanding of what arrays are for, let's see how they work. Here are the steps for building a simple array into a navigational menu:

1. The array is going to be scripted on the first frame. Click the first frame of the actions layer and display the Actions panel in Normal mode. In the

Actions Toolbox, click Actions | Variables and double-click set variable. For Variable, type **info**. For Value, type **new Array**(). Select the Expression check box for Value.

2. Now that we have instantiated our new array, we will populate it with data. Repeat the process in Step 1, double-clicking set variable. Keep double-clicking until you have created a total of 11 lines, including the first one. Now all we need to do is to return to line 2, and enter the Variable and Value. For line 2, Variable, type **info[0]**. For Value, type **Sunny**. Repeat this process for the next ten lines, using the following data:

Variable	Value
info[1]	Partly Cloudy
info[2]	Cloudy
info[3]	Showers
info[4]	Rain
info[5]	Sleet
info[6]	Snow
info[7]	Snow Flurries
info[8]	Downpour
info[9]	Hurricane

The index for the variables is numerical and contained in brackets. Notice the first index entry (Sunny) is [0], the second is [1], and so on.

3. With line 11 selected, click Actions | Variables and double-click set variables. For Variable, type the letter **i**. For Value, type **5** and select the Expression check box. With line 12 selected, repeat the preceding process, but for Variable, type **weather**, and for Value, type **info[i]**. In the preceding script, line 12 defines a new variable, i, that has a numerical value of 4. In line 13, another variable is declared. This time the value of weather = info[i]. The info is the array. The variable i, which is equal to 5 (declared on line 12), becomes a placeholder for the index. When the weather is updated, the person doing the updating simply needs to change the variable i in this script, which is the current index number. In other words, this would involve very little input. All you need to know is which index number corresponds to what element.

14

Now let's script the button that will display the array data in the dynamic text field.

4. Select the first dynamic text field (under the Today's Weather button), and, in the Properties Inspector, give it the Variable name of **todaysWeather**.

5. Click the Today's Weather button, and, in the Actions Panel Toolbox, select Actions | Variables and double-click set variable. Click line 2, and for Variable, type **todaysWeather**. For Value, type **weather**. TodaysWeather is the name of the dynamic text box, and the weather value, if you recall, is a variable on Frame 1. The value of that variable is info[i].

```
1 on (release) {
2     todaysWeather = weather;
3 }
```

Test the movie. When you click the Today's Weather button, index[5] (from the array we created on Frame 1) appears in the dynamic text field.

NOTE

The set variable action is for global variables. You could use the var action instead of the set variable action; but for the var to remain local, it has to be declared within a function.

As you can see, it's pretty easy to set up an array. In addition to the way we just created an array, we can construct our array in a different manner and still yield the same results. Since both methods do the same thing, it's up to you which method you use. Ultimately, the complexity and quantity of information will help you make this decision.

Let's now script the array associated with the last button that we named, "Colors of the Day."

1. Click Frame 1 in the Timeline and, in the Actions panel, click the last line of script (line 13). In the Actions Toolbox, click Actions | Variables and double-click set variable. For Variable, type **dayColor**. For Value, type the following using brackets with the quotation marks: **["brown", "black", "blue", "green", "red", "purple", "orange", "teal"]**. Select the Expression check box.

This array is constructed in a single line; however, the index values are still associated with the elements in sequential order. For example, "brown" is index [0], black is index [1], and so on. Now let's script the button and the dynamic text field where we want to call this array. The finished script on Frame 1 now looks like this:

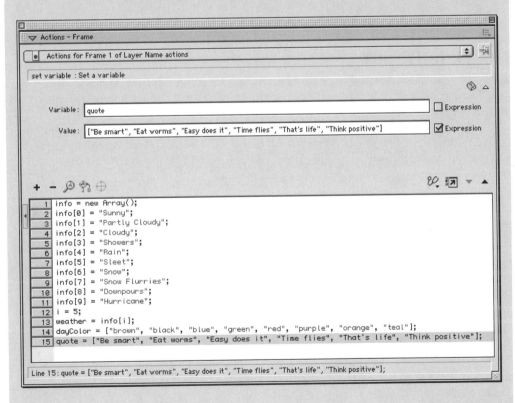

```
1   info = new Array();
2   info[0] = "Sunny";
3   info[1] = "Partly Cloudy";
4   info[2] = "Cloudy";
5   info[3] = "Showers";
6   info[4] = "Rain";
7   info[5] = "Sleet";
8   info[6] = "Snow";
9   info[7] = "Snow Flurries";
10  info[8] = "Downpours";
11  info[9] = "Hurricane";
12  i = 5;
13  weather = info[i];
14  dayColor = ["brown", "black", "blue", "green", "red", "purple", "orange", "teal"];
15  quote = ["Be smart", "Eat worms", "Easy does it", "Time flies", "That's life", "Think positive"];
```

14

2. Name the dynamic text field under the Color Of The Day button. Click it, and, in the Properties Inspector, give it a name of **todaysColor**.

3. Click the Color Of The Day button, and, in the Actions Panel Toolbox, click Actions | Variable and double-click set variable. For Variable, type **todaysColor**. For Value, type **dayColor[7]**.

```
on (press) {
    todaysColor = dayColor[7];
}
```

Test the movie. When you click the Color Of The Day button, the value for the dayColor array, index[7], displays in the dynamic text field named todaysColor.

The third button and text field in the navigation bar, Quote Of The Day, was not scripted. Try to see if you can figure out the procedure for creating and assigning an array on this button following the directions for the previous button. The source file for this array is located in the Chapter 14 source file folder for this book on the Osborne site (www.osborne.com/).

Create a Date Object

There is one other dimension to Figure 14-2 that we haven't covered yet, and that is the date object. The date object is displayed in the dynamic text field under Today's Date when the Today's Date button is clicked.

With the date object, you can return any information relating to the current date or time in relation to your operating system's internal clock or the user's internal clock. To use the date object, you need to first create an instance of the object to call the date object methods. In this script, we will be using the following date object methods: Date.getDate, .getMonth, and .getFullYear.

In Figure 14-2, the second button (Today's Date) contains a script that creates three date objects and calls them on a button event. They are displayed in the dynamic text field under the button when the button is clicked.

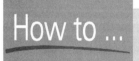 **Create and Retrieve a Date Object**

There are many creative ways in which to use the date object methods. The following are the steps used to display the date when the Today's Date button is clicked in the movie displayed in Figure 14-2:

1. Click the dynamic text field under the Today's Date button, and, in the Properties Inspector, give it a variable name of **whatsToday**.

2. Click the Today's Date button, and, in the Actions Panel Toolbox, select Actions I Variables and double-click set variable. Click it seven times to generate a total of seven variable lines. We will now go in and modify them all. Select line 2 and, for Variable, type **currentDate**. For Value, type **newDate()**. Repeat the process of selecting lines 3 through 8, and for Values and Variables, follow this table for input:

Line	Value	Variable
3	todaysDate	currentDate.getDate();
4	currentMonth	new Date();
5	todaysMonth	currentMonth.getMonth();
6	currentYear	new Date();
7	todaysYear	currentYear.getFullYear();
8	whatsToday	todaysDate+"/"+todaysMonth+"/"+todaysYear;

```
1  on (press) {
2      currentDate = new Date();
3      todaysDate = currentDate.getDate();
4      currentMonth = new Date();
5      todaysMonth = currentMonth.getMonth();
6      currentYear = new Date();
7      todaysYear = currentYear.getFullYear();
8      whatsToday = todaysDate+"/"+todaysMonth+"/"+todaysYear;
9  }
```

After creating all the new objects, on line 8, the variable `whatsToday` (the dynamic text field) has a value of the date (`todaysDate`), plus a string slash, plus `todaysMonth`, plus a slash, plus `todaysYear`. All of these values were defined in this script.

Test the movie. When you click the Today's Date button, the current date will display in the dynamic text field.

Make Functions

If you browse through the Actions Toolbox, you will notice that one of the folders contains functions. A *function* is an instruction or a procedure that the user can define. In other words, it's sort of like writing your own custom code. The syntax is simple, too. All you have to do is give the function a name and then define it.

Why do people use functions? For the same reason you would develop a procedure for any long or repetitive task. For example, let's say you do your laundry every Thursday. You gather up a few clothes and trek all the way downstairs to the washing machine to drop off the clothes. Then you go back upstairs, pick up another few clothes, and walk downstairs again. You repeat this process five times and realize how silly it is to keep running back and forth with laundry. So, you make a laundry basket to put the dirty clothes in, and now you only have to walk downstairs once. Now, when you gather the clothes of your kids or significant other, you only need to use the container once to transport the laundry downstairs. Functions are similar in a way. They define a procedure that can be executed when the name of the procedure is called. The function can do something, like change the property of an object, or it can return a value.

Return a Value with a Function

Although they can get pretty complex, it's relatively simple to create a function. All you need to do is declare the function, then state the parameters and—when you're ready—call the function. In other words, you store a set of instructions you created in your movie until it is called upon to function.

Let's create a simple function that returns a value. In Figure 14-3, there is a button next to some text that tells you to "press button to get mileage total." There is also a dynamic text field underneath it. When the button is clicked by the user, a function is called. The function calculates some numbers as per the instructions in the function.

In the Actions panel, select Expert mode from the Actions panel pop-up options. Insert a keyframe on the first frame of a movie.

Functions should always be defined on the first frame of a movie because, that way, when it is called at any point in the movie, you know it will work. Type the following script:

```
function getMileage(total,mph) {
reimburse = "Total="+""+(total/mph)*33;
}
```

Here's what's going on in the previous script:

- A function is created called getMileage whose parameters, `total` and `mph`, can be defined and changed.

- A variable is declared that is equal to a string (`Total=`) and a calculation of `total` divided by the `mph` and multiplied by 33.

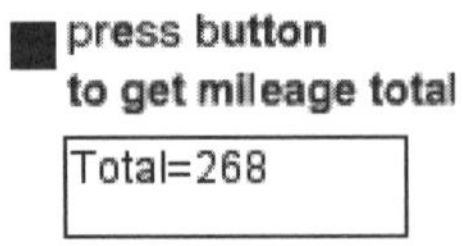

■ press button
to get mileage total

Total=268

FIGURE 14-3 When the button is clicked in this movie, a function is called that displays the results of a calculation in the dynamic text field.

The parameters serve as placeholders. We can change these placeholders and therefore change the result of the outcome on-the-fly.

Now let's see how we get this function to work. We are going to return the function when the button is clicked. The dynamic text field in Figure 14-3 has a variable name of "reimburse." If you recall, in the function we just wrote, the value of the variable `reimburse` is defined.

On the button resides the following script:

```
on (press){
     return getMileage(325,40);
}
```

When the movie is tested and the button is clicked in the dynamic text field, the function is fired. Every time you go in and type different parameters for the `mph` and `total` placeholders, the results change when the button is clicked. The `return` action sets the value for the function being declared.

You may notice that the text field is returning numbers with several places after the decimal. Let's try to use the `Math.floor` method here to round the number out. Alter the script on the first frame a little:

```
function getMileage(total,mph) {
 reimburse = "Total="+" "+Math.floor((total/mph)*33);
}
```

Now when you test the movie, it rounds out the return from the getMileage function. The number rounds off to the nearest whole number.

Change Properties with a Function

Functions are perfect for applications that require mathematical calculations such as we previously created. You can use functions for other purposes, too. In fact, you are only limited by your creativity. Let's examine a function that makes an object grow and shrink. In Chapter 13, we created a couple of buttons that enlarge the width and height of an object when clicked. Here, we will create a function that can be reused simply by calling the function. In this movie, we call the function on a button event. However, you could return the function in any number of ways, such as on a frame or a movie clip event. The function can be easily modified just by changing the parameters assigned to the function.

Figure 14-4 displays a chess piece with a couple of buttons. One button says Grow Up and the other says Grow Down. In the first frame in the Timeline, a function is defined. The function is called growUp. There are three parameters in this function. The first parameter is the name of the movie clip, the second is `wd` (representing the width of the movie clip), and the third is `ht` (represents the height of the movie clip). The Grow Up button calls the `growUp` function and passes parameters that allow you to customize the function, just like a built-in function in Flash.

You could easily create a function that changes any properties of an object by using the same script you just learned. For example, your function could change the rotation, or X and Y coordinates of an object. As your scripts become more complex and you need to reuse scripts, functions will become an important part of your scripting.

14

The buttons in this movie enlarge and reduce the size of the chess piece by calling a function on a button event.

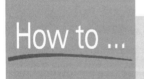

Create a Function That Changes the Properties of an Object

Let's take a look at how to create a function that modifies the width and height of an object, using Figure 14-4 as our example.

1. Create a new movie, make three layers, and give them the following names: **actions**, **buttons**, and **chess piece**.

2. Create a button that says **Grow Up**, and a movie clip. The movie clip used in Figure 14-4 is a chess piece. From the Library, place an instance of the Grow Up button on the button layer and the movie clip on the chess piece layer. To be consistent with our sample, in the Properties Inspector, give the movie clip an instance name of **chess**.

3. Now we will create the function that enlarges the width and height of a movie clip. Click the actions layer and add a keyframe to Frame 1. Display the Actions panel in Normal mode, and, in the Actions Toolbox, click Actions | User-Defined Functions and double-click function. For Name, type **growUp**. For Parameters, type **clip, wd, ht**. GrowUp is the name of the function. The parameter names (clip, wd, ht) serve as placeholders and will be customized when the function is called. With line 1 selected, in the Actions Toolbox, click Actions | Variables and double-click set variable. For Expression, type **clip._width += wd**. With line 2 selected, in the Actions Toolbox, click Actions | Variables and double-click set variable. For Expression, type **clip._height += ht**. The script should appear as it does here:

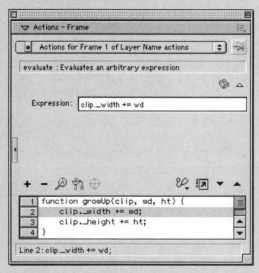

Now let's call the function on the Grow Up button to see what happens.

4. Click the Grow Up button and display the Actions panel in Normal mode. In the Actions Toolbox, click Actions | User-Defined Functions and double-click call function. Leave Object blank. For Function, type **growUp**. For Parameters, type (**chess, 50, 50**). The script on the Grow Up button should look like the following illustration.

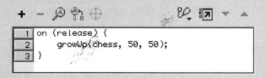

Let's examine the script on the button. The function called growUp (defined on the first frame in the main Timeline) is called on the release of this button. The instance name of the chess piece (chess) has now taken the place of clip. The numbers 50, 50 have taken the place of the parameters, wd and ht.

Test the movie. When you click the Grow Up button, the size of the movie clip grows.

If you want more practice, you can create the second function in this movie, which is the growDown function. This function makes the width and the height of the movie clip reduce in size. To do this, create another button that says **Grow Down**. Click the first frame in the main Timeline and display the Actions panel in Expert mode. On the line under the last bracket of the existing function, type the following:

```
function growDown(clip,wd,ht) {
    clip._width-=wd;
    clip._height-=ht;
}
```

Notice that this function is almost identical to the first function. The Actions panel should now look like this:

```
1  function growUp(clip, wd, ht) {
2      clip._width += wd;
3      clip._height += ht;
4  }
5  function growDown(clip, wd, ht) {
6      clip._width -= wd;
7      clip._height -= ht;
8  }
```

To test this function and make certain it works on other objects, try creating another button. Then create another movie clip. It can be any object you want, since this is just for test purposes. Give the movie clip an instance name. Now call the function on the new button, but this time, in the parameters, use the name of the new instance and type a different wd and ht parameter. Test the movie. As you can see, the new parameters were indeed passed to the new instance when the function was called.

Create a Simple Drag-and-Drop Movie Clip

One of the simplest and most common interactive techniques you see nowadays is the drag-and-drop technique. Drag and drop refers to an interactive technique where the user can click an object and move it to another part of the stage simply by pressing and releasing the mouse. Often, you will see this technique used on puzzles and with interactive shopping carts.

In the next chapter, we will expand upon the drag-and-drop functions by utilizing them in conjunction with several other techniques. In this section, we will cover the basics of creating this technique.

It's quite simple to create a drag-and-drop function. It merely involves creating a movie clip, nesting a button in the movie clip, and then placing the script on the button in the movie clip.

In Figure 14-5, a chess piece appears again, but this time with a drag-and-drop function.

FIGURE 14-5   A simple drag-and-drop function was applied to the object.

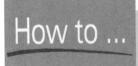

Create a Simple Drag-and-Drop Function on an Object

As you can see here, the steps required to create a simple drag-and-drop function are covered. Let's review the steps:

1. In a new file, make a movie clip, drag the movie clip to the stage, and give the movie clip an instance name. In Figure 14-5, the movie clip is a chess piece and the instance name assigned is **pawn**.

2. Double-click the movie clip instance to enter editing mode. Click the object—in this case the pawn—and press F8 to insert another symbol. In the Symbol Editing dialog box, click Button, name it **button**, and click OK.

3. In editing mode of the button, put a keyframe on the Hit state and draw a rectangle over the boundaries of the object to indicate the clickable area of this button. In other words, this is the area where the user can click to drag the instance.

14

4. Exit button editing mode by clicking down one level to the movie clip in the upper-left corner. You will then enter the movie clip editing mode that the button is nested in.

5. In editing mode for the movie clip, click the object. Notice in the Properties Inspector that the object is a button. Display the Actions panel in Normal mode; in the Actions Toolbox, click Actions | Movie Clip Control and double-click startDrag. Click line 1 of the script and, for Event, select Press and deselect Release. Click line 2 and click in the Target box. Click the Insert Target Path button; in the Target Path dialog box, for Mode, click Absolute. Select the instance name in the Target path area and click OK. Deselect the Expression check box.

6. Select line 3 and, in the Actions Toolbox, select Actions | Movie Clip Control and double-click stopDrag. The script on the button should look like this:

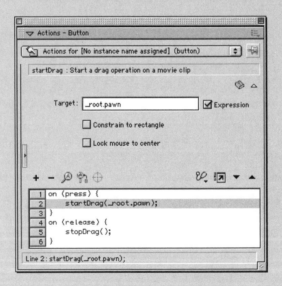

Exit editing mode and test the movie. You should be able to pick up and drag and drop the instance. Notice that when you position your pointer over the object, you see the hand icon commonly associated with button events. The inclusion of the button in the instance is what makes it clickable.

Hide the Mouse

Sometimes, you will see Flash movies where the traditional pointer has disappeared. In its place will be something other than a mouse. This is another ActionScript method in action, called `Mouse.hide`. Basically, it involves a few steps. You hide the mouse and replace it with the movie clip that the script resides on. Then you set the new _x and _y position of the custom cursor. If it sounds pretty easy, that's because it is.

Figure 14-6 shows a movie clip instance of a paintbrush. This movie clip takes the place of the standard cursor. In other words, when the user moves his/her mouse, instead of seeing the usual arrow, the paintbrush appears. Let's take a look at how to hide a cursor and then substitute a movie clip in it's place. The first step is to create a movie clip and then display the Actions panel in Expert mode. If you are more comfortable using Normal mode, you can find the `Mouse.hide` action in the Actions Toolbox | Objects | Mouse | Methods | hide.

On the movie clip instance, type the following script:

```
onClipEvent (load) {
     Mouse.hide();
}
onClipEvent (enterFrame) {
          _visible = true;
     }
onClipEvent (mouseMove) {
     _x = _root._xmouse;
     _y = _root._ymouse;
     updateAfterEvent();
}
```

The script is simple. When the movie clip loads, the mouse hides. Then a variable is set. The variable is the `_visible` property, which returns `True` on entering the frame. On a mouseMove event, more variables are set. The _x and _y values are equal to the _xmouse and _ymouse properties, which simply return the coordinates of the position of the mouse. Test the movie. When you move the pointer, the movie clip moves, too.

We have covered what seems like a lot of ActionScript territory in the last few chapters. In Chapter 15, we further expand upon our ActionScript knowledge base by introducing more scripting techniques and combining various actions, methods, functions, and operators.

FIGURE 14-4   This movie clip instance replaces the cursor using the `Mouse.hide` method.

Experiment with More Complex ActionScript

How to...

- Make movie clips behave as buttons
- Use the `attachMovie` method
- Use the sound object
- Draw with ActionScript
- Design Using the Color Object
- Use the `setMask` method
- Design with components in Flash

Since Flash version 4, ActionScript has experienced a tremendous growth. In fact, ActionScript as it currently exists bares little resemblance to the original Flash scripting environment. Certainly, some simple actions are the same as in earlier versions, but many have been deprecated and the scripting interface looks very different than it used to.

In earlier versions of Flash, the scripting environment offered a straightforward interface that made it easy for Flash designers to add simple interactivity to their Flash movies. In version MX, ActionScript has evolved into an extremely complex, full-bodied programming language, and it takes a lot of study and practice to find your way around the more advanced features.

Although this book provides a solid introduction to the basics of ActionScript, readers interested in the advanced programming aspects of Flash need extensive study and hands-on experience to master ActionScript. If you are a designer, a cursory understanding of ActionScript could be just fine for your purposes. Chapters 11 through 15 provide information and examples that will assist you in creating a variety of interesting scripts. However, if you find your interests lie in the programmable aspects of Flash, the ActionScript in this book will only act as a springboard and point you in the right direction for more advanced ActionScript studies.

TIP   *It's a good idea to download the chapter source files associated with Chapter 15 from the Osborne site (www.osborne.com). You may find that some of the examples in this chapter are easier to follow if you view the source files.*

In this chapter, we will examine some of the new actions, methods, and functions of the latest version of ActionScript. New techniques will be combined with some old techniques so that you can understand the concept of planning out and combining techniques to make your interactive movies multidimensional.

It is assumed in this chapter that you have a basic understanding of Flash and ActionScript, so there is not as much detail included in the description of building the movie and scripting as was provided in earlier chapters. We will also start scripting more in Expert mode, which is kind of like learning to ride a two-wheeler after relying on Normal mode "training wheels." If you prefer to script in Normal mode and you don't know where the Actions are located in the Actions panel Toolbox, you can always go to the bottom of the Actions panel Toolbox and select any action from the Index. Here, the contents of the Actions Toolbox are alphabetically categorized. You can also right-click (Windows)/CTRL-click (Mac) any item listed in the Index to display the context menu. In the context menu, you can select Show Original to take you to where an action is located in the Actions Toolbox. You can also select View Reference to take you to the Reference panel, where you can find a definition for the item you selected. This will help you find an action quickly in the Actions Toolbox (see Figure 15-1).

This chapter will provide you with some additional tools and direction for your ActionScript arsenal, and you can begin to provide your own creativity to these scripts.

Make Movie Clips Behave Like Buttons

In Chapter 11, you learned how to make basic buttons and movie clips. You also learned the basic differences between these two behavior types. To review, buttons are clickable and are generally used to control frame actions and movie clips. Movie clips, on the other hand, are movies on their own Timeline. The power behind movie clips comes from the fact that they have the ability to talk to one another and, as a result, do all sorts of spectacular tricks.

Creating a drag-and-drop effect in a movie generally involves nesting a button in a movie clip and assigning the script that drags and drops the movie to the button nested in the movie clip. So, the nested button (the child) would talk to its parent object, the movie clip. In MX, you can now assign button events to a movie clip object. In essence, what you're doing here is creating a button movie clip by combining button events with movie clips.

Button events are different from movie clip events because movie clip events run when an event is triggered. For example, if you were to assign a drag-and-drop method to two movie clips in the same movie, the clicking and dragging would only work on the movie clip situated on the higher level. In contrast, when you assign a drag-and-drop action on a button in a movie clip, the action becomes specific to the movie clip referenced in the button script. The following would be the script for a simple drag and drop of a movie clip without a nested button:

```
onClipEvent (mouseDown) {
        _root.mc.startDrag();
}
onClipEvent (mouseUp) {
        _root.mc.stopDrag();
}
```

If you copy and paste this script onto another movie clip and give the other movie clip a different instance name, when you test the movie, you will see that the clip event only works on the first clip. So, multiple instances of drag-and-drop movie clips wouldn't work with this script. Let's see what happens when we take a movie clip and assign button events to it. First, let's examine how to assign button events to a movie clip.

Create a Movie Clip Button

It's fairly easy to create a button movie clip, as you will see. You can actually assign up, over, and down properties to the movie clip, similar to a button Timeline. But since you're doing this on a movie clip Timeline as opposed to a button Timeline, the way you create it is a little different.

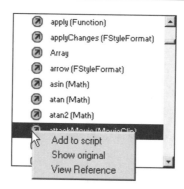

FIGURE 15-1 Right-click/ CTRL-click an action in the Index of the Actions panel Toolbox to find the path of an action or display the action in the Reference panel.

 **Create a Movie Clip That Behaves Like a Button**

Here's how to do it:

1. Create a new movie clip with Insert | New Symbol, and name it **shape**.

2. If your movie clip Timeline has multiple layers like the one portrayed in the following illustration, add them all on the first frame.

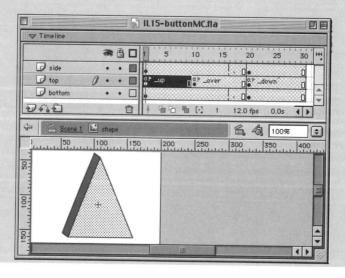

3. To add an _up, _over, and _down state to the movie clips Timeline, insert two additional keyframes on one of the layers. In the case of the illustration, the movieclip/ button changes on the _over and _down states, and an additional keyframe is added to Frames 10 and 20. In addition, regular keyframes are added to Frame 30 so the last frame label can be seen. You must put a label on these frames in order to get these frames to work the right way, so the additional frames give the label enough space to display.

4. Now, click the first keyframe in the top layer (the layer you are changing states on) and type **_up** in the Properties Inspector.

5. Click the second keyframe and type **_over** in the Properties Inspector.

6. Click the third keyframe and type **_down** in the Properties Inspector.

7. Extend the frames on the last keyframe so you can see the _down label. Do this by selecting the last keyframe and clicking F5.

8. Click the first keyframe, and display the Actions panel (F9); in the Options pop-up menu, select Expert mode. Type **stop();**.

9. Repeat this process for the remaining two keyframes (_over and _down). You will now see the letter *a* on each of the three keyframes, indicating that they contain a frame action.

10. Go back to the _over and _down states and change their properties as you would do on any button. In the illustration, the color was changed on the _over and _down states and the position of the object was moved on the _down state.

11. Exit movie clip editing mode and drag an instance of the new button movie clip to the stage.

If you test the button events on the movie clip, you will notice that nothing happens. You don't even get the little gloved hand commonly associated with buttons when you mouse over the movie clip. We have to do a little additional scripting to get this movie clip to act like a button. We have to assign a button event to it. Along with the button event, we'll assign a simple trace action just to make sure the button movie clip is really alive and kicking.

15

12. On Frame 1, select the button movie clip, display the Actions panel in Expert mode, and type in the following code:

```
on(release) {
        trace(_root.shape._y);
        trace(_root.shape._x);
}
```

Test the movie. When you mouse over the button movie clip, it now acts just like a button, changing as per the different states assigned. Each time you click it, as per the script on the button movie clip, an output window appears that traces the position of the X and Y coordinates of the button movie clip, just as the script requested. The path to the trace action in Normal mode is the following: Actions | Miscellaneous Actions | trace.

The button movie clip is a pretty cool feature, but you're probably thinking "so what?" In the next section, we will build a movie around some button movie clips. In addition, we will incorporate some new ActionScript techniques not reviewed yet in this book, as well as some old techniques. This will help give you some idea of how you can put all of these pieces of script together and make them work.

Put Movie Clips with Button Behaviors to Work

There are many things you can do with button movie clips, and the following is a simple example. Figure 15-2 is a movie that uses movie clip button instances for a drag-and-drop function. Let's consider how this movie works.

When the movie loads, you see three cameras on the left and a blank screen to the right. Instructions on the top of the movie tell you to drag the cameras to the screen on the right and drop them. When you do this, for each camera, an image of a painting appears. The images are JPEG files that are accessed remotely if the camera button movie clip hits a particular target.

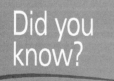

Omitting Trace Actions

When you use trace actions to test a script, you should eliminate them when you publish the Flash file. In the Flash Publish Settings dialog box, you can select the Omit Trace Actions check box to ensure that they are all removed from a script before you publish it. We discuss the Publish settings in detail in Chapter 16.

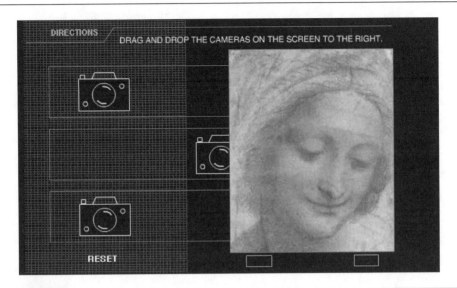

FIGURE 15-2   This movie uses button movie clips to create a drag-and-drop and a
`hitTest` function.

The target is the screen on the right. The screen is a movie clip with an instance name of "box"
that the JPEG files are being loaded into when the camera hits the screen target. This movie clip
is just an outline rectangle with no fill.

There is also a Reset button on the bottom left of the stage, which is just a regular button.
Since the Reset button doesn't have to do anything fancy like the button movie clips, a regular
button works just fine for the purpose of returning all objects to their initial state.

This movie has several actions and functions going on simultaneously. First, button movie
clips are created using the techniques from the previous section. There is also a `hitTest` method
utilized in the script and a conditional (`if`) that evaluates the parameters of the collision between
the movie clips and the screen. If the parameters are true, a JPEG file loads into the screen. For this,
we use the `loadMovie` method. In addition, a function is defined that resets the properties of the
movie to their initial state on a button event. This function is called when the Reset button is clicked.

It's a good idea to test the movie first (loadMovie.fla) so you can familiarize yourself with
how it works and what it does. See if you can spot how and where the previously mentioned
actions, methods, and functions were used.

15

NOTE
*The source files for this movie (as are all source files for every chapter), including
the JPEG files, are located in the Chapter 15 folder for this book on the Osborne site
(www.osborne.com).*

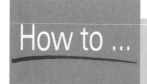

Make a Movie with Draggable Movie Clips That Behave Like Buttons

Understanding that movie clips and buttons can exchange behaviors is an important part of understanding the power of ActionScript. In Chapter 14, we created a simple movie clip with a button nested in it. Here, we actually assign button attributes to a movie clip. With this in mind, let's get to it.

1. Begin a new movie, save it, and give it a black background in the Document Properties dialog box.

2. Create the layers in the Timeline. In this movie, the layers are named as follows:

   - actions
   - GRID
   - reset button
   - directions
   - screen frame
   - direction lines
   - loaded movies
   - mc button 1
   - mc button 2
   - mc button 3
   - reset button
   - background

   Later, when you drag the assets onto the stage, make certain you place them on the layer associated with the object. For example, the movie clip that we will name mc button 1 will go on the mc button 1 layer.

3. Build the various parts of the movie. First, you can make the camera as a movie clip. In the movie clip associated with the example file, the camera is named camera1. As you can see in the camera movie clip Timeline, the same method as was outlined previously was used to create button states on the movie clip. In other words, the _up, _over, and _down states were created. The object changes slightly on each state and a stop action was applied to each keyframe. The camera movie clip is multilayered, with various pieces residing on different layers. The properties of the camera change on the _over (color) and _down (color and position) states.

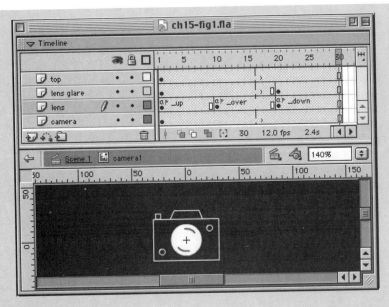

4. If you want, you can create a grid background like the one in the sample movie. If you do, place the background on the background layer and lock it so it doesn't interfere with the rest of the layers.

5. The screen used to load the JPEG files was constructed. This screen (named screenMc) is merely a movie clip rectangle with no fill and no stroke. To create this screen, insert a new movie clip. In editing mode, draw a rectangle with no color. Make the dimensions of this blank rectangle 200 width × 240 height. These are the exact dimensions of the JPEG files that will load into this movie clip. Jot this size down. You will need to use this data later when you make the frame that creates the border of the screen and when you size the JPEG files. Also, in order for the JPEGs to load into the movie clip properly, you must place the registration point of the movie clip in the upper-left corner. This way, the movie will load in the correct spot.

15

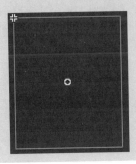

6. Make the Reset button. The button in the example is a plain text button, but you can obviously make any kind of button you like. A script will be added to it in a later step.

7. On the first frame of the Directions layer, type in any instructional text that might help your user navigate the interactive movie. It's not often obvious to a user how they are supposed to respond to a movie, so you often need to spell it out for them. In this movie, the following directions were typed: DIRECTIONS: DRAG AND DROP THE CAMERAS ON THE SCREEN TO THE RIGHT.

8. The screen movie clip that we named screenMc is blank, so you can't see it on stage. Since the user needs to see the target they need to drop the cameras in, we will create a static border that will sit on top of the blank screen. This way, they can see where the target is. On the screen frame layer, make a rectangle of the same dimensions as the screen (width of 200 and height of 240), give it an outline color and no fill, group it, and give it a reference point of top left. An easy way to change the reference point of a graphic is to select it and then select the Free Transform tool from the Toolbox. Drag the middle ring to the top left to change the reference point of the object.

9. Position this rectangle to the right of the stage, approximately where it appears on the finished movie. Record the X and Y coordinates that are used in this rectangle because, when we drop the screenMc on the stage, we will want to make certain it sits directly underneath this graphic. You can get the X and Y coordinates by clicking the rectangle and looking in the Properties Inspector.

10. At this point, any additional, nonfunctional graphics can be added to the movie. For example, the horizontal lines that help guide the user from the cameras to the hit area of the screen can be rendered and placed on the directional lines layer.

11. From the Library, place an instance of the camera movie clip in the first frame of the following layers: mc button 1, mc button 2, and mc button 3. Put the cameras on the left side of the stage, between the directional lines. Select each camera movie clip, and give it an instance name of **mc1**, **mc2**, and **mc3**, respectively, to correspond with the similarly named layer. As you select each camera, type the instance name in the Properties Inspector.

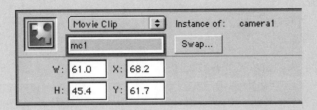

12. From the Library, drag the screenMc onto the loaded movie layer. It is important that you make certain the coordinates match with the screen frame graphic. The top-left reference point of the screen frame box in this movie is X: 250.8, Y: 36.

13. Give the screenMc an instance name in the Properties Inspector of box.

Now let's talk about the mechanics of loading JPEGs into movie clips.

Load a JPEG File into a Movie Clip

Almost every element in the movie is now in place and we are almost ready to add the scripts. The only elements that have not been prepared are the JPEG files that load when the user drags the cameras onto the screen. For this function, we are going to use the `loadMovie` action.

`loadMovie` can be used in a couple of different ways. You can use it to load external SWF files into your current browser window. You can also use `loadMovie` (as we will do in this movie) to load an external SWF or JPEG file into a movie clip. This is a commonly used feature of Flash ActionScript. If you're working with large files, you can keep your files separate from your Flash movie and just have them load when the user wants to see them by clicking a button or some other event. Using this function helps keep your file sizes smaller, which means faster navigation for your users. The other incentive for using this method is that the annoying delay between HTML pages loading in a browser doesn't exist with this method. In other words, an image appears in the same window with no screen refresh delay, which sometimes breaks the flow and spontaneity of the interactive experience.

You can also load external sound into Flash using the sound object. We will discuss that later in this chapter.

Preparing Your JPEGs for the loadMovie Function   The JPEGs will be a part of the interactivity of the movie; they won't be imported into the movie during the design process. Rather, the `loadMovie` action will call the JPEGs and they will appear in the screen movie clip. The JPEGs do have to be prepared beforehand in an external application like Photoshop or Fireworks so that they will look right when the user drags their camera to the hit target screen.

15

Loading Movies in Order

External SWF and JPEG files that are loaded into Flash assume levels, the first movie always being level 0. Subsequent movies load in increments of one, and stack on top of one another. If you need to change the order of multiple movies that are loading, you can do so in your script. Notice the number 1 in the following script:

```
on (release) {
    loadMovieNum("picture.swf", 1);
}
```

This number indicates the level that the movie loads in when the button is clicked. You can also use the Get URL action to load an HTML file or SWF file into your current movie on an event.

After optimizing the files in the external application, you want to make certain the size of the JPEG file is identical to that of the movie clip it is going to load into. Earlier, you jotted down the size and position of the screenMc and the frame graphic, which indicates to the user the borders of the screen. Use this information to make certain the JPEGs that will load are the exact same width and height as the screen before you save them. Additionally, you want to make a notation of the path (location) of the JPEG files. In this movie, the JPEG files are stored in the same folder as the Flash movie we are creating. The movies should remain in the same folder, and this path should be mimicked in its remote location to eliminate any loading problems at run time. If the JPEG files (or SWF files) reside on a remote sever in another directory, you must update the path in the script.

Once you have sized the JPEGs correctly (200 width × 240 height) and stored them in the same folder, you are all set to start scripting. The JPEGs we are going to use are this size, and they have been saved as "ren1.jpg", "ren2.jpg", and "ren3.jpg".

Assigning a Script to the Movie Clips

There are five separate scripts in this movie. Let's start by scripting the cameras. Remember, you gave the cameras an instance name of mc1, mc2, and mc3, consecutively.

Select the first camera movie clip (mc1) and display the Actions panel. In the Actions panel options pop-up menu, select Expert. We will be scripting in Expert mode for now. We first need to let Flash know that this movie clip wants to act as if it's a button. We do this by assigning a button event handler to it. In addition, we want to set up the drag-and-drop action on this clip. Click in the Actions panel and type in the following script in Expert mode. (To find the path for startDrag() and stopDrag() in the Normal mode Toolbox, select Actions | Movie Clip Control | startDrag.)

```
on (press) {
    startDrag("");
}
on (release) {
    stopDrag();
}
```

TIP *You can display your script with line numbers by selecting View Line Numbers in the Actions panel options pop-up menu. The line numbers don't show up in the final script. The line numbers act as a guide to help you navigate through a script, line by line.*

Notice that the actions, startDrag() and stopDrag(), are contained within brackets after the event handlers. Also, notice the semicolon after the actions. A semicolon acts almost like a period at the end of a sentence in ActionScript. The parameters for this startDrag() and stopDrag() are empty. Pay careful attention to the structure of the scripts we are creating, and you will begin to see a pattern. We have discussed the syntax in the last couple of chapters.

To make sure you didn't make a typo, click the Check Syntax button in the Actions panel. If you didn't make a mistake, a dialog box appears telling you so. If you did make a mistake, an output window will appear and will assist you in figuring out what you did wrong.

If you test the movie at this point, you will see that the movie clip drags and releases. Also, the movie clip possesses the properties of a button.

Let's now add the hitTest function to this script. If you recall, the hitTest method evaluates a situation and decides whether the hitTest is true or false. In this case, the hitTest is evaluating whether one of the camera instances (mc1, mc2, mc3) collided with the hit area, the mc instance, whose instance name is box.

To add a hitTest to mc1:

1. Display the Actions panel in Expert mode. You will see the previous script you entered. In the script, position your cursor between the last two lines of code (between lines 5 and 6).

15

Did you know?

Additional Buttons

The Actions panel set in Expert mode has some additional buttons that appear in the panel interface:

- The Check Syntax button checks to make certain you didn't make any errors in the way you input the code. You can also select this from the pop-up Options menu, or use the shortcut key, CTRL-T (Windows)/CMD-T (Mac).

- The Auto Format button formats the script in Flash formatting style. To define Flash formatting style, go to the options pop-up window and select Auto Format Options. Here, you can customize the way spaces and brackets are displayed, among other things.

The Show Code Hint button can remind you how to structure a line of code. With a ToolTip interface, the proper syntax appears, indicating where parameters, events, and properties are supposed to go (see Figure 15-3).

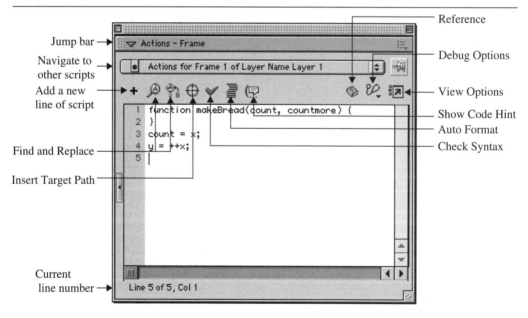

FIGURE 15-3 In Expert mode, the Actions panel buttons are arranged differently and three buttons are added to the panel.

Include the following script. (To find the path of the `if` action in Normal mode, select Actions | Conditions/Loops | if.)

```
if (_root.mc1.hitTest(_root.box)) {
    _root.box.loadMovie("ren1.jpg");
}
```

The final script should look like this:

```
on (press) {
    startDrag("");
}
on (release) {
    stopDrag();
    if (_root.mc1.hitTest(_root.box)) {
    _root.box.loadMovie("ren1.jpg");
}
}
```

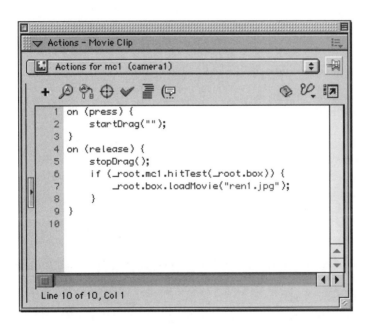

Let's examine what is being said in this script. We have used a conditional statement in this script (`if`) that evaluates whether the mc1 instance has collided with the box instance. Notice the instances are called from the _root level, as an absolute address. If the collision is true, then the next statement is executed, and the file "ren1.jpg" loads into the box instance.

2. Test the movie, and drag the instance of mc1 onto the box instance to see what happens. A JPEG file loads if the `if` condition returns true in the script. Remember, the JPEG files are stored in the same folder as the movie, so they can easily be called in the movie.

3. The script on the other two camera movie clips is almost identical, except the picture that loads is different. Rather than write the script from scratch on the remaining camera movie clips, mc2 and mc3, you can select each instance and, in the Actions panel, copy and paste the script on the first camera. Then you'll go back and modify lines 6 and 7 of the code.

4. For mc2, change the movie being loaded to "ren2.jpg"; and for mc3, change the movie being loaded to "ren3.jpg". The script on mc2 now reads as follows:

```
on (press) {
    startDrag("");
}
on (release) {
    stopDrag();
    if (_root.mc2.hitTest(_root.box)) {
     _root.box.loadMovie("ren2.jpg");
}
}
```

The script on mc3 now reads like this:

```
on (press) {
    startDrag("");
}
on (release) {
    stopDrag();
    if (_root.mc3.hitTest(_root.box)) {
     _root.box.loadMovie("ren3.jpg");

}
}
```

Test the movie to see how it works. Next we will discuss how to make the Reset button.

Create a Reset Function

After the user has dragged these cameras onto the stage, it would be nice to offer the ability for the user to return the screen to its original state. In order to do this, we can set the properties on a button event, which, in this case, is the Reset button. When the user clicks the Reset button, all the clips jump back to their original position on the stage. This is commonly done with a `setProperty` action and is quite simple to do.

There is one other another issue with returning the movie clips to their original position. What appears in the screen (box instance) once the cameras revert back to their original state? Don't we want the screen to appear in its original state, which was a blank screen? We could use the unLoadMovie method to achieve this. This method would remove any movies in the box instance. The problem with unLoadMovie is that if the user wants to go back and load another movie, using this method won't allow for further loading. This is due to the order in which the load and unload methods are executed in a script.

The other way to give the movie the appearance of reverting back to a blank screen when the Reset button is clicked would be to create a JPEG file or a SWF file that is blank (or that matches with the background color of the movie) and load it with the loadMovie method. So, the blank JPEG or SWF would work the same way as the other JPEG files, only it would give the appearance of a blank screen.

To reset the stage using the setProperty action, and load a blank JPEG or SWF file into the box instance, follow these steps:

1. First, create a blank JPEG file or SWF file that is the same dimensions as the other JPEG movies and the box instance (or make the file the same color as the movie background, which, in this case, is black). The size of the screen and the JPEG files in the movie example with the cameras is 200 width × 240 height. Save this file in the same folder with the movie and all the other supporting pieces associated with this file. In the example we are working with, the blank file is a JPEG and it is called "black.jpg".

2. Click all three of the movie clips and jot down their location on the stage. You will need this information to set the position of the cameras back to the way they were when the movie initialized. Get this data from the Properties Inspector or the Info panel (Windows | Info). In the Info panel, you can also define the reference point of the X and Y coordinates.

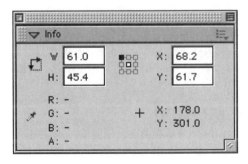

3. Display the Actions panel in Expert mode and click the first frame in the Actions layer. We are going to create a function here. This function will reset the X and Y properties of mc1, mc2, and mc3. Later, we will create an event handler on the Reset button that will call this function. Type in the following script; and if your X and Y coordinates are different from the coordinates listed, type your new numbers in. (For the first line of the script, the path to `function` is the following: Actions | User-Defined Functions | function.)

```
function Reset(_x,_y) {
    _root.mc1._x = 98.4;
    _root.mc1._y = 88.3;
    _root.mc2._x = 98.4;
    _root.mc2._y = 161.8;
    _root.mc3._x = 98.4;
    _root.mc3._y = 236.4;
box.loadMovie("black.jpg");
    }
```

Let's briefly examine the previous script. The function in the first line is named Reset and the parameters of the function are the _x and _y position. The next six lines are variables that basically state that the movie clips' _x and _y position is equal to the number assigned.

The box.loadMovie("black.jpg") line of code is also contained within this function. So, in addition to resetting the _x and _y position of each movie clip, the "black.jpg" file will load in the box instance. Now that the function is defined, let's call the function on a button event.

Call the Reset Function   Now it's time to add the last script to the movie to make it fully functional. Display the Actions panel and click the Reset button. In the panel, type the following script:

```
on (press) {
    _root.Reset();
}
```

When the user clicks the Reset button, the functions defined on the main Timeline are executed.

Test the movie to see how it works. This movie is fairly simple and shows you some frequently used actions in action. One of the hardest tasks in learning ActionScript is conceptualizing what it is you want to make interactive. Examining source files like the preceding example is tremendously helpful in boosting your ActionScript skills. To add to these skills, let's take a look at a couple of other commonly used actions that are similar to the `loadMovie` method.

Use the attachMovie Method

As you probably suspect, `attachMovie` does just what its name says—it attaches a movie to something. More specifically, this method allows you to attach a movie clip from the Library to a movie clip on the stage. Using this method creates a programmable instance of the movie clip, and it gives the new instance a name. The difference between `attachMovie` and `loadMovie` is that the `loadMovie` method loads a SWF or JPEG file from an external source, whereas the attachMovie method loads a movie clip from your Library. You can also attach another movie

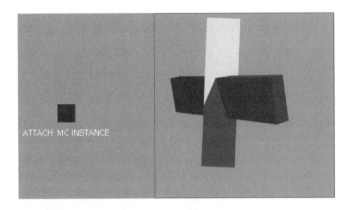

FIGURE 15-4   This movie uses the attachMovie method to load a movie clip into another movie clip on a button event.

clip instance from another Library during run time; but for now, we'll examine how to do this from the file you are currently working on.

Why would you use the `attachMovie` method? For one thing, it's an uncomplicated way of introducing a movie clip that's not currently in the Timeline. If you attach a move from the Library of another SWF file where a linkage identifier was defined, you can reduce the size of the Flash movies that share this movie clip. Let's take a look at how the `attachMovie` method works.

Figure 15-4 shows a movie that loads a movie clip named `beamCenter` into a movie clip on a button event. In the Library of this file, there is a movie clip named `beamCenter`. This movie clip is a simple, 3-D animation imported from Swift3D. (This, by the way, is a great program for generating quick vector-based, 3-D movie clips.) When the movie loads, it plays a brief animation and then stops on Frame 25. At this point, a black button appears. If you click the button, an instance of the movie clip, *beam*, loads into another movie clip on the stage that acts as a frame. You will notice this process is reminiscent of the `loadMovie` function. The difference is that you are attaching a movie clip instance, as opposed to an external JPEG or SWF file.

Use the Sound Object

Sound objects were introduced in Flash version 5. Prior to Flash 5, the only interactive sound control you could build into your Flash movie was the ability to stop all sounds. In this section, we are going to create a sound object whose volume can be dynamically controlled by the user. In addition to being able to control the volume of a sound object, you can also control when it start and stops, and the pan of the sound. The *pan* refers to the speaker balance of the left and right channels. We are going to create a simple sound object with a sliding button. You've probably seen this technique used on many Flash sites. Basically, it involves making a button

15

Attach a Movie to a Movie Clip with the attachMovie Method

Now that you understand how the `attachMovie` method works, lets experiment with actually using it here.

1. First, you need to make a movie clip that the attached movie clip instance is going to load into. Obviously, this movie clip should be either the same size or larger than the movie clip that it will contain. In the movie example (Figure 15-4), the movie clip named frame is what the attached movie will load into. This is a rectangle with no fill and a stroke of 1, sized large enough to accommodate the SWF movie that's going to be loading into it.

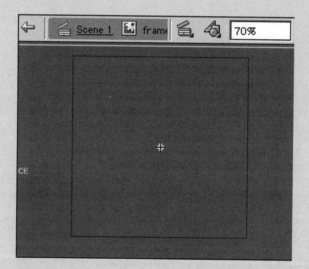

2. When you make this movie clip that acts as the frame, it needs to have a reference point of center. Likewise, the movie clip that is being attached should have a reference point of center. This way, the movie clip instance will attach to the center of the first movie clip acting as the frame.

3. Then, you need to create a movie clip that will attach. The movie clip in the following example is named `beamCenter` in the Library, and the frame movie clip is named frameMc.

4. Drag an instance of the movie clip that acts as a frame onto the stage and give an instance name in the Properties Inspector. If your main Timeline is multilayer, make sure you drag it onto the correct layer. In the example, the frame was placed on the frame layer and put on Frame 25, so you don't see it when the movie loads.

5. The frame needs an instance name, so give it one in the Properties Inspector. In the example, the instance name given is `frame`.

6. In the example, the `beamCenter` movie attaches to the frame on a button event, so our directions will use a button event handler. You could also use this method in conjunction with other event handlers, including frame events. Create a button and put it on the appropriate layer and frame. In the example, a button is on Frame 25 of the button layer.

7. The instance of the beamCenter movie clip that will attach to the frame movie clip instance needs an instance name. The question is, how do we give an instance name to something that does not yet exist? In the Linkage Properties dialog box, you can assign a linkage name for an instance that will attach. The linkage name becomes the instance name of the attached movie. To assign a linkage name to the movie clip that will attach, in the Library, right-click (Windows)/CTRL-click (Mac) to display the Library pop-up Options menu and select Linkage.

8. In the Linkage Properties dialog box, check Export For ActionScript. In the Identifier box, type in a name. In this example, "beamer" was entered as an identifier name. Select Export In First Frame if you want the movie clip to load before the first frame.

15

This is a small movie, and the movie clip instance can load on the button event we will assign, so leave it deselected.

```
                    Linkage Properties
    Identifier  beamer                                    OK

    Linkage:  ☑ Export for ActionScript                Cancel
              ☐ Export for runtime sharing
              ☐ Import for runtime sharing               Help
              ☐ Export in first frame

        URL:
```

9. To script the button, select the button, display the Actions panel in Expert mode, and type the following. (The path to attachMovie in the Normal mode Actions Toolbox is: Objects | Movie Clip | Methods | attachMovie.)

```
on(press){
_root.frame.attachMovie("beamer","beamer2",1);}
```

> NOTE *In this script, you don't need to use absolute addressing because all movie clips are on the main Timeline. You could, if you wanted to, leave the _root off the second line of code.*

In the script, when the user clicks the button, a movie is attached to the frame instance onstage. Contained in the parentheses is the argument, or parameters, of the method. The first parameter ("beamer") is the instance name being applied to the beamCenter movie clip. This is the linkage name you typed in the Linkage Properties dialog box. The second name ("beamer2") is the instance, which is being targeted as the attached movie clip. It becomes a child to the frame movie clip. The number 1 represents the depth of the instance. Here, you can indicate the depth, or the level in which the movie clip instance loads. Our simple example doesn't require a depth because we are only attaching one movie clip. However, 0 is the base level, so a depth of 1 would load on top of 0.

Test your movie. Your movie clip should load when the button is clicked. Linkage IDs can also be used to attach a sound to a Flash movie. Once a sound is attached to your movie, you control certain properties of the sound, like the volume or when it plays. In the next section, we will examine the process of attaching a sound and controlling it in Flash.

movie clip for the slider button, putting a script on the button, and nesting the button movie clip in another movie clip of the slider line (see Figure 15-5).

Create a Volume and Pan Control with the Sound Object

Using the sound object in Flash can be a little confusing the first time. Understanding the process and following the basic steps will help you build a successful sound object. Let's examine the process here.

1. Since this lesson is really about sound, let's start by importing a sound loop (File I Import) into Flash. The sound used in this lesson is called loop.aif. The source file can be found in the Chapter 15 folder for this book on the Osborne web site.

2. We need to give the sound a linkage identifier. Select the sound in the Library and display the Library pop-up Options menu (or right-click in Windows/CTRL-click on Mac). Select Linkage. In the Linkage Properties dialog box, give an identifier name of **loop**, and select Export For ActionScript and Export In First Frame. Close the dialog box. The identifier acts as an instance name for the sound object.

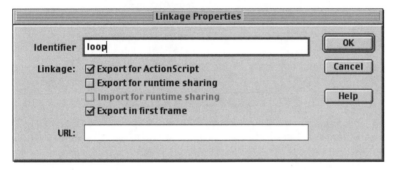

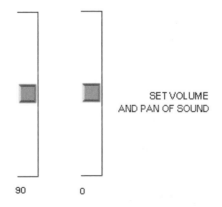

FIGURE 15-5   You can build user-controlled movie clips that alter the properties of a
sound object.

3. Add a new layer to the top of the main Timeline and name it **actions**. We are going to create a sound object and add some sound methods. Click the first frame of the layer, and display the Actions panel (F9). On this frame, type the following script. (For Normal mode, the path to line 1, set variable, is Actions I Variables I set variable.)

```
techno = new Sound();
techno.attachSound("loop");
techno.start("", 999);
```

4. Make a button with a center registration point and name it **button**. In the example, the button is yellow, but you can make it any way you want.

5. Make a movie clip (Insert I Movie Clip) and name it **buttonMc**. Drag an instance of the button into the movie clip and center it on the stage cross hairs (0,0) using the Properties Inspector as a guide. Exit editing mode. The only content of the movie clip is this button:

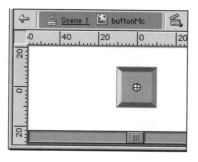

Instead of nesting a button in a movie clip, you could also make a movie clip and script it with button events in the movie clip Timeline (_up, _over, _down) like we did in Figure 15-1. That way, you bypass the process of nesting a button in the movie clip. To make a button movie clip with only a movie clip, follow the instructions we used for Figure 15-1. In other words, on the movie clip Timeline, indicate the _up, _over, and _down states as labels in the Properties Inspector. Then, apply the script in Step 4 to the movie clip instance as if it were the button. However, some Flash users are accustomed to using the old method of nesting a button in a movie clip, and that's what we are using in this example.

6. While still in movie clip editing mode, click the button, display the Actions panel in Expert mode, and type the following script. (For Normal mode, the path to line 1, startDrag, is Actions I Movie Clip Control I startDrag.)

```
on (press) {
    startDrag("", false, 0, 90, 0, -90);
}
```

```
on (release) {
    stopDrag();
}
```

Note that in the script, the dragging range is constrained to –90 and 90, the total of which will equal the height of the slider bar. We will make the slider bar in the next step. The parameters listed after `startDrag` refer to the following: The "" refers to the object itself; false is a Boolean value that indicates the mouse is not locked to the center; the 0, 90, 0 , –90 numbers refer to the left, top, right, and bottom parameters to which this movie clip is restrained. In other words, these parameters are what makes the button draggable on a straight path.

7. Next, create another movie clip and name it **slideMc**. In the example (refer to Figure 15-5), the slider is 180 pixels in height, which correlates to the dragging range of the button movie clip (–90 to + 90). This way, when the button movie clip slides on the slider, it will stop at the beginning and end of the slider bar. Make sure the slider is centered on the editing stage cross hairs (0,0). In the slideMc Timeline, create a new top layer for the button and name it **button**. You can name the second layer **slider**.

8. On the button layer of the slideMc, drag an instance of the button to the slideMc Timeline. Center the button on the stage cross hairs (0,0). Give the button an instance name of **but**.

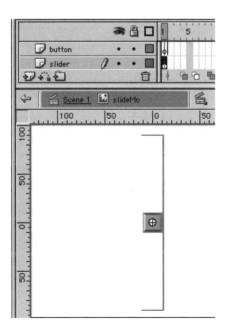

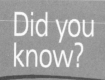

Knobs & Faders

In the Common Libraries Buttons folder, there is a folder called Knobs & Faders. In this folder are three scripted sliders with buttons. So, if you need a slider in a hurry, and don't want to spend the time putting buttons in movie clips and so forth, you might want to check these out.

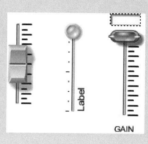

9. Exit the slideMc editing mode, and drag a copy of the slideMc movie clip from the Library to the stage. Test the movie. You should be able to drag the button movie clip up and down the slider you made.

We can also dynamically display the level of the sliders by making a Dynamic text field and scripting it on the volumeMC and the panMC. So, let's set up the text fields and give them a variable name.

10. Create a Dynamic text field under the volumeMC instance. In the Properties Inspector, give it a variable name of **VolTxt**. Copy this text box and paste it on the stage. After you make the PanMc movie clip (to the right of the VolumeMc), you can position this new text box under the panMC movie clip. Select the text, and in the Properties Inspector, change the variable name of the text to **panTxt**.

> TIP *To make a quick copy of text or an object, hold down the ALT/OPT while you drag. This is the equivalent to copying and pasting an object. To copy and paste an object and constrain the new object on the same horizontal or vertical plane as the original, use SHIFT-ALT/SHIFT-OPT to drag to copy the text field.*

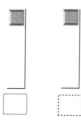

11. Now that we have made the slider, we just need to drag another instance on the stage to create the pan slider. Drag another copy on the stage and arrange the two movie clips. Create another layer that will only be used for static description text. Here you can add text to indicate which slider controls the volume and which controls the pan. Give the volume slider an instance name of **volumeMC** and the pan an instance name of **panMC**. Don't forget to position the Dynamic text box we made in Step 10 underneath the panMc movie clip.

12. Now we're going to put a script on the `volumeMC` instance in the main Timeline. Click the `volumeMC` instance and display the Actions panel in Expert mode (F9). Type the following script:

```
onClipEvent (load) {
_parent.volumeMC.but._y 90;
}
onClipEvent (enterFrame) {
    vol = _parent.volumeMC.but._y+90;
    _parent.techno.setVolume(vol);
    _parent.volTxt = Math.round(vol);
}
```

The _y property of the instance (child of the parent movie clip, `volumeMC`) is 90. Then you declare a variable named `vol` for the `but` movie clip (child of the parent movie clip, volumeMC) and define it with a _y property, which is +90. In addition, the `setVolume` method is used to set the volume of the sound named `techno`. Finally, the text field variable, `volTxt`, equals the `Math.round` method whose parameter is the variable, `vol`. The `round` method will round out the value of the `vol` variable to a whole number.

13. Click the panMC and, in the Actions panel, type the following script:

```
onClipEvent (enterFrame) {
pan = 2*_parent.panMC.but._y;
_parent.techno.setPan(pan);
_parent.panTxt = Math.round(pan);
}
```

This script is similar to the script on the volumeMC; but in the instance, we are using the `setPan` method, which allows you to control the sound balance in left and right channels.

Test the movie. The sound should load on the first frame. The volume control increases the amplitude as you drag the button up the slider, and does the reverse when you drag it down. Concurrently, the pan slider travels from the left and right channels, respectively, as you drag it up and down.

There are several other ways you can control the sound object. You can add `stop` and `play` functions. You can also use the `onSoundComplete` method, which is used to launch an event once a sound has ceased to play. The deconstruction of making volume and pan sliders for the sound object will give you a basic idea of how this object works. Speaking of objects in Flash, let's now take a look at the drawing object and see what it's about.

15

Draw with ActionScript

If you've gotten this far in the book, you are most likely very familiar with how to draw in Flash. You know how to select drawing tools and assign properties such as fill and stroke color to an object.

You can also create programmable drawings in Flash that can be assigned a size, position, fill, and stroke. In other words, you can create a drawing with nothing more than a script. This process is done by creating an empty movie clip object, and then defining the parameters and properties of this object.

With a little creativity and a lot more interactivity, you can do some amazing things with drawing methods. For example, you can build a movie with a user interface that allows users to draw in the Player file. This is good news for gaming and educational developers. You can also create self-generating automatic drawings. In the Chapter 15 source file folder on the Osborne site, I have included some more complex examples of the drawing methods in action. If you are ready for a more complex examination of the drawing methods, you can download these examples. In the interim, let's review the basic process of drawing with ActionScript.

You can make any kind of shape you want, with a fill and stroke, or just one or the other. The form of the shape is controlled by the parameters you enter. Let's start with a simple circle. Figure 15-6 displays a circle that was created with a script. In addition to the circle, there is also a button in the bottom-right corner, instructing the user to click it to duplicate the circle. Although

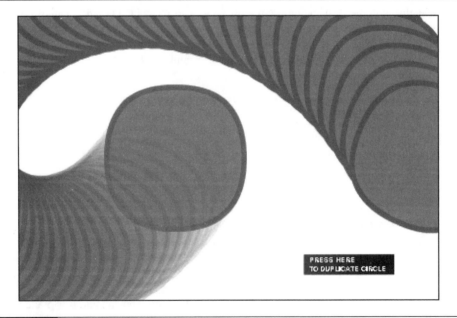

FIGURE 15-6 This movie draws a circle using the drawing object and duplicates several of its properties on a button event.

this figure won't win any design awards, it demonstrates a few basic ActionScript concepts. First, the circle is generated with a script. Second, on a button event, the movie clip instance of the new circle duplicates several times. Third, the duplicate circles' instances change their properties according to the script.

To make a simple circle in ActionScript:

1. Display the Actions panel in Expert mode and click the first frame of the Timeline.

2. Type the following script. (For Normal mode, the path to line 1, createEmptyMovieClip, is Objects | Movie | Movie Clip | Methods | createEmptyMovieClip.)

```
_root.createEmptyMovieClip( "cir", 3 );
with ( _root.cir ) {
    lineStyle( 8, 0xBB2000, 60 );
beginFill( 0xff0055, 60 );
    moveTo( 200, 300 );
    curveTo( 300, 300, 300, 200 );
    curveTo( 300, 100, 200, 100 );
    curveTo( 100, 100, 100, 200 );
    curveTo( 100, 300, 200, 300 );
    endFill();
}
```

The following is a breakdown of the above code:

- The createEmptyMovieClip() method creates a child movie clip of the movie clip object. The parameters inside the parenthesis () assign an instance name and a depth to the new movie clip.

- The lineStyle and beginFill methods define the stroke and fill of the object. The parameters for the lineStyle include stroke, RGB color, and alpha. The parameters for beginFill include RGB color and alpha.

- The moveTo parameters indicate the X and Y coordinates of the instance in relation to its registration point.

- The curveTo method creates the curve of the circle. The parameters for the curveTo method include the X and Y position (first two numbers) of the first point in relation to the registration point of the parent movie clip. The last two numbers of the parameter indicate the X and Y position of the point that the first point is connecting to. In other words, these parameters build one path that connects from one point to another.

- The endFill method fills the area and completes the circle.

Once you have a basic structure, you can alter the object by adjusting the parameters of the object. The beginFill method can be eliminated to create an object with a stroke only.

15

Duplicate a Movie Clip

The `duplicateMovieClip` method creates an instance (or multiple instances) of the current movie clip. In Figure 15-6, there is a button in the right corner that uses the `duplicateMovieClip` method.

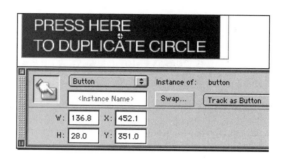

When you click the button, it duplicates the circle many times. In addition, it changes the rotation, position, and alpha of each instance according to the math calculations in the script. There are many ways in which you could do this. Another way to script this would be to randomly duplicate the instances and randomly change the properties using the `Math.random` method. To better understand the basics, let's change the properties using simple variables and operators.

To duplicate the circle instance that we created previously (or any movie clip instance):

1. Create a button, drag it to the stage in the main Timeline, and then select it and display the Actions panel in Expert mode.

2. Type the following script. (For Normal mode, the path to line 1, `set variable`, is Actions I Variables I set variable.)

```
     on (release) {
i = 1;
while (i<300) {
duplicateMovieClip(_root.cir, "c2"+i, i);
setProperty(eval("_root.c2"+i), _rotation, i);
setProperty(eval("_root.c2"+i), _x, i);
setProperty(eval("_root.c2"+i), _y, i);
i += 30;
}
}
```

A variable i is declared and given a value of 1. The letter *i* is often used in scripts for simple counting equations.

A `while` loop is used here to evaluate a condition (i<300). The action will continue to evaluate as long as the condition is true. While this condition is true, the lines within the curly brackets execute. This includes duplicating the movie clip instances; giving the first and subsequent instances names; and setting the properties, which are evaluated and changed on each instance.

You can try experimenting with different operators and operands in this script to see what different results they yield. Plus, once you have a basic script, you can expand upon it or revise it to customize a particular project.

Design Using the Color Object

The properties you can change on a movie clip may seem limited at times. Sure, you can change the position, alpha, scale, and rotation, to name a few, but you can't change the color using properties. However, you can use the `color` object to create movies that dynamically allow a user to change colors.

There is an excellent example of a movie (Color_picker.fla) that utilizes the color object in the Flash MX Samples, FLA folder in your Flash application folder. Take a look at the source file and navigate around the movie so you can see how the interface works (see Figure 15-7).

In the Color_picker.fla movie, the user can custom select a mix of RGB colors from draggable sliders. The text fields on the bottom of the sliders dynamically update the hex and RGB equivalents of the dragged slider color selection. The user also has the option of typing either the hex or the RGB colors in these text fields. The third way for a user to pick a color in this movie is to click one of the color swatches to the left of the sliders. To see the color selection, the user clicks the Apply button in the bottom-right corner. This makes the car to the right change color. This sample file demonstrates one of the many different ways in which you can

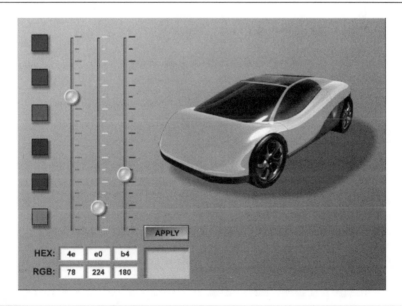

FIGURE 15-7   This movie (Color_picker.fla) demonstrates the use of the color object.

15

use the color object. With a little more work, you can also create dynamic sliders that change the color of an object on-the-fly.

NOTE   *A sample of the Color_picker.fla file from Macromedia is also in the Chapter 15 source files for this book on the Osborne site (www.osborne.com).*

In this section, we will create a movie that utilizes the color object. Figure 15-8 has a simple interface that does the following: when the user clicks on a butterfly, the butterfly changes color and identifies the type of butterfly. This movie also uses dynamic text to identify the butterfly on a button event. The button in this case is nested in the butterfly movie clips. The script resides on the button in the movie clip. The following instructions walk you through the steps of making this movie.

Here's how to use the color object in a movie:

1. As always, you need to plan layers and gather up all your assets before you apply the interactivity. Name the layers in the following order:

    ■ **text** (for a title and instructions)

    ■ **bronzeCopper**

    ■ **purplishCopper**

    ■ **blueCopper**

    ■ **ruddyCopper**

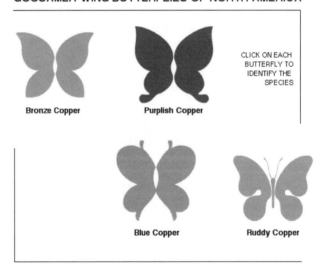

GOSSAMER-WING BUTTERFLIES OF NORTH AMERICA

CLICK ON EACH
BUTTERFLY TO
IDENTIFY THE
SPECIES

Bronze Copper   Purplish Copper

Blue Copper   Ruddy Copper

FIGURE 15-8   Using the color object, the butterflies in this movie change color on a button event.

2. Create all four butterfly graphics as movie clip symbols. Flash files like this can become very confusing when there are many pieces that are similar. Because of this, the movie clip symbols are all named to correlate with the final butterfly type, just as was done on the layers. Likewise, you will notice this practice is carried through in the naming convention of the instances, too, if you take a look at them in the Library.

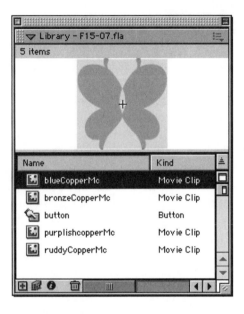

3. Make one blank button with a hit state approximately the same width and height as the biggest butterfly movie clip.

4. Open each butterfly movie clip in the Library. Place an instance of the button in each movie clip. It's a good idea to make a top layer in the movie clip Timeline and place the blank button on the new layer.

5. Arrange each button movie clip on the stage, placing each instance on its own layer.

6. Name each movie clip instance in the Properties Inspector. In Figure 15-7, the movie clips are named to correlate with the Timeline and the name of the movie clip. The following instance names were used for the movie clips:

Movie Clip Name	Instance Name
bronzeCopperMc	bronze
purplishCopperMc	purple
blueCopperMc	blue
ruddyCopperMc	ruddy

15

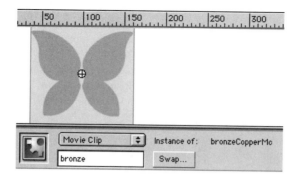

7. Select the Text tool and create the text fields that will dynamically display the name of the butterfly when the user clicks the movie clip. In the main Timeline, position the first text field under the first butterfly. In the Properties Inspector, give the text field a font, font size, alignment, and color. Most important, indicate the Text Type as Dynamic in the Properties Inspector pop-up list.

8. Once you have created the first text field, select it with the Arrow tool, duplicate it, and move it under the next butterfly. Do this by holding down the ALT/OPT key while you drag.

9. Once all text fields are duplicated, click each one with the Text tool and give each text field a variable name in the Properties Inspector. The text field variable names again correspond to the movie clip they are associated with:

Movie Clip Name	Text Field Variable Name
bronzeCopperMc	bronze.txt
purplishCopperMc	purple.txt
blueCopperMc	blue.txt
ruddyCopperMc	ruddy.txt

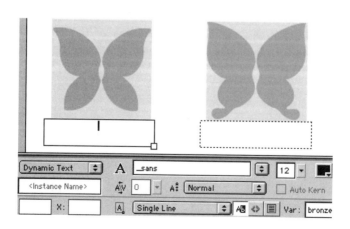

10. Now that everything is in place, the movie clips have instance names, and the text fields have variable names, the scripts are ready to be generated. Double-click the first butterfly movie clip instance (in this case, the *bronze* instance) and display the Actions panel in Expert mode. Select the button you nested in this movie clip; and in the Actions panel, type the following script. (For Normal mode, the path to line 1, `set variable`, is Actions I Variables I set variable.)

```
on (press) {
    mycolor = new Color(_parent.bronze);
    mycolor.setRGB(0xCC9933);
    _root.bronzeTxt = "Bronze Copper";
}
```

Let's discuss how this script functions. The variable named `mycolor` on line 2 is given the value of `new Color` (in Normal mode, select Actions I Variable I set variables). The parameter of `new Color` is bronze, the new instance name given to this color object. The path is indicated as `_parent` because the bronze movie clip is the parent of the button. The button is, in effect, talking to its parent.

On line 3 of the script, `mycolor` is defined with the `setRGB` method (in Normal mode, select Objects I Movie I Color I new Color). The parameter for this method is the hex (hexadecimal) equivalent of the color, which, in this case, is 0xCC9933.

On line 4, a variable defines the value of the text field, "Bronze Copper", which is the text that pops up on the button event.

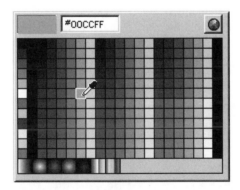

15

TIP   *You can get the hex equivalent of a color in any of the swatch panels. Just put "0x"
before the hex code when you indicate the color parameter.*

Rather than retyping the script on the remaining three buttons, the script on the first button can be copied and pasted into the buttons nested in all the subsequent movie clips. Then, you can go back and modify the variables and parameters for each button. For example, on the second button, the `new Color` parameter is the name of the next movie clip, purple. The hex color is now purple, so the parameter for `setRGB` changes to "0x663399". In addition, the text field value now changes to `Purplish Copper`.

```
1  on (press) {
2      mycolor = new Color(_parent.purple);
3      mycolor.setRGB(0x663399);
4      _root.purpleTxt = "Purplish Copper";
5  }
6
```

When you are done, test the movie to make sure it functions correctly. The source file for this movie can be found in the Chapter 15 folder on the Osborne site.

Make a User-Controlled setMask

In Flash, it's quite easy to create a mask using the layers in the Timeline. In Chapter 9, we created a mask from a bitmap picture of water and some text. If you recall, the text masks the water layer, so the text appears to be filled with a bitmap of water. The water bitmap moves so the water appears to be flowing behind the word (refer to Figure 9-14).

You can also create masks in ActionScript. This is a very cool feature and there are many exciting effects you can achieve using the `setMask` method. A good example of this method can be found in your MX application folder | Samples | FLA | ScriptableMask.fla.

Figure 15-9 utilizes the `setMask` method to create a spotlight over a darkened background. After the `setMask` method is called, the functionality of the circle movie clip (that creates the spotlight effect) is scripted. The circle follows the mouse as the user moves it. This part of the script defines a few simple variables, using the `_x` mouse and `_y` mouse properties and a little math to make the circle movie clip follow the mouse as the user moves it.

The remainder of the script involves simple button actions that go to frames in the main Timeline, to display the opaque version of the car background and a Reset button that returns all elements to their original state. In this section, we will examine the basic functionality of this movie. This includes the `setMask` method and the process used to create the effect of the circle following the mouse. Let's examine how to make this movie:

1. Set the movie up. In Figure 15-9, the background of the movie is black. Create all assets, and import any external elements into the Library. This movie uses a JPEG file named traffic.jpg, located in the Chapter 15 source files folder for this book on the Osborne site. The circle is a simple movie clip. There are two buttons: one that says TURN ON THE LIGHT OVER HERE and another that says RESET. These are simple text buttons. Your setup should also include preparing the layers. The objects placed on stage all reflect the names of the layers. This movie contains the following layers:

■ actions

■ hit

■ alpha cars

15

FIGURE 15-9   This movie utilizes a `setMask` method along with a function that makes a circle mask follow the mouse while the user moves the mouse.

- dot
- sound
- background cars

2. The following objects are located in the Library and can be made prior to creating the movie:

- **cars_mc** This is the car background movie clip and the alpha overlay. The imported JPEG, traffic.jpg, is in this movie clip.

- **circle** This is the spotlight circle movie clip that masks the background.

- **turnOn_button** This is the button Turn On The Light Over Here, which makes the playhead go to Frame 36 on the main Timeline where the mask no longer resides.

- **Reset_Button** This button is used to return the playhead to Frame 1 on the main Timeline.

- **sound** This movie clip (a movie clip with a sound attached to it that plays when the circle movie clip instance is pressed) is played when the circle movie clip instance is pressed.

- **traffic.jpg** This JPEG is the imported picture of the cars used for the background movie clip. This is nested in the cars_mc movie clip.

- **Visor Hum Loop** This is a sound from the Common Sound Library that is used in the sound movie clip.

3. To start building the movie, place an instance of cars_mc on the background layer in Frame 1. Click this instance of cars_mc and select Edit | Copy. Now click the alpha_cars layer and select Edit | Paste In Place on Frame 1 to paste a copy of the cars_mc instance. Give the cars_mc instance on the alpha_cars layer a 20 percent Alpha in the Properties Inspector. You will now be able to see through the circle mask to the bottom movie clip when you test the movie. In other words, this is what creates the smoky-colored backdrop that the spotlight shines through. This is also done by deliberately putting the alpha_car layer above the background and the circle that is masked out on the dot layer located between both the car layers. Because the background of the movie is black, the car_mc instance (on the `alpha_cars` layer) with the 20 percent alpha effect appears dark. Lock the alpha cars and the background layers so they don't move.

4. On the actions layer, click Frame 1 in the Timeline and display the Actions panel in Expert mode. Type **stop();**.

5. Drag an instance of the circle movie clip to the dot layer. Give it an instance name of **circle**.

6. Drag an instance of the turnOn_button to the hit layer, Frame 1.

7. In the main Timeline, insert a keyframe on Frame 36 of the hit layer and drag an instance of the Reset button to the bottom right of the stage on this frame and layer.

8. Drag an instance of the sound movie clip to the sound layer. Double-click it to enter movie clip editing mode. In editing mode, create two layers. Name the first layer **actions** and the second layer **sound**. Insert a keyframe on the actions layer and put a stop action on this frame (Actions panel | Expert mode, and type **stop();**). Put another keyframe on Frame 3 and add another `stop` action following the previous step. Place a keyframe on Frame 2 of the sound layer and drag an instance of the Visor Hum Loop to this frame. Exit editing mode for this clip.

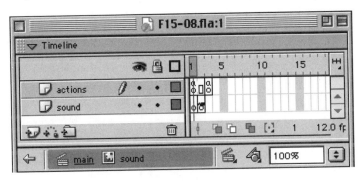

9. On the hit, alpha_cars, dot, and sound layers, click Frame 35 and insert frames (F5).

10. On the actions layer, insert keyframes on frames 35 and 36, and put a `stop` action on frames 35 and 36 as outlined previously. Click the Reset button in the hit layer on

Frame 36. In the Actions panel, Expert mode, type the following script. (This script will send the playhead back to Frame 1 when the Reset button is clicked.)

```
on (press) {
        gotoAndPlay(1);
}
```

11. On the hit layer, click turnOn_button and add the following script in the Actions panel, Expert mode. (This script will send the playhead to Frame 36 when turnOn_button is clicked.)

```
on (press) {
gotoAndPlay(36);
}
```

12. On the background layer, insert frames to Frame 36.

13. Now let's add the body of the script. Click the circle in the dot layer. Give this movie clip an instance name of **circle** in the Properties Inspector. Most of the script will reside on this instance. Display the Actions panel in Expert mode and type the following. (For Normal mode, the path to line 1 in the Actions Toolbox, setMask, is Objects | Movie Clip | Methods | setMask.)

```
onClipEvent (enterFrame) {
        _root.cars.setMask(_root.circle);
}
```

Test the movie. You will see that the circle instance has masked out the background. As mentioned before, the car instance with the 20 percent Alpha setting sits above the mask so it is not affected by the mask. Now let's go back and add the rest of the script to make the circle instance follow the user's mouse movement.

14. With the circle selected and the Actions panel displayed in Expert mode, click at the end of line 2 (_root.cars.setMask(_root.circle);), and press the ENTER key to create a new line 3. Type the remainder of the script:

```
diff_x = _x-_root._xmouse;
        diff_y = _y-_root._ymouse;
        _x = _root._xmouse+(diff_x/1.2);
        _y = _root._ymouse+(diff_y/1.2);
}
onClipEvent (mouseDown) {
        setProperty(_root.circle, _width, 250);
        setProperty(_root.circle, _height, 259);
}
onClipEvent (mouseDown) {
        _root.hum.gotoAndPlay(2);
```

```
}
onClipEvent (mouseUp) {
     setProperty(_root.circle, _height, 143);
     setProperty(_root.circle, _width, 143);
}
onClipEvent (load) {
     if (_root.circle.hitTest(_root.hit)) {
          gotoAndPlay(36);
     }
}
```

```
Actions - Movie Clip

Actions for circle (circle)

 1  onClipEvent (enterFrame) {
 2       _root.cars.setMask(_root.circle);
 3       diff_x = _x-_root._xmouse;
 4       diff_y = _y-_root._ymouse;
 5       _x = _root._xmouse+(diff_x/1.2);
 6       _y = _root._ymouse+(diff_y/1.2);
 7  }
 8  onClipEvent (mouseDown) {
 9       setProperty(_root.circle, _width, 250);
10       setProperty(_root.circle, _height, 259);
11  }
12  onClipEvent (mouseDown) {
13       _root.hum.gotoAndPlay(2);
14  }
15  onClipEvent (mouseUp) {
16       setProperty(_root.circle, _height, 143);
17       setProperty(_root.circle, _width, 143);
18  }
19  onClipEvent (load) {
20       if (_root.circle.hitTest(_root.hit)) {
21            gotoAndPlay(36);
22       }
23  }
24
```

Test the movie. You will now see that the circle movie clip follows the mouse when the user drags it. Notice also that the pointer always returns to the center of the circle instance when the mouse movement stops. This function was scripted with simple variables in lines 3–7 of the script that instruct the circle instance to follow the position property of the mouse (_xmouse and _ymouse) and always return to the center as instructed in lines 5 and 6 of the script.

There are many different effects you can achieve using the setMask feature. You can combine this method with many other ActionScript and animation techniques. Let's now take a look at components in Flash, another exciting new feature of the new MX.

Use Components in Flash

Components are a very exciting and useful feature in Flash MX. If you worked in version 5 of Flash and you were familiar with Smart Clips, then you will appreciate components. Smart Clips were prescripted, ready-made movie clips that had parameters you could change by editing the information in a simple panel. Some of the typical Smart Clips were for functions like ready-made preloaders, drag and drop, and scroll bars.

Components are a derivative of the old Smart Clips in Flash. They are customizable movie clips whose behavior is defined as a component, and that allow Flash designers to add user interface elements like scroll bars, scroll panes, buttons, and menu lists. The Flash components that ship with MX are stored in the Components panel, shown in Figure 15-10.

Flash ships with seven components. You can download additional components from the Macromedia site; and if you rummage through the Samples | FLA folder in your Flash application file, you can find a couple of additional components. There are also several button components in the Buttons Common Library (Window | Common Libraries | Buttons.fla) that you can use for a quick, interactive design. In addition, you can find components on many web sites that offer source files for download, or you can build your own. Sites where you can download source files can be found in Appendix A.

Components are helpful for designers who don't want to spend a lot of time learning the fine points of ActionScript, but require interactivity in their movies. They are also perfect for developers who want to eliminate time-consuming repetitive tasks in programming.

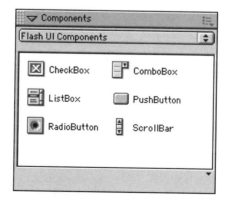

FIGURE 15-10   The Components panel in Flash

Use Component Skins

Components are stored in the Library in a folder called Flash UI Components. If you expand this folder in the Library and examine its contents, you will notice that the folder has many files and folders associated with it. Components you create or acquire from third-party developers appear as a 3-D block icon. Components from Flash appear in the Library just like they do in the Component panel.

One of the folders in the Flash UI Component panel is called Component Skins. The Component Skins folder contains movie clips used to build the component, some of which are shared by other components. Every time you drag another component to the stage, additional skins folders related to that component appear in the Component Skins folder. In fact, some components share the same skins.

Components can be modified in the Library just like any other movie clip. For example, if you wanted a `CheckBox` check to display in a different color, you could open the FCheckBox Skins folder and open the movie clip named fcb_check. In movie clips editing mode, you could then modify the color. You cannot modify the actual component in the Library; only the skins in a component. To get to know components better, let's examine some of the components that ship with Flash MX

Examine the Flash Components

Flash MX comes with seven prebuilt components, all of which are stored in the Components panel. You can access the Components panel from Windows | Components (refer to Figure 15-10).

The parameters of the Flash UI components can be changed in the Properties Inspector. You can also edit the parameters from the Component Parameters panel (Windows | Component Parameters).

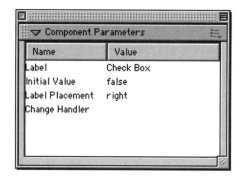

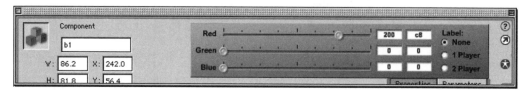

Displaying Parameters

Some parameters will not display in the Components panel. When the author defines the component, he can opt to have the display of the component in the Components panel be true or false. Also, some component authors develop graphical user interfaces that appear in the Properties Inspector. The parameter is then modified in the user interface displayed in the Properties Inspector, which cannot be displayed in the Components panel.

To use a component from the Flash Components panel, just drag it onto the stage from the Components panel. Then, select the component on the stage; and in the Properties Inspector (or the Components panel), change the parameters to suit your particular application. Figure 15-11 shows the CheckBox component on the stage. Notice that in the Properties Inspector, you can change the parameters of the CheckBox component.

You can choose from the following components in the Components panel:

- **CheckBox**   This component is a typical check box that might be used on an interactive form (shown in Figure 15-11). The parameters that can be changed include the CheckBox label, the position of the label, the `True` or `False` value (state of the check when the movie loads), and a `Change Handler` that allows you to call a function on value change.

- **ListBox**   The ListBox gives you a function in which the user can select single or multiple entries. Multiple selections can be made if Select Multiple is set as `True` in the Properties Inspector. The user can make the multiple selection by holding down the SHIFT key. The user can also scroll up and down the list with the UP and DOWN ARROW keys. The parameters that can be changed include the actual labels in the list, the data associated with the labels, and a Change Handler (as described in the preceding paragraph).

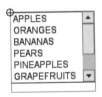

- **RadioButton**   The RadioButton component is similar to the CheckBox, but a user can select only one RadioButton. The parameters that can be changed in a RadioButton are the Label of the button, the Initial State of the RadioButton (whether it is selected or not

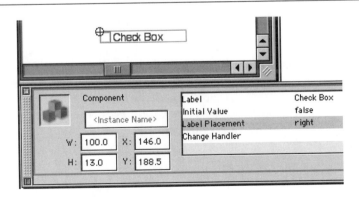

FIGURE 15-11   Change the parameters of a component in the Properties Inspector.

15

when the frame loads), `Group Name` (referring to the group of RadioButtons this button is a part of), Data associated with the button, the Label Placement, and a Change Handler.

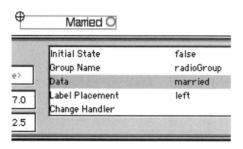

- **ScrollPane** The ScrollPane is used for displaying movie clips in which you can scroll either horizontally or vertically. The parameters that can be changed include the Scroll Content, which is the movie clip identifier; Horizontal Scroll and Vertical Scroll, which can be set to `True` or `False`; and Drag Content (the ability to drag the contents), which can also be set to `True` or `False`.

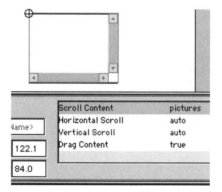

- **ComboBox** The ComboBox is used to create editable and static pop-up list menus. The only parameter that can be changed in a ComboBox is the Editable state, which can be `True` or `False`. An Editable box (`True`) allows the user to type in the box as a text field. A Static box (`False`) allows the user only to scroll down and select from the pop-up list. The other parameters include Labels, Data, Row Count, and Change Handler, all of which were discussed previously.

■ **PushButton** PushButtons are just what their name says: simple buttons that change on press and release. The parameters that can be changed in a PushButton include the Label and a Click Handler. The Click Handler parameter is the function that is called on the button event.

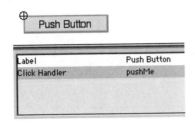

■ **ScrollBar** The ScrollBar is used to scroll text horizontally or vertically. You can add a ScrollBar component to either a Dynamic or input text field. The parameters that can be changed on a ScrollBar are the Target TextField, which is the name given to the text field, and the `Horizontal` parameter (`True` or `False`), which when `True` makes the ScrollBar horizontal instead of the default vertical position.

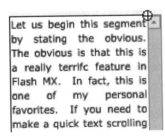

TIP *If Enable Live Preview is selected (Control | Enable Live Preview), you can get an idea of the way your component will appear in the final movie. This setting allows you to see labels and get a basic idea of the size of the components as they will appear.*

Make a ScrollPane

With the ScrollPane, you can quickly and painlessly display movie clips in a scroller window. Although it's an easy process, it still involves a few steps that might seem confusing. In Figure 15-12, the ScrollPane is made from an imported JPEG sequence file that was reconstructed as a movie clip.

Make a ScrollBar

Like the ScrollPane, ScrollBars allow you to scroll content either horizontally or vertically. However, whereas the ScrollPane allows you to scroll movie clips, the ScrollBar allows you to scroll text. If you worked with earlier versions of Flash, you will really appreciate this easy-to-use component because scrolling text is a frequently used feature in Flash movies.

FIGURE 15-12   The ScrollPane allows the user to dynamically scroll through a movie clip.

How to ... Make a ScrollPane

Components save a lot of scripting time. Let's walk through the steps of how you would actually use one.

1. If you are using any external elements (like JPEG files), import them into the Library of your movie.

2. Create a movie clip (Insert | New Symbol). In Figure 15-12, the JPEG sequence was constructed horizontally across the movie clip using the center cross hairs as a guide. When you're done, exit movie clip editing mode.

3. Right-click (Windows)/CMD-click (Mac) the movie clip in the Library and in the context menu. Select Linkage. In the Linkage Properties dialog box, click the Export For ActionScript button and the Export In First Frame button. In addition, give the clip an identifier name. In Figure 15-12, the identifier name is *scroll*.

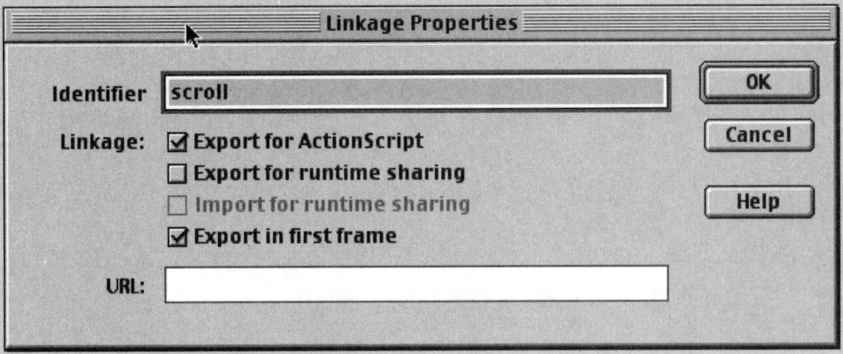

Linkage Properties

Identifier	scroll	OK
Linkage:	☑ **Export for ActionScript**	Cancel
	☐ **Export for runtime sharing**	
	☐ Import for runtime sharing	Help
	☑ **Export in first frame**	
URL:		

4. Display the Components panel. Drag an instance of the ScrollPane onto the stage and click it. In the Properties Inspector (or the Components panel), for Scroll Content, type in the name you assigned to the movie clip in the Linkage Properties dialog box. For Horizontal Scroll and Vertical Scroll, leave on the auto setting. For Drag Content, select either True or False. True makes the movie clip scrollable.

5. Test the movie. Now the movie clip will scroll when you drag the scroll bar.

Create A Scroll Bar   Figure 15-13 has a ScrollBar attached to a text field. The text was input directly into the text field. You can also copy and paste text from a word processing program directly into your text field. Let's review the process used to make this text field.

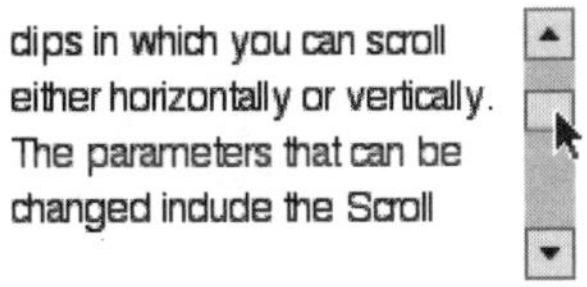

clips in which you can scroll
either horizontally or vertically.
The parameters that can be
changed include the Scroll

FIGURE 15-13   A ScrollBar attached to a text field allows the user to dynamically scroll the text in the field.

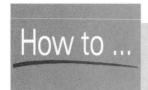

Attach a ScrollBar Component to a Text Field

Only if you have made a ScrollBar from scratch could you appreciate the convenience of being able to drag and drop this function onto a text field. Let's walk through the steps of how to create a scrolling text field with the ScrollBar component.

1. Create a text field on the stage using the Text tool in the Toolbox.

2. In the Properties Inspector, give the text field an instance name. In Figure 15-13, an instance name of "text" was given. In the Properties Inspector, you also need to indicate the other properties of the text you are going to put in this text field, including alignment, font, size, and so forth. Also, make sure you select Multiline for Line Type.

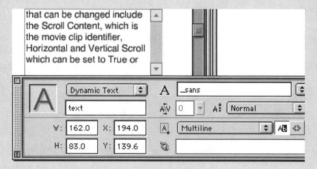

3. Click the text field and select Text | Scrollable from the menu. This will ensure that the text will scroll in the movie.

4. Type your text in the text field. You can also copy and paste text into this text field from a word processing application.

5. Display the Components panel. Click the ScrollBar icon and drag it onto the text field. It will attach itself. Click the ScrollBar; in the Properties Inspector, for Target TextField, type the name of the text field instance (in Figure 15-13, the instance name is "text"), and for Horizontal, select False.

6. Test the movie. The text field will scroll when you click the arrows or drag the scroller.

Use a Video Component

If you dig deep within the layers of the sample files provided by Macromedia, you will find a video control component. Fortunately for you, I have done the digging so you don't have to. You can find the video control component along with the source files and QuickTime video sample in this section in the Chapter 15 folder files for this book on the Osborne site. Figure 15-14 displays

FIGURE 15-14 This movie uses a video component that enables you to control the playback of embedded video clips in Flash.

a QuickTime movie imported into Flash that uses the video component. This figure provides a good example of how easy it is to add a component to a graphic. Another thing you want to think about when locating a component is identifying a use for it. In this case, the video control component is pretty cut and dry in terms of what it does. It acts as a virtual VCR, allowing you to stop, rewind, and loop the video. Let's examine how to import the movie and attach this component.

How to ... Create a Video with Controls in Flash Using a Component

15

Being able to embed video in Flash is a wonderful feature in MX. Let's look at a quick way to attach a video component to a video clip that allows the user to control the playback of the video.

1. Import a movie into Flash (File | Import To Library) as an embedded movie. Flash supports QuickTime (.mov), Digital Video (.dv), Audio Video Interleaved (.avi), Motion Picture Experts Group (.mpg and .mpeg), and Windows Media File (.wmv).

2. Open the Library of the file that contains the component (videoControl_hand.fla). Do this by selecting File | Open As Library. You can also get this controller out of the file called Import_Video.fla from the Samples | FLA folder in your Macromedia application folder.

3. From the Library, drag a copy of the component onto the stage. You can put it on its own layer if you want to keep it separate from the video.

4. Test the movie. You will be able to control the play of the movie. Notice you can position the controller anywhere you want on the stage and it still controls the movie.

Make Your Own Component

Suppose you're searching and searching and you can't find a component that works for your purposes. The good news is that you can create your own components in Flash. Components begin as movie clips, so any movie clip that contains properties or variables that can change easily is an ideal candidate for a component.

In this section, we're going to review the process of making your own custom component. Figure 15-15 displays a very simple custom-made component that is a button with some text over it. You can create something far more sophisticated than this button; but for the sake of understanding the process, we will walk through the making of a very simple component. Once you understand the process, you can conjure up something exciting.

A component is simply a movie clip that has been defined as a component in the Component Definition dialog box located in the Library pop-up Options menu. In fact, just like a movie clip, you can edit the custom component and the script associated with it by double-clicking the icon in the Library to enter the component's editing mode.

Ready-Made Templates

Flash comes with a set of ready-made templates. These templates include typical layouts with properties preassigned to objects. The templates address a need to make it easy for beginners or nondesigners to make attractive Flash layouts without the design expertise. To begin a new file using a Flash template, go to File | New From Template. Here, you can select from templates ranging from Ad layouts to Mobile Device layouts. To save a Flash file as a template, simply select File | Save As Template. In the dialog box, you specify a Name, Category, and a Description. Nondesigners will find this a welcome addition to Flash MX.

my display

FIGURE 15-15   Custom-built components can be made in Flash.

Let's walk through the process of making the simple button represented in Figure 15-15 into a custom component:

1. In a new file, insert a new movie clip. Name it **red bar**. On the first layer in the red bar Timeline, create a button. Name the layer the button is on.

2. Make a second layer on top of the first and name it **text**. Place a text field on this layer. In the Properties Inspector, pick a font style, size, color, alignment, and so forth. Also in the Properties Inspector, make the text field Dynamic, and give the text field an instance name of **myLabel**.

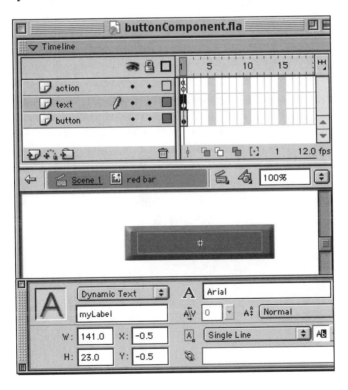

15

3. Create another layer and name it **actions**. Display the Actions panel in Expert mode and click the first frame in the Actions layer on the movie clip Timeline. Type the following script:

```
myLabel.text=mlt;
myLabel.textColor=mlc;
```

The instance name of the text field is `myLabel`. Parameters for the text object are `text` and `textColor`; **text** is the text you enter, and `textColor` is the hex color of the `text` object. Exit editing mode.

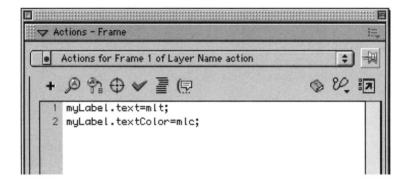

4. Right-click/CTRL-click the red bar movie clip in the Library. From the context menu, select Component Definitions. In the Component Definition dialog box, we will now use the variables we assigned in the movie clip. Click two times on the + in the top-left corner to create two new entry fields in the Parameters window. Input the following information:

Name	Variable	Value	Type
message	mlt	defaultValue	String
text color	mlc	#000000	Color

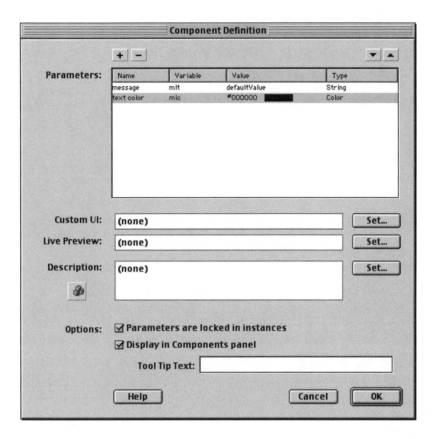

You will notice that to the right of each row, you can select a type of parameter from a pop-up menu. These parameters include Array, Object, List, String, Number, Boolean,

Font Name, Color, and Default. The message is a string and the text color is obviously a color parameter. You can return later and add more parameters to this component.

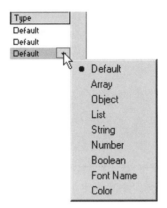

5. At the bottom of the Component Definition dialog box, check Parameters Are Locked In Instances (to prevent users from deleting parameters). If you check Display In Components Panel, the component will display in the Components panel. However, in order to see it, you have to export the component as an SWF file and place the SWF file in the Components folder of your system. Otherwise, you can simply access it from your Library.

To use this component or any component in a Flash file, you must import it from the Library of the source file (where you created it) to the Library or the stage of the new file. In other words, it must appear in the new file's Library. So, when you create a component file, the file is only used for storing the component, not for actively using it in that file.

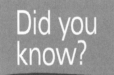

Choices, Choices

If you drag an object from the stage to the Library, it becomes a symbol. There are a few other choices you have in this box, too:

- You can attach a custom icon to this button by clicking the cube icon (or the default icon, as it is called) and selecting a different style.

- You can add a component definition in the Definition box. The definition can explain to other users what the component is and how it works.

- You can create a ToolTip that displays when you mouse over the component in the Components panel, if you opt to place your component there.

Create a Custom Interface

You can use a custom design to display your component. So, if you want to use something a little fancier than just text input fields in the Properties Inspector to change the parameters on a component, you can use an interactive SWF file to change the parameters of your component.

To make a component with a custom user interface, you first need to create a Flash file that is small enough to appear in the Properties Inspector. Create the interface and script using the component. The other important ingredient is that, in the original file that is going to serve as your component, you must create a blank movie clip with an instance name of xch that needs to reside somewhere on the stage. This xch movie clip instance is an Exchange movie clip whose sole purpose is to pass values from the SWF file to the component. In other words, the custom interface communicates with the component via xch as the user makes changes to the custom interface in the Properties Inspector. This process is the equivalent of changing the values of parameters in the Properties Inspector using the standard text field input, only better looking (assuming you build a good-looking interface).

To make a custom interface:

1. Build an interactive Flash file whose dimensions are small enough to fit into the Properties Inspector. Create an empty movie clip, and give it an instance name of **xch**. Drop it somewhere in the movie. Export it as an SWF file.

2. Return to the file with the movie clip you're making into a component. Right-click (Windows)/CTRL-click (Mac) the movie clip in the Library and open the Component Definition dialog box. Click the Set button next to Custom UI to display the Custom UI dialog box. In the Custom UI dialog box, select Custom UI In External .SWF File or Custom UI With .SWF File Embedded In Flash File. For Custom UI In External .SWF File, browse to the SWF file the custom interface is in and click OK. As before, you also want to click the options at the bottom of the Component Definition dialog box, Parameters Are Located In Instances and Display In Components Panel.

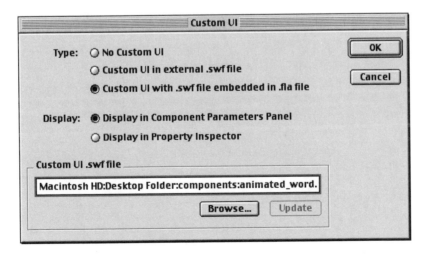

Now, when you click your component on the stage, in the Properties Inspector, you can adjust the parameters of the component with a custom UI. For a good example of a custom UI, see the Flash Samples | FLA | Live Preview-custom_UI.fla or Pill_button_preview.fla. Examine the components' definitions in the Library and the scripts on the components. If you are serious about making your own components, it's a good idea to examine previously made components.

In the next (and final) chapter, we will examine the process of publishing your Flash movie, as well as the debugging process. Learning how to publish your movies correctly is crucial to the success of your final project.

Chapter 16

Test and Publish Your Flash Movies

How to...

- ■ Optimize your movie
- ■ Test your movie locally
- ■ Use the Flash Player
- ■ Interpret the Bandwidth Profiler
- ■ Build a preloader
- ■ Debug a movie
- ■ Test in different file formats
- ■ Export your movie
- ■ Publish your movie

Once your Flash movie is finished, you need to prepare it for delivery to your audience. This is when the real test begins. Flash designers always have one goal in common: to marry efficient playback with good design in their Flash movie. In order to do this, you must step back and critically view, assess, test, and debug your work before presenting it to the audience. If your Flash movie is part of a web site, it can be very embarrassing to find out from your audience that a sound didn't play, the movie froze, or they got an erroneous error message indicating they don't have the correct plug-in.

Although all mistakes can't be caught 100 percent of the time, many mistakes in your movie can be spotted and corrected before delivery. If a Flash project is bound for the Web, most large-scale production houses will release the Flash project in alpha and beta stages. In the alpha stage, they ask friends and industry acquaintances to test the movie to see if they can spot any problems. In the beta stage, the movie is released to include a larger audience, including the client, but still not the wider audience. On launch, when it is finally delivered, the production house constantly checks to make certain everything is still working the right way. Nurturing a large-scale project can be quite a daunting task.

Getting back to smaller-scale projects, you need to double-check to make certain all the pieces (objects, bitmaps, sound, and movie clips) are working correctly and will download quickly enough to keep the low-bandwidth user occupied. You need to decide who your audience is and what kind of computers they have. Is your Flash movie part of a web site or is it a stand-alone projector file on a CD-ROM or DVD? Does your audience use Macs or PCs? Or, do you just need to export to a static file format like GIF or JPEG?

Once you have tested the movie and made decisions about your audience, the movie is ready to be published so it can be ported to its final destination. In this chapter, the final phases of movie delivery are examined. The aspect of movie making, the actual delivery of the movie, is perhaps the most exciting and crucial part of Flash production.

Optimize Your Movie

When a Flash movie is published or exported (which we discuss later in the chapter, in the section "Export Your Flash Movie"), elements residing in the movie are optimized to make certain the movie will compress to as small a size as possible. However, the onus still falls on you, the author, to make sure all elements in a movie are as compact as possible before getting to this point. Adding sound and bitmaps to a movie can automatically increase the file size. There are a myriad of other issues you may not even be aware of that can contribute to a larger file size. The following is a checklist of issues you should make yourself aware of to help keep the file sizes down:

- Grouping and/or making symbols of objects helps keep a file size down, because the object is then addressed in the Flash environment as one object rather than several objects.

- Animation can take up a lot of frames, which means bigger file sizes. Tweening can help keep files smaller, as opposed to frame-by-frame animations, which use many keyframes. The tweening process eliminates repetitive data, thus eliminating a bit here and there. In addition, movie clips are more compact than graphic symbols and yield smaller file sizes. Keep in mind, we may just be talking about a bit here and a bit there of data, but the sum of many bits can accumulate in a large movie.

- As mentioned throughout this book, using symbols for graphics that are reused frequently is a very efficient method for keeping file sizes down. Symbol data is stored in the first frame on which it appears. Any other instances of that symbol are linked to the first. Thus, the bulk of the data on the symbol only loads once, resulting in a smaller overall file size. Also, colorizing symbols with the Properties Inspector's Color Effects adds color without compromising file size.

- If you need to animate a bitmap, try to limit the amount of time the animation lasts. Make sure you either use a file in a compressed format (JPEG or PNG) or compress the file in Flash using the Properties dialog box on that graphic, as shown next. Large bitmaps and animated bitmaps increase overall file size.

16

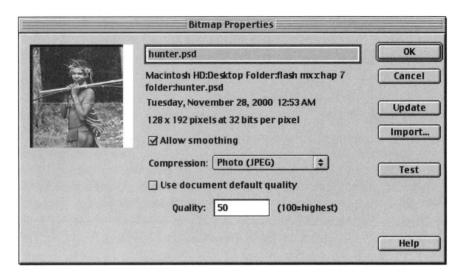

- Whenever possible, make the movie dimensions as small as possible. Any unnecessary part of the stage should be eliminated. You can always match the background of the Flash movie to your browser so the audience can't detect whether a movie is sized smaller.

- Optimize your shapes using the Modify | Optimize | Curves command to smooth them out. This eliminates unnecessary data used to describe shapes.

- Whenever possible, use device fonts (_sans and _serif), as opposed to embedded fonts. Embedded fonts are the fonts on your system. Device fonts don't embed the font information in the SWF file, thus resulting in a smaller movie size. If you embed fonts, try to use as few font families as possible. Each embedded font can cost you 20–40KB if the whole set of characters is embedded into the SWF file. Also, sans serif fonts generate smaller file sizes; so, if you need to shave off a bit or two on your file size, font type is another issue to consider.

- Try not to use a lot of gradients, as they increase file size.

- Increasing your frame rate from the default 12 fps will increase the file size. Concurrently, decreasing the frame rate will result in a smaller movie.

- If you're using Flash components, test the size of your movie (SWF file) frequently. They may increase the size beyond your size limit.

TIP *To check the size of your SWF file when you test the movie (Control | Test Movie), display the Bandwidth Profiler (View | Bandwidth Profiler). Here, you can preview the file size and many other statistics. The Bandwidth Profiler is covered later, in the section "Interpret the Bandwidth Profiler."*

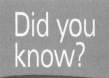

More on Compression

Flash does recompress bitmaps, so you need to recheck the quality of JPEGs after the movie is exported. Since JPEG compression is a lossy format, your image quality may be degraded a significant amount. PNG compression is lossless and will ensure the same quality as the original; and ditto for PSD format, which is also not compressed. You can also customize your compression settings on a JPEG in the Bitmap Properties dialog box on the object you have selected. To access the custom compression settings, deselect the Use Document Default Quality box. When you do this, you can enter any number from 0 (lowest compression) to 100 (highest compression). You will only see the results of this compression when you test the movie.

Before you even begin the design process, you should design your Flash movie for optimization. Decide what the maximum file size should be for your project before you begin. Periodically check the size to make sure you don't stray too far off this target size. These tips, along with using simple logic, will help keep the size of your Flash file smaller.

Test Your Movie Locally

Testing your movie is crucial to the successful delivery of your Flash movies because of the broad range of variables that come into play from the development stage of your movie to the end user/audience stage. While developing the movie, you must consider the Internet connection; the browsers being used; the browser versions; and the viewer's computer configuration, including processing speed and video display. All of these things have a significant impact on the way your movies will play back. You need to make sure that your movie is viewable by the majority of your audience.

The movie needs to be tested and retested throughout the entire production process. Even after it's up and running, you should still check the movie constantly, as problems can always pop up along the way. This will help ensure that problems are minimal. This section discusses checking the movie locally (testing and previewing it on your computer). If it all looks good on your computer, then it's time to take it to other platforms, browsers, and configurations to rule out potential viewing problems that could ruin the experience of your movie.

Throughout this book, you've been testing movies on the spot using the Control | Play And Control | Test Movie menu option. This is a form of quick local testing. Testing the movie often throughout its development, as well as sticking with some good optimizing common sense, puts you in a more successful position when the movie is ready to be published.

16

Use the Flash Player

When you test your movie using Test Movie from the menu, an SWF file is automatically generated in the folder where the movie resides. So, you're actually previewing the movie as it appears as an SWF file. You will recognize a Flash Player format file (SWF) on your computer's desktop by the Flash Player icon by the Type listing of Flash Player File, or by the .swf extension. When viewing in Test Movie mode, you are seeing the Flash Player file, not the FLA file you're working on.

Flash installs the Flash Player when you install Flash on your computer. In addition, it allows you to install the Flash Player plug-in on your browser (Netscape Navigator, Internet Explorer, and Opera, among others). With the Flash Player MX, you can view any SWF file that was exported as Flash 6 or lower on your system. If you are previewing a file in Flash Player, you can open and play other SWF files while in the Player window by selecting File | Open from the menu. By previewing an SWF version of a movie, you will get a good idea of what your audience will be seeing.

It should be noted that the plug-in the viewer uses to see your movie in a browser (or even a self-playing version of your movie) will not have the same extended menu options available in their Player window as you do. These additional menu options, such as Bandwidth Profiler, Streaming, and Debugging options, are discussed in the next section.

If your movie is exported in the Flash 6 format, viewers that have older Player versions will not be able to see it. If you suspect your audience may still be using older versions, you can publish your movie all the way back to version 1. Take note that functions in your movie that were not available in older versions will be dysfunctional when published to earlier versions of the Flash Player.

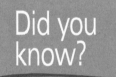

Flash Player Usage Information

According to the Macromedia site, to date, approximately 97 percent of Internet users have Flash Player loaded on their systems. Since many viewers already have the Flash Player, you can rest assured that a large portion of your audience will be able to see your movie. The most important decision for you will be which version of the Flash Player to publish to. As of this writing, most users will at least have version 4 or 5. Since version 6 is new, make sure to offer a link to the Macromedia downloads page (www.macromedia.com/downloads/) so that a member of your audience who doesn't yet have the version of the Flash Player you're targeting can easily download it.

There are several operating systems and browsers that will install the Flash Player. The OSs include Macintosh OS 8.1 and later, Windows 95 and later, Linux, UNIX, Solaris, IRIX, and Pocket PC. Browsers include Netscape Navigator and Communicator, Microsoft Internet Explorer 4.5 and later for Mac, Internet Explorer 5.5 and later for Windows, AOL, Prodigy, Opera, Intel Web Outfitters CD/Web, and NeoPlanet.

Interpret the Bandwidth Profiler

When you test a movie locally, it generally appears to play pretty quickly, regardless of how big it is. When it loads remotely on the Web, that's another story. If the file contains big elements on some frames that bloat the movie's file size, it could take a while to load on your viewer's computer. Hit load time will very depending upon their bandwidth. Since Flash streams, an unbalanced frame load can cause erratic playback on the viewer's end. There could be pauses and skips in the stream if you don't anticipate this potential behavior upfront. So, utilities like the Show Streaming feature and the Bandwidth Profiler are important in helping you to measure the efficiency of the playback of the movie in the real world, as opposed to playback on your desktop.

To prepare the entire movie for the best-case scenario in playback, you need to find out where problems might be hiding in your movie's frames. The Bandwidth Profiler visually shows you which frames are causing the problems, like a long download, so that you can rework the components of your movie for smoother animations, synchronized sounds, and quicker downloads.

To display the Bandwidth Profiler, you first need to be in Test Movie mode. When in this mode, select View | Bandwidth Profiler or press CTRL-B (Windows)/CMD-B (Mac) while in Player mode. Accessing this tool will help you check frames for download speed and smoothness of streaming with a visual representation.

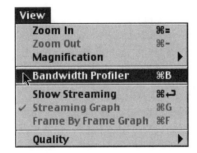

The Bandwidth Profiler displays a graph above the movie in Player mode (see Figure 16-1) in two columns. The column to the left generates important data regarding the file. The following Movie Settings are available in this column:

- Dimensions of the movie
- Frame rate
- Size of the Player file
- Duration of the movie in frames and seconds
- Preload in frames and seconds

16

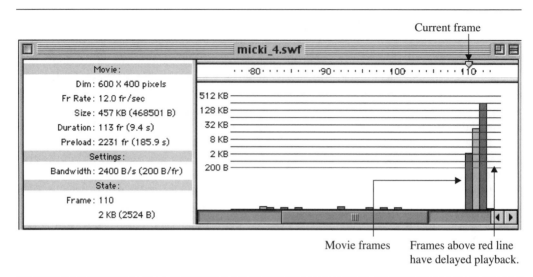

FIGURE 16-1 The Bandwidth Profiler displayed as a frame-by-frame graph on a movie gives a visual representation of the movie's playback on different bandwidths.

In the Bandwidth Profiler, the column to the right represents each frame in the movie. Frames are depicted as alternating bars of dark and light gray. The frames can be displayed as two different types of graphs, depending upon your purpose for viewing the information. These two kinds of graphs are the frame-by-frame graph and the streaming graph.

View the Bandwidth Profiler as a Frame-by-Frame Graph

In the Bandwidth Profiler, the column to the right is the actual graph where you can gather information about individual frames. In Figure 16-1, the bars are depicted as a frame-by-frame graph. View the graph in this mode by selecting View | Frame By Frame Graph or pressing CTRL-F/CMD-F. When you view the Bandwidth Profiler as a frame-by-frame graph, the graph displays the size of each frame in varying bar heights. Viewing in the frame-by-frame mode makes it particularly easy to spot large frames that might give you trouble on playback. You can easily spot and return to the problem frames and do some doctoring on them to bring the load time/size ratio down.

In the frame-by-frame graph, the bars in the graph are representative of the size (in bytes and kilobytes) of each frame in the movie. The corresponding vertical kilobyte (KB) scale gives you a rough indication of the height of each frame in relation to the surrounding frames. The red horizontal line in the graph serves as a warning that any bars above this line will take longer to load, therefore potentially causing erratic behavior at this point in the download. Any frames displayed below the red line should load quickly. Keep in mind that this loading preview is directly related to the sample baud rate you choose in the Debug menu. The Debug menu is discussed in the upcoming section "Test with Different Baud Rates."

View Bandwidth Profiler as a Streaming Graph

As mentioned previously, the Bandwidth Profiler can be viewed as a streaming graph by selecting View | Streaming Graph or by pressing CTRL-G/CMD-G. A streaming graph depicts how a movie will stream into a browser. In a streaming graph, if frames contain very little information, several bars appear stacked on top of one another in a single time unit. Frames with a lot of data cover several time units (see Figure 16-2). Frames alternate in light and dark gray shading, and are sized according to the time each one takes to download.

You can also click an individual frame in the graph to get data on that one frame. This is particularly helpful when you do have some frames much bigger than others. It can help you isolate the element(s) in the frame that is causing the heaviness on that frame.

Show Streaming

Should you decide at any time that you would like to view a download progress bar from Flash Player's Control menu, select View | Show Streaming or press CTRL-ENTER/CMD-ENTER. While the movie streams, the Timeline at the top of the Profiler displays frames in the process of streaming within a green streaming bar. You can see the green bar creep across the frame counter while the frames load. The white arrow pointing to a frame in the frame counter represents the frame currently playing. The streaming bar and arrow help you see the download process as the movie streams, while the actual animation is playing in the test window. It also gives you a real time simulation of streaming in different settings that you can select from the Debug menu, which is discussed in the next section.

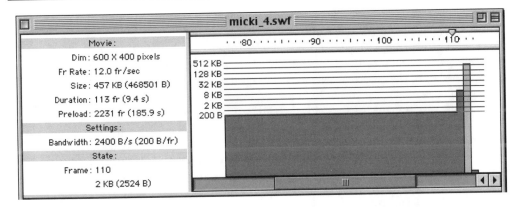

FIGURE 16-2   The Bandwidth Profiler displayed as a streaming graph depicts frames containing a small amount of data stacked on top of one another.

16

Having the ability to see the streaming of a movie is like having an extra pair of eyes to witness the download of the movie on another computer. The streaming feature becomes particularly important when viewing a movie with a lot of peaks and valleys represented in the streaming graph. It can be quite surprising to witness frame-loading delays that you might not have otherwise known about had you not witnessed them yourself. This convenient feature will help you determine if your movie requires a preloader or some other kind of adjustment, like repositioning frames with large content to other frames. The process of building a simple preloader is discussed in the section "Build a Preloader."

Test with Different Baud Rates

The Bandwidth Profiler needs to work in conjunction with one other feature in order to provide you with a full set of testing tools. In the Debug menu (in the Flash Player window), you can emulate several different baud rates. Depending upon what rate you select in the Debug menu, your Bandwidth Profiler will respond accordingly. The reason for the various baud rate selections is that your audience will consist of viewers with many different bandwidths.

There are three modem simulations for you to choose from: 14.4 Kbps, 28.8 Kbps, and 56 Kbps. These simulations simulate real Internet connection rates.

To create a customized setting for a connection speed, choose Customize from the Flash Player's Debug menu and specify the test names and rates in the Custom Modem Settings dialog box (see Figure 16-3). Here, you can also indicate a custom speed you wish to simulate in the Bit Rate box. For example, if you wanted to test a movie at a DSL or cable-modem setting, you could create and save it in the Custom Modem Settings dialog box. Three additional places to store extra settings include User Setting 4, 5, and 6.

Each time you select a different modem rate while testing the streaming of a movie, depending upon how complex the movie is, the streaming will change dramatically from one modem setting to another. Nowadays, it's more likely your audience will be using cable or DSL

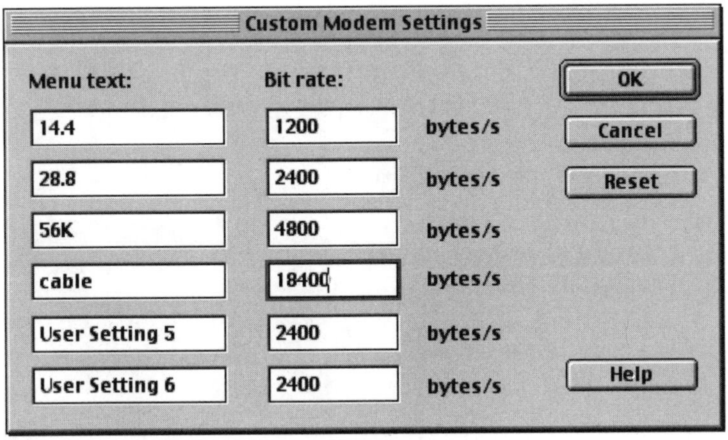

FIGURE 16-3   The Customize dialog box can be accessed from the Debug menu in Player mode.

baud rates, as opposed to 14.4 Kbps. But when publishing a movie, you may need to weigh all possible scenarios against one another and set priorities accordingly.

Build a Preloader

When discussing streaming in Flash, it's hard not to mention preloaders. A common item on many Flash sites today, preloaders allow you to display a message for your audience to let them know there's more of your movie to come, if they can handle the wait.

You've probably seen preloaders many times. Some are simple and just say something like "Please Wait" or "Loading." Others indicate the percentage of the movie that has loaded so your audience can anticipate how much longer they have to wait. Still others are elaborate and provide information while the viewer is waiting—anything to keep them waiting for your Flash movie until it loads.

Your preloader can be as simple or as complex as you want, but it always serves the same purpose: to entertain the audience while frames are loading in the background. Preloaders can solve erratic loading problems, ensuring that everything (or a portion of frames) has loaded up front before the bulk of the movie starts playing. In the following "How To," you will learn how to make a simple preloader. Using the same basic script and instructions, you can adopt this method for your preloaders (see Figure 16-4).

16

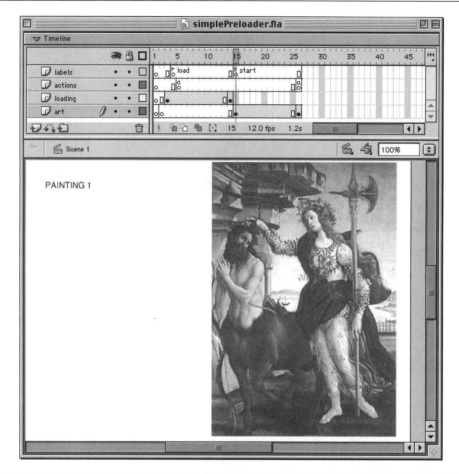

FIGURE 16-4 This preloader holds back the bulk of frames in the movie until all frames have loaded.

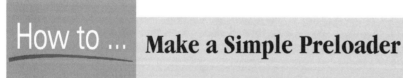 **Make a Simple Preloader**

Creating a simple preloader may seem a little complex at first. I outline the process for this, as follows:

1. Build a movie that's big enough to warrant a preloader. Put things in it that will weigh it down, like bitmaps and lots of frames. Begin the movie on Frame 15, creating blank frames in Frames 0 to 14. The number of blank frames is up to you. The idea here is to leave enough blank frames for the art and labels that will all be used to construct the preloader. In Figure 16-4, the movie only occupies 57 frames and is comprised of five bitmaps distributed among these frames. After you build your movie, test the movie in the Bandwidth Profiler and turn on View | Streaming Graph and View | Streaming. In the Debug menu, make sure you've selected 28.8 Kbps so you can witness the streaming of your movie at a low bandwidth.

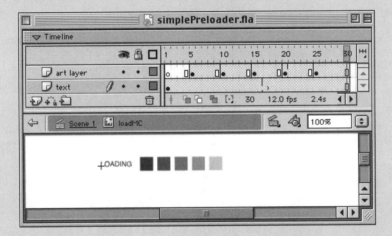

   While streaming, if the movie gets hung up on a frame while loading because it encounters a large element in the frame, you'll know your movie is a perfect candidate for a preloader like the one displayed in Figure 16-4. Name the layer your movie is on. In Figure 16-4, the bitmaps in the movie are all on the art layer.

2. Build a preloader. The preloader can be an animated movie clip, plain old static text, or anything that will indicate to the viewer that something is going to occur momentarily. The preloader in Figure 16-4 is just a movie clip that says "load" with an animated bar to the right. Keep in mind that you want this message to load immediately, so make it small and compact.

3. Create additional layers on top of the existing art layer. These layers will help us build the preload sequence. In Figure 16-4, the layers are as follows:

   ■ labels

   ■ actions

   ■ loading

   ■ art

16

4. On the labels layer, insert a blank keyframe on Frames 4 and 15 (Insert | Blank Keyframe). Note in the Timeline in Figure 16-4 that Frame 15 is also where our movie begins on the art layer. Click Frame 4 in the labels layer and, in the Properties Inspector, type **load**. Click Frame 15 in the labels layer and, in the Properties Inspector, type **start**.

5. Insert a keyframe on the loading layer, Frame 3. Drag the preloader from the Library onto this frame. The frame sequence on the loading should end on Frame 14; so, to shorten the frame sequence, press CTRL (Windows)/CMD (Mac), position your pointer over the last frame (which will appear as a double-headed arrow) in the sequence, and drag it to the left so the frame sequence ends on Frame 14.

6. Add the script. Insert a keyframe on Frame 5 of the actions layer. Display the Actions panel in Expert mode and type the following:

```
var doneLoading = _totalframes;
if (_framesloaded = = doneLoading) {
  gotoAndPlay("start");
} else {
  gotoAndPlay("load");
}
```

Let's examine what the script is instructing the Timeline to do. First, a local variable (var) is being declared (doneLoading), the value of which is the property _totalframes. The _totalframes property defines the total number of frames in the Timeline. A conditional statement (if) tests the equality (= =) of the _framesloaded property and the variable, doneLoading. The _framesloaded property does exactly what its name says it does: it indicates the number of frames loaded. If the condition is true (if (_framesloaded = = doneLoading)), then the frame with the label "start" will play. This happens to be Frame 15. If the condition is not true (else), then the frame with the label "load" plays.

7. On the actions layer, insert a keyframe on Frame 57. In the Actions panel, Expert mode, type **stop();**. This will stop the playhead from looping back to Frame 1.

Test the movie and view the Bandwidth Profiler while Show Streaming is selected. You will be able to see firsthand how the movie streams at whatever baud rate you selected.

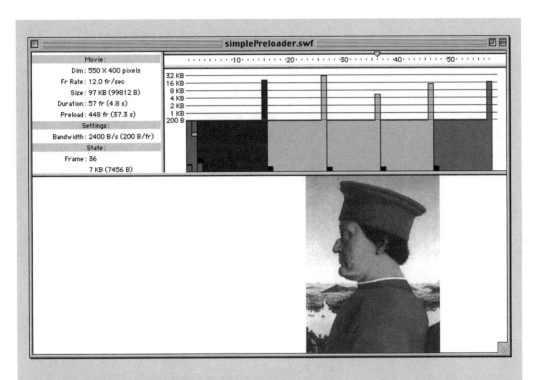

There are many other ways to create preloaders, such as preloaders that dynamically display the percentage of frames loading as they load, but the preceding script provides an easy way to create a simple preloader.

Debug a Movie

Whether you're a programmer, web developer, or designer, a major issue to reckon with in designing movies is to ensure that the movie plays properly and the ActionScript works flawlessly. If you can analyze what happens within your movie as it is playing, you stand a better chance of getting rid of the bugs in your movie before you bring it to the Web or its final destination.

To debug a movie, you simply select Control | Debugger from the menu. This displays the Debugger window and plays the SWF file. As new elements are introduced into the movie during playback, they appear in the upper-left corner of the Debugger window, as shown in Figure 16-5.

16

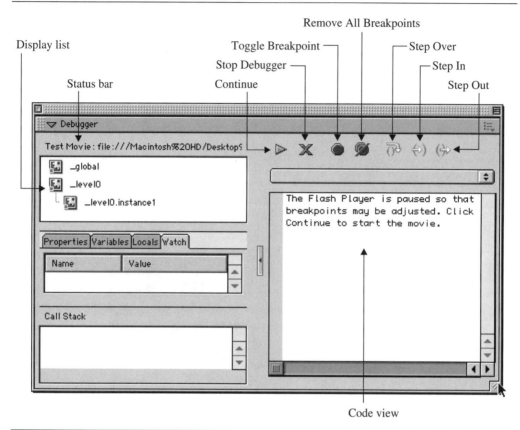

FIGURE 16-5 The Debugger window in Flash allows you to spot errors in your movie's playback.

The status bar at the top of the Debugger window tells you the location of the movie you are debugging. If it is remote, it will indicate the URL.

Notice the following additional tabs in the Debugger window, all of which allow you to further dissect the structure of the movie and edit it on-the-fly:

- **Properties** This tab allows you to view the properties and values of properties of a selected movie clip and change them as the movie runs. To do this, click a movie clip in the top display list and, in the Properties tab that appears, double-click any of the active values to type in a new one.

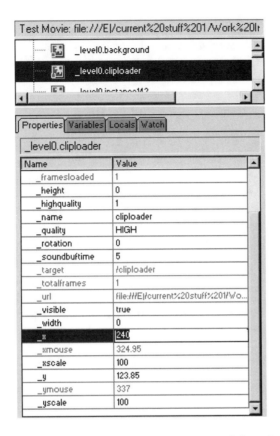

- **Variables** This tab allows you to view the variables and the values of variables on a selected movie clip. To do this, click the Variables tab. Here, you can change a value on a variable the same way you can change the value of a property, by double-clicking the value in the Value column.

- **Locals** This tab displays local variables in the movie.

- **Watch** This tab allows you to monitor certain variables closely. You can add variables to this list from the Debugger pop-up menu (Add or Remove Watch).

The Debugger window is useful from two perspectives. You can track and watch various pieces of your movie while it's playing, and you can debug a movie while it streams from a server.

16

NOTE *To debug a Flash Player (SWF) file remotely, select the Debugging Permitted check box on the Flash tab in the Publish Settings dialog box under Flash Editor. Then set a password in the box for this purpose. You will need to enter this password to access the SWF file from a remote computer to debug the file.*

Options:	☐ Generate size report
	☐ Protect from import
	☐ Omit Trace actions
	☑ Debugging Permitted

From a remote location, you can use the stand-alone Player to debug. When you publish the movie with Debugging Permitted selected, an SWD file is created. This file holds all the debugging information. This file must reside in the same folder as the SWF file in order to debug remotely. For more information about debugging remotely, refer to your Flash MX reference manual.

Set Breakpoints

In Figure 16-5, you will notice there is a button in the Debugger window called Toggle Breakpoint. Breakpoints are a wonderful feature in Flash MX. Breakpoints allow you to set breaks in the script, so when you test the movie in the Debugger window, the script will stop where you inserted a breakpoint. Why would you want it to stop playing at a certain point? If your script contains complex variables, conditionals, properties, or math functions, you may need to pause the script to check it or revise a value. Otherwise, the script could go whizzing by you as the movie plays. So, if you know there are some complex lines in the script that may need extra attention in the Debugger, these are the lines you want to insert breakpoints on.

Breakpoints are set in the Actions panel and controlled in the Debugger. Although you can set a breakpoint in the Debugger, you generally start out setting them in the Actions panel. To set a breakpoint on a line of code in the Actions panel, do the following:

1. Make sure the line numbers are visible (Actions panel options | View Line Numbers).

2. Select a line of code.

3. Click the Debug Options icon in the Actions panel. This icon appears as a stethoscope and displays a pop-up menu.

4. Select Set Breakpoints from the pop-up menu. Note that you can also remove breakpoints from this pop-up menu, too. To remove a breakpoint, select a breakpoint line and then select Remove Breakpoints from the pop-up menu.

5. A red stop icon will appear on the lines of the script with breakpoints in the Actions panel.

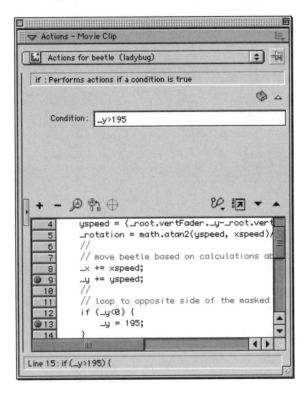

6. When you debug the movie (Control | Debug), an alert will appear that says, "The Flash Player is paused so that breakpoints may be adjusted. Click Continue to start the movie." Click the Continue button to play the movie.

16

7. As you play the movie in the Debugger window, the breakpoints you selected in the Actions panel appear in the Debugger window as red stop sign icons that correspond to the Actions panel.

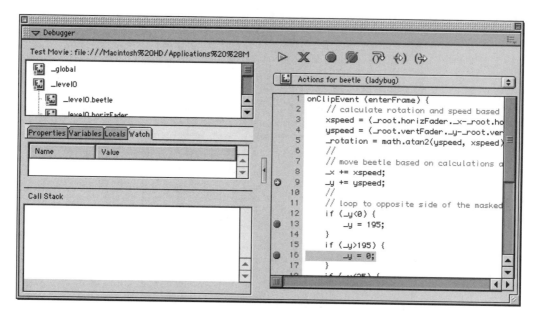

To continue to play the script until it reaches the next breakpoint, click the Continue button. To add another breakpoint in the Debugger window, select a line of code and click the Toggle Breakpoint button. You can remove all breakpoints by clicking the Remove All Breakpoints button. To skip over a breakpoint, click the Step Over button.

 As you click the Continue button to navigate through breakpoints in the Debugger, the current breakpoint icon (red stop sign) will contain a yellow arrow to indicate which one is the current breakpoint.

Use the Features in the Output Window

Throughout the book, we have periodically glimpsed the Output window in action. By now, I'm certain you have typed in a script the wrong way, especially if you're new to scripting in Expert mode. When you make a mistake, the Output window alerts you and even tells you which line the error is on. It also prompts you as to what kind of error it is. This is a tremendous help when you're learning how to script, because you can easily correct a scripting problem when you know what's causing it and where it's located.

```
Scene=main, Layer=dot, Frame=1: Line 1: '{' expected
    onClipEvent (enterFrame); {

Scene=main, Layer=dot, Frame=1: Line 8: onClipEvent handlers may not nest within othe
    onClipEvent (mouseDown) {

Scene=main, Layer=dot, Frame=1: Line 1: Statement block must be terminated by '}'
    onClipEvent (enterFrame); {

Scene=main, Layer=dot, Frame=1: Line 24: Syntax error.
```

When you test a movie, if there is a mistake in the script, the Output window will appear. While you're writing the script, if you click the Check Syntax button in the Actions panel, a message will alert you if there are syntax errors and tell you that they will be listed in the Output window. The Output window can also be viewed in the test movie mode if you select Window | Show Output from the menu.

Use the Output Window to Trace Actions

The Output window also displays the results of the `trace` action when you test a movie. Throughout the book, we have used the `trace` action many times to make sure a script is working properly. For example, you may use a `trace` action on forms to make certain the values the user is returning are correct.

Here's a simple example of a `trace` action used in a script with a variable named `total`:

```
salary = 200;
wages = 200;
total = salary+wages;
trace (total);
```

When the movie is tested, the Output window looks like the following illustration:

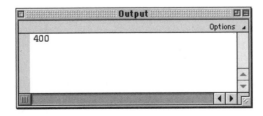

16

The value of `total` checks out OK (400), so we know the script is working the right way. The `trace` action should be deleted before the movie is published, because it is useless at publication time and only adds to the file size. You should make certain you click the Omit Trace Actions button in the Flash Export dialog box when exporting to SWF format. This will remove the `trace` action from the SWF file but not from the movie itself. We will cover the Flash Export dialog box in the upcoming section "Export Your Flash Movie."

List Objects and Variables

There are additional ways to gather data on a movie in Test Movie mode. When a movie is playing, you can select List Objects or List Variables from the Debug menu.

When you select List Objects, an Output window appears, listing all shapes, symbols, and their instance names on the stage, with their respective levels and paths indicated also. This gives you the opportunity to make sure targets are addressed properly. It also helps you find elements that may be nested several levels deep.

```
Output                                                         Options ▾

 Movie Clip: Frame=1 Target="_level0.instance1"
    Shape:
 Movie Clip: Frame=1 Target="_level0.vertFader"
    Button: Target="_level0.vertFader.instance2"
      Movie Clip: Frame=1 Target="_level0.vertFader.instance2.instance3"
        Shape:
      Shape:
 Movie Clip: Frame=1 Target="_level0.instance4"
    Shape:
 Movie Clip: Frame=1 Target="_level0.horizFader"
    Button: Target="_level0.horizFader.instance5"
      Movie Clip: Frame=1 Target="_level0.horizFader.instance5.instance6"
```

The List Variables window lists all the variables in the current stage and their hierarchy in the Output window. You can check to make sure the values are properly assigned to each variable and that they're working correctly. The list appears in the Output window, as do the objects.

The objects and variables in the Output window do not refresh as the movie plays, as happens in the Debug window. In other words, the Output window lists the objects and their hierarchy only once.

Test in Different File Formats

In addition to being able to generate an SWF file when you export a Flash file, you can also export to other file formats. For example, if your SWF file is bound for the Web, you may want to address portions of your audience who don't have the Flash Player plug-in. For this audience, you can alternately publish your file in several static file formats, as well as alternative movie formats. Then, these alternative files can be either embedded in an alternate HTML page or inserted, depending upon whether the format requires a plug-in or not. Because there still may be a few dinosaurs in your audience lacking the Flash Player, you may need to build an alternative version of your web site for limited configurations. Rather than create graphics over again, you can save certain images in GIF or JPEG format, and use them to rebuild static versions of your web site.

Flash allows you to preview what art will look like in alternative formats. This way, you can preview what the art will look like before actually publishing to that format. A fine gradient in Flash can look very banded as a GIF file. A fluid Flash animation may look too jerky as an animated GIF, and you may decide a static image looks much better. Opacity and transparency may not translate well in alternative formats. There are too many variables that could go wrong without testing before you establish what the best-quality alternative format might be.

To preview the movie in different formats within a browser:

1. Display the Publish Settings dialog box (File | Publish Settings). In this box, click the settings you want to preview. For example, if you want to preview a file as a JPEG, select JPEG. Then click OK. You also use this box to customize the settings of your export. We discuss the Publish Settings dialog box later, in the section "Use the Publish Settings Dialog Box."

2. Select File | Publish Preview. Whatever settings you selected will be listed here. The default settings for the Publish Preview include Default, Flash, and HTML.

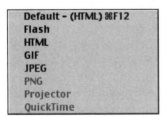

Export Your Flash Movie

Once you have tested and previewed your movie sufficiently, you are then ready to prepare the movie for its final destination. You do this by either exporting the movie or publishing the movie using the Publish Settings dialog box. The Publish Settings dialog box is used for exporting your files in multiple formats with an optional HTML file. It also allows you to pinpoint settings related to those file formats.

Although exporting a movie is similar in nature to publishing a movie, it's important to understand the difference between the two. Also, both the Export Movie dialog box options and the Publish Settings dialog box options offer additional details that are not offered in both dialog boxes. Exporting is fine for SWF movies and updating an SWF that's embedded in an HTML page.

16

There are two different ways you can export your movie: export single frame images of your movie, and export the entire movie and every frame associated with it.

Single Frame Export

Export a single frame if there's a static piece of art, like a logo, you may want to use in another movie or a printed piece. To export a single frame in a multiframe movie, select the frame in the movie you want to export with the playhead. Go to File | Export Image. Give the file a name and choose from one of the available file extensions:

- .swf, .spl, .wmf (Windows only), .eps 3.0, .ai 7.0 and under, .dxf, .bmp, .jpg, .gif, and .png.

Movie Export

To export a movie, select File | Export Movie. This setting is very useful if you need to export a series of sequential frames to another program. For example, you could save a frame sequence in a PNG format and open each frame individually in FreeHand, Fireworks, or any other program that accommodates sequential files. Or, you could export frames in the AI format and open each file as a frame sequence in Adobe Illustrator. There are many different ways you can export sequential frames into other programs by using the Export Movie command.

The following file extensions are available for saving your movie frames in sequential still frames: .wmf, .eps, .ai, .dxf, .bmp, .jpg, .gif, and .png.

The following file extensions export a movie in a movie format: .swf, .swt, .spl, .avi, .mov, and .gif; and for sound, .wav or .aif.

Although there are many formats to choose from, most often, you will be exporting to an SWF file. During this conversion from FLA to SWF format, Flash will eliminate extra information, sounds, timelines, and bitmaps that are contained in the FLA file to compress the SWF file as small as possible. Sound and bitmap files are also automatically compressed, which also pares down the size of the SWF file tremendously. You might want to take special note of your FLA file size versus the SWF file size. The SWF file is much more compact so it's perfect for use on the Internet, where low bandwidths always need to be addressed.

Export in Different File Formats

When you export movies to different file formats from the Export Movie dialog box, once you select the format, an additional dialog box related to that particular export option will prompt you for special information. For example, if you were to export a movie to a QuickTime form at (MOV), you would name the file and select .mov as the Save As Type. Then, a QuickTime Settings dialog box would allow you to further customize the export with Alpha settings, how to read Layers, Compression For Streaming Sound, what kind of movie controller you want, Playback options, and Flatten Movie options (see Figure 16-6).

If you export a movie or image from Flash for web delivery, you must insert or embed your own image/movie into an HTML document. Unlike the Publish command, the Export commands do not automatically generate an HTML file with your SWF file embedded in it.

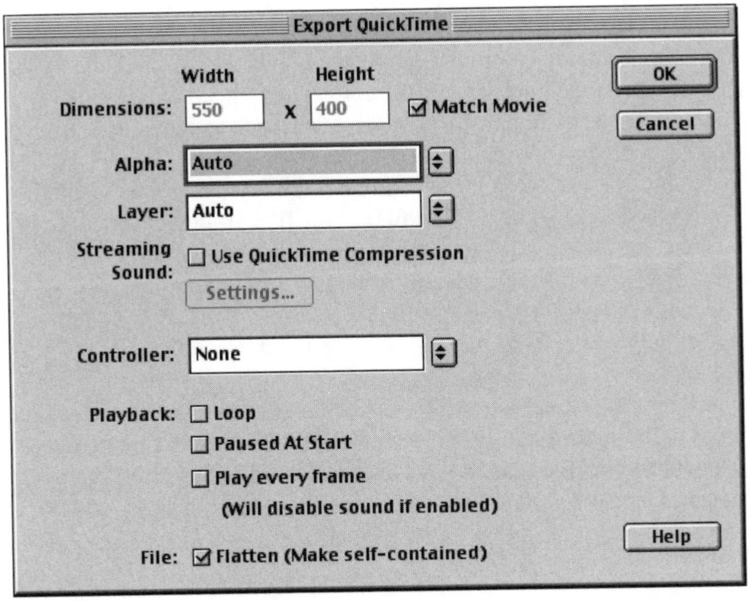

FIGURE 16-6 If you export a movie to a QuickTime format (MOV), a dialog box displays where you can customize your settings.

Publish Your Movie

For a multimedia project that's bound for the Web, or even for a self-playing projector file, the most commonly used exporting mode is via the Publish Settings dialog box. This offers the most comprehensive set of export options and enables you to preview and select all the different settings from the same parent dialog box. In this section, all the elements of the Publish Settings dialog box are examined.

As discussed previously, you can export to many different file formats in addition to the Flash SWF format, so the delivery of your animation and interactivity to an audience who might not have access to Flash plug-ins becomes an attainable alternative. This is easily accomplished with the Publish command, which affords you the ability to publish your Flash movie in up to eight different formats simultaneously. This feature will also generate an HTML document so that your published file has the SWF movie already embedded in it.

You may be wondering at this point what the difference is between exporting a file and publishing a file. Some of the options for exporting and publishing offer more flexibility and customization than others. For example, when using the Publish Settings dialog box, you are offered the choice to remove gradients from GIF files to keep the file size small. But in the Export GIF dialog box, that choice is not available. Another difference between publishing and exporting is that Flash will save the publish settings with the movie file, so if you choose to reuse them in subsequent movies or new projects, they are still available as native Flash files. In addition, you can automatically generate an HTML file when you publish.

16

To select a movie's publishing format, open the Flash document that you want to publish. Choose Publish Settings from the File menu or press CTRL-SHIFT-F12 (Windows)/CMD-SHIFT-F12 (Mac). The Publish Settings dialog box will display (see Figure 16-7). Click the Formats tab.

When you select a type in the Formats tab, the corresponding tab will appear on the top of the dialog box. You can select as many file formats as you wish to generate. When you publish the files, they will all save in the root folder.

To choose the options for a selected format, simply select the tab aligned with that format. For example, if you wanted to generate a JPEG file, select JPEG and then click the JPEG tab. Here, you can fine-tune your selection. Flash will utilize these settings each time you choose the Publish or Publish Preview command. If you enter test mode (by selecting Control | Test Movie or Control | Test Scene), Flash will use a file's current publish settings. For example, if you selected PNG as your only format type in a movie, when you tested the file, the movie would display in PNG format.

There are eight file format choices in the Publish Settings dialog box, which include Flash (.swf), HTML (.htm), GIF image (.gif), JPEG image (.jpg), PNG image (.png), Windows Projector (.exe), Macintosh Projector, and QuickTime (.mov). The custom settings for these formats are discussed in the next section.

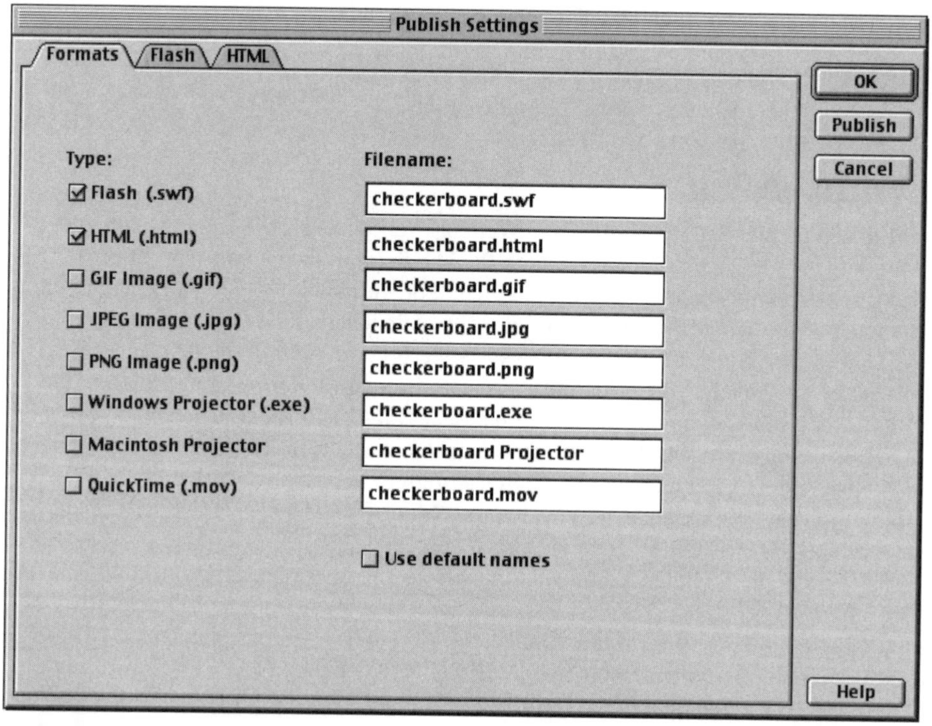

FIGURE 16-7   The initial dialog box that displays when you select Publish Settings from the File menu

Use the Publish Settings Dialog Box

The Publish Settings dialog box looks small, but its settings are many. Some settings can be quite complex if you don't know what they mean. When you first open the dialog box, there are only three tabs generated from the three default settings (refer to Figure 16-7):

- **Formats**   This is where you select the type of files you want to export and assign filenames.

- **Flash**   It's assumed that most often you intend to import in a Flash format, so Flash is the default publish setting.

- **HTML**   Although you don't have to publish an HTML document, again, it's assumed you probably will. When you select HTML as a type, the Flash format (SWF) always publishes with the HTML page.

Depending upon your selection in the Type column, the tabs will change. Each time you select another type for export, a tab is added to the right of the other tabs. Since the selections are numerous in this little dialog box, we will review the different export options and media elements available in the proceeding paragraphs. Let's examine the various options for different file formats.

The Flash Tab

The Flash tab includes the following settings:

- **Version**   Choose the version of the Flash Player you are targeting. You can choose from versions 1 to 6.

- **Load Order**   If you want to select the order in which Flash loads the layers of your movie, you need to address how the first frame of your movie will load. In the Load Order pop-up menu, select from the following two options. If playback on the Web is slow, Flash will start to display individual layers as they download.

  - **Bottom Up**   This selection loads the movie in a browser from bottom to top.

  - **Top Down**   Downloads and displays the top layer first and then continues down the page to the bottom.

- **Options**   The Options section includes the following check boxes:

  - **Generate Size Report**   Generates an automatic text file from Flash that supplies you with a detailed report about the size of each frame and the various events that take place in your movie.

  - **Protect From Import**   Prevents viewers from importing the SWF file and converting it into a source file.

  - **Omit Trace Actions**   Deletes any trace actions in your movie on export.

  - **Debugging Permitted**   Allows you to debug your movie from a remote location using a password.

  - **Compress Movie**   Compresses your movie using the SWF compression methods.

16

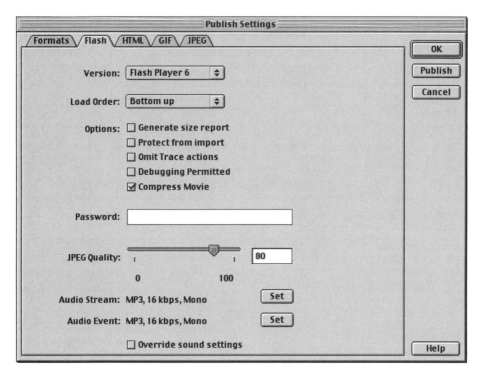

The Publish and Publish Preview commands automatically generate filenames in the Publish Settings dialog box. So, if you want to publish several versions of a movie, each containing different settings, you need to ensure that you don't copy over the original, published file. You will need to rename the new file versions, bring the files to a different location, or provide a different name in the Formats tab of the Publish Settings dialog box. You must do this to maintain the integrity of your various versions and avoid potential confusion. To rename them, deselect the Use Default Names check box on the Formats tab.

- **JPEG Quality**   You can adjust the JPEG quality by using a slider or by entering a value in the field from 0 (low quality) to 100 (high quality).

- **Audio Stream or Audio Event**   Use either one of these options if your sound is streaming or occurs on an event. You can select from MP3 (Compression), 16 Kbps (Bit Rate), or Mono. When you click Set, the Sound Settings dialog box appears, offering you the following options:

  - **Compression**   You can set the sound compression parameters for MP3 (the default), ADPCM, or Raw Format, or disable sound altogether.

  - **Bit Rate**   Choices are offered for 8 Kbps, 16 Kbps, 20 Kbps, 24 Kbps, 32 Kbps, 48 Kbps, 56 Kbps, 64 Kbps, 80 Kbps, 112 Kbps, 128 Kbps, and 160 Kbps.

- ■ **Quality**   You can choose from Fast, Medium, or Best.
- ■ **Override Sound Settings**   This setting overrules the settings used in the Library Sound Properties dialog box.

The HTML Tab

To select HTML as a file format to be included with your SWF file, select HTML on the Formats tab of the Publish Settings dialog box. Then, click the HTML Formats tab on the top of the dialog box. The following are the customizable settings in the Publish Settings dialog box:

- ■ **Template**   Under this option, you can select from several different templates. The templates generated by your selection will provide a fill-in-the-blanks HTML page with the appropriate script generated for a particular outcome. When you select each template, a description of the code that's generated appears to the right of the selection when you click the Info button. For example, if you choose Image Map and click the Info button, the following message displays: "Description: Publish bitmap with a client side image map. In Publish, select GIF, JPEG, or PNG." The filename is also indicated at the bottom of the dialog box.

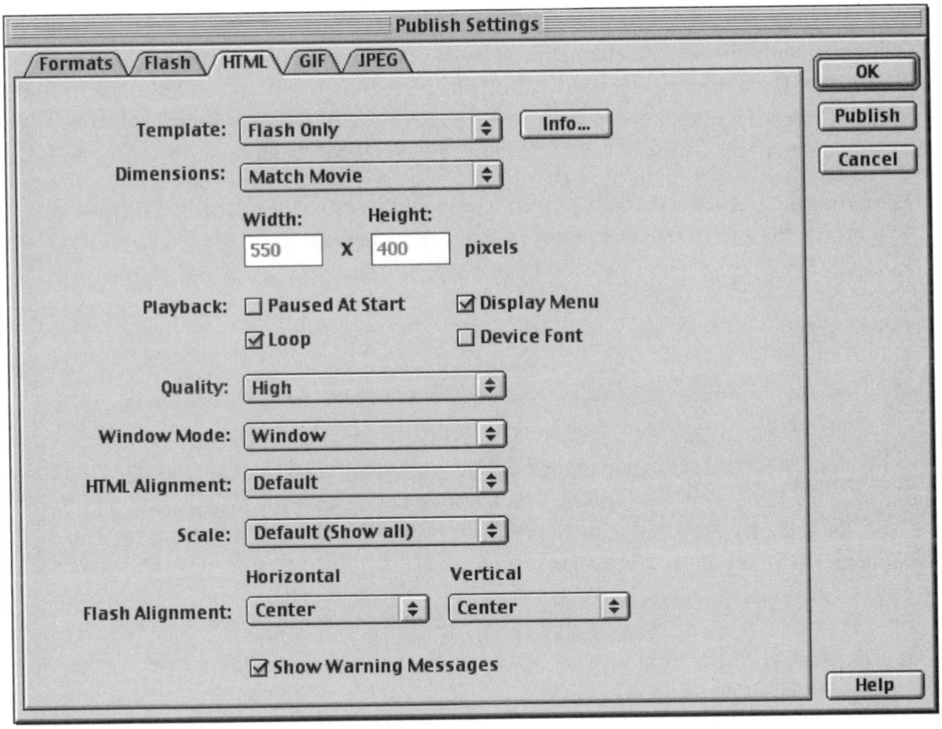

OBJECT and EMBED Tags

The OBJECT and EMBED tags in HTML address the two most popular browsers: Netscape and Explorer. The OBJECT tag addresses Explorer technology (ActiveX) and the EMBED tag addresses Netscape issues (SWF plug-in). Both of these tags are necessary in the HTML code to address both browsers. Both the OBJECT and EMBED tags are automatically included in the HTML document when you publish a movie and choose Flash (.swf) and HTML (.html) in the Publish Settings dialog box.

When you choose Flash Only (the default) from the Template pop-up menu, you have selected the most simplistic way to set your HTML code. It will use the OBJECT and EMBED tags so that your Flash movie is displayed and seen by the viewer with the Flash Player plug-in.

The HTML default will automatically make the background color of your web page the same as the background color of your Flash movie. To use a different color, create a template, which you can then modify. Be sure to open the default template, save a copy, and give it a new name. In the Flash Only (default) option, change the line of code and give it a name like Flash Only (insert your name) (Background). This will allow Flash to recognize it and add it to the available templates in the Template menu. In the HTML tag, replace the line code with HTML code for a specific hex color and save the new template in your Flash HTML folder.

- **Dimensions** Assists you with determining your movie's placement in the browser. The following selections are available in the Dimensions pop-up menu:

  - **Match Movie** Allows you to establish the dimensions of your movie.

  - **Pixels** Allows you to type in values within a range of 0 to 32,000 for Width and Height.

  - **Percent** Allows you to type in values within a range of 1 to 100 for Width and Height.

If you input a different width and height from your original Flash movie, you need to tell Flash how you want the new movie scaled. When you decide to resize a movie, keep in mind that it may not fill the rectangle and that gaps may occur around the borders of your page. This is a minor design consideration that can be fixed easily, but should be anticipated nonetheless.

- **Playback** This option offers your viewers several playback choices:

  - **Paused At Start** This option allows your viewer to begin the movie with an event like a button press.

- **Display Menu**   Choose this option if you want to develop your own playback options and make them available to your audience.

- **Loop**   Select this option if you want the movie to repeat itself and start over again when it has reached its last frame.

- **Device Font**   This option enables Windows viewers to speed playback on their systems by substituting device fonts (_sans or _serif) whenever a Flash movie uses system-installed fonts from the viewer's computer.

- **Quality**   To ensure that your movie plays back at the best quality possible, use this option to select from Low to Best. These choices will control smoothing and antialiasing in the Flash movie. The following settings are available:

  - **Low**   Flash will set the antialiasing to off.

  - **Auto Low**   Flash will begin playing back your movie with antialiasing off. If Flash should decide that the viewer's system and Internet connection can control the antialiasing and not disrupt the movie's frame rate, Flash will turn antialiasing on.

  - **Auto High**   Flash will turn on antialiasing to start the publishing, and turn it off if the playback falls below the frame rate established for the movie's downloading time.

  - **Medium**   With this setting, you are at the 50-50 mark, where Flash will handle minor antialiasing but not address smoothing out bitmaps.

  - **High**   Flash will apply antialiasing to all graphics except animated bitmaps.

  - **Best**   This option allows Flash to maintain antialiasing in the on position throughout the course of publishing the movie.

The overall function of the Quality setting is to balance image quality with playback speed in a published Flash movie.

- **Window Mode**   The following settings are available for Window Mode:
  - **Window**   This is the regular default window mode that plays the movie in a regular browser window.

  - **Opaque Windowless**   If you want to just play the movie in its own web page window, select Opaque Windowless. This will allow you to block out the background and other elements of the web page with transparent sections.

  - **Transparent Windowless Effect**   For your Windows Internet Explorer user audience, choose this option to allow your web page elements to show through.

- **HTML Alignment**   The alignment selected will be added to the HTML template. Choose from the standard HTML settings of Default, Left, Right, Top, and Bottom.

16

■ **Scale**   This option gives you three choices:

   ■ **Default (Show All)**   This option defaults to the user's browser settings.

   ■ **No Border**   Enables you to fill most of the rectangle.

   ■ **Exact Fit**   Enables you to change the movie's height and width to the new specifications so that it appears to reproportion the movie.

■ **Flash Alignment**   From Flash Alignment, you can pick the Horizontal pop-up menu and choose from Left, Center, and Right. From the Vertical pop-up menu to the right of the Horizontal, you can select Top, Center, and Bottom.

■ **Show Warning Messages**   When you select this check box, any problems or conflicts that occur when you publish your file will be brought to your attention. For instance, having QuickTime 4 or over installed on your computer before Flash MX is installed is crucial. If you select QuickTime as a file format for testing and delivering your movie, and you don't have QuickTime 4 or over installed, you will be alerted about this conflict. This option is helpful for spotting potential problems.

For more details about writing, placing, and formatting the HTML code for the Flash aspects of your web page, you should familiarize yourself with HTML (if you haven't already done so). There are many excellent books available on the subject. Following are two books that I recommend for brushing up on your HTML skills:

■ *HTML 4 for the World Wide Web: Visual QuickStart Guide, 4th Edition*. Elizabeth Castro, Peachpit Press.

■ *HTML & XHTML: The Definitive Guide*. Chuck Musciano, Bill Kennedy, O'Reilly.

The GIF Tab

As you probably know by now, you can also create static GIF, JPEG, or PNG images of the first frame of your movie, as well as multiple-image, animated GIFs.

GIFs are limited to a 256-color palette (indexed color). When you choose a GIF format, you need to define the color characteristics for the file in the lower section of the dialog box. Also important to keep in mind is that animated GIFs are made up of bitmap images, so the files they generate may be large, especially if your Flash movie is long. Be sure to keep an eye on the size of the files.

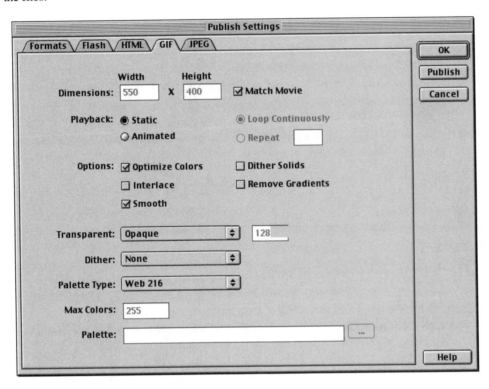

The following settings are available on the GIF tab of the Publish Settings dialog box:

- **Dimensions**   You select the Width and Height, or select Match Movie to match the size of the frame in the movie.
- **Playback**   Playback can be static or animated. It can also loop continuously.
- **Options**   Additional options include
  - **Optimize Colors**   You can optimize the colors of a file saved in a GIF format in the GIF tab. Selecting Optimize Colors will help reduce the colors in an image to make it fit within the 256-color parameters of the GIF format.

16

- **Dither Solids**   This option allows you to reduce the number of colors used in your image by replacing solid colors with dithered colors.

- **Interlace**   When you select Interlace, you are specifying that the GIF generate the file so that it can be viewed as the end user downloads. The end user's perception is that of the file downloading more quickly, when, in fact, interlacing increases or decreases file size in negligible increments.

- **Remove Gradients**   If you select this check box, you will combine colors and reduce the overall number of colors required to view your image. This option is very much like the Dither Solids box.

- **Smooth**   When you select Smooth, elements become vector based prior to the generation of the GIF file.

- **Transparent**   Set the transparency of a GIF image here. This option also allows you to selectively identify a color as Opaque or Transparent, or give a particular color an Alpha setting.

- **Dither**   The Dither settings include None, Ordered, and Diffusion.

- **Palette Type**   You can select from the following GIF-appropriate palettes:

  - **Web 216**   The standard web-safe palette.

  - **Adaptive**   You would use this option if your end user does not have color-viewing limitations.

  - **Web Snap Adaptive**   This option will yield color results somewhere midway between an 8-bit color palette and your customized or adaptive colors.

  - **Custom**   If your viewer's capability is not limited, such as on an intranet, you can use this option. It enables you to load Photoshop Swatch files to help in setting up your image's color palette.

  - **Max Colors**   This setting allows you to control the number of colors used in the color palette. Using smaller color palettes helps reduce the size of the overall GIF file.

  - **Palette**   This setting allows you to load a color palette from another source. For example, if you have created a custom palette in Fireworks or Photoshop, it can be loaded here and applied to the GIF image you are creating.

The JPEG Tab

JPEGs are usually used for continuous tone without a lot of flat color. The following settings are available on the JPEG tab of the Publish Settings dialog box:

- **Dimensions**   You can manually indicate the Width and Height or Match Movie.
- **Quality**   Use the JPEG Slider to adjust the compression of a JPEG bitmap from high, to medium, to low quality.

  Use the JPEG Quality Field option to manually enter a specific value in the JPEG Quality field to the right of the slider. When you adjust this setting, you control how Flash will compress your bitmaps as it exports your movie. Using a setting of 0 offers the most compression at the lowest quality. If you use a setting of 100, your bitmaps will be the least compressed at the best quality. JPEG images seem to download quickly because they are read instantaneously even though the entire image is not yet downloaded or visible.

- **Progressive**   This is the JPEG equivalent to interlacing. A low-resolution image appears; and as the image progressively loads, it becomes clearer.

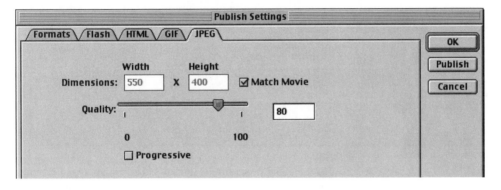

The PNG Tab

Since an 8-bit PNG file is similar to the GIF format, the settings on the PNG tab of the Publish Settings dialog box are almost identical to those on the GIF and JPEG tabs, except you can choose a bit depth of 24 or 8 bit. Also, with PNG files, you can select filtering options. There are five filtering options in the Filtering Options menu. These filters (Sub, Up, Average, Path,

16

and Adaptive) perform a mathematical, line-by-line compression that helps keep the PNG file size down.

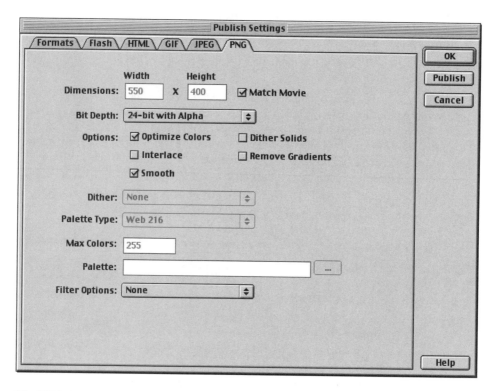

The PNG format provides most of the capabilities of GIF and JPEG in one format. The big difference is that, unlike the JPEG format, which offers lossy compression, PNG file compression is lossless and will retain its quality over multiple generations.

Projector Files

Projector files are primarily used for distributing movies on various media formats, such as CD-ROM, DVD, desktop presentation formats, or e-mail. Projector files in Flash Player aren't cross-platform compatible. A projector file you create in a Mac format cannot be used on a Windows-based system, and vice versa. However, you can create projector files for both Windows and Macintosh platforms separately. Neither projector file setting generates a Tab to a dialog settings box. You can select either setting from the bottom of the Formats tab.

- **Windows Projector and Macintosh Projector**   Use this setting to create a stand-alone file that plays in Windows. Windows Projector files can only be run in Windows. Concurrently, Macintosh Projector files can only be viewed on the Mac. You can address both platforms by creating a hybrid CD-ROM with both file formats on it.

The QuickTime Tab

The QuickTime movie format can be used both on the Web and for disk presentations. QuickTime version 4 and later provides Flash tracks in its architecture to help fully take advantage of sound and media in your Flash movie.

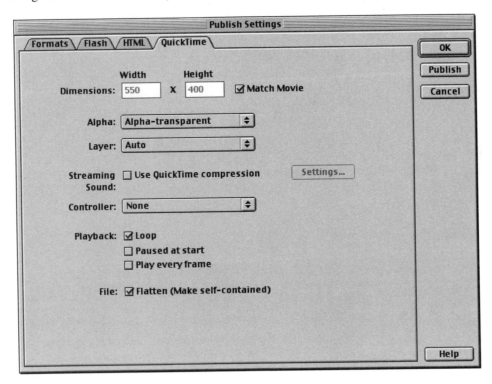

The following settings are selectable on the QuickTime tab of the Publish Settings dialog box:

- **Dimensions** You can set the size of the movie in dimensions by typing the new Width and Height, or selecting Match Movie to match your original Flash movie.

- **Alpha** You can control the transparency background of your Flash page on top of QuickTime. You can select from Auto, Alpha-Transparent, or Copy.

- **Layer** You can decide where the Flash track lies in the stacking order of QuickTime tracks. Select from Auto, Top, or Bottom.

- **Streaming Sound** Use compression to export streaming sound to QuickTime sound track.

- **Controller** You can select a QuickTime Controller interface for your QuickTime movie. Select from None, Standard, or QuickTime VR.

16

- **Playback**   The following Playback options are available for QuickTime movies:

  - **Loop**   This option causes the movie to repeat itself and start over again when it has reached the last frame.
  - **Paused at Start**   This option will pause the movie before it starts playing.
  - **Play Every Frame**   This option will ensure that all the graphical components of the QuickTime file are retained, to ensure smoothness.
- **Flatten**   Flattening makes a movie self-contained and eliminates layers.

Evaluate Your Movie

Even with all the distribution methods made available to you for delivering your Flash movie to your audience, it is highly unlikely that it will be picture perfect all the time for all audiences. To ensure success, you need to keep testing your movie frequently to anticipate all possible problems that may arise.

Appendix A

Flash Resource Guide

Over the last several years, Flash has continued to assume a dominant role on the Web. Nowadays, Flash-driven sites are synonymous with good design practice. More and more designers, programmers, and web developers are using Flash to build web sites. Because Flash is so popular and so expansive in terms of its scope, there are many resources offered on the Web for Flash developers. If you are serious about learning Flash, you will probably need to turn to external resources at some point in your studies.

Keep in mind that many of these sites can be cross-referenced in other categories. In other words, if you don't find what you're looking for in one category, feel free to go to another. For example, a site I recommend for sound loops might just as well contain tutorials on something else Flash-related. The purpose is to give you some initial direction, but you can find out additional information on these sites by poking around.

This appendix is a list of resources to help you keep your skills fine-tuned. Because version MX is so new, some of the information in these resources may refer to older versions of Flash. Not to worry though; Flash is still Flash regardless of the version number attached to it. If a resource relates to an older version, the information can generally be adapted to relate to the newer version. Also, by the time you read this book, the resources may very well have been updated. In either case, you are bound to find valuable information and inspiration when you browse through these links.

Training/Tutorial/Technical Sources

There is no shortage of free and fee-based Flash tutorials on the Web. At the time of this writing, Flash MX tutorials are scarce because the program is relatively new. However, more and more Flash MX tutorials and training tips go up on these sites every day, so keep checking back periodically for updated information. In the meantime, if you are new to Flash ActionScript, version 5 tutorials might help tweak your skills, too. And you certainly can use older source files to help you figure out some cool techniques you can achieve through scripting. Either the techniques will be accomplished the same way in MX, or you can easily research the "new-and-improved" way of doing a technique once you've identified what that effect you want to achieve is all about.

Many tutorials offer sample movies (source code) that can be downloaded. Unlike HTML, you can't view the source code of a Flash Player (SWF) file; unless you're a hacker (in which case, you wouldn't be reading this book), you need to obtain the FLA version (original movie) of the file to see how it was made. Being able to view the code in a movie you really like is a great resource in itself.

The following sources currently are recommended for training and tutorials:

www.ultrashock.com   This site offers tutorials in Flash. You can download free goodies and links to third-party tools, conferences and trade shows, educational links, fonts and typography, inspiration, music, sound effects, and source code.

www.flashweb.com   If you're looking for real-world how-to techniques, this is a good source. It offers good, general information and useful tutorials.

www.flashplanet.com   This is a fascinating and well-made site. With all its resources, tutorials, and links, it can be a handful, so patience is necessary, but it navigates well and easily. The Flash tutorials offer a wide variety of subjects, such as the sound object, functions, and show/hide mouse cursor techniques. Additionally, you can sharpen your motion graphics skills. There's a level three for advanced users, and they offer tutorials in different languages.

www.flashlite.net   This site is excellent for tutorials, source files, and additional resources. If you want a tutorial-style learning, browse under Tutorials when you enter the site. You are given several choices of subjects. You can view tutorials in an HTML format or PDF file.

www.were-here.com   This site offers a myriad of tutorials for ActionScript, such as creating mouse trails, arrays, drag and drop, dynamic text, and controlling a movie clip with a slider. This is an excellent and well-respected source for free tutorials on the Web.

www.flashguru.co.uk   This site contains Flash examples with downloadable source files. There also are links to other noteworthy, Flash-driven sites here.

www.flashkit.com   Flashkit is another well-respected source for Flash tutorials on the Web. The scope of the Flash community is apparent on this site with contributors from all over the world. This is a great place to exchange ideas and learn from one another.

www.lynda.com   Lynda offers Flash training in her books, her online site, and at her training facility in Ojai, California. Throughout the year she does numerous road shows all over the U.S. on Flash and other Web-related topics. In addition, her site is packed with Flash tips, downloads, links, and techniques.

www.doeducate.com   This is a great educational site with plenty of Flash usage and moderately priced classes in Flash and related applications.

www.ipw.internet.com   This is a developer resource site that offers information and links to audio, device management, HTML authoring, JavaScript, Java, publishing, rich media, site tools, and reviews of all types of products for Flash development and related areas.

www.creativemac.com   This site offers tools and techniques for Mac users. There are tutorials available for many topics under the Mac umbrella, including Flash features and functions.

www.juxtinteractive.com   This is an award-winning site with plenty of good design and a wealth of inspiration for would-be and experienced designers. Periodically, Juxt puts together training seminars offered on their site in Newport Beach, California. These training sessions are only for the truly advanced ActionScripter. Since the Juxt people are Flash innovators, it's got to be a great experience. For more information on these seminars, contact them on their web site.

www.virtual-fx.net   This site offers information on classes and Flash tutorials, discussion boards, source files, and more.

A

www.presstube.com   This site is an inspiration for all aspiring designers. There are a million incredible links to great stuff, plus an unbelievable number of animations to get your juices flowing.

Flash Animation

Animation, of course, is one of the main staples of Flash. The thing about Flash animation is that there are so many different ways you can create it. There are thousands of sites out there with great Flash animation, and here are a handful you can browse through to see how different designers utilize it.

www.melondezign.com   Very beautiful and hip Flash animation on this site. This is not exactly your run-of-the-mill kids' cartoon animation, but a very inspirational and innovative style of animation.

www.hopbot.com   This is a well-designed site with plenty of artfully rendered animation. It uses an interesting combination of pictures, text, and random markings, and will show you some interesting things that can be done in Flash.

www.rooneydesign.com   This site offers great looping animation on a group of clever zoom transitions.

www.egomedia.com   This site provides a good example of vectorized video animated silhouettes of people for this digital design agency site.

www.cartoonnetwork.com   If you are interest in animated cartoons in Flash, this site provides a cartooning extravaganza.

www.atomfilms.shockwave.com   This site offers many Flash films and shorts in every genre from comedy to drama.

www.geocities.com   This site has a short comic book movie that incorporates animation with conventional print techniques.

www.animfactory.net   At this software company, you can buy many animations created by a group of artists.

Audio

Since Flash is the ultimate in multimedia, it would be pretty boring if it weren't capable of incorporating sound. If you're new to Flash, you may need a little help figuring out where to go to get loops and sound effects. Although sound sources are just too numerous to mention, here are a few suggestions to get you pointed in the right direction:

www.flashkit.com   Among other tutorials, open source code and sound files are available through downloading. You can check out tutorials in which you import sound and create movie symbols, buttons, and actions. Tutorial source files are available for download on this site, too. Additionally, you can download sound loops for use in Flash projects. This site holds a huge library of royalty-free music loops.

www.were-here.com   This site offers a huge music loops section, which you can download for the Macintosh in AIF format and WAV format for Windows.

www.webdevelopersjournal.com   *Web Developer's Journal*. This is a great site, and the resources are endless. You can download multimedia Mac, PC, SWF files, and web development tools from this site. You can also download streaming media servers and MP3 search clients, such as free Napster, CuteMX (a real-time MP3 search engine), Scour Exchange, and iMesh, where you can search for MP3 audio, video, and graphic files. There are looping and sampling software applications such as Fruity Loops, Hammerhead, Tuareg, Acid, and Electrifier Pro. Beatnik and MOD Play software also are available.

www.creativepro.com   You can find some great info here about Flash including optimizing your audio.

www.panic.com   You can download Audion (a MIDI-like application) from Panic, as well as graphical faces to use in your Flash web designs. Also, go into Audion 2 from the Panic site, where you can learn to handle all your audio playing needs, MP3s, and streaming network audio, and encode, mix, edit, and so on.

www.loopz.com   At $1 a loop, there's a wide selection of quality audio loops to add sound to your site or any multimedia application you may be using. You can actually compile your own set of loops, and demo loops are played as Flash movies.

Audio-Editing Applications

There are many applications you can use for sound editing. If you are doing serious sound editing, the following applications will be out of your league. If you need something quick and inexpensive, then these may be of help to you. Don't feel you need to limit yourself to these applications. Flash can import AIFF, WAV, and MP3 formats. You can walk on down to your local computer store, go to the sound applications software section, and try out some loops right off the shelf.

- ■ **Rebirth** by Propellerheads offers techno music making at its best. It comes with a mixer so you can modify loops. You can download a free trial version at **www.propellerheads.com**.

- ■ **Groovemaker 2.0** enables you to create hypnotic, nonstop professional dance tracks in real time. You can mix them, layer in some loops, and create a totally new remix.

A

The interface is space age; and even if you don't like this kind of music, it sure is fun to play with the cool buttons and synthesizer. Download a free trial version from **www.groovemaker.com**.

- **Acid Pro** by Sonic Foundry is another loop-based music creation tool. Download a free trial version from **www.acidplanet.com**.

- **SmartSound for Multimedia** is an inexpensive program that comes with prefab loops you can throw together in sort of a wizard-like fashion. Compared to the other applications, some of the loops are a little on the corny side. If you're in a hurry and need something quick, and it doesn't have to be a Grammy Award–winning track, you can try this **www.smartsound.com**.

Tips and Techniques

Flash ActionScript brains are abundant. It is through their designs and implied answers to technical questions that we will learn great techniques and grow. So, whether it is to review techniques about loops, build ActionScripts, or create special text effects in Flash, the following designer sites should help you obtain most of the answers to your questions:

www.moock.org   This is Colin Moock's site, a well-respected Flash expert and author of *ActionScript, The Definitive Guide* (O'Reilly Press, 2001). If you haven't heard of him yet, you will, eventually. On his site, Colin offers answers to technical questions and inspiring examples from the popular to the obscure. In addition, there are very helpful ActionScript tutorials on this site.

www.canada.cnet.com   This site offers a "help" section with how-tos and tips. You can review the materials online or print out tips and techniques regarding loops, recycling scripts, optimizing, audio, and printing, to name just a few.

www.flaxfx.com   Here you can create text effects for Flash in real-time. Be sure to check out the samples at this site. It has 31 special-effect groups that can be tweaked using sliders and buttons to create a wide array of unique special effects.

www.macromedia.com   Of course, Flash's manufacturer, Macromedia, has a great site with lots of pertinent and helpful information. Be sure to look under Macromedia Flash Usability to find usability tips, downloadable source files, and guidelines with extensive hyperlinks to relevant and useful information. Also, check out the Flash gallery and "site of the day" section. Each day they feature a new site. There's also a Designer and Developer Resource section where they provide articles on writing maintainable code and designing for efficiency.

Source Code

We could all use a little help now and then with scripting. Sometimes you will know you want to create a particular effect, but you just won't know how to build it. If you can find something similar, and if the author has been kind enough to post the source code, then this may solve your problem. On these sites, you can search for open code for your Flash movies:

www.flashplanet.com   This is probably the best Flash site around for viewing source files. In addition to great tutorials, if you check out Flash Arena, you will find a plethora of ActionScript source files, such as time functions, buttons that load content into frames, creating recordable movement with playback, how to avoid the pirating of your source files, text substrings, building a progressive percentage preloader, and how to build a virtual shopping cart.

www.were-here.com   This site offers a lot of source code available for downloading from preloaders to shopping carts.

www.macromedia.com   Check out Macromedia's source code and guidelines.

www.flashpro.nl   You can download Flash movies to view, along with 100 new effects and source files. If you click new archives, there's a list of Flash materials. There's a Help section covering ActionScript beginner techniques, games, and more. There is also a Review section that includes links to noteworthy sites. Additionally, there's always a Featured ActionScript tutorial.

www.flashguru.co.uk   This site offers Flash samples with downloadable source files. Two tutorials worth checking out are collision detection and random function. Check out the resources at this site, and links to other Flash sites and projects.

Gaming Sites

Gaming in Flash has never been hotter—many gaming applications are now created in Flash. Here is a sampling of some interesting game sites. So, if this is your major field of interest, it will give you some game inspiration.

www.Globz.com   This site contains many games that are beautifully executed. They are intelligent, hip works of art. This isn't your everyday arcade-style site. If you're interested in game design, you definitely want to check this one out.

www.rocketsnail.com   Many cool games await you on this site. You can license the use of their games to use on your site, too. Games on your web site could certainly draw more traffic to a site.

www.sarbakan.com   This site is the Arcane OnLine Mystery Series, which is a very ambitious Flash game with professional illustration and animation created with Flash.

www.yenz.com   This site is the Secret Garden of Mutabor, which is a well-animated game site that is easy to navigate and play.

www.flashkit.com   This site offers many links to games developed in Flash.

A

www.sadisticboxing.com This site offers a high level of scripting, and, although bloody, it's very engaging.

www.huihui.de This site offers a mini-arcade interface with Frogger, Space Invaders, and Tetris.

www.electronictank.com This site offers an incredible collection of real-time multiuser games.

www.titoonic.dk This site is an unbelievable, highly playable game. It contains beautiful art work, superior sound effects, and great animation.

www.ferryhalim.com This site offers 21 short, sweet, funny, and fun games that are beautifully illustrated.

Cartooning Applications

For Flash designers interested in cartoon animations, you can purchase or download a trial version of **www.toonboomstudio.com**, a very cool cartooning application. Create 2-dimensional cartoons that export to SWF file format. You can also import Toon Boom SWF cartoons directly into Flash MX using the Toon Boom Studio Importer. Once they are in Flash, they can be made interactive.

Noteworthy Flash Movies

These sites are noteworthy because of their technical brilliance and use of design elements. Well-structured Flash sites always provide inspiration when you need to get your creative juices flowing.

www.macromedia.com/showcase-site of the day This site changes every day. Showing your work on this site is a real honor.

www.digitalorganism.com This is a well-known site with a good mix of sound, motion graphics, interactivity, and color.

www.flashplanet.com As mentioned before, this is probably one of the best sites around for Flash materials. Be sure to go into the site and check out Clip Art, which contains galleries of ready-made symbols to add to your Flash libraries. The gamut runs from basic symbols and backdrops to anatomical figures and symbols.

For further inspiration, go into the Directory of Web Sites at this site, and take a look at the 40 or so sites listed at the time this book was written. They are all Flash resource sites, most of which contain outstanding Flash materials. Two worth mention are **www.thesocalled.com**, which contains interesting games in Flash, and **www.twilomedia.com**, which won the Webmaster Award and Golden Web Award and truly is brilliant.

www.were-here.com This site offers "design" links to many beautiful Flash sites for a plethora of creative ideas.

There's also a "site check" location at this site that enables you to review other Flash sites people have created. By "reviewing" these sites, you can get some fresh ideas for your own Flash creations.

www.shop4software.online.com   Be sure to investigate this site so you can purchase Flash Master. This program creates screensavers from Flash files, eliminating the problem of building fully interactive multimedia screensavers. You also can preview sample screensavers made with Flash Master.

altpick.com   Art Mill shows incredible work in these interactive design sites, which are a testimony to magnificent design inspiration.

www.dvhandbook.com   This is an animation test site for The Idea Exchange. It's an excellent site for inspiration.

www.portfolios.com   You can view many designers' Flash portfolios on this site. Also, be sure to go into Folio Finder so you can review interactive portfolios created in Flash, as well as other interactive software. For the experienced gurus out there, you can set up your own portfolio to procure work.

www.creativepro.com   This site is for professionals. It holds some interesting links, such as a stock photography search, and they also offer a Personal Portfolio Hosting service.

www.secondstory.com   This site offers more than 40 interactive features on subjects ranging from the visual arts to music and history, all explored through a fabulous timeline of collected works. Again, if you're looking for inspiration, try this site.

www.theremediprojects.com   This site is a collection of unique Flash utilization.

www.heavy.com   This site offers great music and Flash animation.

www.pepsiworld.com   This site is all Flash and Shockwave; it's constantly updated, with great games as well, which keeps its perspective fresh and appealing to pop culture.

www.becominghuman.org   This site is a web documentary that traces the evolution of man. It's a feast of Flash applications and is incredibly beautiful.

Flash Interface Design

Everyone is always looking for a great Flash idea. These sites are representative of outstanding Flash features with clever interfaces.

www.virtualpulse.com   This site employs many Flash features and excels at all of them. It uses extremely cool space design, a clever interface, and great design elements throughout the site. Aside from this, it provides very useful information.

A

www.vrlx.net   This site offers a tour of the world, and it's incredibly well done. There's a lot going on here; however, the interface is very clever—it holds your attention and is very intriguing.

www.searchbots.net   This is an incredible Flash search engine.

www.greets.com   This is a greeting card site with an intuitive gaming interface and elements that jump out and grab you. You can create a multimedia greeting card and save it as a CD-ROM.

www.mnh.si.edu   This site employs extremely sharp and crisp photography, great use of Flash, and great scripting tricks that keep the navigation synchronized with the browser back button. This interface very much emulates a museum-type environment.

www.archpark.org.il   This site has an unbelievably brilliant timeline highlighting periods of time with crisp photography, Flash animations, and interactive maps. The site is representative of an archaeological attraction in Jerusalem.

www.philbrown.bc.ca   This outrageously designed site offers a true narrative experience that is fully balanced with the navigation of the site. It also utilizes liquid mask transitions.

Flash 3D

Swift 3D is an inexpensive vector-based program that allows you to export in an SWF format, making **www.erain.com** the ideal 3D Flash companion. Electric Rain is the maker of Swift 3D, and on their site you can purchase Swift 3D and also check out what other designers created using Swift 3D and Flash.

Miscellaneous Resources

If you don't own Flash MX yet, you can download a trial version from the Macromedia web site. This could be extremely helpful if you bought this book and you don't yet own Flash MX.

You will also find on the Macromedia site trial versions of Macromedia's Dreamweaver, Fireworks, FreeHand, Director, UltraDev, and other programs. To evaluate these programs, you can download them from **www.macromedia.com/downloads**.

If you use other programs to create your vector, bitmap art, or HTML, Macromedia's products are a wonderful complement to Flash. The interface on all these programs has a familiar look, as does the language used.

The Flash MX Player can be downloaded from this site, too. You might want to direct visitors to your Flash site (who don't have the correct Flash plug-in) to the Macromedia site to get the proper plug-in.

Keep in mind that the Web is an ever-changing form of media and is constantly being updated. Although all the previous web sites and references were in existence at the time of this writing, some might be changed, gone, or rerouted by the time you arrive.

Appendix B

Frequently Used Shortcut Keyboard Commands

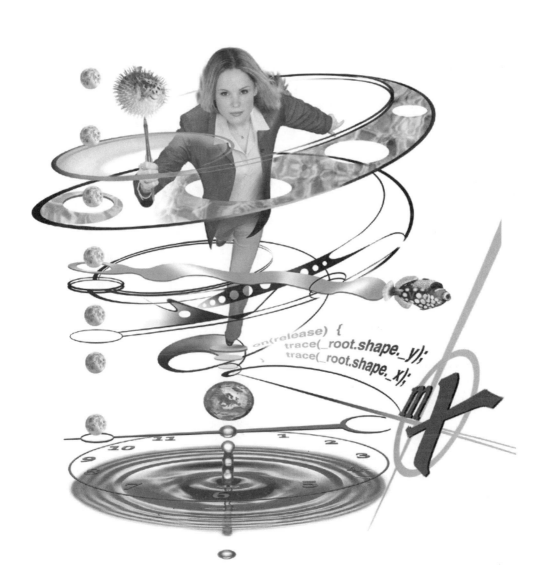

Command	Menu	Windows	Macintosh
100%	View | Magnification	CTRL-1	CMD-1
Action Panel	Window	F9	F9
Add Shape Hint	Modify | Shape	CTRL-SHIFT-H	SHIFT-CMD-H
Align	Window | Panels	CTRL-K	CMD-K
Align Center (Text)	Text | Align	CTRL-SHIFT-C	CMD-SHIFT-C
Align Left (Text)	Text | Align	CTRL-SHIFT-L	CMD-SHIFT-L
Align Right (Text)	Text | Align	CTRL-SHIFT-R	CMD-SHIFT-R
Blank Keyframe	Insert	F7	F7
Bold (Text)	Text | Style	CTRL-SHIFT-B	CMD-SHIFT-B
Break Apart	Modify	CTRL-B	CMD-B
Bring Forward	Modify | Arrange	CTRL-↑	CMD-↑
Bring to Front	Modify | Arrange	ALT-SHIFT-↑	OPT-SHIFT-↑
Clear Keyframe	Insert	SHIFT-F6	SHIFT-F6
Close (File)	File	CTRL-W	CMD-W
Convert to Symbol	Insert	F8	F8
Copy (Selection)	Edit	CTRL-C	CMD-C
Copy Frames	Edit	CTRL-ALT-C	CMD-OPT-C
Cut (Selection)	Edit	CTRL-X	CMD-X
Cut Frames	Edit	CTRL-ALT-X	CMD-OPT-X
Debug Movie	Control	CTRL-SHIFT-ENTER	CMD-SHIFT-RETURN
Decrease/Increase (Tracking)	Text | Tracking	CTRL-ALT-LEFT	CMD-OPT-Left arrow
Default (Publishing)	File | Publish Preview	F12	F12
Deselect All	Edit	CTRL-SHIFT-A	CMD-SHIFT-A
Duplicate (Selection)	Edit	CTRL-D	CMD-D
Edit Symbols	Edit	CTRL-E	CMD-E
Enable Simple Buttons	Control	CTRL-ALT-B	CMD-OPT-B
Export Movie	File	CTRL-ALT-SHIFT-S	CMD-SHIFT-OPT-S
Frame (Add)	Insert	F5	F5
Grid (Show/Hide)	View | Grid	CTRL-'	CMD-'
Group (Selected Items)	Modify	CTRL-G	CMD-G
Guides (Show/Hide)	View | Guide	CTRL-;	CMD-;

TABLE B-1 Keyboard Commands

Command	Menu	Windows	Macintosh
Import	File	CTRL-R	CMD-R
Increase (Tracking)	Text | Tracking	CTRL-ALT-→	CMD-OPT-→
Italic (Text)	Text | Style	CTRL-SHIFT-I	CMD-SHIFT-I
Justify (Text)	Text | Align	CTRL-SHIFT-J	CMD-SHIFT-J
Keyframe (Add)	Insert	F6	F6
Library (Show/Hide)	Window	CTRL-L/F11	F11
Lock (Group)	Modify | Arrange	CTRL-ALT-L	CMD-OPT-L
Lock Guides	View | Guide	CTRL-ALT-;	CMD-OPT-;
Movie (Properties)	Modify | Document	CTRL-J	CMD-J
Movie Explorer Panel (Show/Hide)	Window	ALT-F3	OPT-F3
New Symbol	Insert	CTRL-F8	CMD-F8
Open as Library	File	CTRL-SHIFT-O	CMD-SHIFT-O
Paste (Clipboard Contents)	Edit	CTRL-V	CMD-V
Paste Frames	Edit	CTRL-ALT-V	CMD-OPT-V
Paste In Place	Edit	CTRL-SHIFT-V	CMD-SHIFT-V
Plain (Text)	Text | Style	CTRL-SHIFT-P	CMD-SHIFT-P
Play (Movie)	Control	ENTER	RETURN
Print	File	CTRL-P	CMD-P
Publish	File	SHIFT-F12	SHIFT-F12
Publish Settings	File	CTRL-SHIFT-F12	OPT-SHIFT-F12
Redo	Edit	CTRL-Y	CMD-Y
Remove Frames	Insert	SHIFT-F5	SHIFT-F5
Reset	Text | Tracking	CTRL-ALT-↑	CMD-OPT-↑
Rewind	Control	CTRL-ALT-R	CMD-OPT-R
Rulers	View	CTRL-ALT-SHIFT-R	CMD-OPT-SHIFT-R
Save	File	CTRL-S	CMD-S
Save As	File	CTRL-SHIFT-S	CMD-SHIFT-S
Scale and Rotate	Modify | Transform	CTRL-ALT-S	CMD-OPT-S
Select All	Edit	CTRL-A	CMD-A
Send Backward	Modify | Arrange	CTRL-↓	CMD-↓

B

TABLE B-2   Keyboard Commands *(Continued)*

Command	Menu	Windows	Macintosh
Send to Back	Modify | Arrange	CTRL-SHIFT-↓	OPT-SHIFT-↓
Snap to Grid	View | Grid	CTRL-SHIFT-'	CMD-SHIFT-'
Snap to Guides	View | Guides	CTRL-SHIFT-;	CMD-SHIFT-;
Snap to Objects	View	CTRL-SHIFT-/	CMD-SHIFT-/
Test Movie	Control	CTRL-ENTER	CMD-RETURN
Test Scene	Control	CTRL-ALT-ENTER	CMD-OPT-RETURN
Timeline	View	CTRL-ALT-T	CMD-OPT-T
Transform	Window | Transform		CMD-T
Undo	Edit	CTRL-Z	CMD-Z
Ungroup	Modify	CTRL-SHIFT-G	CMD-SHIFT-G
Unlock All	Modify | Arrange	CTRL-ALT-SHIFT-	CMD-OPT-SHIFT-L
Work Area	View	CTRL-SHIFT-W	CMD-SHIFT-W
Zoom In	View	CTRL-=	CMD-=
Zoom Out	View	CTRL--	CMD--

TABLE B-3   Keyboard Commands *(Continued)*

Index

INTERNATIONAL CONTACT INFORMATION

AUSTRALIA
McGraw-Hill Book Company Australia Pty. Ltd.
TEL +61-2-9417-9899
FAX +61-2-9417-5687
http://www.mcgraw-hill.com.au
books-it_sydney@mcgraw-hill.com

CANADA
McGraw-Hill Ryerson Ltd.
TEL +905-430-5000
FAX +905-430-5020
http://www.mcgrawhill.ca

**GREECE, MIDDLE EAST,
NORTHERN AFRICA**
McGraw-Hill Hellas
TEL +30-1-656-0990-3-4
FAX +30-1-654-5525

MEXICO (Also serving Latin America)
McGraw-Hill Interamericana Editores S.A. de C.V.
TEL +525-117-1583
FAX +525-117-1589
http://www.mcgraw-hill.com.mx
fernando_castellanos@mcgraw-hill.com

SINGAPORE (Serving Asia)
McGraw-Hill Book Company
TEL +65-863-1580
FAX +65-862-3354
http://www.mcgraw-hill.com.sg
mghasia@mcgraw-hill.com

SOUTH AFRICA
McGraw-Hill South Africa
TEL +27-11-622-7512
FAX +27-11-622-9045
robyn_swanepoel@mcgraw-hill.com

**UNITED KINGDOM & EUROPE
(Excluding Southern Europe)**
McGraw-Hill Education Europe
TEL +44-1-628-502500
FAX +44-1-628-770224
http://www.mcgraw-hill.co.uk
computing_neurope@mcgraw-hill.com

ALL OTHER INQUIRIES Contact:
Osborne/McGraw-Hill
TEL +1-510-549-6600
FAX +1-510-883-7600
http://www.osborne.com
omg_international@mcgraw-hill.com